AF574825

Underwater **Photography**

Dedication

With many thanks to Matt Murphy of the Sherkin Island Marine Station, County Cork, Ireland, who deserves considerable credit for sparking my interest in underwater photography and leading me into a career path that I could never have otherwise envisaged!

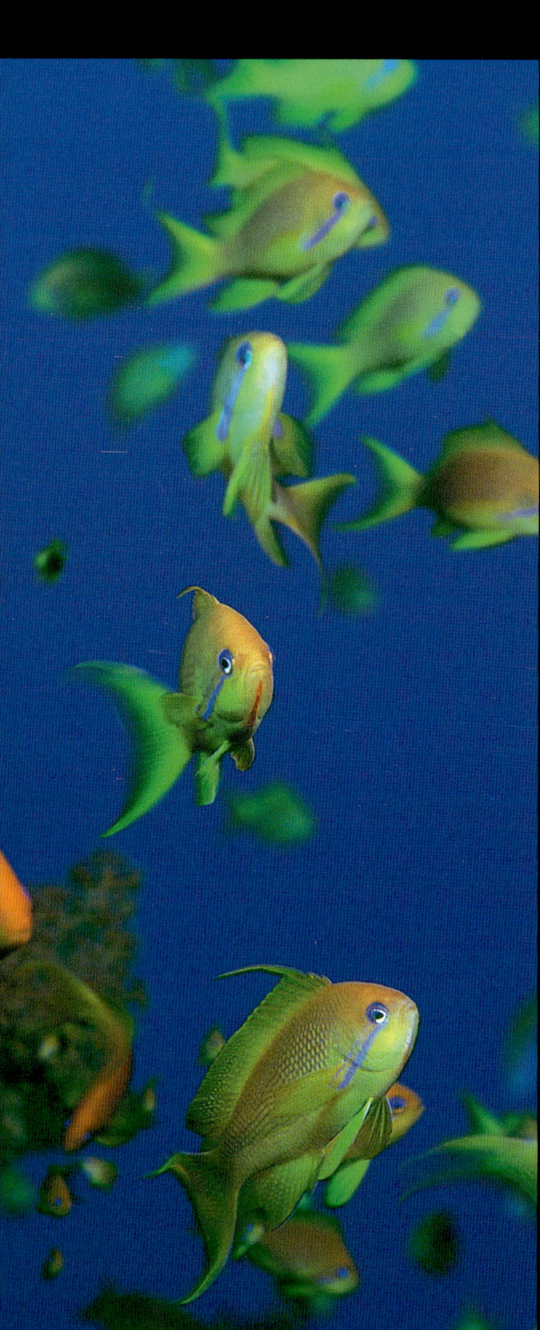

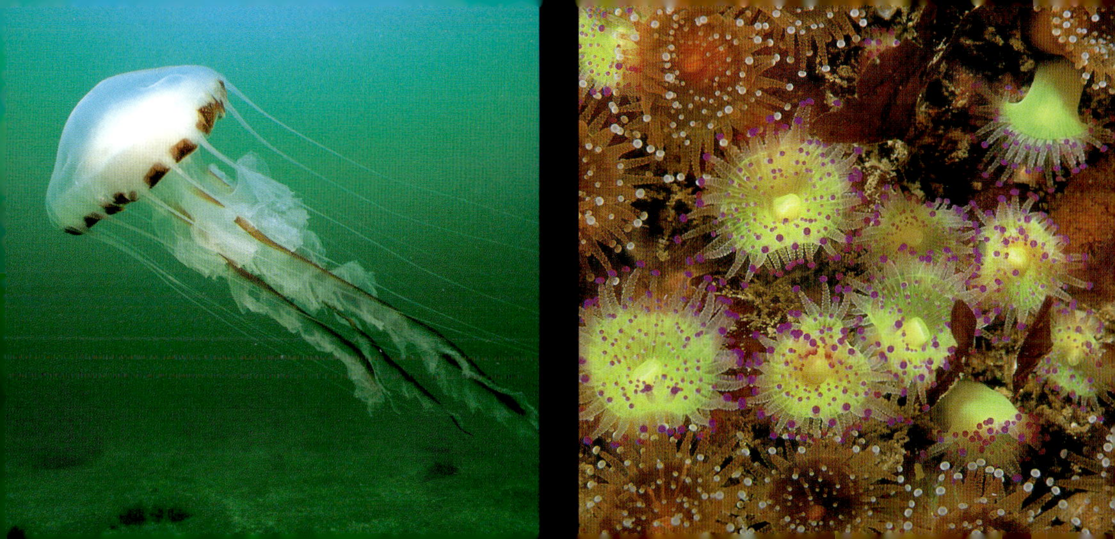

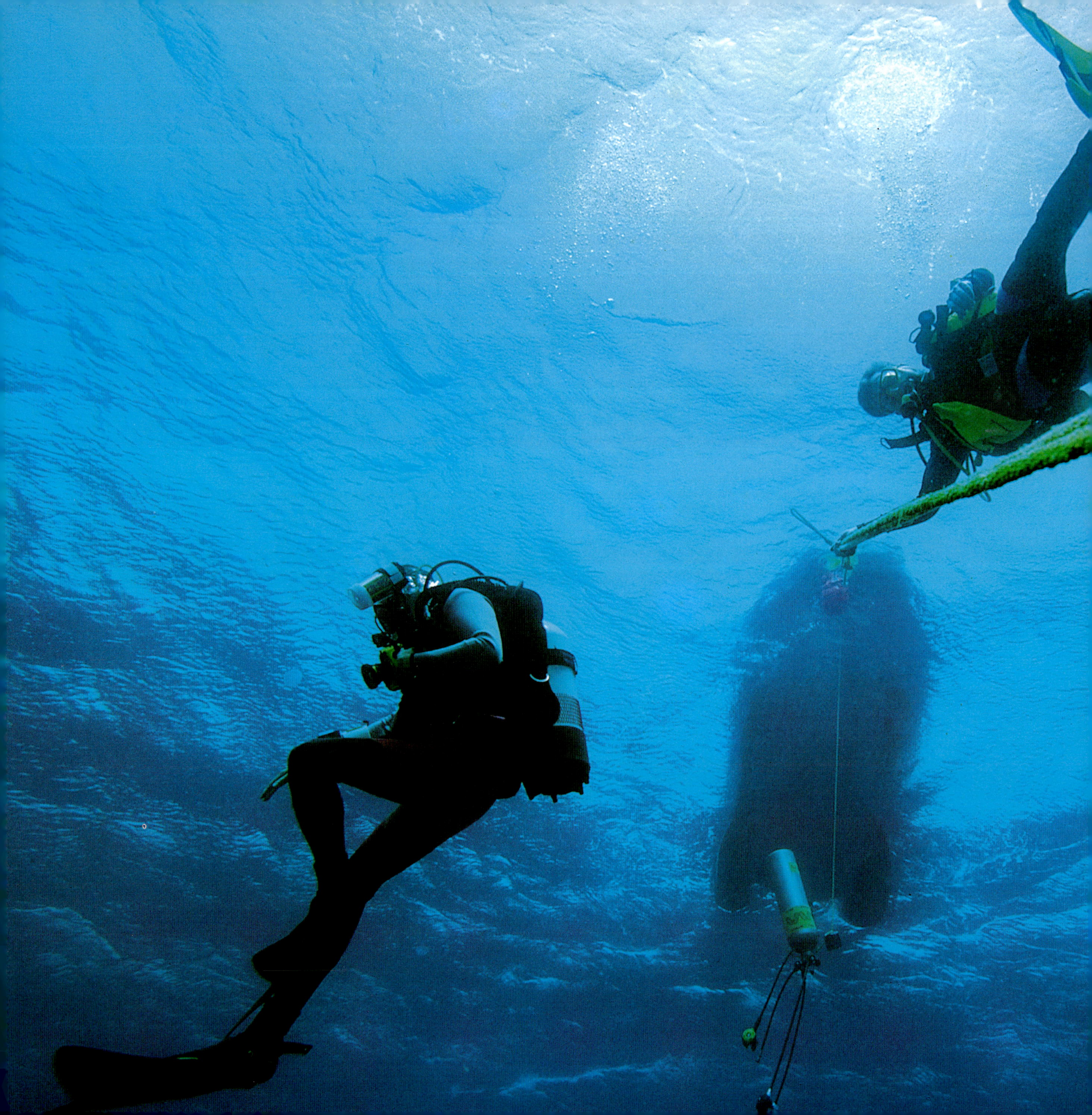

Composition is a difficult area, and often there is little control over the actions of a subject. Therefore, when an interesting shot is seen, it has to be captured immediately. Here, the two decompressing divers maintained this position for just a very short time and the image had to be grabbed.
Subal-housed Nikon F100 and 17–35mm lens set at 17mm, with two diffused Nikon SB105 flash units. 1/30s at f/11 on Fuji Provia 100 ISO

introduction

In the 1950s, books and films by the likes of Jacques Yves Cousteau and Hans Hass began to popularize an exciting new world – the undersea. Also at about this time, the aqualung started to become available. Its introduction enabled many people to explore this hitherto inaccessible area of our planet for themselves. Since then, scuba diving has grown in popularity, and has now burgeoned into a sport taken up by many millions.

Underwater photography actually pre-dates the introduction of the aqualung, but despite its late nineteenth-century origins, it remained a very problematic and specialized area of photography, undertaken by a few who were prepared to work hard for their images. Today, with the help of modern technology, it is a well-established and fast-growing area of interest.

Many of us who scuba dive are fascinated by what we are able to see, and inevitably we want to capture images of the undersea and its inhabitants. For many divers, this is the first time that they take up photography of any sort.

Underwater photography has its own particular set of problems. Some of these are associated with operating relatively complex photographic equipment in an alien environment; others are due to the physical effects that being underwater has on optics and light, as well as on us.

There is no simple, single reason for taking underwater photographs. Each of us will have his or her own specific desires regarding the images produced.

Perhaps it is the desire to show the underwater world to those who cannot be there and see its beauty in person. Some divers simply want to have a record of the fascinating

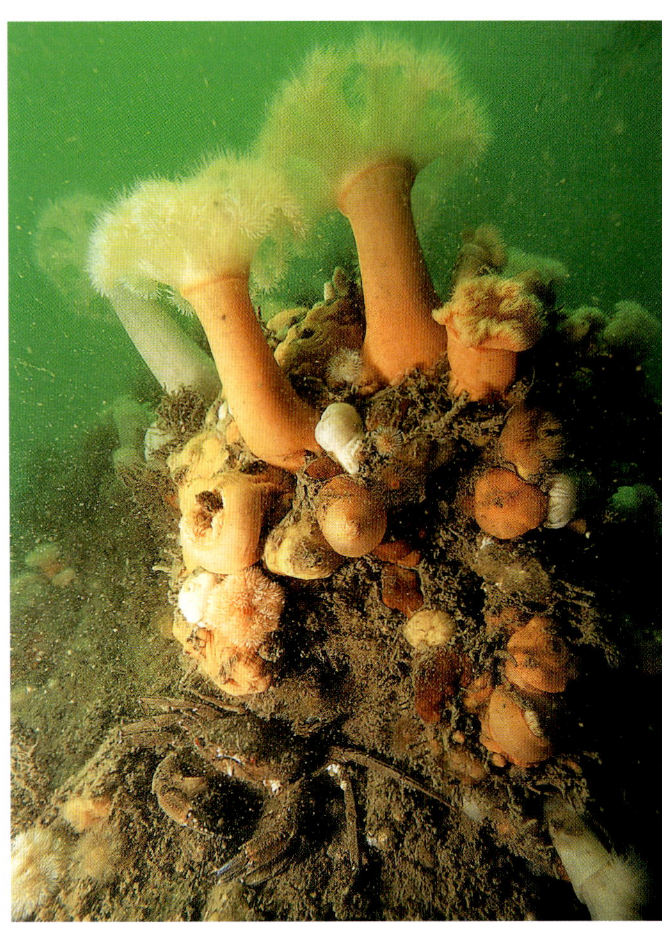

Taking pictures in low visibility is a real challenge. Often the results are imperfect, but at least they allow non-divers to see what lives in places they are unlikely to visit for themselves, such as off the east Anglesey coast in North Wales.
Subal-housed Nikon F100 and 17–35mm Nikkor lens set at 17mm, with a diffused Nikonos SB105 flash. 1/4s at f/16 on Fuji Provia 100 ISO

creatures encountered on a dive, perhaps in order to be able to identify them later. Then there are those interested in natural history or shipwrecks, who may use photography as a tool for making a technical or scientific record.

Whatever the reason for taking underwater photographs, hopefully everyone who takes one will always experience the thrill of producing a new image of the underwater world. It is always exciting to look through fresh photographs – whether they are slides, prints, or now even digital images – and experience the satisfaction of having achieved the desired result, despite operating within in the problematic undersea environment. This should be an emotion that doesn't fade.

Before attempting to take underwater photographs, it is important to consider what they will be used for and

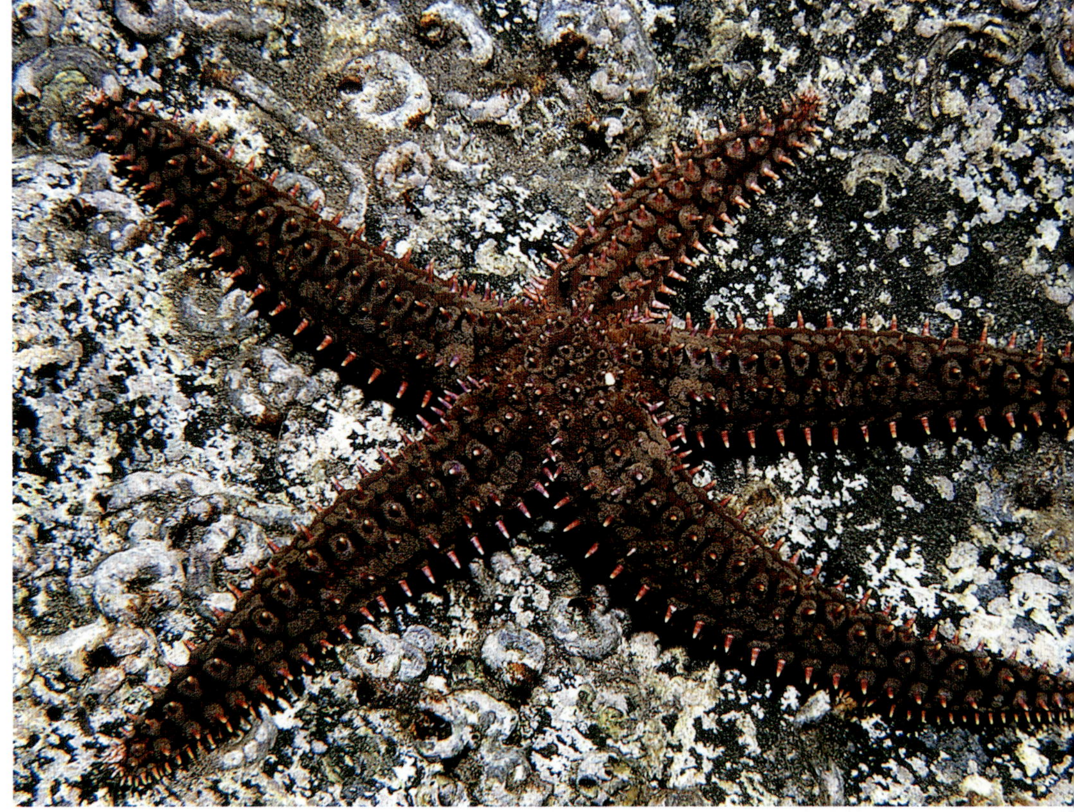

Although taken in only a couple of metres of well-lit water in La Gomera, Spain, a flash was used to create sufficient contrast to show this spiny starfish against a lighter background, and to avoid problems with motion caused by the swell.
Subal-housed Nikon F80 and 28–105mm Nikkor lens set at 50mm, with a single Nikonos SB105 flash. 1/60s at f/22 on Fuji Provia 100 ISO

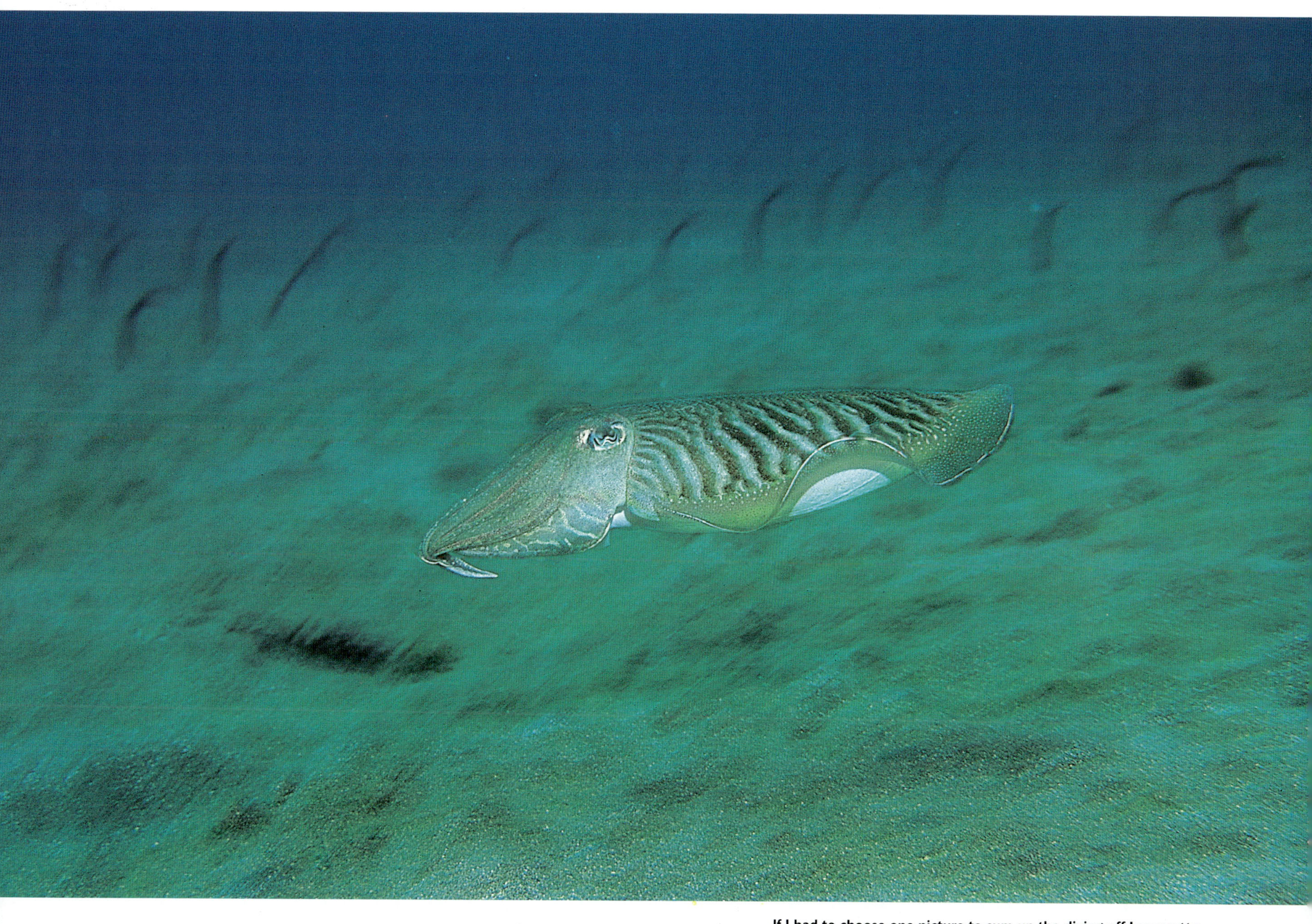

If I had to choose one picture to sum up the diving off Lanzarotte, it would be this. It shows a common cuttlefish (*Sepia officinalis*) swimming slowly along in clear blue water, and in the background are numerous garden eels – a very evocative picture.
Subal-housed Nikon F100 and 17–35mm lens set at 28mm, with a Nikon SB105 flash unit. 1/8s at f/11 on Fuji Provia 100 ISO

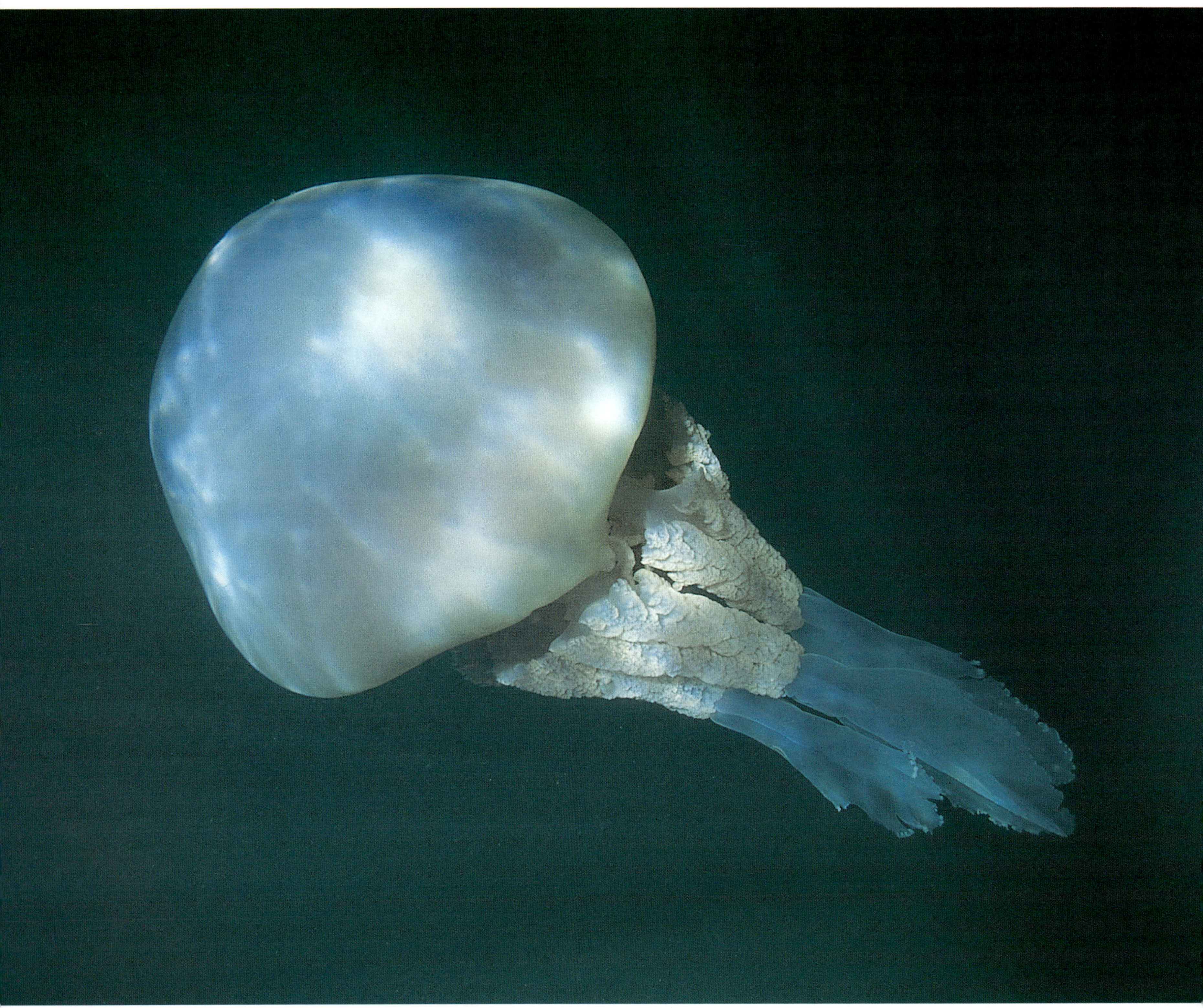

Left: Opportunities need to be taken when spotted. After a dive in Hell's Mouth, North Wales, I glanced down to see this barrel jellyfish (*Rhizostoma octopus*) drifting slowly by the boat. I slipped over the side with what remained of my film and shot the creature by available light while snorkelling. ***Subal-housed Nikon F100 and 17–35mm lens set at 17mm. Aperture priority at f/5.6. Fuji Provia 100 ISO***

why they are to be taken. This is because, as with all forms of photography, the end use of a photograph will determine how it should be taken and what equipment and film should be used to take it. Underwater photographic equipment is expensive and there is a steep learning curve involved with using much of it, so making some considered decisions beforehand can save both time and money.

The equipment needed to record a tropical diving holiday and produce some acceptable, handy-sized prints that are easy to show around can be very different from that required to take photographs intended for high-quality publication. These are very different sets of requirements.

In the first case, a small, relatively inexpensive camera that will fit in a stabilizer (or buoyancy compensator) jacket pocket may be a good choice, particularly as it could be used or put away whenever desired. For the second, a housed 35mm (or perhaps even digital) single-lens reflex (SLR) camera plus a full range of accessories would be essential, but this set-up will dominate a dive.

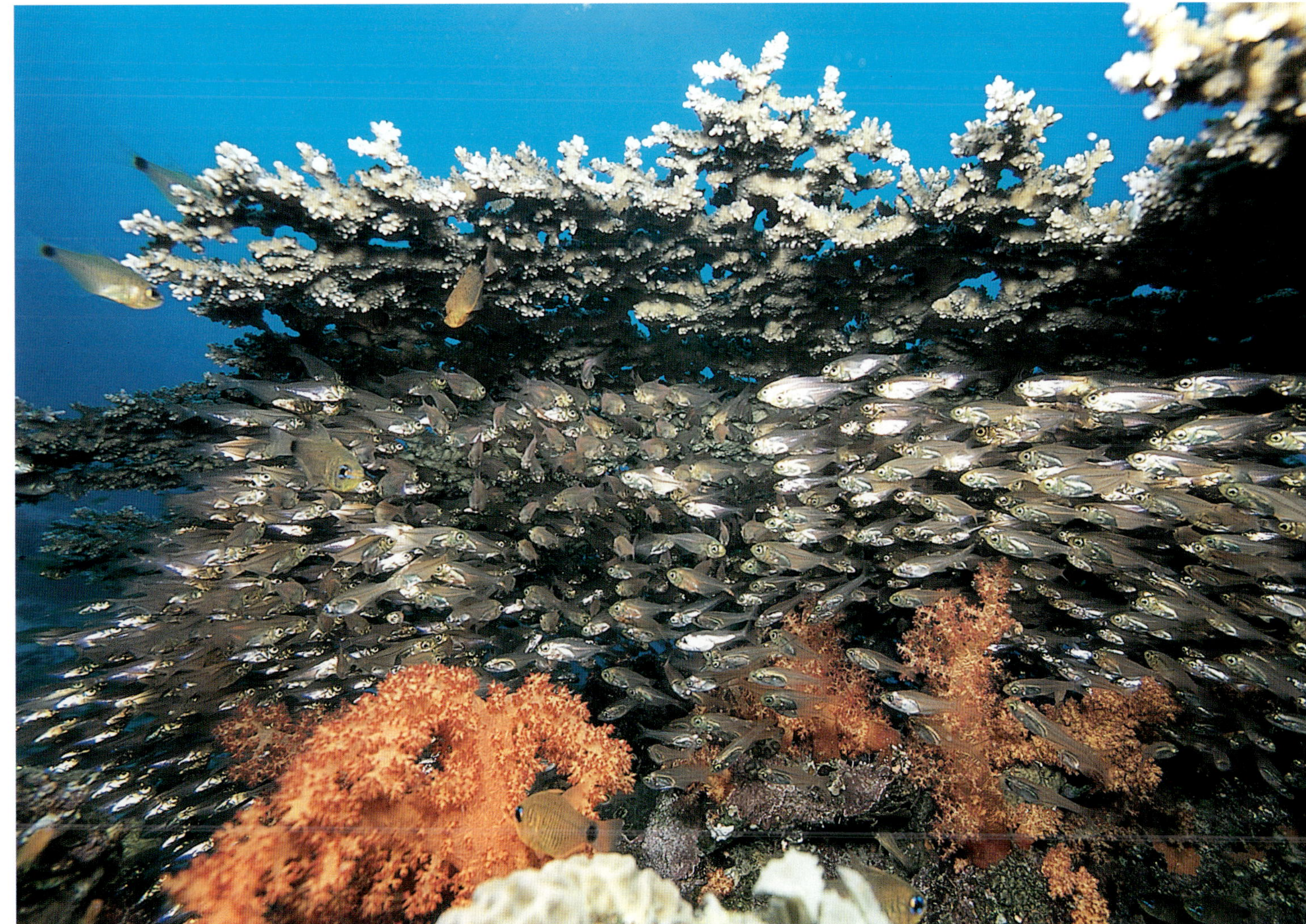

Coral reefs, such as those found in the Egyptian Red Sea, are one of nature's marvels, and it is often difficult to do anything more than capture a tiny fragment of the quantity and diversity of their inhabitants. Not surprisingly, coral reef photography attracts many divers to underwater photography in the first place. ***Subal-housed Nikon F100 and 20mm Nikkor lens, with a Nikon SB105 flash unit. 1/60s at f/16 on Fuji Provia 100 ISO***

There are also factors such as weight, bulk and ease of use to think about. Complete systems are usually heavy and can cause transportation problems, especially on aircraft. In addition, as much (if not more) time can be taken up cleaning, testing and experimenting with equipment as actually using it. The overall effort required to maintain and learn about using underwater photographic equipment is considerable, and this may not be everyone's idea of fun. So before tackling underwater photography, it is useful to decide just how far it is to be taken.

My purpose in writing this book is to help readers make an informed decision regarding choice of equipment; to know what it is capable of and how it can be used. It is not definitive – no single volume could be. Although there is a considerable amount of information in this book, there are many other techniques, methods and ways of doing things that are only mentioned briefly, or are not covered at all. There will also be those who successfully use methods that I adjudge potentially problematic. What this book aims to do is to provide an overview.

For anyone with some photographic experience, Part One of the book should be straightforward and might seem quite basic. However, given the complexities encountered in the underwater environment, it is essential to understand the fundamental concepts of photography.

It is worth remembering that the definition of a good underwater photograph is one that fulfils the photographer's reasons for taking it. This is true whether the photograph is merely a snapshot or a technically difficult and complex scientific study.

Safety

Taking underwater photographs is a very rewarding extension to exploring the undersea world, but working in this alien environment has great safety implications. Scuba diving is now accepted as being a relatively safe adventure sport, but it does retain the potential for serious and even fatal accidents.

For the untrained or inexperienced diver, I hope that this section will instil caution until sufficient underwater experience has been acquired to enable photography to be undertaken without any additional risk. For trained divers it should be seen more as a useful reminder. Please don't skip it, or be put off by anything it contains.

The undersea environment is potentially hazardous, and it should go without saying that an underwater photographer must never dive outside his or her capabilities. No photograph is worth dying for.

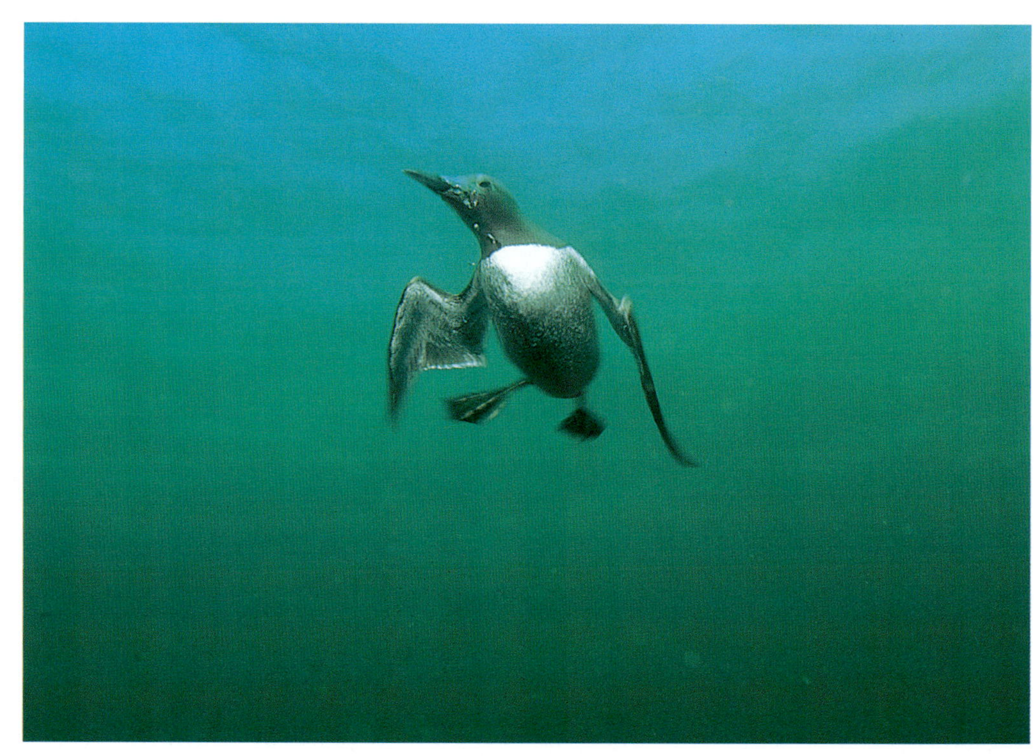

This bizarre photo was taken at the entrance to the Sugar Loaf Caves in the Isle of Man, UK. It shows an inquisitive guillemot halting in mid-water in order to peer at me – a strange, air-belching undersea creature. While not perfect from a technical perspective, this shot is so evocative of the dive that it remains one I really enjoy viewing. ***Subal-housed Nikon F100 and 17–35mm lens set at 35mm, with two diffused Nikon SB105 flash units. 1/8s at f/16 on Fuji Provia 100 ISO***

I hate wasting film, but there are usually opportunities for using up the odd shot left after a dive – even while decompressing. This shot delighted the dive organiser as it captured that satisfied feeling of having enjoyed a good dive in the blue water of the Red Sea. ***Subal-housed Nikon F100 and 17–35mm lens set at 17mm, with two diffused Nikon SB105 flash units. 1/8s at f/16 on Fuji Provia 100 ISO***

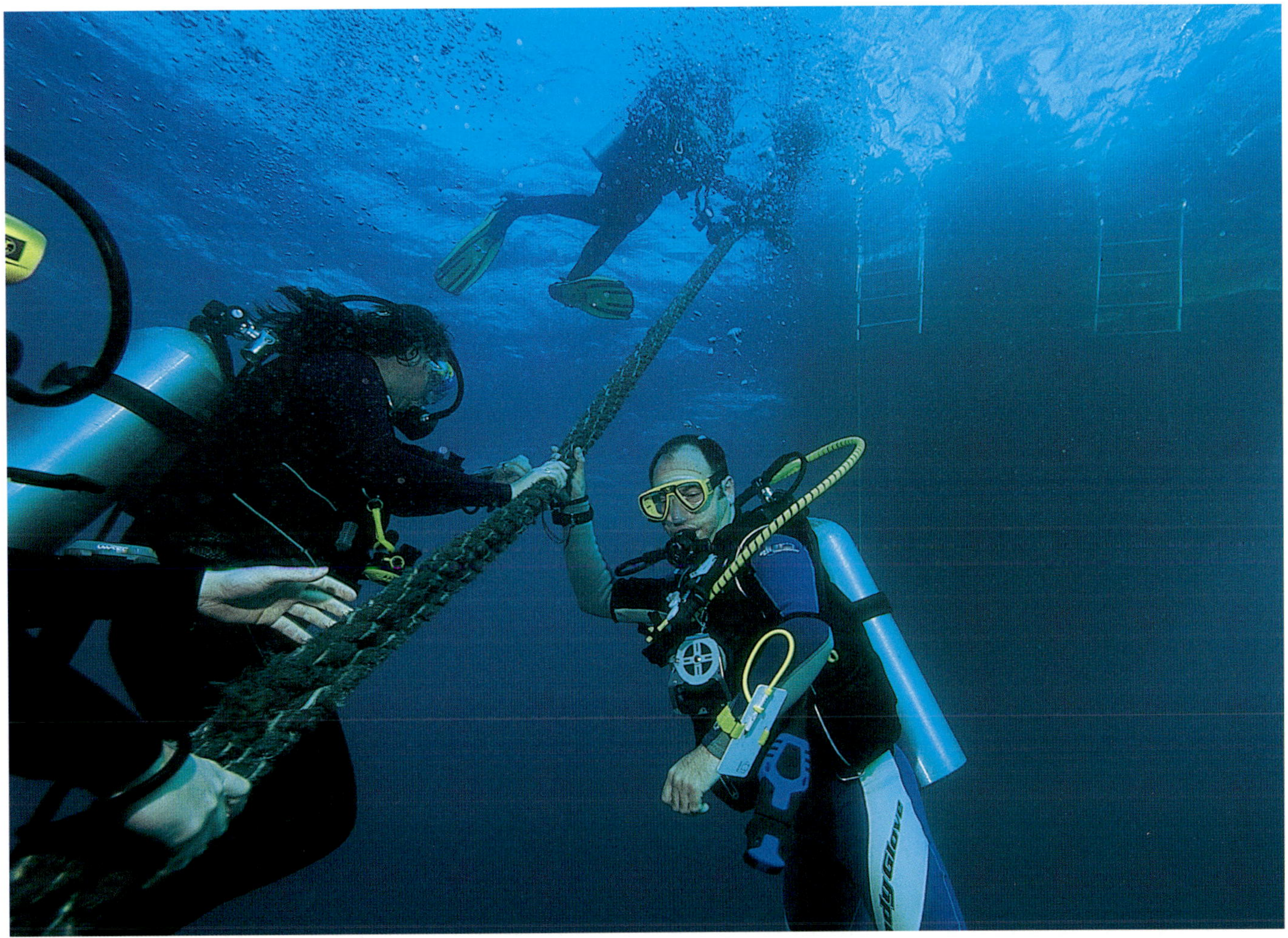

Training

Scuba diving requires extensive training. Before any underwater photography is undertaken, a diver must be fully trained to an internationally recognized standard, as well as conversant with the underwater environment and all appropriate safety procedures. Ideally, an underwater photographer should not only be qualified for diving under the conditions (whether temperate or tropical) in which underwater photography will occur, but experienced in them too.

Buoyancy control is taught during standard diver training, but in order to operate successfully as an underwater photographer, a diver must have very precise buoyancy control. Accurate buoyancy control is absolutely essential and should be so ingrained as to be instinctive; this cannot be stressed enough. It is a skill that can only be achieved by constant practice. Instability while underwater is not only an irritation to the photographer, but can also result in damage to plants and creatures, as well as stirring up silt, mud and suchlike. At best this will annoy nearby divers, and at worst it can be dangerous.

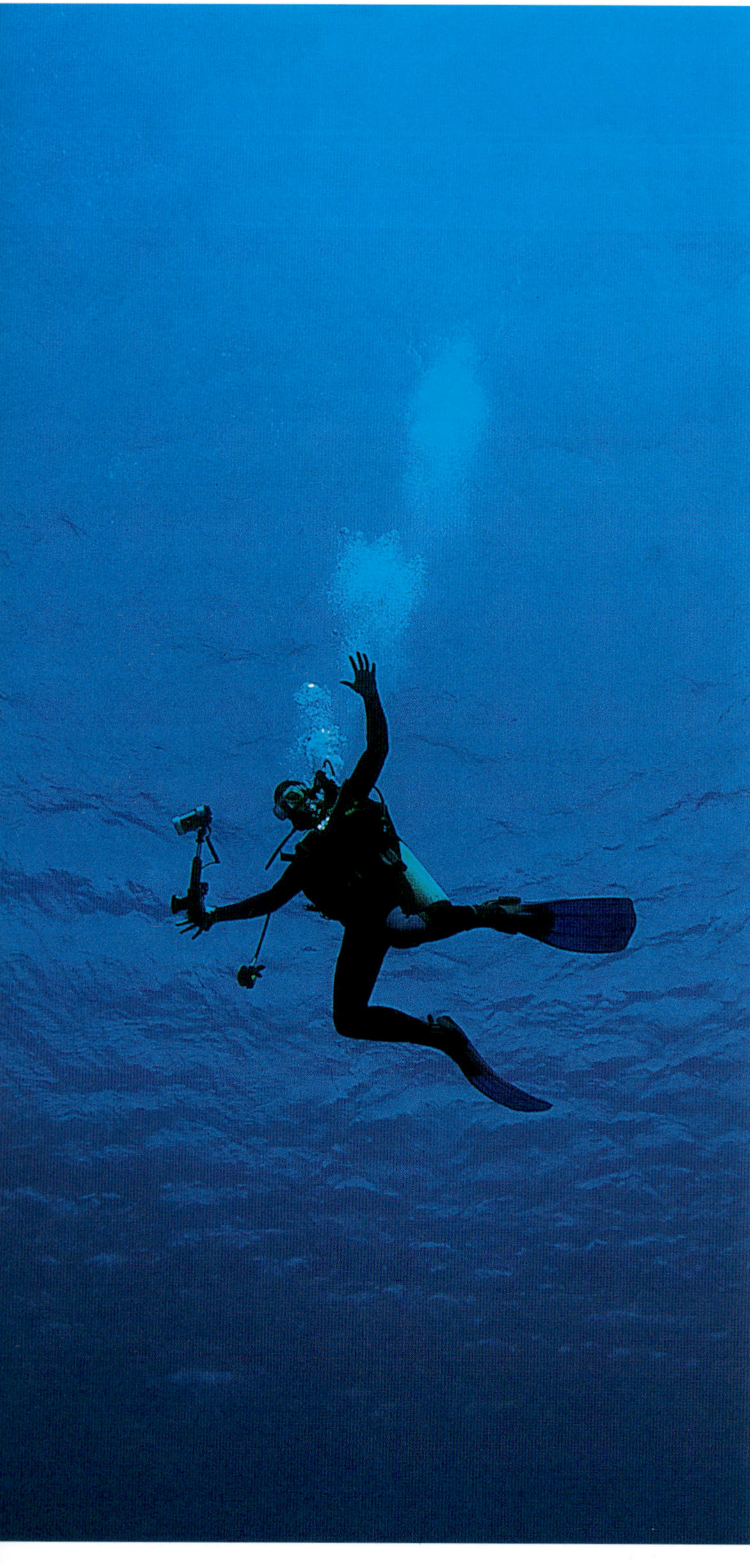

An underwater photographer in free fall – a picture illustrating that diving is not just about taking pictures. Shot by available light in the Red Sea. ***Subal-housed Nikon F100 and 17–35mm lens set at 17mm. 1/60s at f/5.6 on Fuji Provia 100 ISO***

The wreck of the Fairweather V, in the north of Scotland, lies in the dark water of a sea loch. It has been transformed beautifully after ten years underwater, but is difficult to capture in the gloom. The other photographer kept very still during exposures, displaying superb buoyancy control. ***Subal-housed Nikon F100 and 17–35mm lens set at 17mm, with two diffused Nikon SB105 flash units. 1/2s at f/16 on Fuji Provia 100 ISO***

Diving overweight is a temptation for many underwater photographers as it creates stability and allows them to settle onto the seabed. However, it is considered bad dive practice as it decreases inherent buoyancy margins, and should be refrained from (unless it is really essential, is not damaging to the seabed, and has been compensated for in terms of additional buoyancy capability).

If a dive requires the use of unfamiliar techniques (for example, the use of a dry suit for diving in cold water or using a gas mix other than air), these skills or techniques should be learnt before adding a camera into the equation. An underwater photographer should also be familiarized with all equipment and procedures to be used on a dive.

Experience

Newly trained divers usually find that they have enough to do underwater just concentrating on the techniques and practicalities of diving. Taking underwater photographs can divert attention away from issues such as regularly monitoring air, depth and lapsed underwater time. Before taking a camera underwater, such actions should become an established routine that is second nature and does not require any prompting.

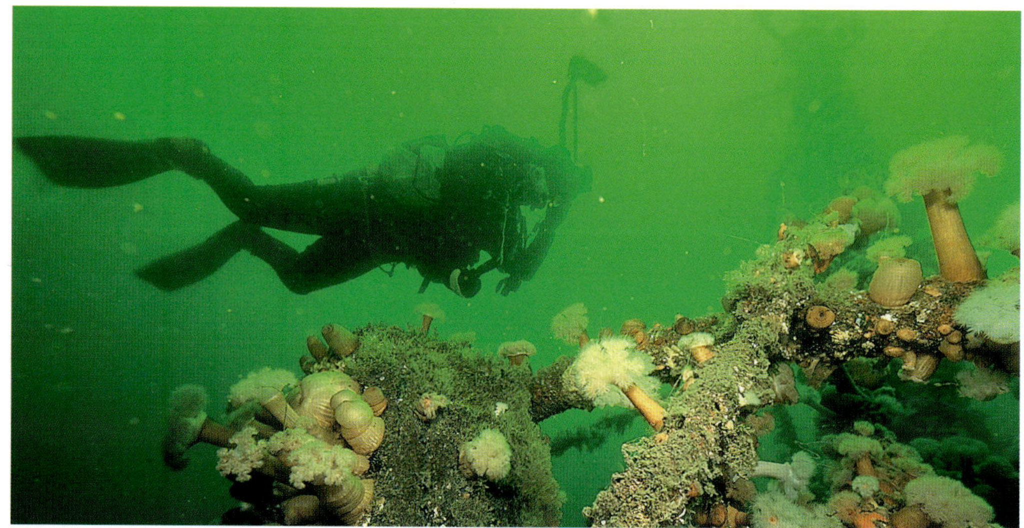

Even when considerable underwater experience has been built up, it should be realized that operating a camera can be extremely diverting, and care needs to be taken by experienced divers to ensure that they do not become complacent or negligent about other diving skills. I have inadvertently drifted into decompression on more than one occasion, and had my 'buddy' (my wife, who is also an underwater photographer) tap me on the shoulder to inform me.

There is also a very significant difference between diving in warm tropical seas and colder temperate waters. Cold-water dive gear is generally far more restrictive, the visibility lower, and the physical stresses experienced before, during and after diving are often higher than those associated with diving in warmer water. Any warm-water trained diver should become thoroughly familiarized with the changes in conditions, technique and equipment required for diving in temperate waters before taking an underwater camera into them.

Decompression, whether precautionary or necessary, is a boring task. Any film left over from the dive can be put to good use practising techniques such as balancing light, testing which shutter speeds are effective while the camera is hand held, and so on. Dive buddies are very useful for practising on, although they don't always like it!
Subal-housed Nikon F801 and 60mm micro-Nikkor lens, with a Nikon SB105 flash unit. 1/15s at f/16 on Fuji Provia 100 ISO

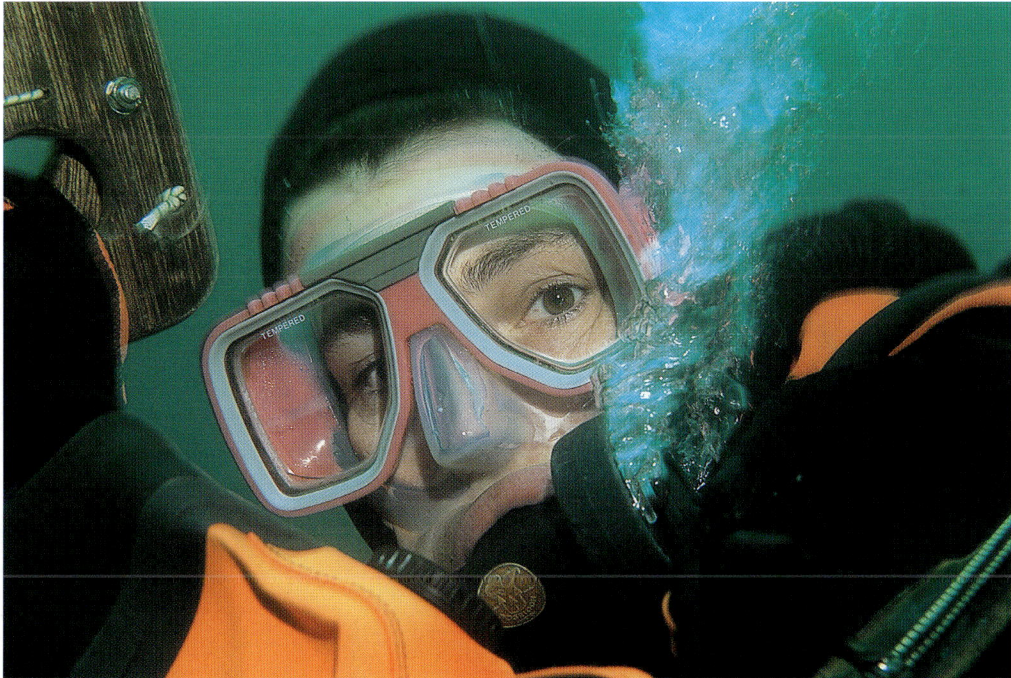

Nitrogen narcosis is assumed to be a problem only beyond certain depths, but many divers will testify that concentrating while underwater at any depth is not as easy as above water, even for those who are experienced and narcosis aware. Many underwater photographs are not as good as they could be for no obvious reason. Just being aware of this, and concentrating more to compensate, may help improve the percentage of useful photographs taken.

Dive equipment

It is essential to put diving equipment before camera gear. Clearly, to take good photographs an underwater photographer has to be comfortable, as well as safe, in the anticipated dive conditions. Being comfortable underwater makes a big difference in terms of the ability to concentrate in a difficult environment. This means that the dive suit (wet or dry) should be a good fit and as thermally efficient as is required to keep body temperature up. Water conducts heat away from the body very efficiently and long dives, even in warm water, may need warmer suits. I tend to use a dry suit in all but the warmest water as I do not want to have to think about cooling down at all.

Equipment should be well maintained, serviced according to its manufacturer's recommendations, and in good working order. Scuba gear is life-support equipment, and as such needs to be treated with the respect that it deserves. This is true of all of the equipment used, not just breathing apparatus.

Photography raises specific issues with regard to certain items of equipment. Demand valves should not need to be squashed or pushed into the mouth in order to look into a camera viewfinder. Most valves vent exhaust air from below and to either side of the mouth. Many underwater photographers prefer side-venting regulators, as these expel exhaust air from one side of the mouth, away from the camera viewfinder.

Trying to take a photograph looking upward and seeing a constant stream of bubbles that can be traced to a leaking detachable air connector is infuriating. All air connections should be in good condition in any case, but this is an important additional reason.

Rebreather units are becoming more widely accepted, and some underwater photographers find these very successful, especially in terms of getting close to fish and other creatures usually frightened by air bubbles and the noise they generate. Using rebreathers requires extensive additional training and experience. They also seem to be far more demanding in terms of monitoring (when in use) and maintenance (when not in use) than conventional equipment.

For those who wear glasses, a dive mask with corrected, or prescription, lenses is a must. While some camera viewfinders have adjustable dioptric correction built in, many housings use reducing optics to provide a small but complete view of the viewfinder image. This is often at a fixed 'virtual' distance from the eye, and may require an optician's advice as to which corrective lens to fit to the 'taking-eye' side of a mask.

The diving buddy should also be aware of the photographic requirements of a dive so that no interference occurs. Many underwater photographers claim that solo diving has its place, but undertaking this does increase the risk factor. No training agency sanctions this type of diving as being as safe as diving using the 'buddy system'.

My own preference is to dive with my wife, Lucy. While she does carry and use a camera too, she understands my way of diving (and vice versa) and I feel attuned to her underwater. This is a result of many years of diving together and its value cannot be underestimated.

Lastly, there are a few divers who seem to believe that 50 metres is only a nominal limit for scuba diving on air, despite the plethora of data which supports this figure as being 'acceptable' as an air limit. Anyone who intends to exceed this depth on air while using a camera is fooling nobody; it dramatically increases the risk levels, and photographs taken while suffering from high levels of nitrogen narcosis will probably be of poor quality anyway.

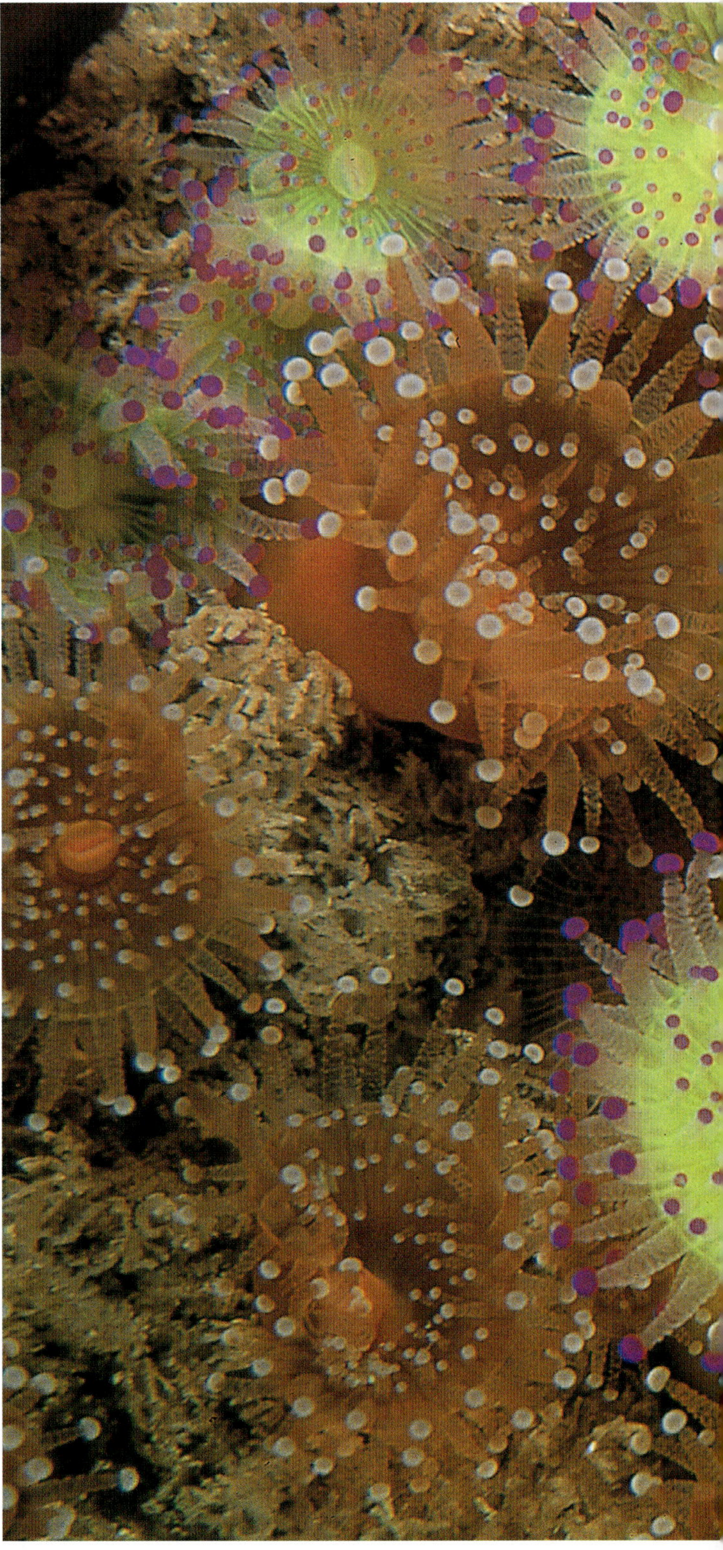

Jewel anemones (*Corynactis viridis*) are among the most photographed of temperate species. Trying to take a different photograph of them is tricky, but can be done. Searching out different colour morphs (at the edges of sheets of similarly coloured anemones) is one way, and certainly produces a striking image. ***Subal-housed Nikon F100 and 60mm micro-Nikkor, with Nikon SB105 flash unit. 1/30s at f/16 on Fuji Velvia 50 ISO***

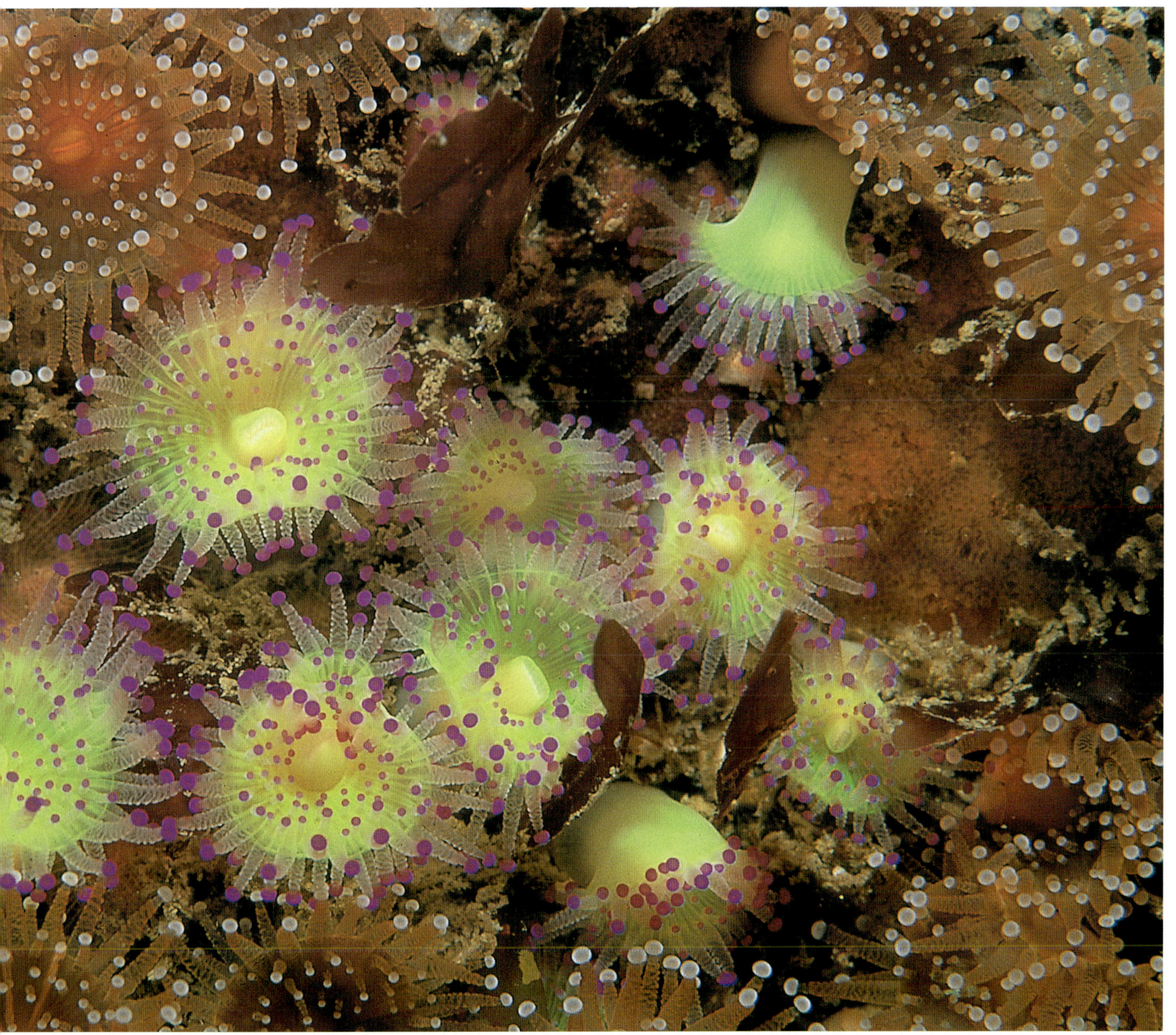

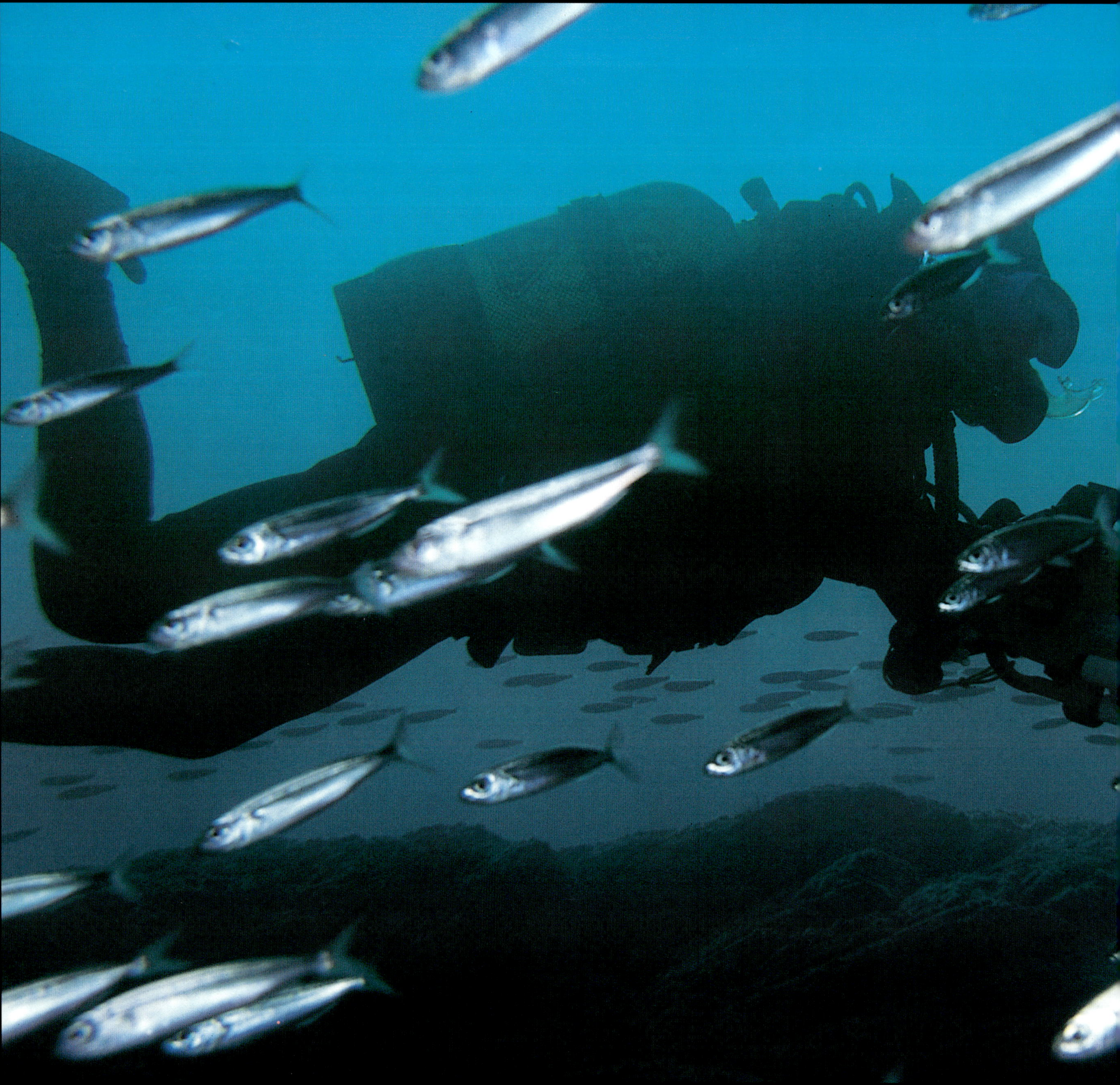

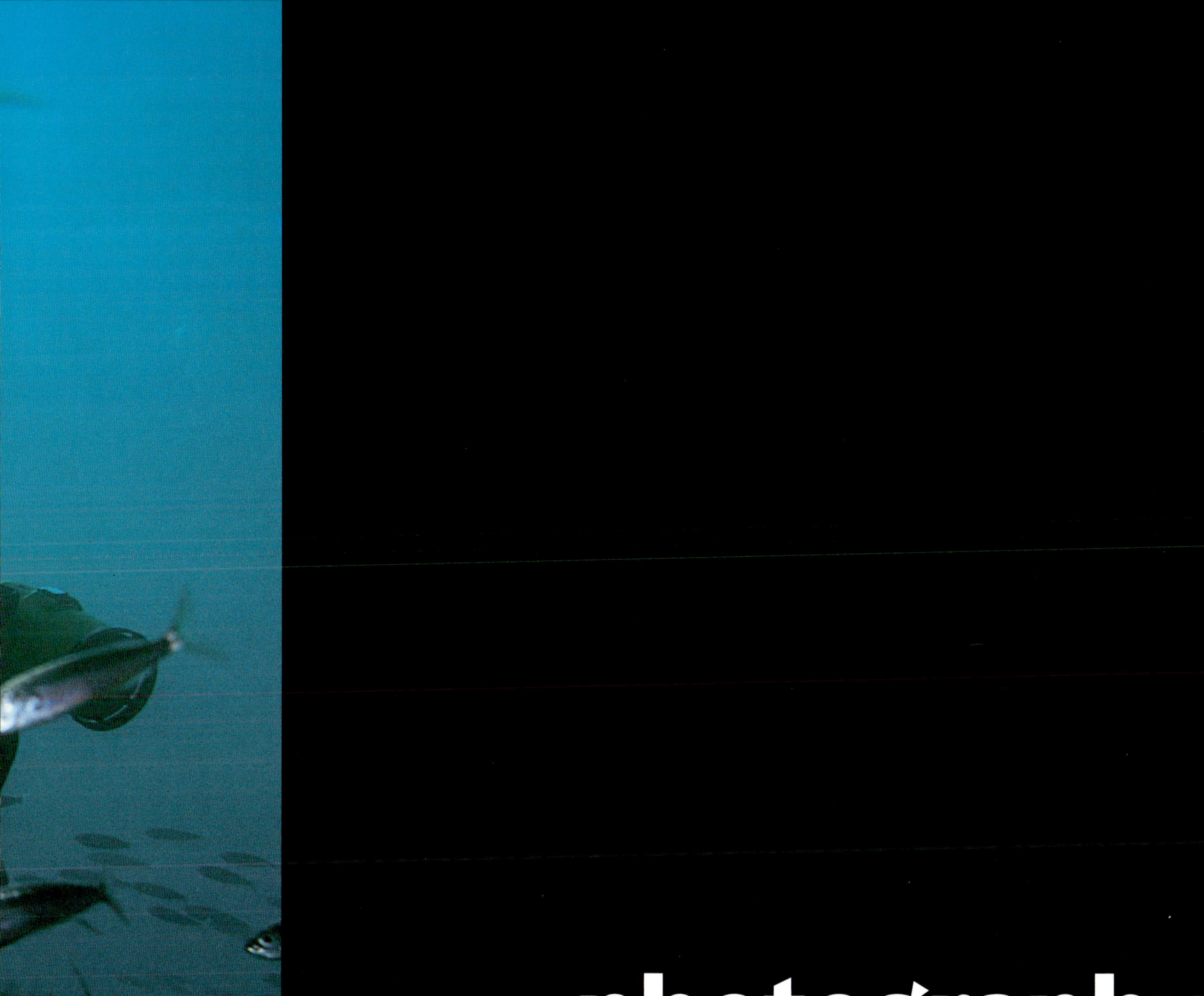

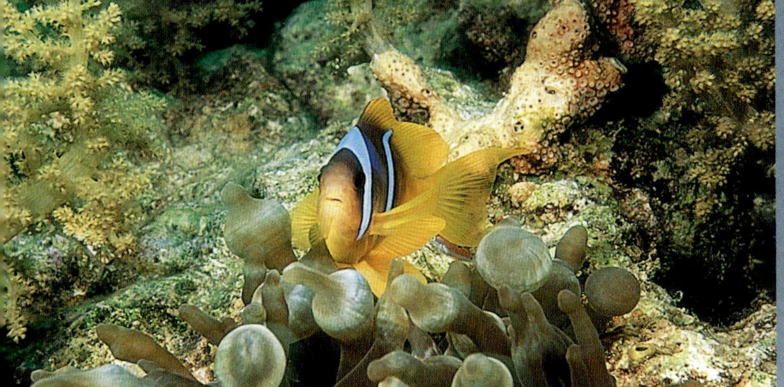

photographic basics

Many scuba divers decide that they would like to take up underwater photography, but most of them have little or no existing knowledge of photography. As underwater photography can be technically demanding, this chapter is intended as an introduction to some of the basic principles of photography, which will be of use to anyone wanting to it take up.

It may also be useful as a refresher for anyone already familiar with various photographic techniques, but who no longer tends to work through basics. While this book is inevitably limited in terms of the amount of theory that it can go into, it does cover the basic essentials that underwater photographers really do need to know.

The concept of photography

Photography literally means drawing with light (it is derived from the Greek *photo* meaning light and *graphos* meaning to draw). This sums up photography perfectly – producing an image by using light.

In practical terms, what this actually involves is using a lens to project an image onto a light-sensitive material (usually film, but now also an electronic device) that can be used to produce a permanent record. A camera is used to do this, and most have various controls to enable the amount of light passing through them to be regulated. This is so that a correctly exposed image (i.e. an image of the appropriate intensity) can be projected onto the light-sensitive material.

So, in essence, a camera is simply a light-tight container, with a lens and light-regulating mechanism, that contains a light-sensitive material. In the case of a film camera, after the light-sensitive material has been exposed to a specific amount of light, the film is placed into various chemicals so that a visible image is produced (this is known as processing). Processed images can be either slides (transparencies) or negatives. Both of these can then be printed onto paper, and slides can also be projected.

Today, digital technology is starting to replace conventional, chemically processed films. However, the fundamental mechanism used to produce the image still remains the same, and there is no real change in basic photographic principles. Film and digital devices both still require a specific amount of light to activate them correctly, and lenses and light-regulating mechanisms will still be incorporated into cameras for the foreseeable future.

The only difference between a camera used underwater and one used on land is that the underwater one needs to be waterproof. The way it works remains fundamentally the same.

This image remains one of my most satisfying. It captures the essence of diving in the kelp forest surrounding Staffa in the Inner Hebrides, Scotland. I love temperate diving, and to me this sums up the movement, colour and beauty to be found off the west coast of Scotland.
Subal-housed Nikon F100 and 17–35mm lens set at 17mm, with two diffused Nikon SB105 flash units. 1/8s at f/11 on Fuji Provia 100 ISO

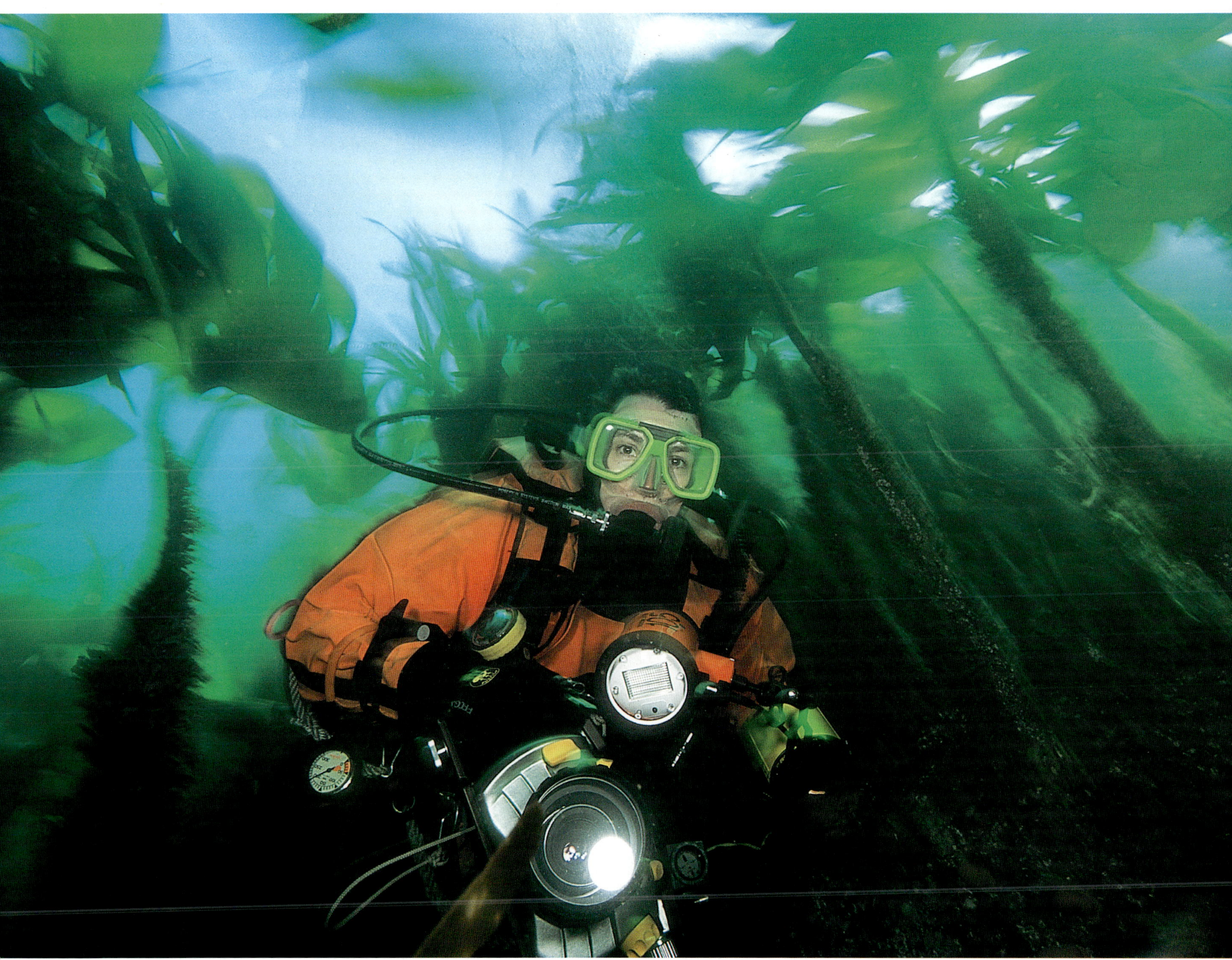

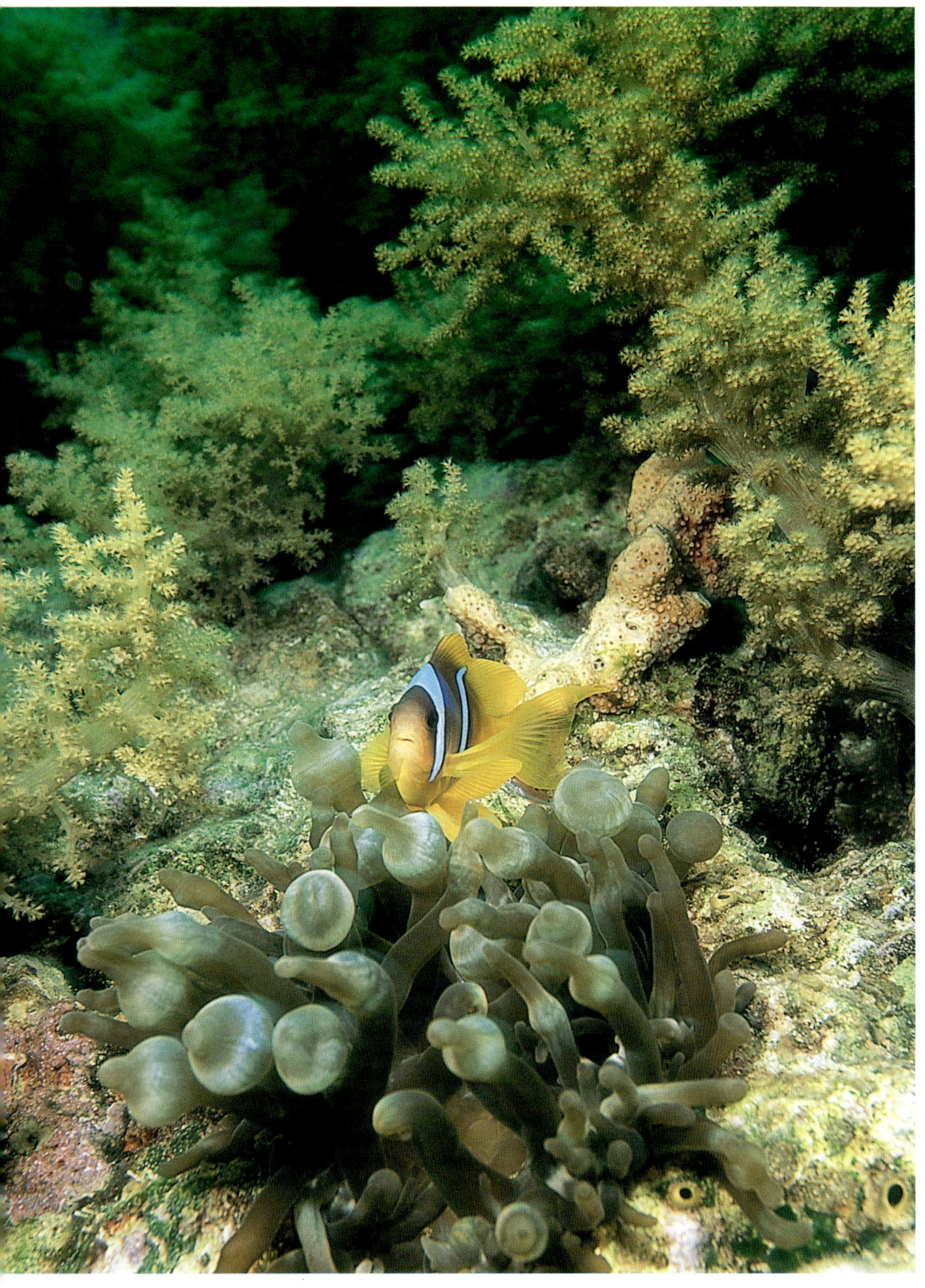

Photographic formulae

While many people may not like having to deal with equations, there is one essential formula in photography, necessary to understand the photographic process, and this is:

Exposure = **Intensity** (of light) x **Time** (for which light falls onto the film) or **E** = **I** x **T**

Exposure (**E**) is a term used to describe the process of actually capturing an image, whether it is on light-sensitive film or by digital means. The two variables in our formula are Intensity (**I**) and Time (**T**). These are adjusted by two camera controls: light intensity is altered by varying the aperture, and time by altering shutter speed.

An exposure is made using the combination of aperture and shutter speed that will produce the desired image. This sounds very straightforward, and it is. No matter what camera is used, it will always use a combination of aperture and shutter speed.

Most pictures of anemone fish (this is a two-banded one, *Amphiprion bicinctus*, from Aqaba in Jordan) are photographed in close up. This shot shows the habitat and background, so that the fish is placed in its correct context.
Subal-housed Nikon F100 and 60mm micro-Nikkor lens, with a Nikon SB105 flash unit. 1/15s at f/16 on Fuji Velvia 50 ISO

exposure

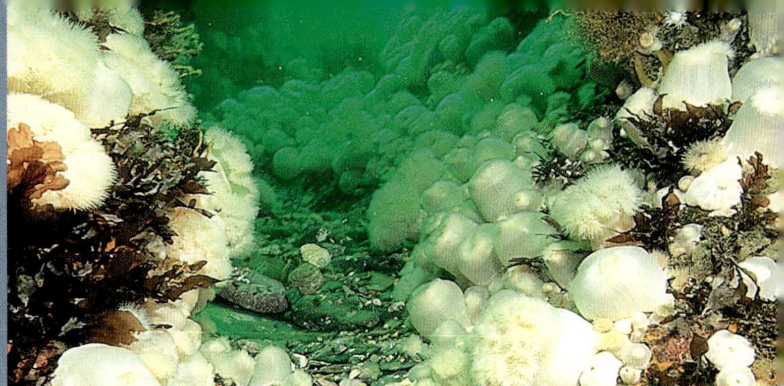

Precisely what constitutes a 'correct' exposure can be a matter of personal preference. Older cameras and hand-held meters worked on the assumption that they were measuring light that would reproduce a mid-tone grey (i.e. a grey that reflects 18% of the light falling onto it). This is fine in simple situations, but does not take into account contrast or the colour of light and so on. Today's sophisticated reflex cameras, and many digital cameras, take into account all sorts of factors when assessing what is the 'correct' exposure. These include contrast, predominant colours and more.

Determining an exposure to be made underwater is still problematic, as contrast and light levels are often low. Many different aspects of assessing exposure will be covered in the following sections of this book, but it is important at this stage to appreciate that a correct exposure is one that results in an image showing the same range of colours and tones that were envisaged when it was taken.

If the final photo is too light, it is termed as being overexposed; it is underexposed if too dark. This statement can be applied not only to the whole photograph, but also to areas within it. Thus, a photo of a diver against a blue coral reef may show the blue water and coral reef as intended, but the diver may be too dark. Lightening the diver by adjusting either aperture or shutter speed may result in the diver being fine, but the reef and water appearing overexposed. This is an example of a photograph that needs some additional illumination in order to light up the diver while keeping the water and reef correctly exposed. To do so some flash lighting may be used, and the

A shot such as this one, taken to illustrate the poor visibility often found in the Menai Strait in North Wales, is more difficult to produce than one taken in better conditions. Combining a slow shutter speed with an aperture that allows flash, available light and torch light to be exposed correctly is tricky.
Subal-housed Nikon F801 and 20mm Nikkor lens, with a Nikon SB105 flash unit. 1/4s at f/8 on Fuji Provia 100 ISO

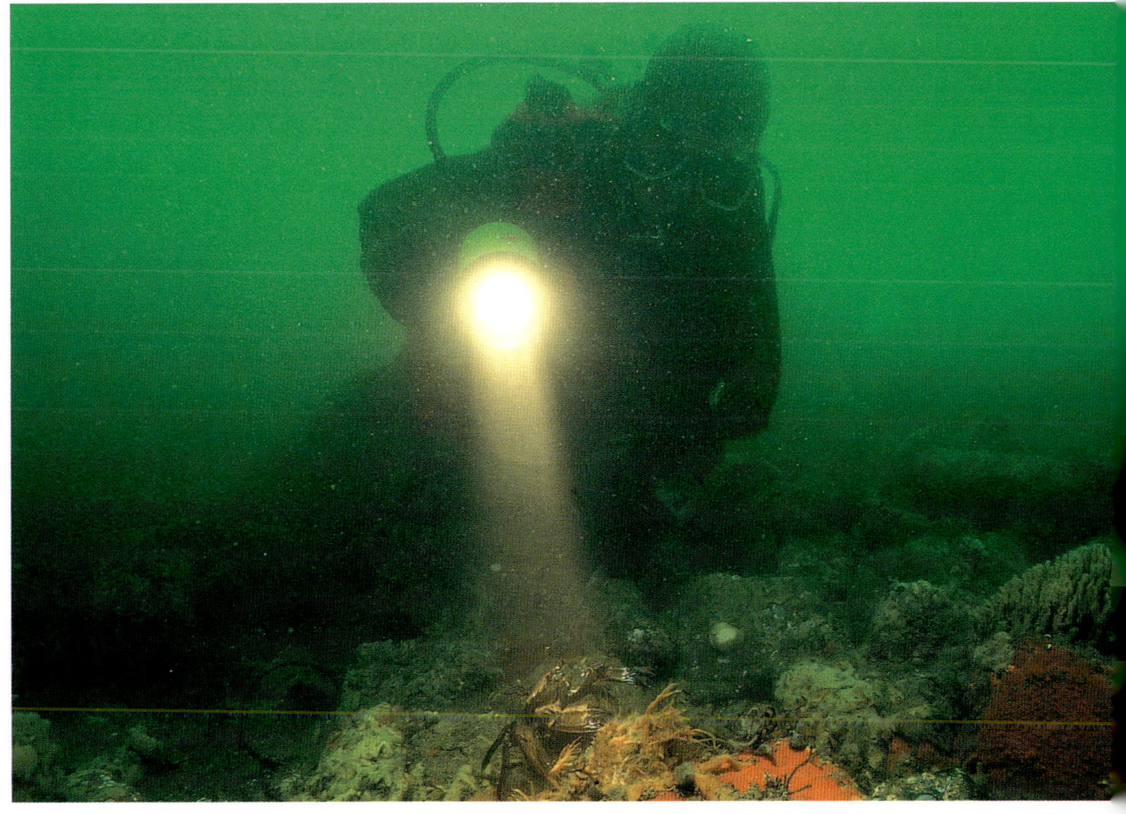

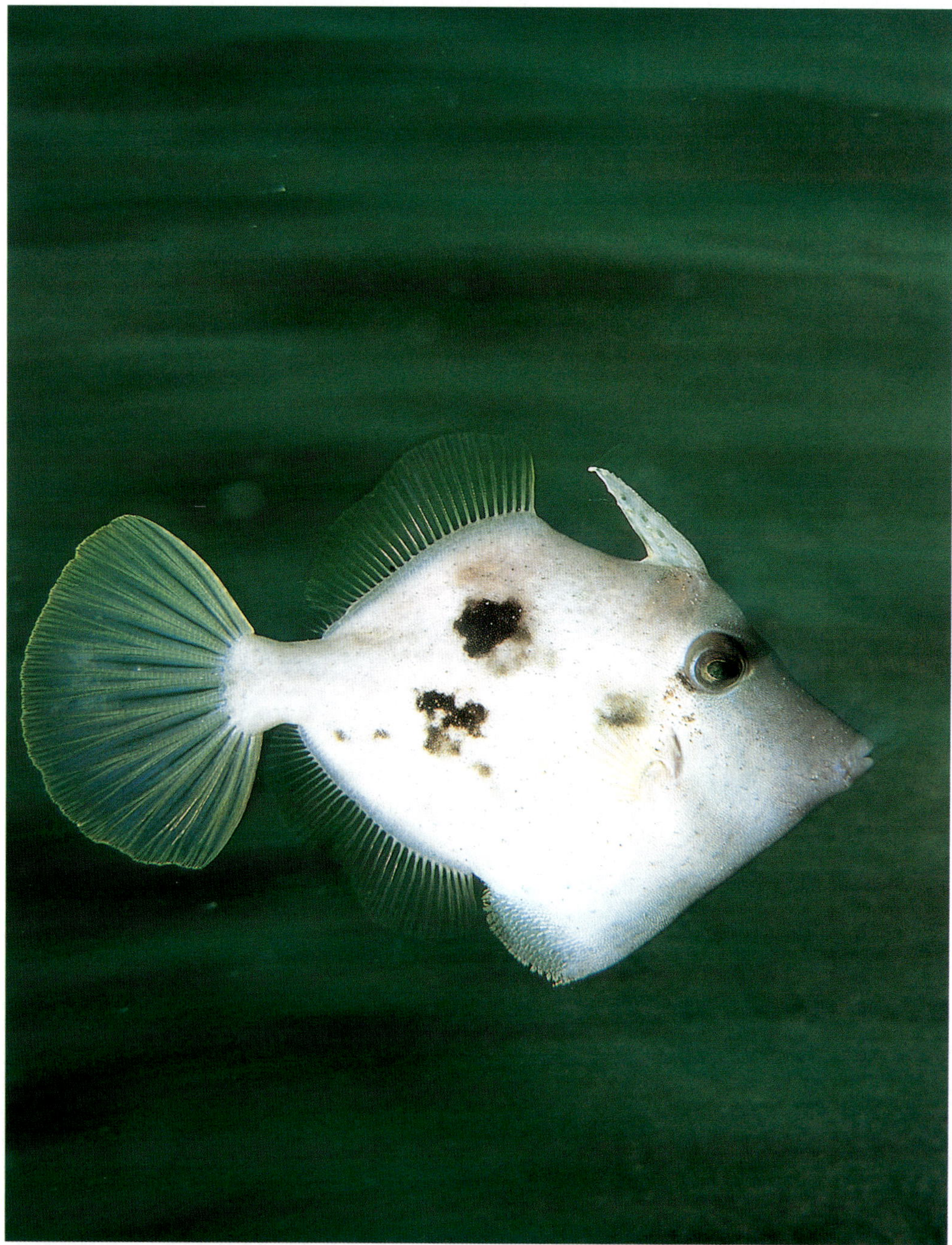

Panning is a technique used to blur the background into streaks. It is used above water, but using this technique underwater is complicated by the addition of flash. It does produce interesting images, but relies on moving the camera with the subject, even if it is only a few centimetres long. Pygmy filefish (*Stephanolepis hispidus*), taken off Lanzarotte.
Subal-housed Nikon F100 and 60mm micro-Nikkor, with Nikon SB105 flash unit. 1/30s at f/16 on Fuji Velvia 50 ISO

photograph would be taken using 'fill-flash' or 'balanced light'. The section on techniques (see page 90) will cover this type of photography, explain how exposures are determined and suggest when to use certain approaches.

Apertures

The intensity (**I**) of light falling onto the film is adjusted by using the aperture control. In most cases the aperture is actually a multi-bladed diaphragm set within the camera lens that is only activated when an exposure is actually made. The intensity of light that this permits can be adjusted by varying the size of the 'hole' that it forms.

Apertures are numbered, and shown on lenses as follows:

1, 1.4, 2, 2.8, 4, 5.6, 8, 11, 16, 22, 32, 45, 64

Each increasing figure represents a halving of the light intensity allowed to fall onto the film. Aperture values are usually written as an f-number (e.g. f/5.6) to show that the figure is an aperture.

For the technically minded, this number is the ratio of the diameter of the aperture to the focal length of the lens. So a 50mm lens with an effective aperture diameter of 50mm would be described as being an f/1 lens. A 50mm lens with an effective aperture diameter reduced to 25mm would be an f/2 lens, and so on.

Also for the technically minded, the actual intensity of light from an aperture of f/2 compared with f/1 is a quarter. The intermediate number f/1.4 represents the halving of intensity because it represents an increase in the area of the aperture by the square root of 2, which is the increase required to double the light intensity. The scale is actually a logical mathematical progression.

This is how apertures are numbered, but it is not essential to understand the mathematics. All that is necessary is to appreciate that the apertures represent a reduction (or increase) in light intensity through a halving (or doubling) system.

The intermediate figures shown in the sequence below are 'one-third stop' differences in aperture. These are found on some lenses and in the displays of the more expensive and sophisticated cameras.

1, 1.1, 1.2, 1.4, 1.6, 1.8, 2, 2.2, 2.5, 2.8, 3.3, 3.5, 4, 4.5, 5, 5.6, 6.3, 7, 8, 9, 10, 11, 12.5, 14, 16, 18, 20, 22, 25, 28, 32

Apertures are often referred to as stops, a term that comes from when they were physical light 'stops' (plates with holes of differing size in them), which were used to vary the light passing through the lenses of very old cameras by 'stopping' some of it. Now a stop is the photographic term used to denote a full doubling or halving of either aperture, shutter speed or film sensitivity. Differences of a half and even a third of a stop in exposure are often quoted, which is why figures differing by these amounts are shown in the sequences of ISO ratings, apertures and shutter speeds.

Shutter speeds

The mechanism used to control the amount of time for which light is allowed to fall onto the film is the camera shutter. This normally remains closed until an exposure is made, at which point it opens for the duration required.

Shutter 'speeds' are the duration for which the film is exposed to light. They are shown in terms of seconds or fractions of a second (known as reciprocals), some of which are approximated. For example, 1/15s should really be

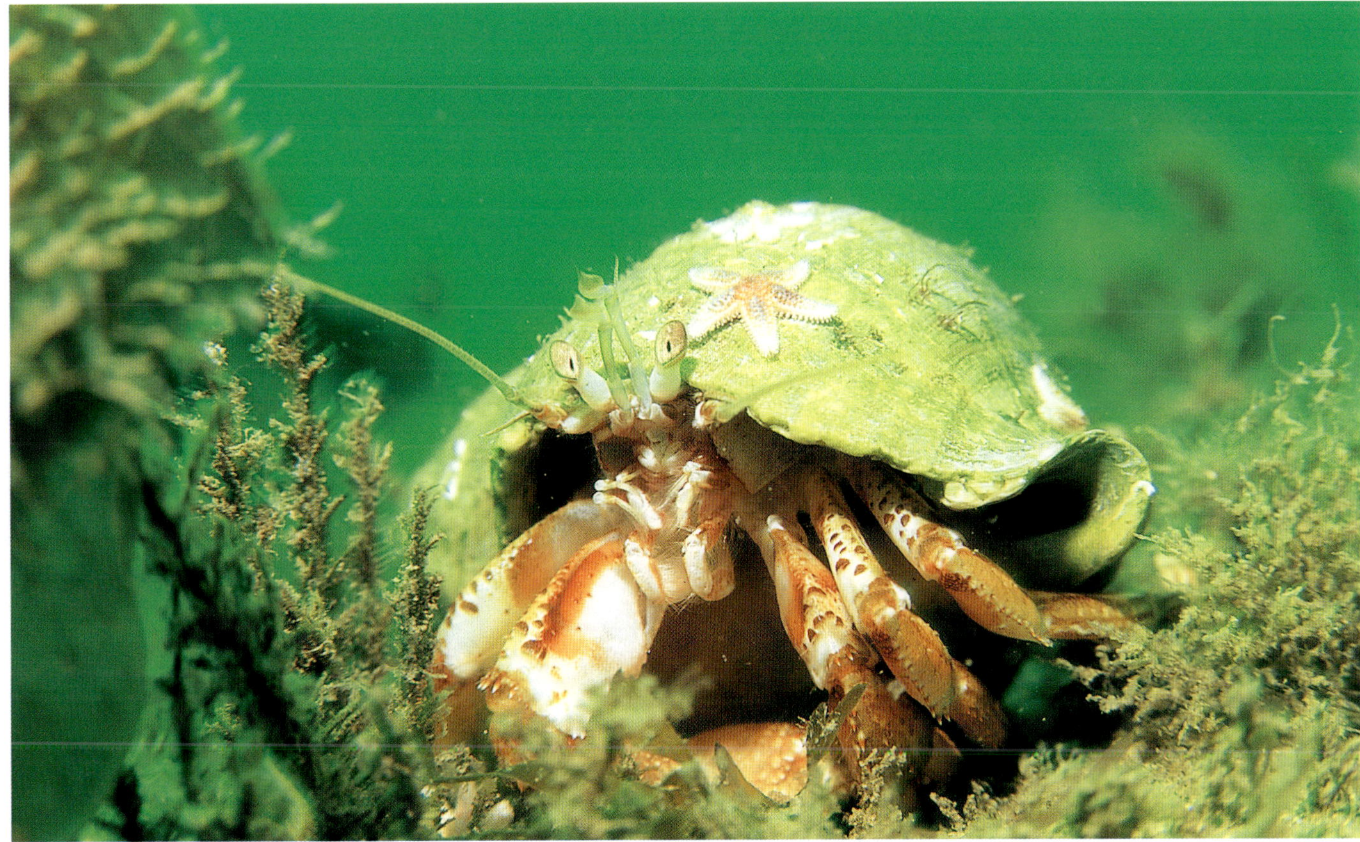

This hermit crab in Cardigan Bay, North Wales, was in a suitable position to enable the use of a slow shutter speed to capture the rich green of the seawater. The effect is almost surreal in its emphasis on strong colour.
Subal-housed Nikon F100 and 60mm micro-Nikkor lens, with a Nikon SB105 flash unit. 1/4s at f/16 on Fuji Velvia 50 ISO

1/16s, 1/30s should be 1/32s, and so on. As with apertures, intermediate figures represent intermediate speeds that are available on some cameras. These come in either one-third or one-half stop increments depending on the camera. The series for one-third stops is shown below:

8", 6", 5", **4**", 3", 2.5", **2**", 1.6", 1.3", **1**", 1.3, 1.6, **2**, 2.5, 3, **4**, 5, 6, **8**, 10, 13, **15**, 20, 25, **30**, 40, 50, **60**, 80, 100, **125**, 160, 200, **250**, 320, 400, **500**, 640, 800, **1000**, 1250, 1600, **2000**, 2500, 3200, **4000**, 5000, 6400, **8000**

The " is used to denote seconds; all the other numbers are an approximate fraction of a second (e.g. 1/250s). **Bold** figures denote 'standard' shutter speeds, each of which represents a halving (or doubling) of the open time.

At this point it is worth mentioning something known as exposure latitude. This is the term used to indicate the amount of inaccuracy that a film will tolerate in exposure while still producing an acceptable result. Even a film with little latitude – such as a slow, fine-grained slide film – will not show a significant difference when exposures made vary by as little as one third of a stop. So this is generally the precision to which most cameras and their meters are built to operate.

Exposure values

Combinations of shutter speeds and apertures that allow the same amount of light to expose the film are said to have the same exposure value (**EV**). For example, 1/60s at f/5.6 is equivalent to 1/125s at f/4, which is equivalent to 1/30s at f/8, and so on. As one parameter is adjusted in one direction, the other needs to be adjusted in the other; using a smaller aperture means also using a slower shutter speed, and using a larger (or wider) aperture means setting a faster shutter speed.

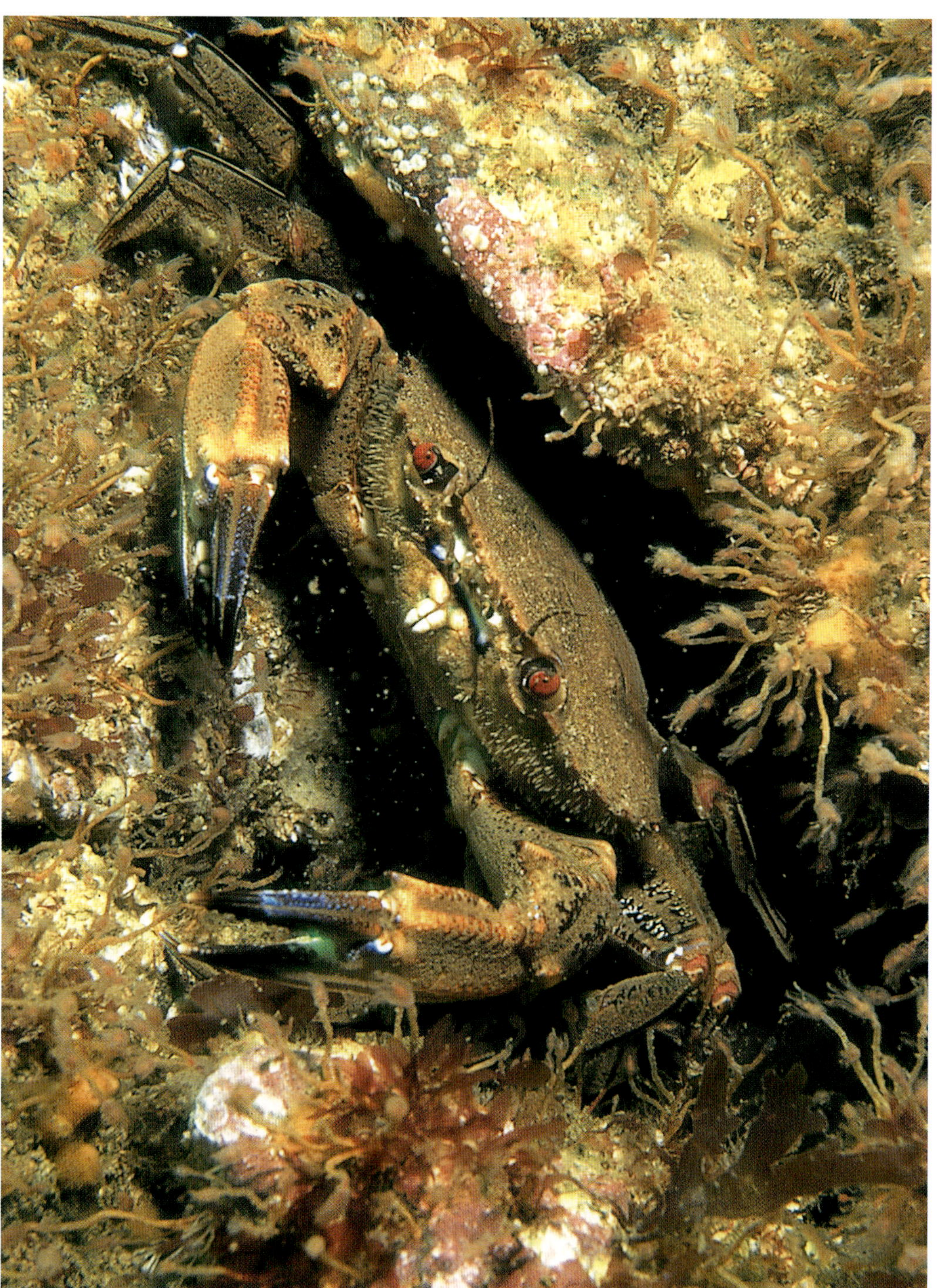

Velvet swimming crabs (*Liocarcinus puber*) may be vicious animals, but they still like to retreat into a crevice when necessary.

Subal-housed Nikon F801 and 60mm micro lens, with a Nikon SB105 flash unit. 1/60s at f/16 on Fuji Provia III 100 ISO

effects of aperture and shutter speed

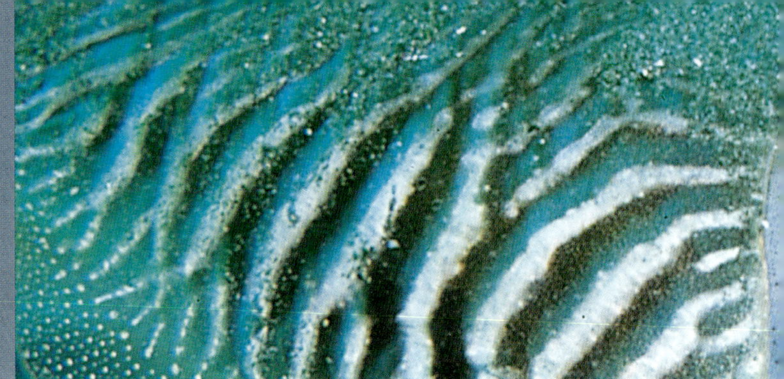

Changing the aperture has further effects that need to be considered when taking a photograph. By far the most important of these is depth of field. This is quite a simple concept, but it has such an impact on the resulting image that it needs to be thoroughly understood so that it may be used appropriately.

Depth of field is the phrase used to describe the area of a photograph that is in focus (i.e. sharp). A rule of thumb is that approximately one third of the depth of field extends in front of the point focused on, while two thirds extend behind it.

Wide apertures (i.e. small f-numbers) give little depth of field, while small apertures (i.e. large f-numbers) produce photographs in which far more is in focus. However, the focal length of a lens and the distance to the point of focus also affect depth of field. Using a wide-angle lens at a small aperture while focusing on a distant object will result in a very large depth of field. Conversely, using a long lens at a large aperture and focusing on a close object will result in a very shallow depth of field (and thus a very limited plane of sharpness).

It is possible to use what are known as hyperfocal settings. These settings allow for maximum depth of field in a photograph when a subject includes infinity in it (in an above-water scene). By using predetermined scales (which can either be engraved on the lens or supplied in its instruction booklet) as a reference, the furthest point that will be in focus can be set to infinity for any given aperture, thus ensuring that the maximum possible amount of the photograph is in focus.

Although the fish is swimming away from the camera, blurring (achieved by panning the camera) has resulted in an image where the photographer appears to be following the fish into the dark and mysterious sea. I like this shot, taken off Gozo, but it is a matter of personal taste.

Subal-housed Nikon F801 and 35mm Nikkor, with a Nikon SB105 flash unit. 1/8s at f/16 on Fuji Velvia 50 ISO

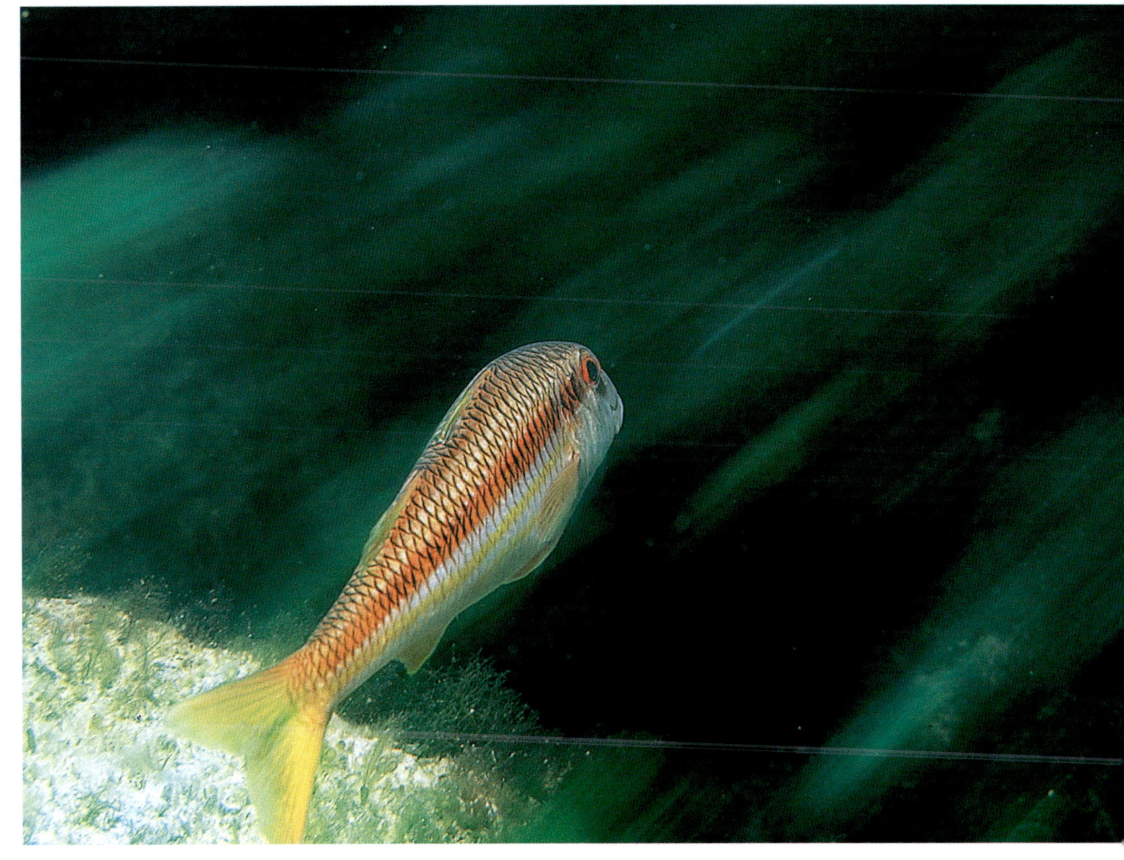

Unfortunately, depth-of-field scales are usually unreadable on underwater photographic systems (although some Nikonos lenses have a very accurate moving-pointer mechanism to indicate depth of field). However, it is useful to know about such settings when considering certain types of photograph, so that depth of field can be maximized.

While the depth of field dictates how much of a photograph is in focus, the aperture can also be used to influence how out of focus the rest of the image appears. Generally, this effect can only be seen once film has been processed, and is not viewable when using a camera underwater. Therefore, it is something that can only be learnt through the experience of using a specific lens.

The shutter speed used to take a photograph can have a marked effect on the final picture. A high shutter speed can freeze movement in a photograph, whereas a slow speed may produce blurred (usually unacceptable, but sometimes intentional and effective) results.

The choice of shutter speed in determining exposure usually has less direct relevance than aperture in underwater photography, but this does not mean that it lacks importance. Because so much use is made of flash

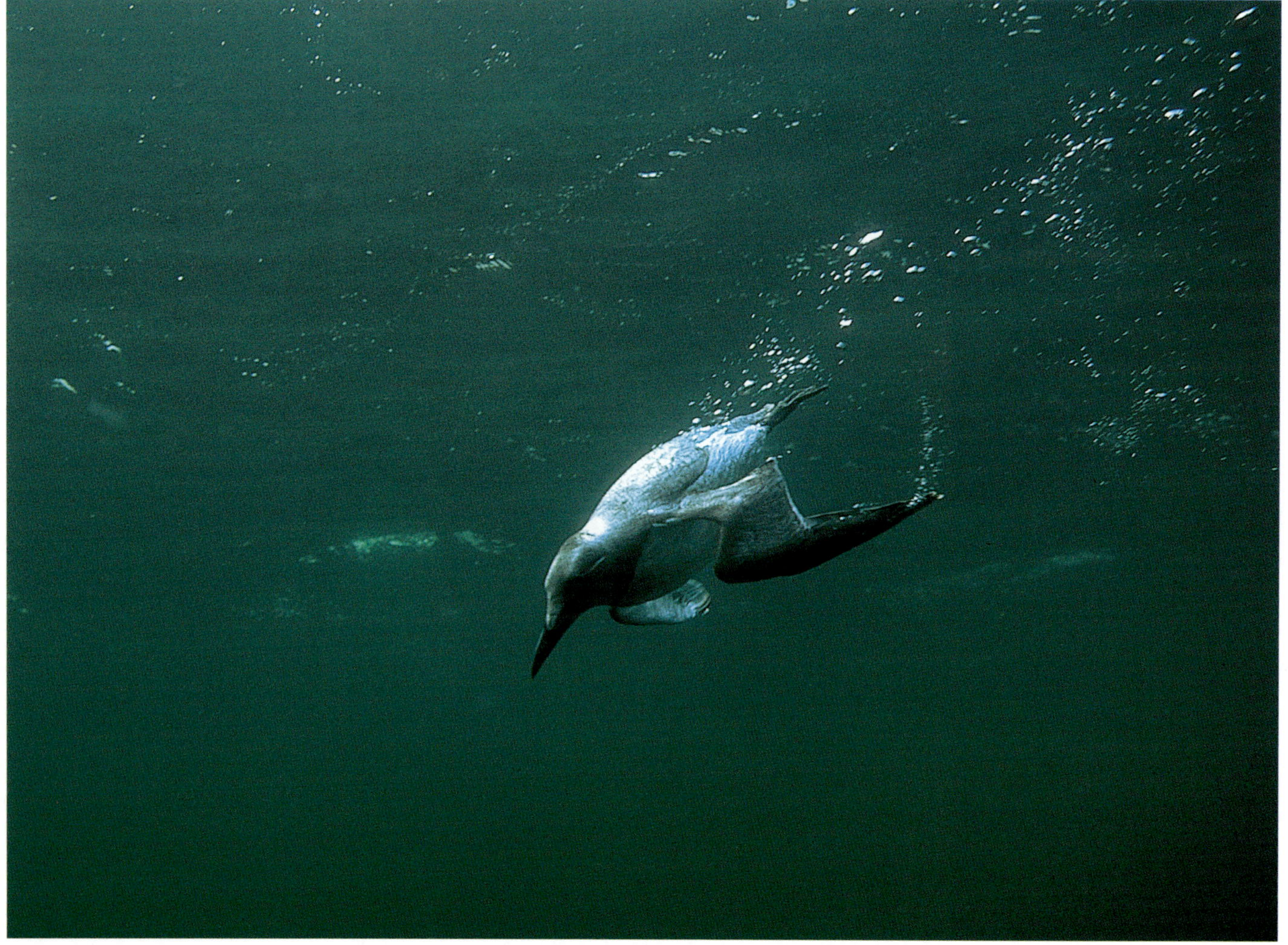

Using available light only relies on having a viable shutter speed. In this shot of a guillemot, 1/60s is marginal but, at f/5.6, was as fast as Fuji Velvia (pushed to 100 ISO) would allow. Taken off the Isle of Man, UK.
Subal-housed Nikon F100 and 17–35mm lens set at 35mm

underwater, there is a tendency not to use techniques involving slower shutter speeds. While the aperture generally dictates how much of a scene will be in focus, the shutter speed dictates whether anything at all will be sharp. If a shutter speed is too slow and no flash illumination is used, the whole picture might be blurred as a result, so primary consideration has to be given to what shutter speed is suitable when the photograph is taken.

Unlike above water, there is a damping medium entirely surrounding the underwater photographer. This means that some slow shutter speeds deemed unacceptable above water (as they would produce image blur), can, with care, be used underwater without the need for a tripod.

A rule of thumb above water is that a shutter speed approximately equal to the reciprocal of the focal length of the lens should be the minimum used to ensure a sharp photograph. So for a 50mm lens a 1/60s shutter speed would be the minimum; and for a 28mm, 1/30s. (This varies slightly from person to person, depending on how still each individual can hold a camera.) Underwater, it is possible to use shutter speeds of one, two or even more stops slower. Thus, for a 50mm lens it might be possible to use 1/30s or

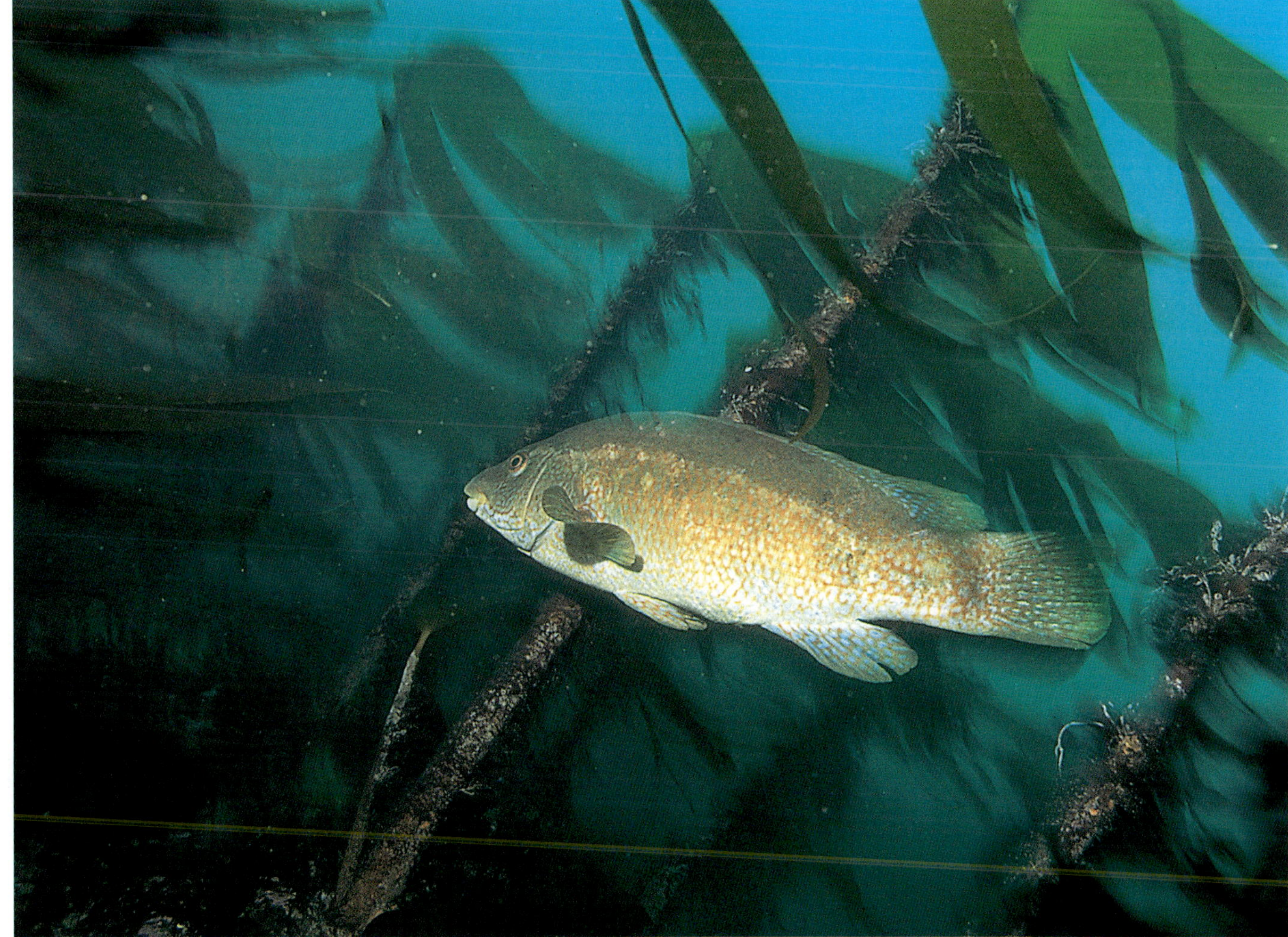

Using slow shutter speeds to allow the background to expose correctly can result in some ghosting (or double imaging), but is generally acceptable for shots like this of a ballan wrasse (*Labrus bergylta*) off the Kerry coast in Ireland.
Subal-housed Nikon F100 and 17–35mm lens set at 24mm, with two diffused Nikon SB105 flash units. 1/8s at f/11 on Fuji Provia 100 ISO

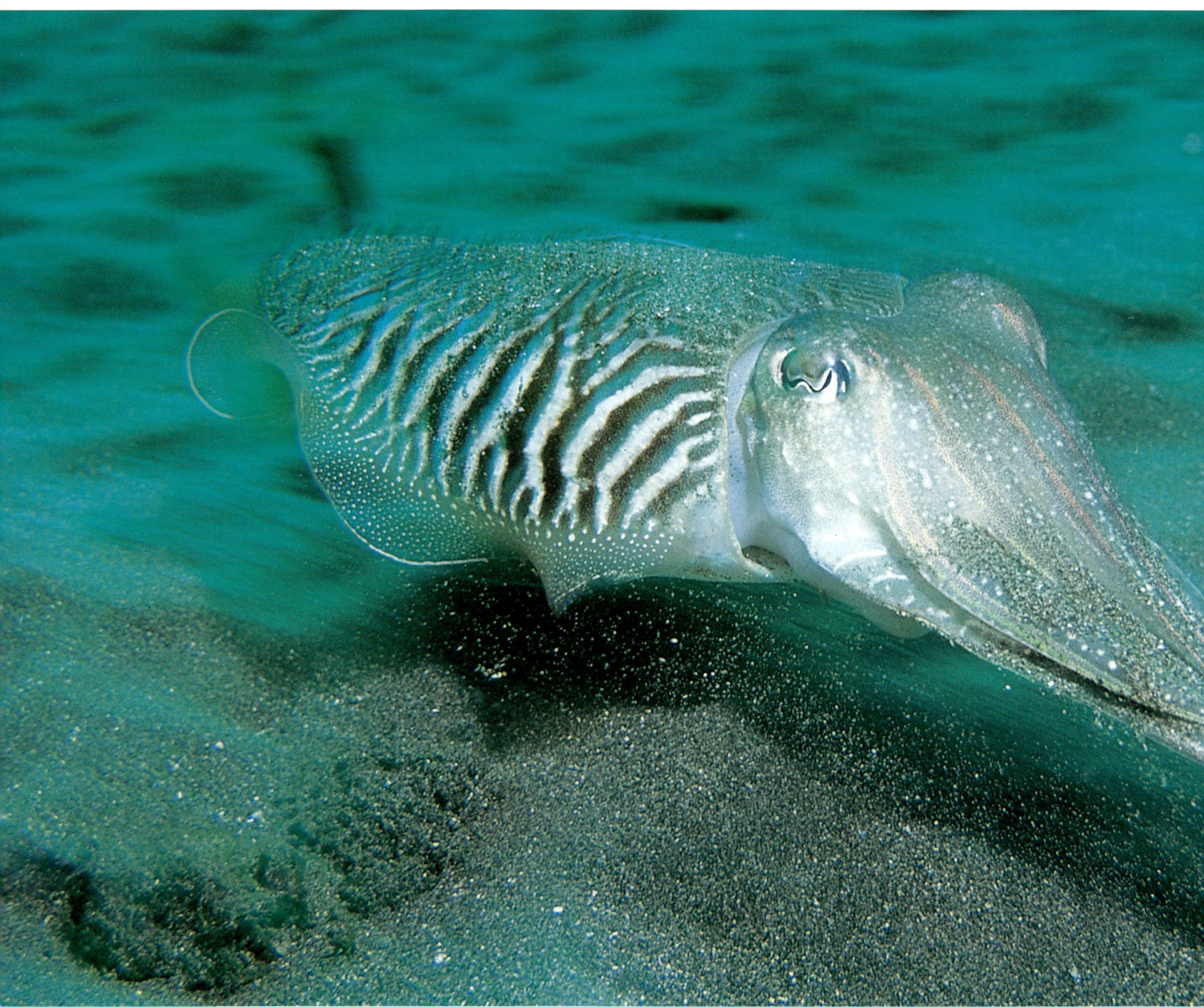

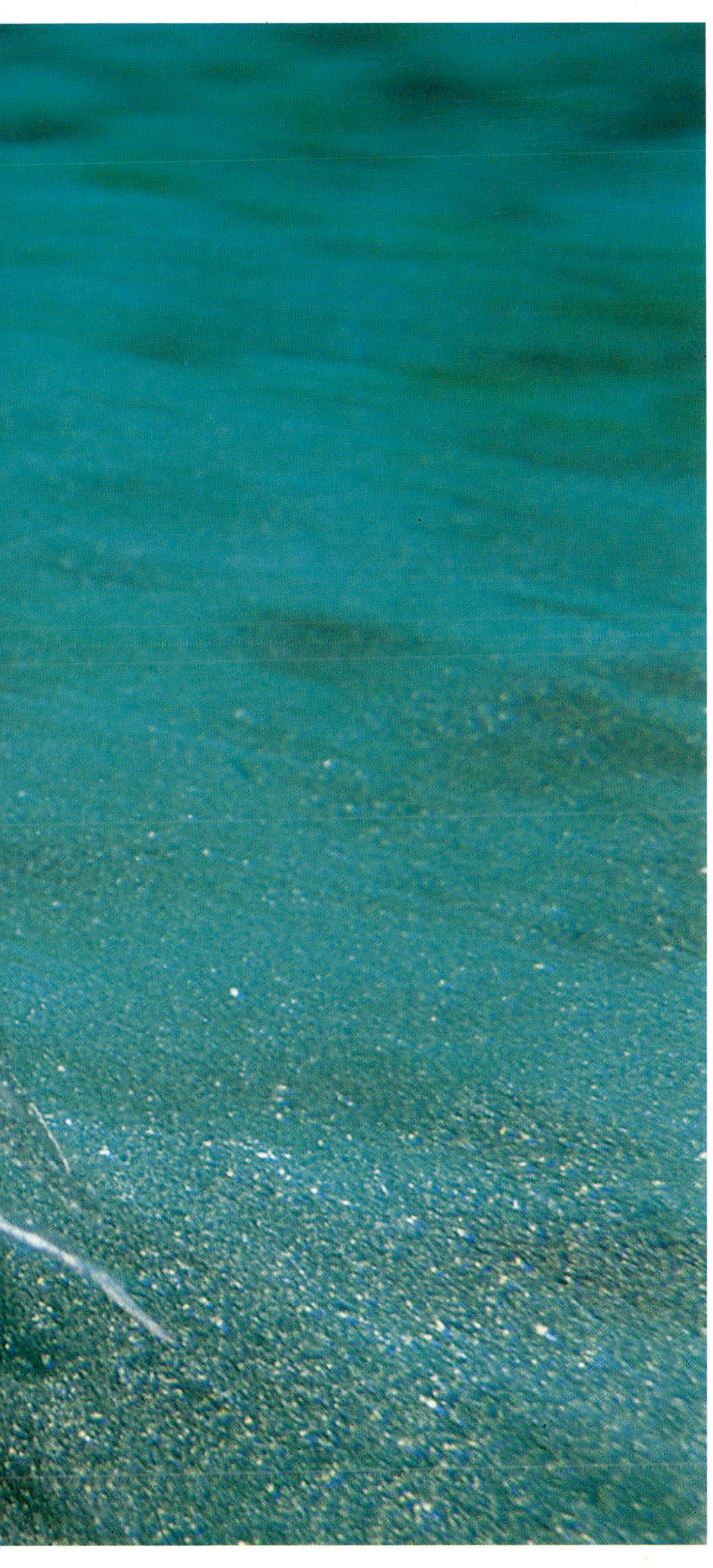

even 1/15s. If some flash is used, shutter speeds can drop even further because the flash freezes motion and makes the photograph appear sharp. To an extent it is a matter of trying slow speeds until results become acceptable. I have, on one occasion, managed to take a sharp photograph using a 4-second exposure, with some flash employed to sharpen it up, which was used on the cover of a diving magazine.

In most cases, flash only makes up a proportion of the light producing the exposure, as some will also come from the available light. With care this can result in lower 'back scatter' (see page 118). If appropriate slow shutter speeds are used, the bright highlights that the back scatter is made up from receive less flash illumination, and so are less intrusive in the finished product.

It is possible to use slow shutter speeds to produce image blur, and this can convey an impression of movement. When also combined with some flash illumination, the resulting photographs can be very effective indeed, but advanced techniques such as rear-curtain sync may also be required (see page 143).

There are many factors to take into account when deciding what combination of aperture and shutter speed to use when taking a photograph. Assessing exposure, too, means making choices. Fortunately, these are quickly narrowed down because other factors will reduce the possibilities of what can be used.

Combining an appropriate slower shutter speed with flash and panning produces a feeling of smooth movement rather than speed, and accurately describes what was happening when this picture of a common cuttlefish (*Sepia officinalis*) was taken off Lanzarotte.
Subal-housed Nikon F100 and 17–35mm AFS Nikkor set at 35mm, with a Nikon SB105 flash unit. 1/15s at f/16 on Fuji Velvia 50 ISO

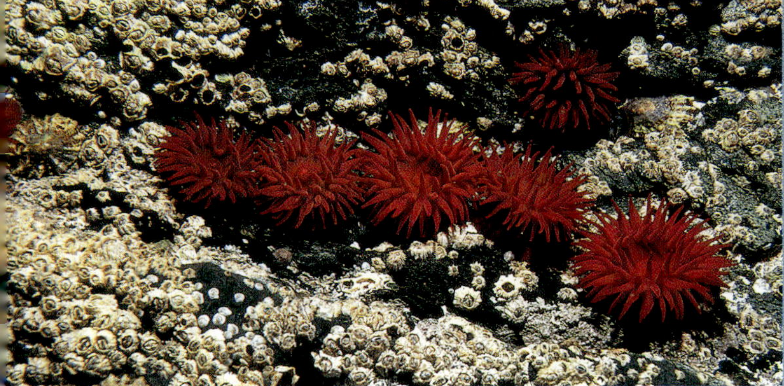

film

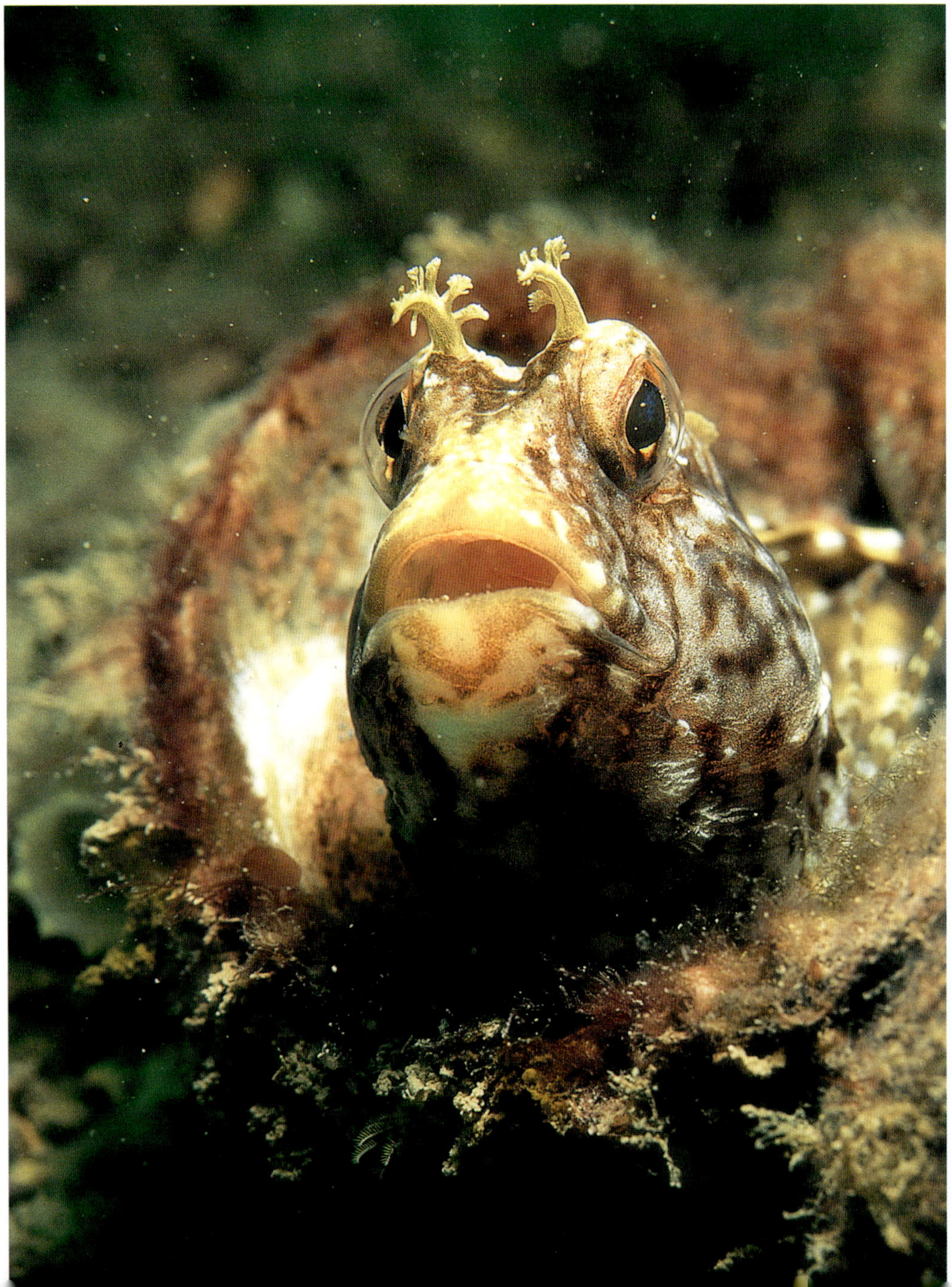

Film consists of a thin, transparent plastic base covered in a light-sensitive film emulsion made up of several layers. These layers – some of which contain silver halide – are made up of a variety of chemicals, which produce a visible image after they have been exposed to light and put through a chemical process.

Film speed or ISO ratings

As we have seen, film requires a fixed amount of light to expose it 'correctly', but first it is necessary to know something about the film's sensitivity to light. A standard system has been adopted, which classes films in terms of their sensitivity by giving them a number. This is often referred to as 'film speed' and is termed as an ISO rating, which will be found marked on the film packaging. A film with a specific ISO rating requires a known quantity of light to produce a precise and measurable effect in the final image after processing. ISO ratings are also applied to digital cameras, where the film is replaced by light-sensitive electronic components and processing is electronic rather than chemical.

This small butterfly blenny (*Blennius ocellaris*) refused to leave the shell in which he sat, as he was guarding the eggs laid inside. He was still curious and remained at the entrance to be photographed several times. St Tudwal's Islands, North Wales.
Subal-housed Nikon F100 and 60mm micro-Nikkor lens, with a Nikon SB105 flash unit. 1/4s at f/16 on Fuji Velvia 50 ISO

Black backgrounds have almost become a separate genre within underwater photography. They do have their place, as this shot (actually on a very dark green background) shows, but black tends to show up suspended particulate matter. Stinging jellyfish (*Cyanea lamarkii*), taken off the Orkney Islands, north Scotland.
Subal-housed Nikon F801 and 60mm micro-Nikkor lens, with a Nikon SB105 flash unit. 1/60s at f/16 on Fuji Velvia 50 ISO

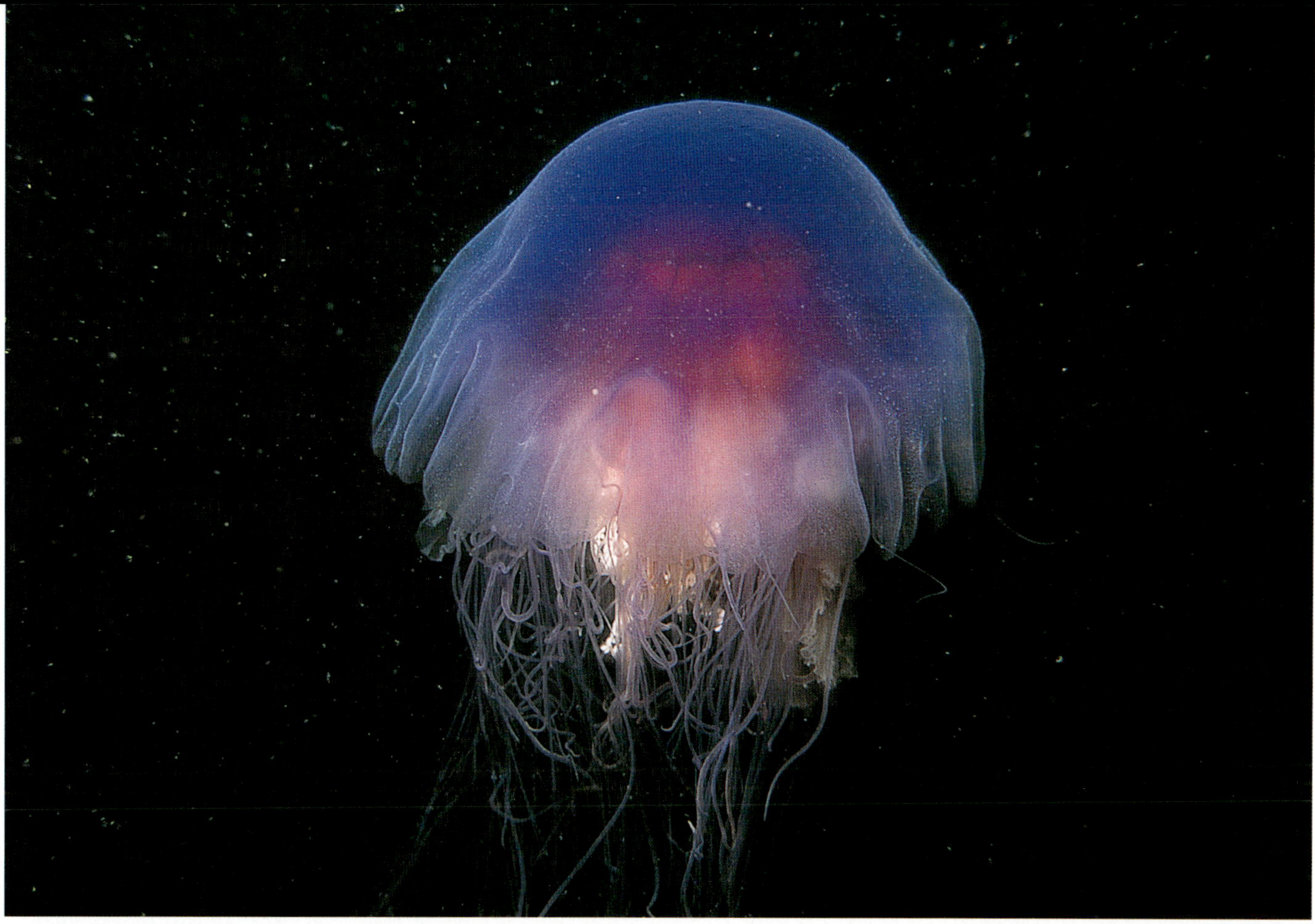

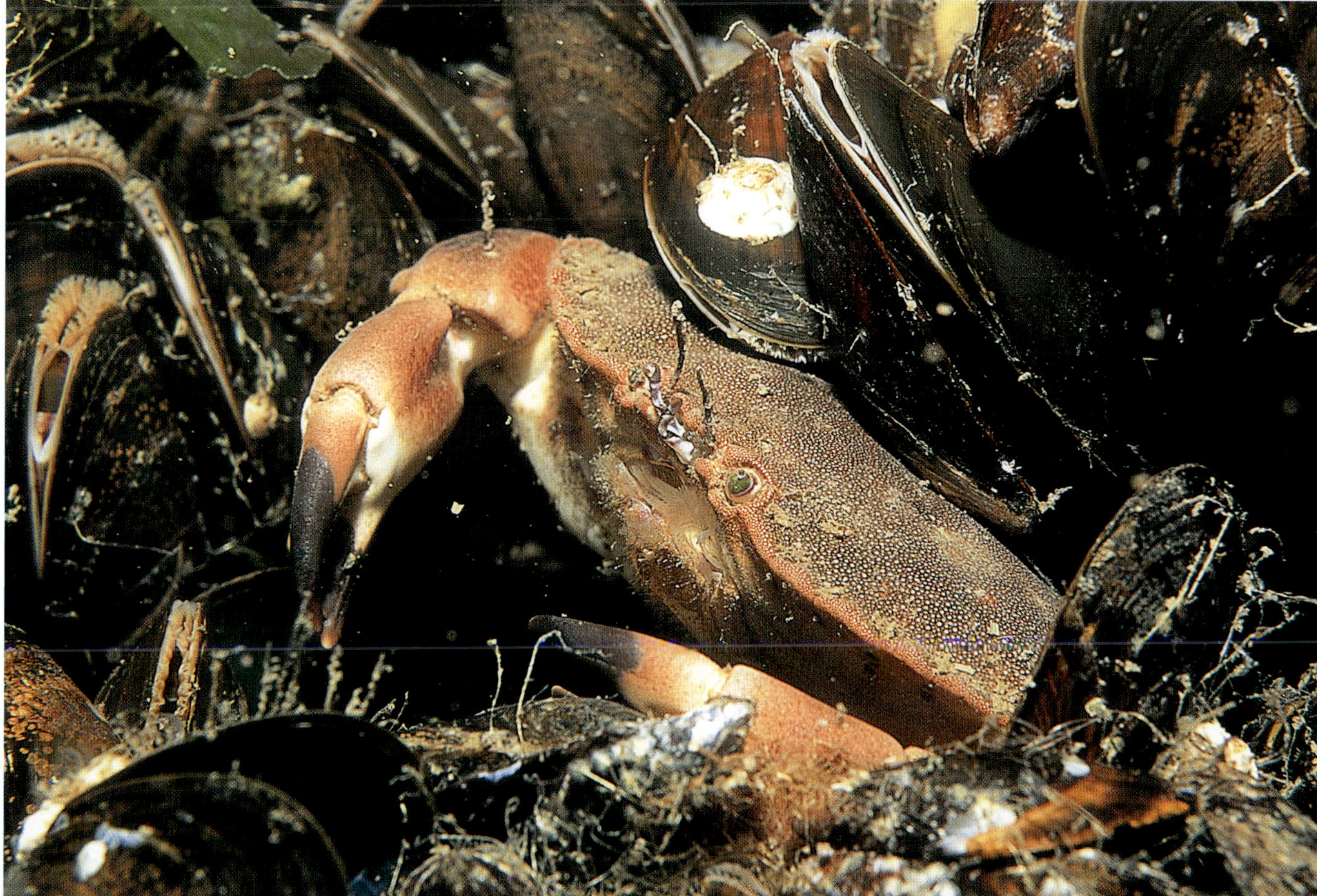

An unusual picture of an edible crab (*Cancer pagurus*) living in a mussel bed within the Menai Strait. An interesting, but unobtrusive, background enhances the subject.
Subal-housed Nikon F801 and 60mm micro-Nikkor lens. Single-flash illumination only. 1/60s at f/16 on Fuji Velvia 50 ISO

Films with higher ISO ratings are more sensitive to light, so less light is needed to expose these correctly than is required for lower-rated films. As mentioned, sensitivity to light is often referred to as 'speed'; higher ISO films are referred to as 'fast' films, while lower ISO films are known as 'slow' films. Whatever the case, all films with the same ISO rating require an identical quantity of light to produce the same effect on them. So our previous equation could be written as:

E (100 ISO) = **I** x **T** for 100 ISO film

Common ISO ratings are shown in the following sequence, with the ratings most often encountered in **bold**:

25, 32, 40, **50**, 64, 80, **100**, 125, 160, **200**, 250, 320, **400**, 500, 640, **800**, 1000, 1250, **1600**, 2000, 1500, **3200**

25 ISO film is half as sensitive to light as film rated at 50 ISO, which in turn is half as sensitive to light as 100 ISO film, and so on. The intermediate speed ratings shown in the table (32, 40, etc.) are one-third stop increments.

Slow films are capable of producing very sharp photographs that can contain very fine detail, and which can have large areas of smoothly and evenly reproduced colour. In comparison, faster films will look less crisp and can have a grainy, coarse appearance, especially in areas of even tone and colour. In digital terms, using a higher ISO setting will increase the noise present in an image ('noise' being a term used to describe pixels operating incorrectly, giving the image a speckled appearance not dissimilar to graininess).

Usually the decision of which film speed to use has to be made before putting film in the camera, as once this has been done it is fixed until another film is loaded. Many modern 35mm cameras use a system called DX coding, which reads the film's speed automatically when it is inserted into the camera. Most films have a fixed film speed, but a few can have their speed adjusted during processing.

A view through a kelp-lined gully, taken in about 5 metres of water on a bright, sunny day off Papa Westry in the Orkney Isles, north Scotland. Some flash was used (a single, medium-power diffused unit).
Subal-housed Nikon F801 and 14mm Sigma lens. 1/30s at f/11 using Fuji Provia 100 ISO

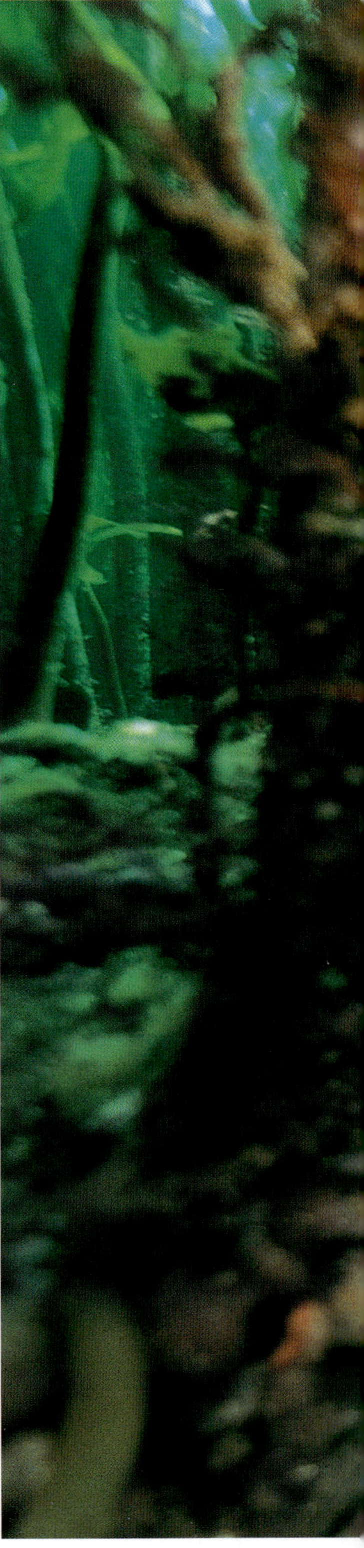

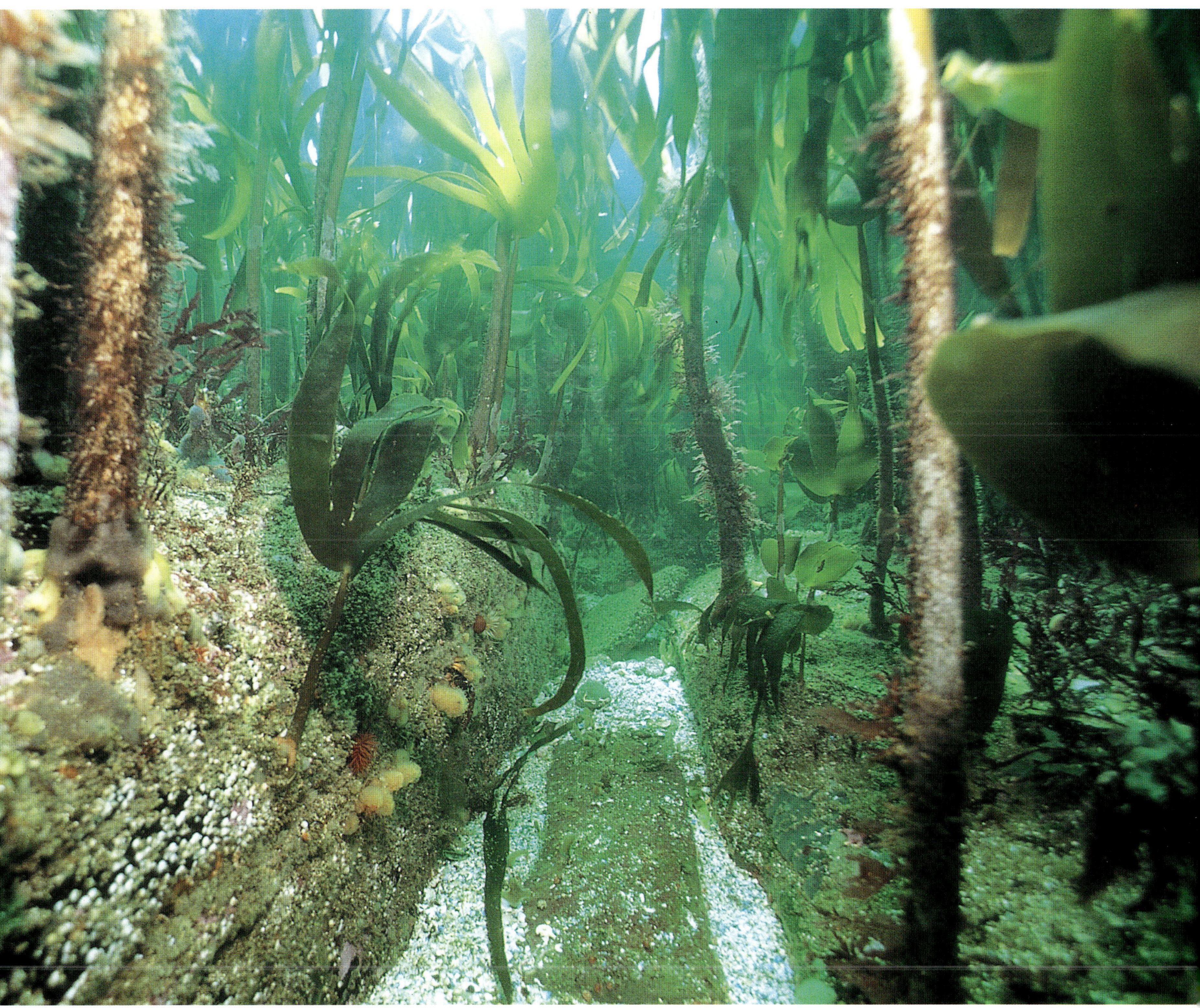

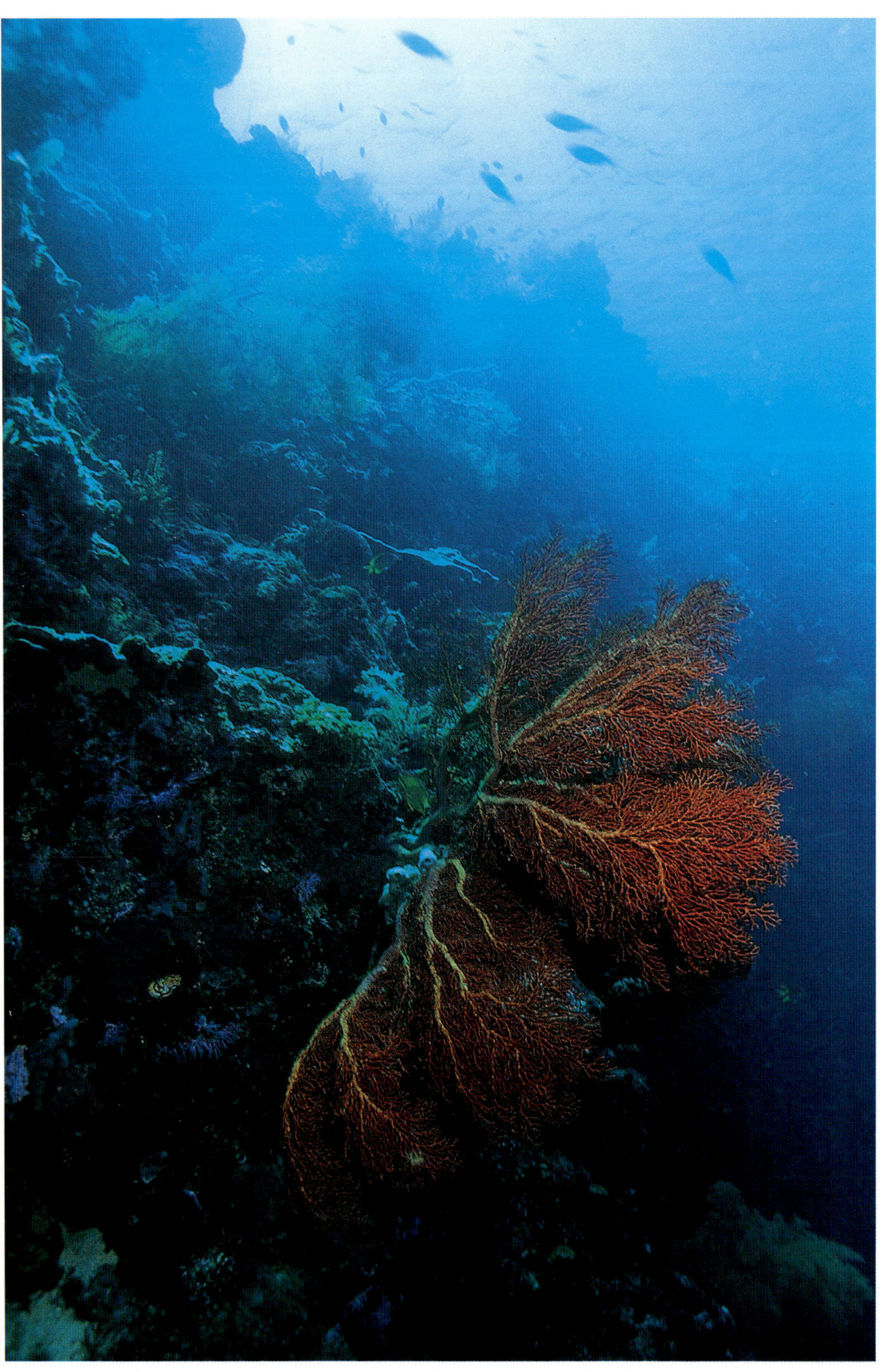

Film types

There are an enormous number of different films on the market today, but the broad categories of film types available for underwater photography are: black-and-white print films, colour print films (negatives) and colour slide films (transparenies).

Black and white

Black-and-white film produces monochrome images, and is often used by photographers who are interested in processing the film and using darkroom techniques. While it is used underwater, it is relatively specialized and requires a good understanding of photographic techniques beyond the scope of this book.

Negatives

Colour print films are by far the most widely used films above water (although digital photography may change this). They are used underwater as well, but generally in less sophisticated cameras, where their good exposure latitude can be used to compensate for inaccurate exposure

Above right: Divers rarely see Beadlet anemones (*Actinia equina*), as they are generally shore or rockpool dwellers. This picture illustrates that working in shallow water at high tide can be rewarding in terms of finding unusual compositions.
Subal-housed Nikon F100 and 60mm micro-Nikkor lens. 1/60s at f/16 on Fuji Velvia 50 ISO

The beautiful, clear blue waters of the tropics (such as seen here off Bali, Indonesia) allow for great depth within photographs by using gradation of tone. Using flash light to illuminate foreground detail can help to enhance this further, but requires care so that it does not become too dominant.
Subal-housed Nikon F801 and 20mm Nikkor lens, with a diffused Nikon SB105 flash unit. 1/60s at f/11 on Fuji Velvia 50 ISO

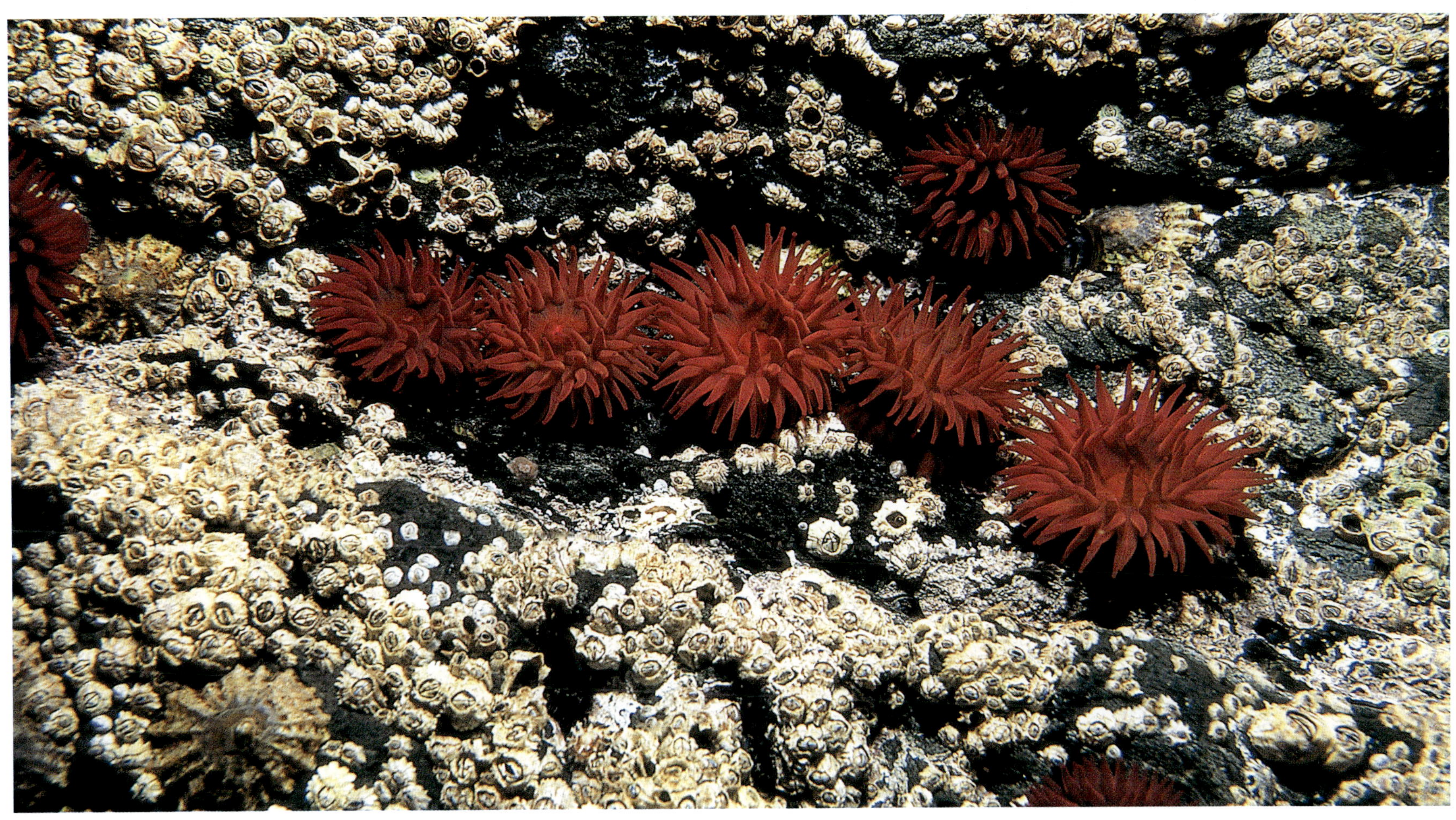

metering systems. This means that a relatively 'incorrect' exposure may still yield a reasonable print, which is part of the function of print film.

Colour negative film is readily available in a variety of ISO ratings, typically 100, 200, 400 and 800. Processing is possible just about anywhere and often quickly (less than one hour, if required). Reprints of various sizes can be made from negatives, while the first print is retained for viewing. Today, some of the digital printing systems in use can produce extremely high-quality prints from even relatively cheap cameras.

Transparencies

Slide films produce transparent photographs the same size as negatives, which can be projected to an audience. As a result, slide films are often thought of as being relatively specialist, but they are used extensively in sophisticated cameras underwater.

Slide film produces the highest-quality images when published, and so has traditionally been the choice of professional and serious amateur photographers. Slide films have less latitude than negative films and need accurate exposure to produce good results. The best are capable of producing extremely sharp and vibrantly colourful pictures.

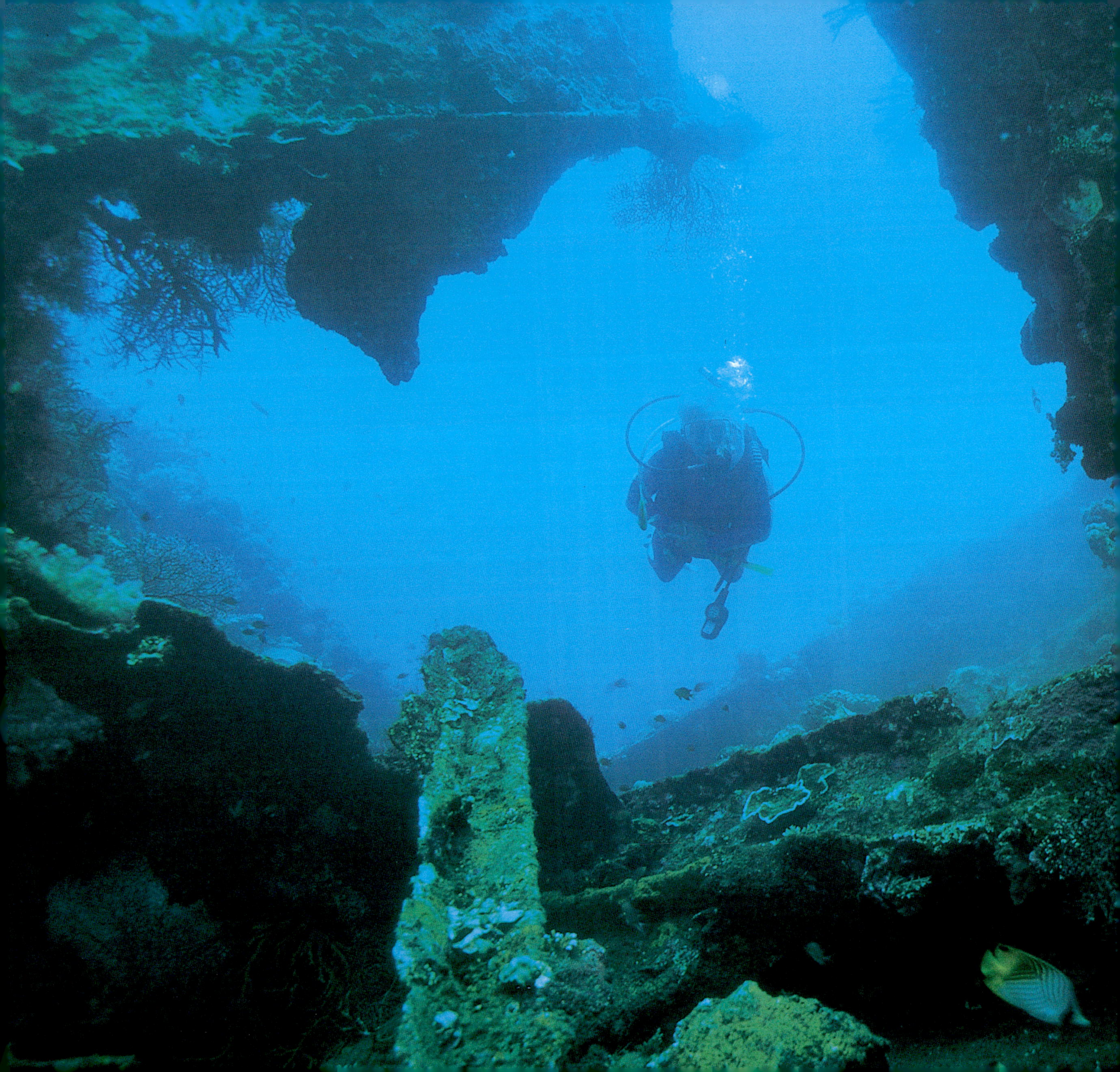

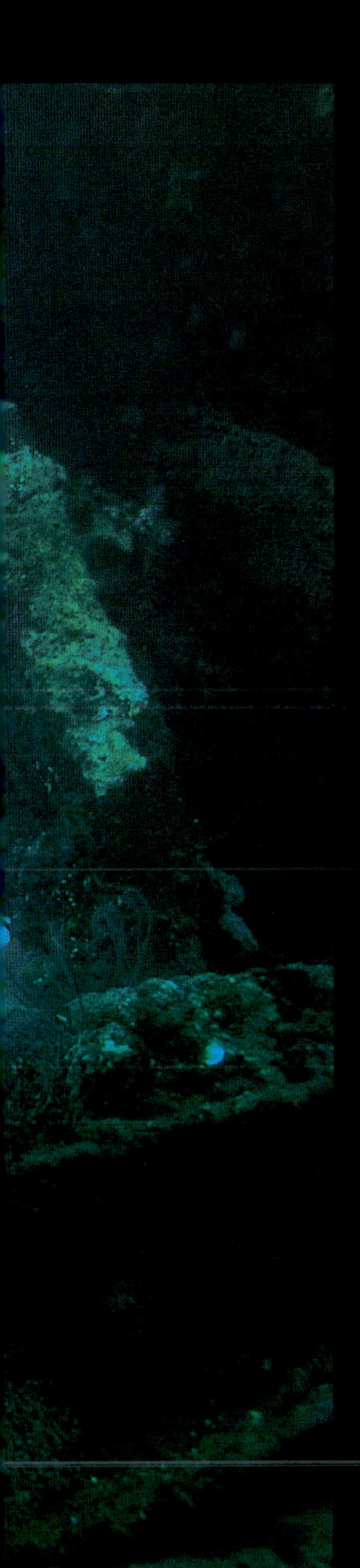

equipment

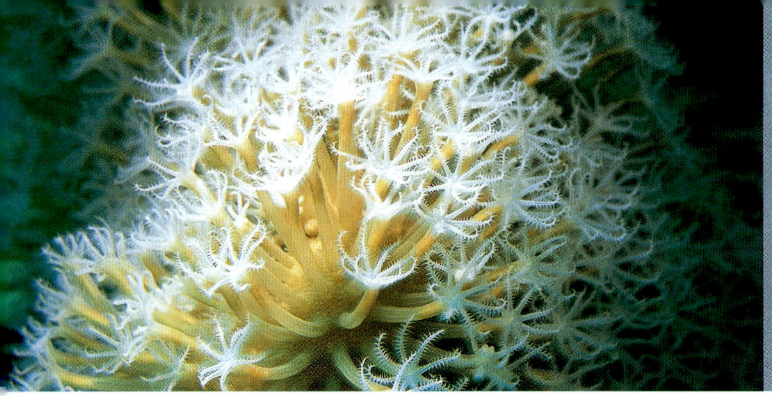

choosing a camera

Despite the claims made by manufacturers, there are many pitfalls waiting for those wanting to buy and use their first underwater camera. In essence, choosing an underwater camera is a matter of deciding what it is to be used for and what budget is available – although these two factors can often prove to be quite incompatible.

Having taught underwater photography courses, I realize how much the expectation of good results is a part of underwater photography. The biggest problem I have found when divers undertake a course is that they buy a camera believing it to be capable of quality results. This is because they have seen high-quality pictures produced by the same model, either in advertisements or in the photographs of others. And yet they find things much more difficult when they try to use it for themselves, and are unable to achieve anything similar.

It is quite possible to obtain superb results from virtually any underwater camera. However, the proviso is that the person taking the photographs must use it under conditions ideal for the type of camera, or be prepared to shoot vast quantities of film in order to obtain a few good pictures. Some divers persevere with camera models that are awkward to master, but can produce excellent results once they have gained sufficient experience.

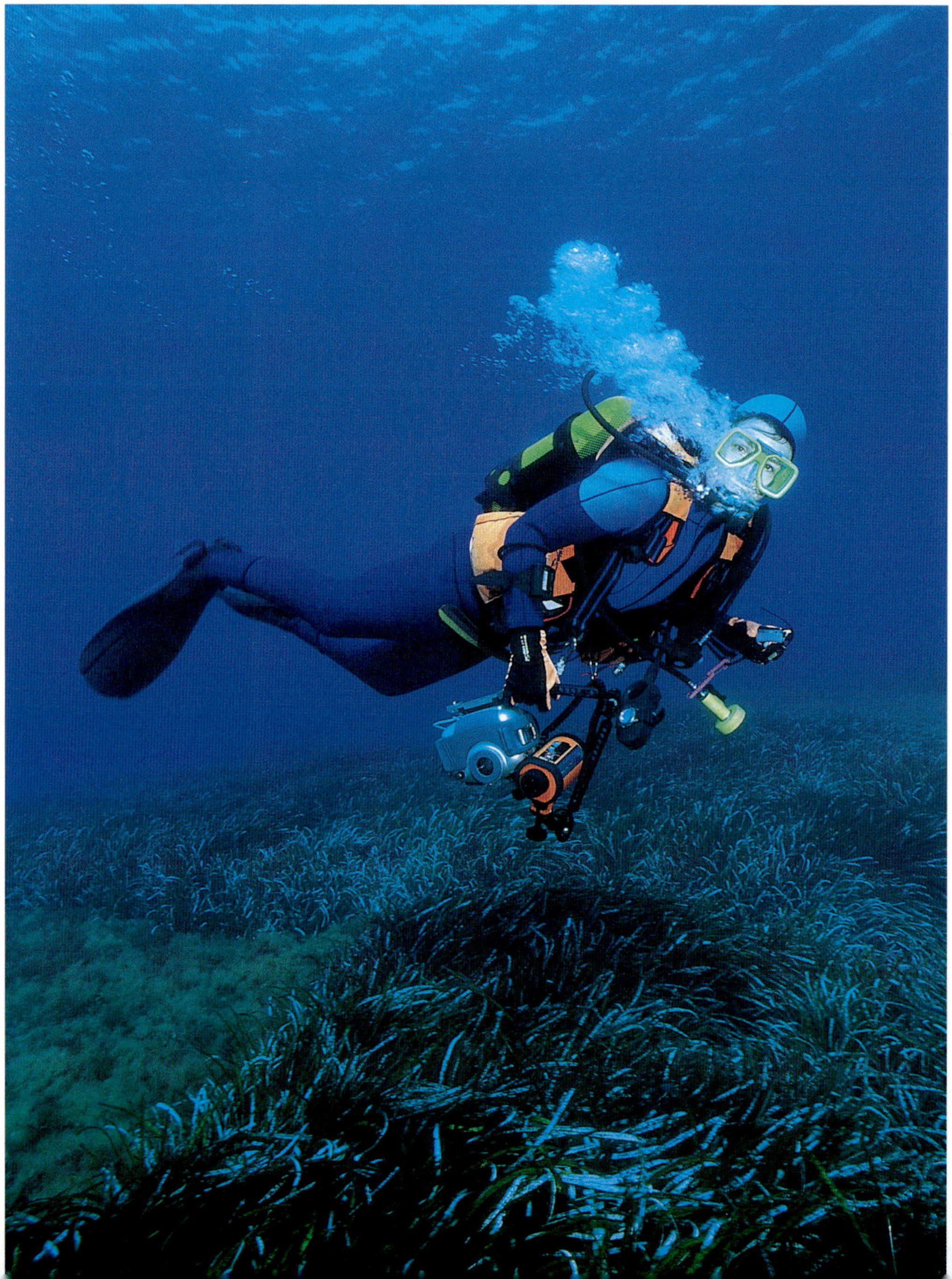

Seagrass is not often considered to be a photogenic subject, but does make a good backdrop for other divers – in this case another underwater photographer.
Subal-housed Nikon F801 and 20mm Nikkor lens, with a diffused Nikon SB105 flash unit. 1/30s at f/11 on Fuji Provia 100 ISO

Using a mix of flash and available light to photograph delicate coral polyps (probably *Sarcophyton* sp.) in Jordan provides depth, but requires a very steady camera.
Subal-housed Nikon F801 and 60mm micro-Nikkor, with a Nikon SB105 flash unit. 1/4s at f/16 on Fuji Velvia 50 ISO

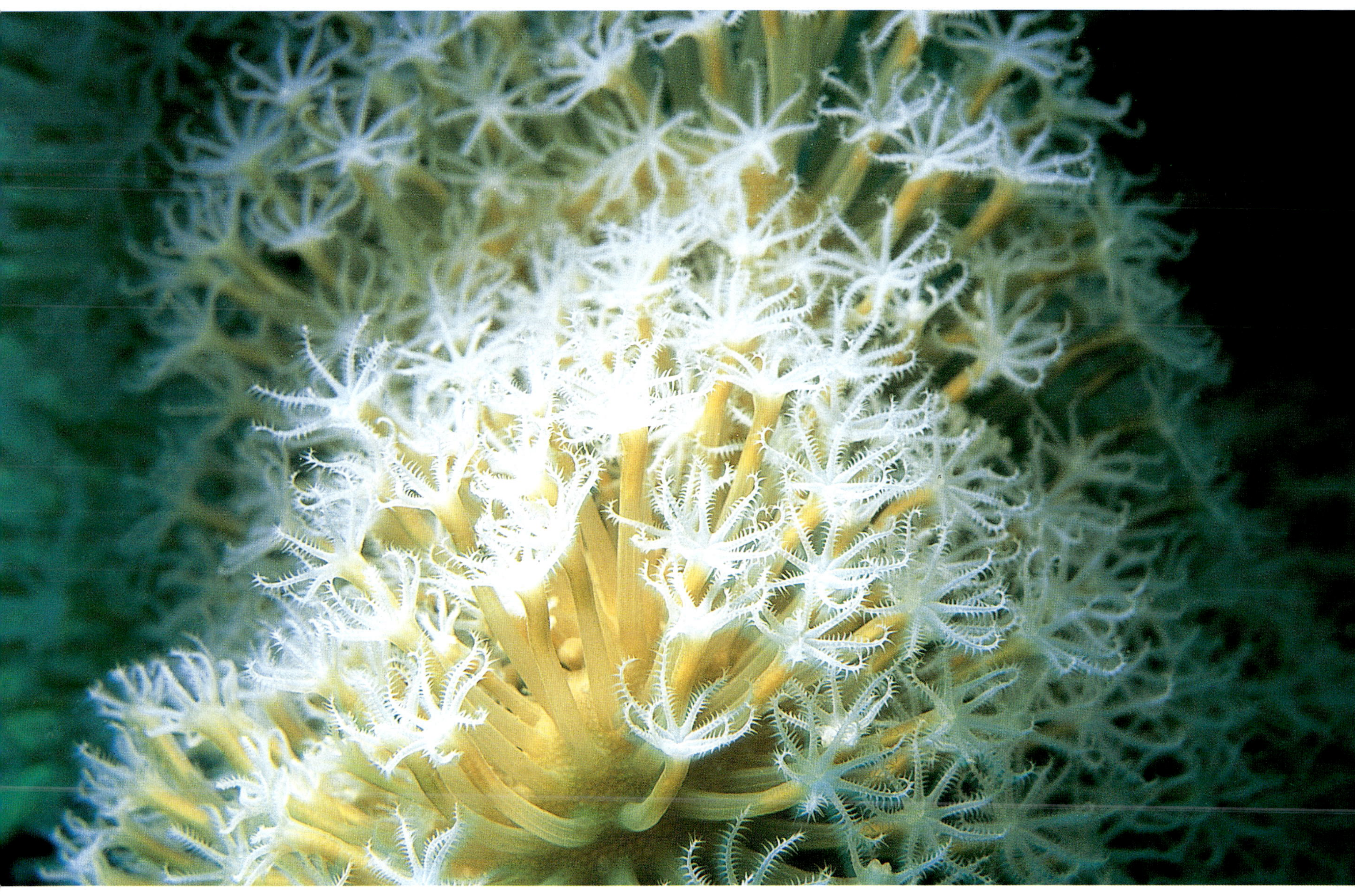

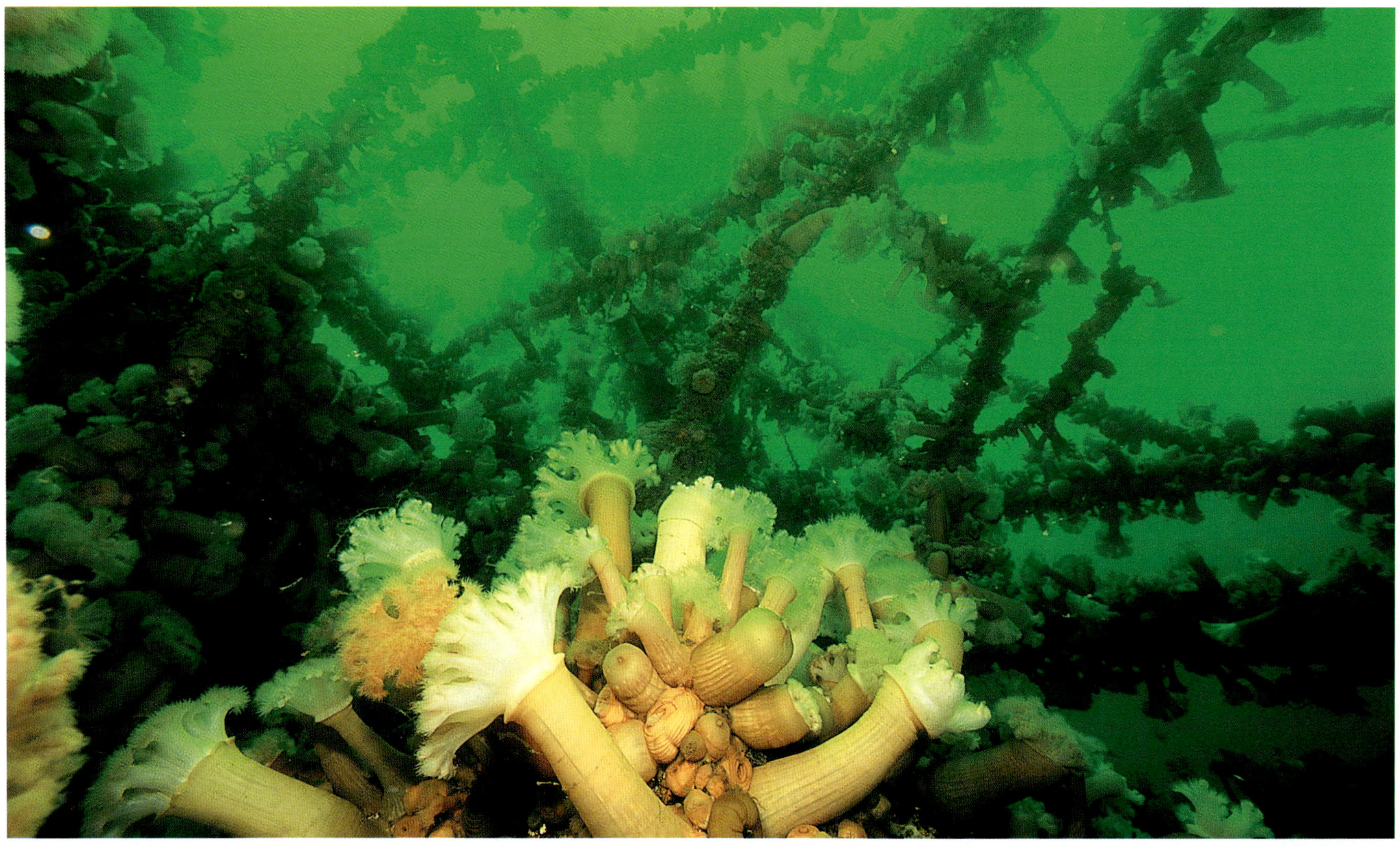

These plumose anemones (*Metridium senile*) seem to mirror the chaotic angles of the masts and rigging of this shipwreck, producing an almost abstract composition.
Subal-housed Nikon F100 and 17–35mm lens set at 17mm, with two diffused Nikon SB105 flash units. 1/2s at f/16 on Fuji Provia 100 ISO

At this point I should stress that the difference between a non-reflex and an autofocus reflex camera when used underwater is dramatic. An autofocus reflex camera will provide sharp photographs immediately, whereas non-reflex cameras only produce correctly focused pictures consistently after a great deal of practice.

In underwater photography you tend to get what you pay for and, unfortunately, it could be added that you 'get what you pay a great deal for'. There is no denying that quality underwater photographic equipment can be very expensive; adding the word 'underwater' to a camera seems to add a zero to the price.

Given that anything other than the very simplest and cheapest underwater cameras represent a significant investment, any decision on which to buy needs to be thought through very carefully. Additionally, buying a camera is only part of the story, as most require essential items of additional equipment to make them viable to use. Such items simply don't exist for many of the cheapest cameras, so these have to be viewed as very limited in their use.

non-reflex cameras

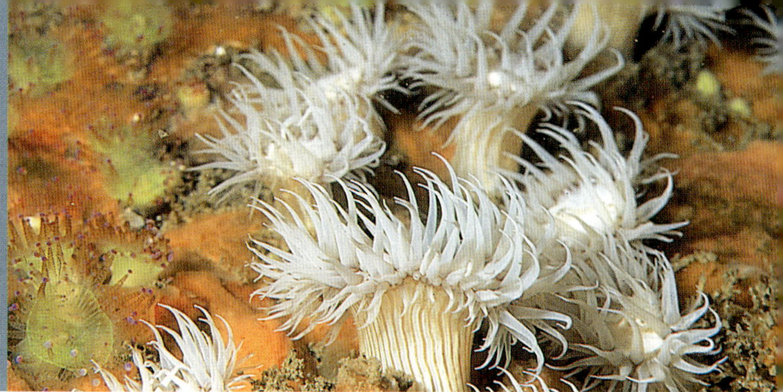

Other than being made waterproof, most underwater cameras are little different to those used on land. While the most sophisticated underwater cameras available today are the housed reflex cameras (see page 45), there are many other types on the market.

Most do not allow the photographer to view or focus through the lens, and these are known as non-reflex cameras. The non-reflex models available for underwater use vary in terms of specification and price, and each model has specific applications and capabilities. Inevitably, there are the trade-offs between cost, versatility, size, ease of use, and so on.

The key to taking good photographs is to use the right equipment for the job in hand, and this is also true underwater. It is all too easy to get carried away with technical specifications and to end up using a sledgehammer to crack a nut.

A small, low-cost non-reflex underwater camera may well be the best choice if the intention is simply to take a few straightforward snapshots in well-lit tropical waters. This is especially true if photography is not to dominate a dive, as a small camera can be put into a suitable pocket when not in use, and so doesn't need to be thought about constantly. If photography is to be about more than just

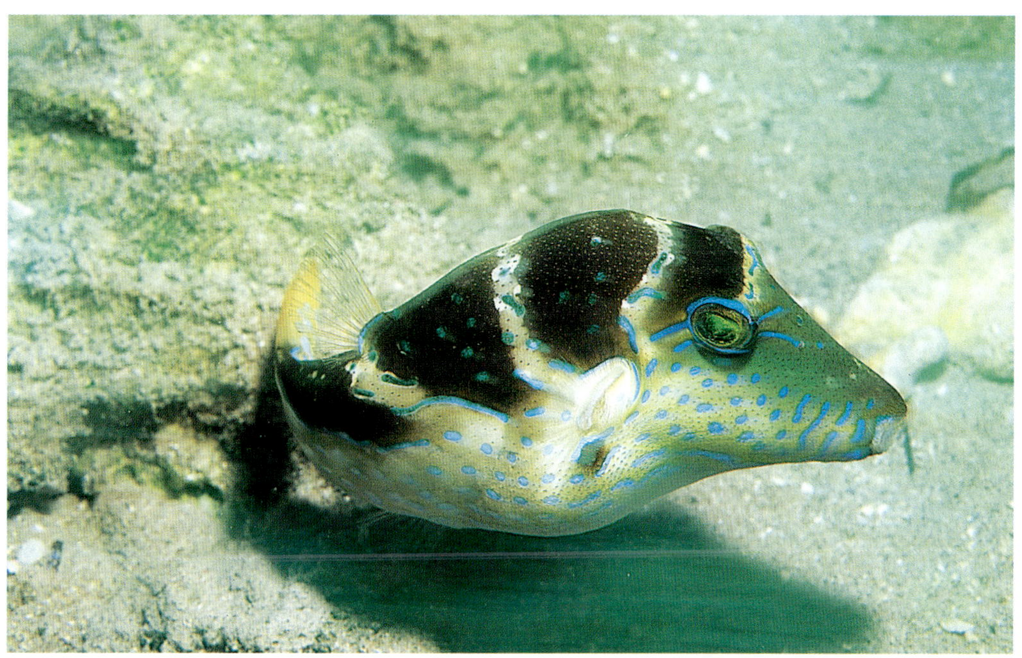

The available-light component of this photograph of a crown toby (*Canthigaster coronata*) is most noticeable in the shadow of the fish. This is sea blue rather than black.
Subal-housed Nikon F100 and 60mm micro-Nikkor lens, with a Nikon SB105 flash unit. 1/30s at f/16 on Fuji Velvia 50 ISO

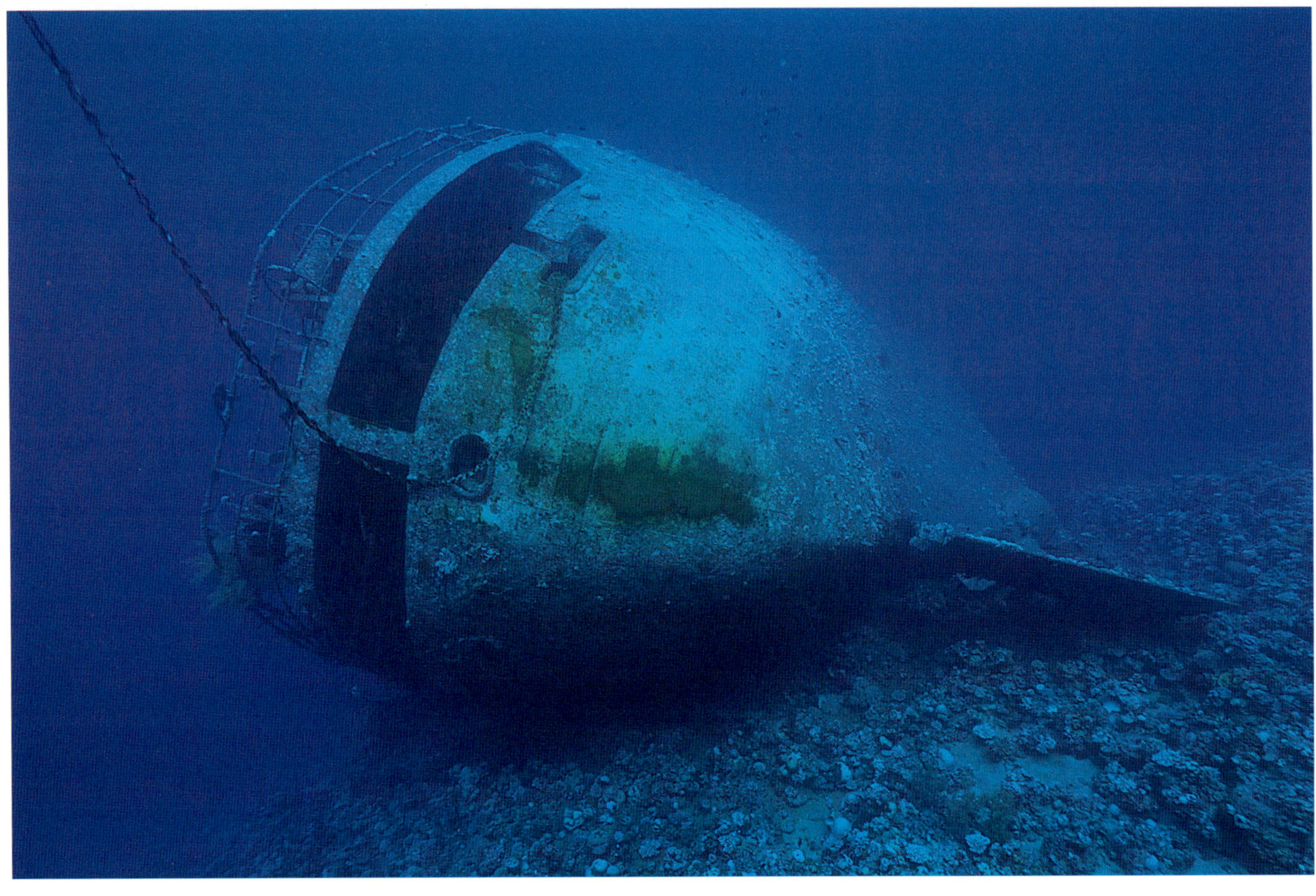

In well-illuminated, superbly clear water, it is possible to shoot underwater 'landscapes' using available light. This was the case with this shot of the purpose-sunk wreck of the Cedar Pride, in Aqaba, Jordan. ***Subal-housed Nikon F100 and 17–35mm lens set at 17mm. 1/15s at f/8 on Fuji Provia 100 ISO***

taking an occasional record, then something a little more sophisticated may be needed.

Few underwater cameras are available in film formats other than 35mm. Some housings have been, and are, made for medium-format cameras, but these are heavy, cumbersome and really only intended for very specific work that demands extremely high-quality results. Such cameras are very expensive and much the exception underwater, and so are not covered in this book.

At the other end of the scale are the very cheapest underwater cameras, such as disposable cameras. These are similar to low-cost above-water cameras and, like them, require both bright light and decent contrast to produce good results. This is because they use fixed or very limited apertures and shutter speeds, and often rely on film exposure latitude to make up for inaccuracies (and so should only be used with print film). Nevertheless, they can produce reasonable results if used in clear, well-lit water (perhaps in the shallows over tropical reefs) and so are ideal for a casual underwater photographer who wants a few prints as a reminder of a tropical diving holiday.

While some of the cheapest underwater cameras do have built-in flash, this is invariably positioned very close to the lens axis. As a result, they are prone to back scatter (see page 118) in all but the clearest water. Any underwater camera with an in-built flash of this type should be treated with real caution and used only in ideal conditions. Such cameras are only capable of taking 'snaps', and most are likely produce many failures in anything other than superbly clear water.

Slightly more sophisticated cameras have flash units that are positioned away from the lens axis or that can be used 'off-camera', which reduces back scatter. These may still have quite simple specifications, but can be used in less-perfect conditions and on many more subjects.

The versatility of such cameras is determined by the extent to which the flash can be adjusted (often this is very limited), as well as by the specifications and controls of the camera. Higher-specification models may even have a very basic system of accessories, usually close-up and wide-angle attachments. Again, these are often very simple and limited in their scope, but capable of reasonably good results in good conditions, especially when used with print film.

Lastly, sophisticated non-reflex cameras are available with an extensive array of accessories, including a variety of lenses or lens attachments, viewfinders, various close-up devices, and a selection of different flash units. These cameras might also feature through-the-lens (TTL) flash metering, have a wide range of shutter speeds and apertures, and allow a variety of film ISO ratings to be selected.

Although production has now ceased, the Nikonos range of cameras were all non-reflex (with the exception of the Nikonos RS), and they fall into this last category. Despite their drawbacks, many underwater photographers still use non-reflex Nikonos cameras, some solely because of the quality of its superb 15mm lens, which is fully corrected for underwater use. However, the majority of professional photographers have now switched over to the more versatile reflex systems.

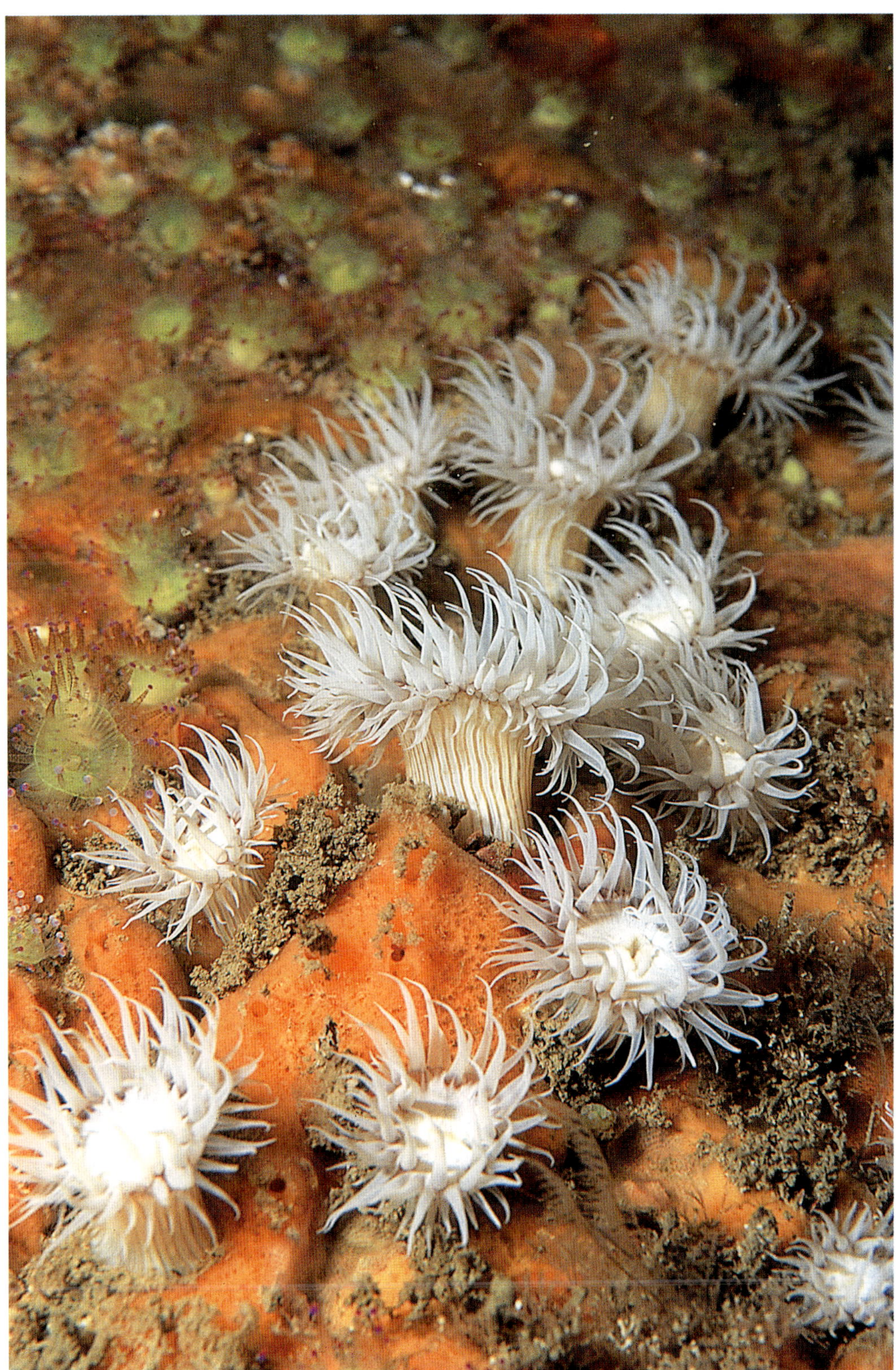

Temperate waters offer as much colour as tropical ones, as is shown in this flash-lit shot of anemones (*Actinothöe sphyrodeta*) surrounded by green jewel anemones on a rock encrusted with orange sponge.
Subal-housed Nikon F801 and 60mm micro-Nikkor lens, with a Nikon SB105 flash unit. 1/60s at f/16 on Fuji Velvia 50 ISO

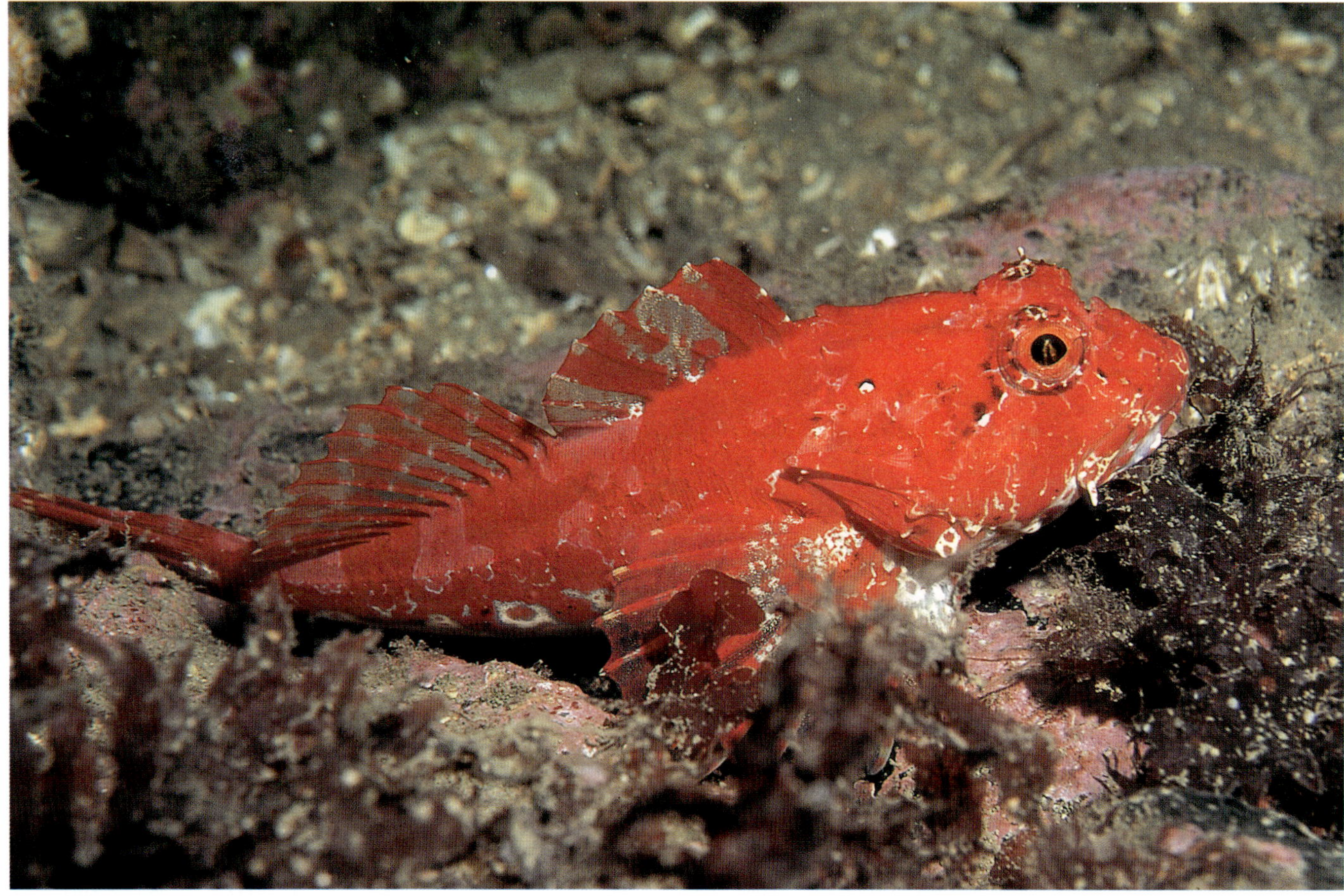

A strikingly coloured long-spined sea scorpion (*Taurulus bubalis*) taken off the coast of Lewis in the Outer Hebrides, north-west Scotland.
Subal-housed Nikon F100 and 60mm micro lens, with a Nikon SB105 flash unit. 1/60s at f/16 on Fuji Provia III 100 ISO.

Disadvantages of non-reflex cameras

No non-reflex cameras feature the sophisticated metering systems found on reflex cameras, and few give very much information regarding available-light levels. While many are fully adjustable and so capable of producing high-quality results, these are relatively difficult to achieve simply because the photographer has little data to work with. Photographers who work extensively with such cameras are either very experienced with them or they tend to bracket exposures whenever possible (or both).

Non-reflex cameras also suffer in comparison to reflex cameras because they rely on physical or estimated means of focusing. This is a very fundamental difference given that distances underwater are apparent (the higher refractive index of water makes everything under the surface appear closer than it actually is). This means that estimates of distance underwater need to be corrected, which often leads to confusion and inaccuracy.

Various methods are used to overcome the difficulty of estimating distances underwater. The simplest is to have a close-up device fitted to the camera. This features either a prong or a framer system, which is placed over or around the subject so that it is certain to be in focus. Such systems are fine for static subjects, but obviously become problematic for more mobile ones such as fish.

There are no other areas of photography, where quality results are required, which rely on estimates or physical means for focusing, and so, while such cameras are capable of high-quality results, they rarely provide superb photographs without considerable experience in their use. They are difficult to operate with confidence without such experience.

When using a non-reflex camera, the subject is viewed through a viewfinder, which uses a separate viewing lens. To compensate for this, many viewfinders come complete with appropriate markings that represent the edges of the resulting picture. Some also have a variety of marks to show views at different distances, and a few can even be pivoted to show the change in view for different distance settings. At best, viewfinders give a bright and reasonably accurate impression of the picture to be taken, but at worst they are tricky to use and not particularly precise.

Most available non-reflex underwater cameras are built from some form of plastic (the Nikonos was metal though). This has the advantage of being lightweight, non-corroding, and allowing cost-effective mass production. However, few plastics are as strong as metal, and so there are often limitations on their use in terms of their maximum pressure (depth) rating and the physical hardships that they will endure.

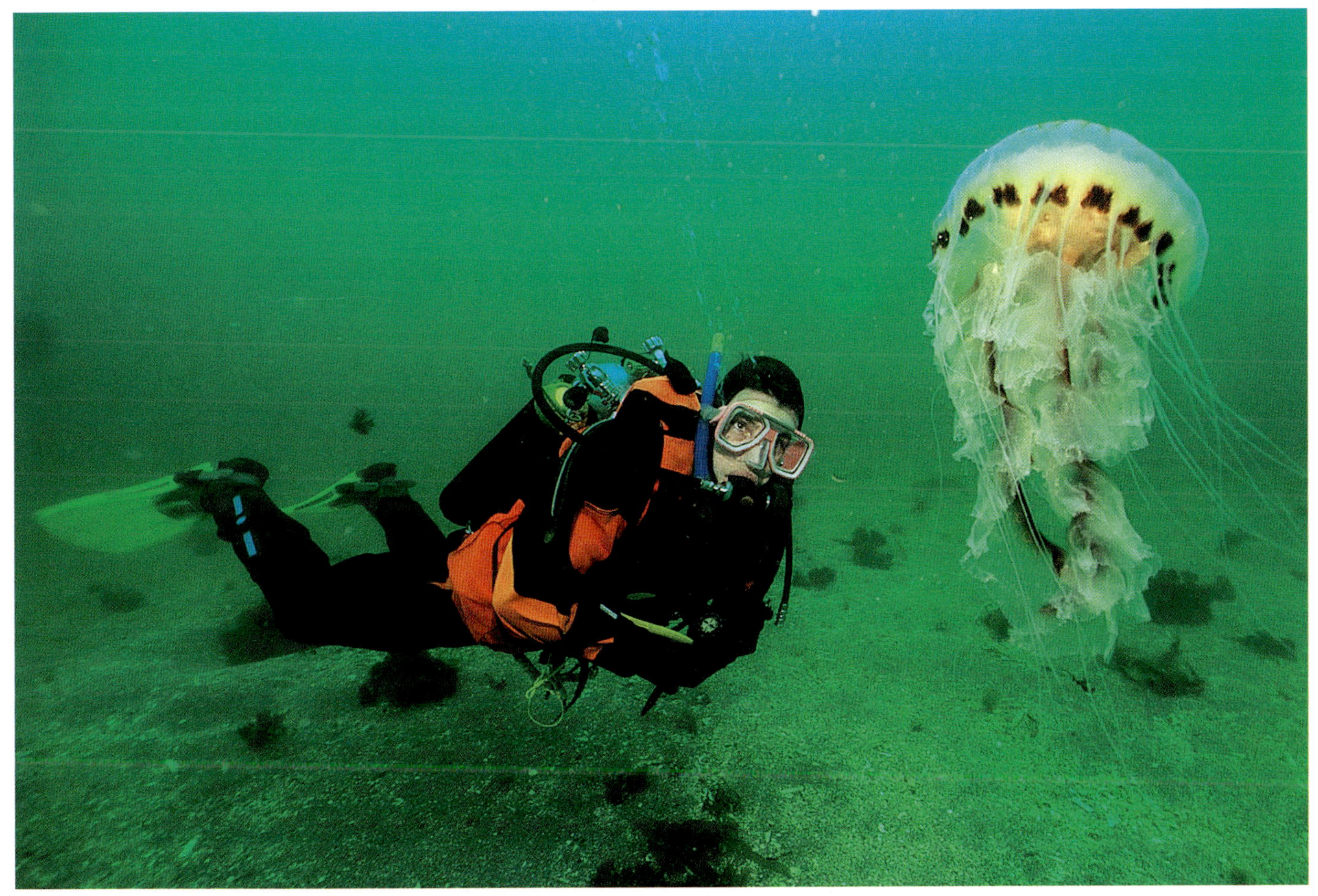

Adding a diver to a composition can provide scale, as it has in this shot of a compass jellyfish (*Chrysaora hysoscella*) off the Aran Islands in Ireland.
Subal-housed Nikon F801 and 20mm Nikkor lens, with a diffused Nikon SB105 flash unit. 1/30s at f/11 on Fuji Velvia 50 ISO

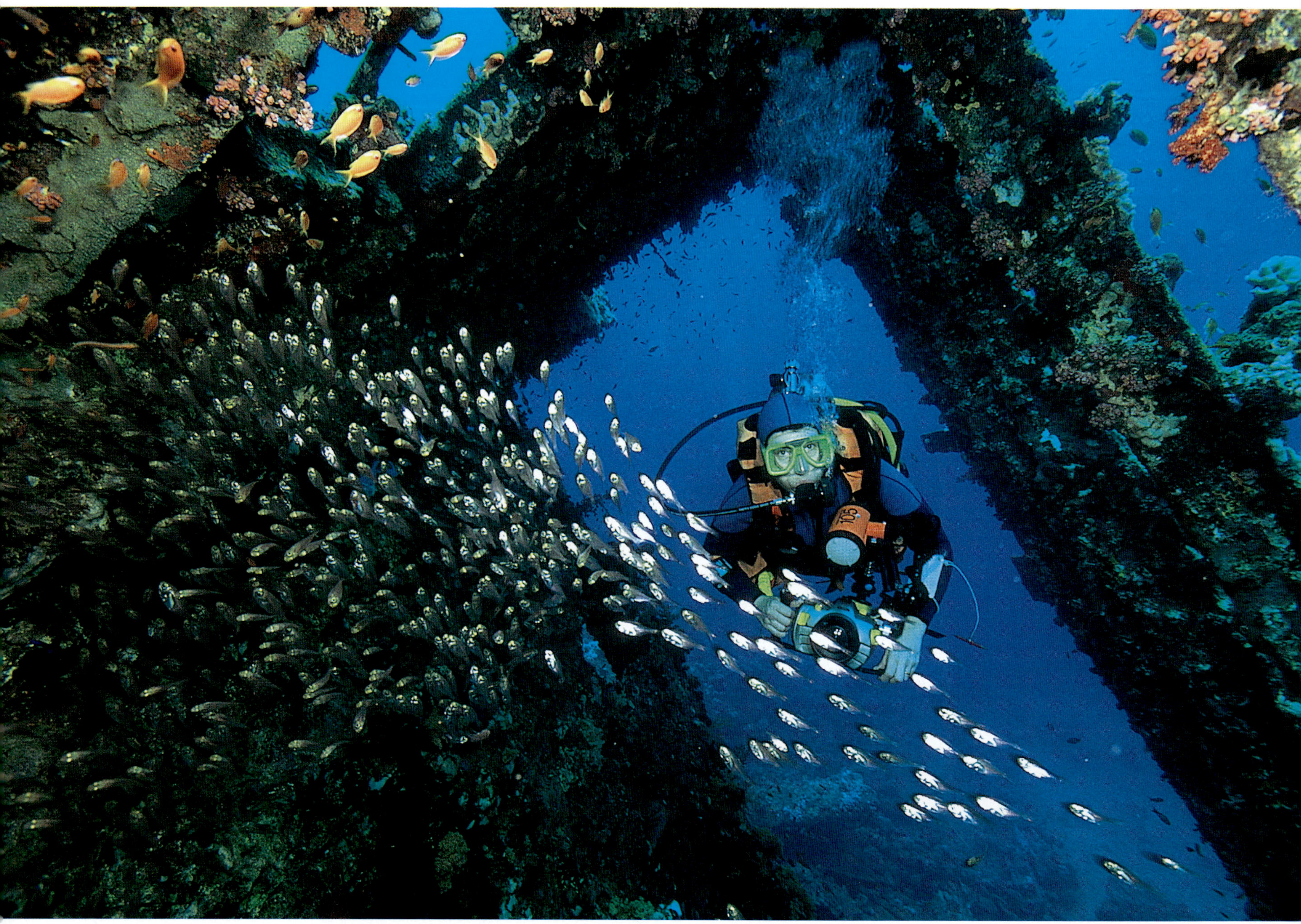

Wrecks such as the Carnatic in the Red Sea provide superb subject matter – in themselves, their inhabitants and their visitors. The change that this vessel has undergone as a result of being underwater is breathtakingly beautiful.
Subal-housed Nikon F100 and 17–35mm lens set at 17mm, with two diffused Nikon SB105 flash units. 1/8s at f/16 on Fuji Provia 100 ISO

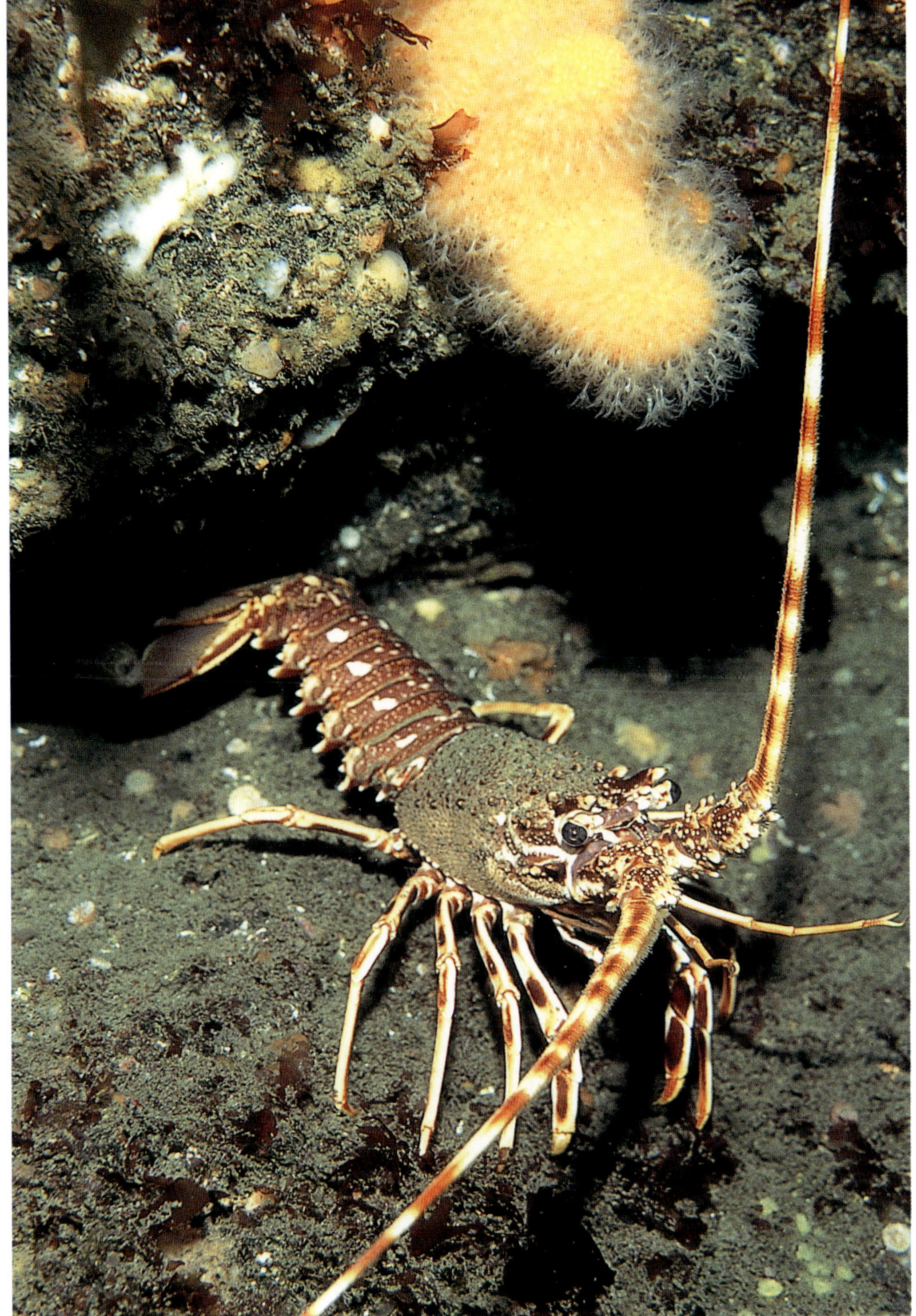

Crawfish (*Palinurus elephas*) are difficult subjects to photograph because they are hard to find (sadly their numbers have diminished in recent years), and because they have long antennae that get in the way all too often. This young creature placed its antennae in an ideal position as it emerged from under a limestone overhang off the Aran Islands, Ireland.
Subal-housed Nikon F801 and 35mm Nikkor lens, with a Nikon SB105 flash unit. 1/60s at f/16 on Fuji Velvia 50 ISO

Advantages of non-reflex cameras

This does not mean that non-reflex equipment is irrelevant – far from it. Non-reflex underwater cameras have some real advantages that are not yet available in reflex equipment.

Non-reflex underwater cameras are smaller and lighter than housed reflex cameras. If air travel is an essential part of a photographer's diving trip, then weight is something that can become a real factor. A complete non-reflex outfit – including camera, lenses, close-up equipment and flash – can weigh as little as or even less than one complete housed camera.

Reflex cameras can be very versatile, but this does come at the expense of being more demanding in use. Underwater photography is often undertaken in less than ideal conditions. There can be water currents, narcosis due to depth, or other divers to keep an eye on. A simple close-up framer outfit on a non-reflex camera can yield high-quality results with minimum fuss, while a housed reflex camera can be complex, time consuming and, potentially, dangerously absorbing to use.

A further consideration is when extreme wide-angle photography is being undertaken. Prime, purpose-designed underwater lenses made specifically for non-reflex underwater cameras will produce superbly crisp results, even into the corners of the picture. The same is not always true of the extreme wide-angle lenses used behind dome ports in housings. Many exhibit blurred picture corners unless the aperture is well stopped down. This, combined with flare resulting from shooting into the light, remains a real and as yet largely unresolved optical problem with large dome ports, which are also very vulnerable to scratching.

Current non-reflex cameras

While the Nikonos V (the last camera in the Nikonos range) is no longer made, several manufacturers do make non-reflex cameras for which a whole system of accessories is available, including close-up and wide-angle units. Some, such as Sea & Sea's Motormarine range or Bonica's models, are capable of very good results, but even these are not very sophisticated in terms of their metering systems or exposure information displays.

When used in the tropics these cameras can produce excellent photographs, even on transparency film. Elsewhere, and certainly in less than ideal conditions, they are less likely to produce consistently good photographs (no doubt many will disagree, and have the pictures to prove it). My own experience of teaching people how to use such cameras is that it is an uphill struggle and that a considerable amount of effort is required to overcome their (not insurmountable) shortcomings, most specifically the art of correct focusing.

Lastly, but very importantly, a non-reflex camera without additional accessories is of very limited use. Either a close-up unit or a wide-angle attachment is needed to make them viable, and this will of course increase the initial price.

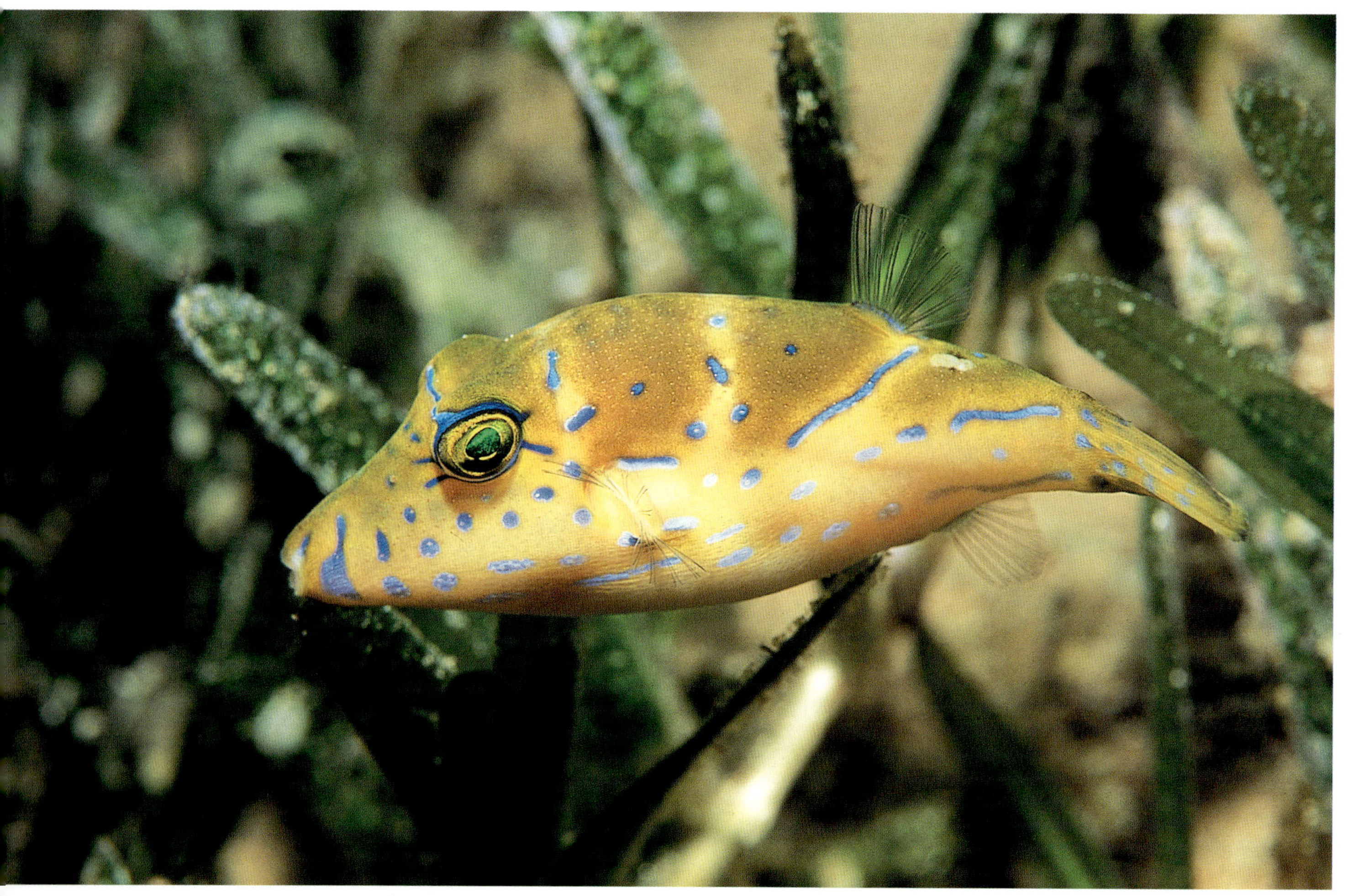

Diving destinations like Aqaba, on Jordan's Red Sea coast, cannot provide the highly spectacular reefs found in some destinations, but do provide easily accessible and varied marine creatures. This pygmy toby (*Canthigaster pygmaea*) was shot over sea grass in just 2–3 metres of water.
Subal-housed Nikon F100 and 60mm micro-Nikkor, with Nikon SB105 flash unit. 1/60s at f/16 on Fuji Velvia 50 ISO.

reflex cameras

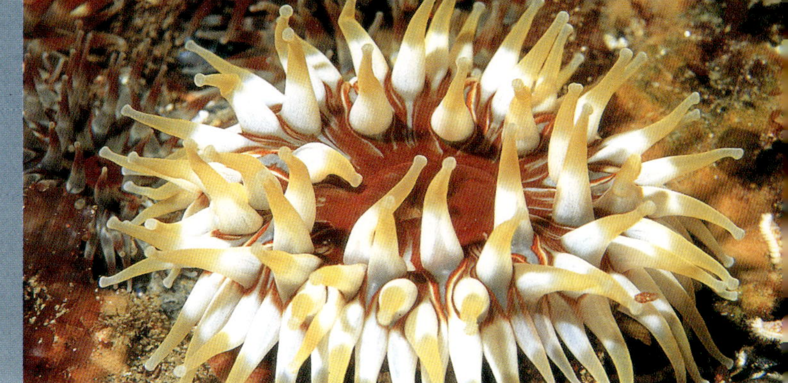

Operating a reflex camera underwater is very different to a non-reflex camera. Current reflex cameras are more expensive, but they yield such consistently better results that this alone should make them worth considering, if financially possible.

Underwater photography has a very specific set of requirements from a camera. Most photographs taken underwater use either flash alone to illuminate the subject, or a mixture of flash and available light. Any camera used underwater needs to be able to operate flash in automatic

A spiny spider crab (*Maja squinado*) walking across a seabed of dead men's fingers. Shot using a mix of available and flash (twin, diffused strobes) light in the Aran Islands, west Ireland.
Subal-housed Nikon F100 and 17–35mm Nikkor lens. 1/15s at f/16 on Fuji Provia 100 ISO

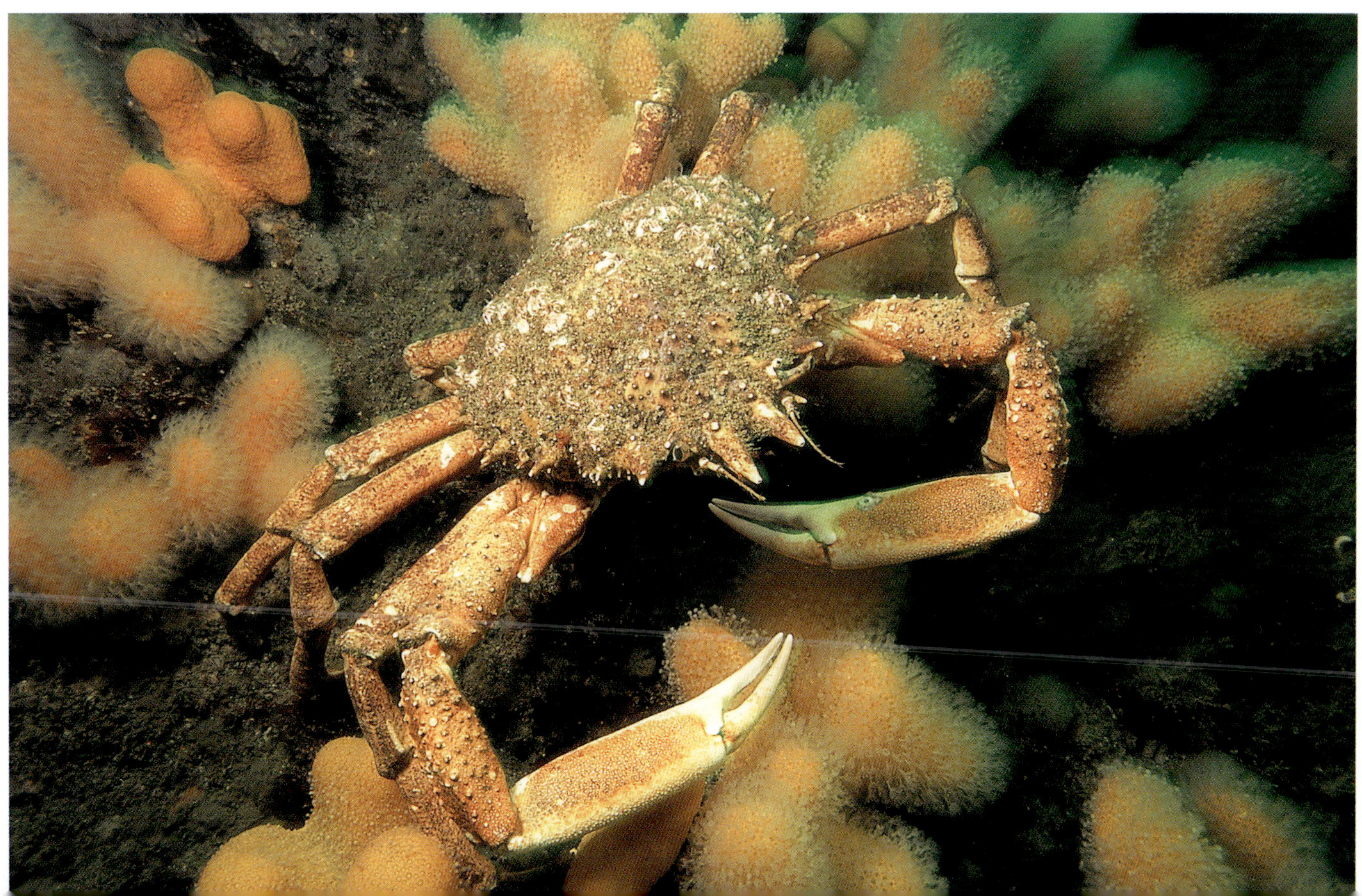

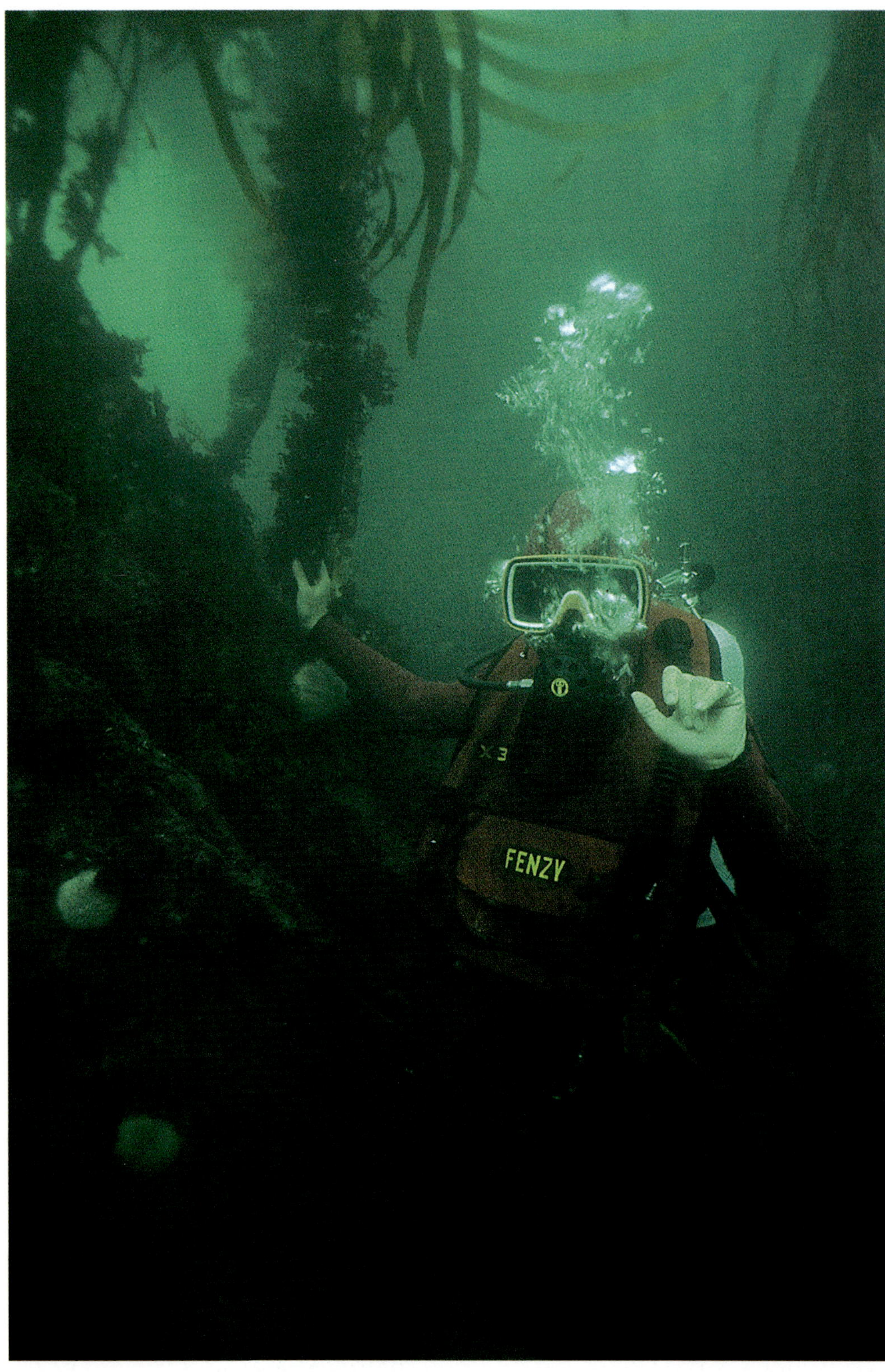

Back in 1983, autofocus did not exist and shots like this one were taken using very different equipment to that available today. Film technology has changed dramatically too. A Nikon F with a 20mm lens was used in an Ikelite housing to take this ambient-light shot at a depth of 6 metres off Sherkin Island in County Cork.

and manual modes, and to meter available light accurately. While these two requirements are straightforward enough with modern cameras, and are incorporated into most, the underwater photographic world has evolved in a rather different way to the topside one.

This is because the underwater camera that popularized underwater photography, and which the others have been judged against, was the Nikonos. Paradoxically, while Nikonos cameras were not (until the last model) reflex cameras, their evolution led to what currently remains arguably the best available option in underwater photography: the housed Nikon autofocus reflex camera. This provided underwater photographers with an excellent and versatile tool with which to undertake underwater photography, and while the light-sensitive material may change, it is unlikely that the reflex camera will be usurped from its position until fundamental technological changes provide something substantially better.

Housings

The real change in underwater photography came when Nikon introduced their F801 model in 1988. Soon, various housings for this camera followed it onto the market. The one feature of this camera that redefined underwater photography was viable automatic focus. This ensured sharp photographs; something that previously had been difficult to achieve underwater.

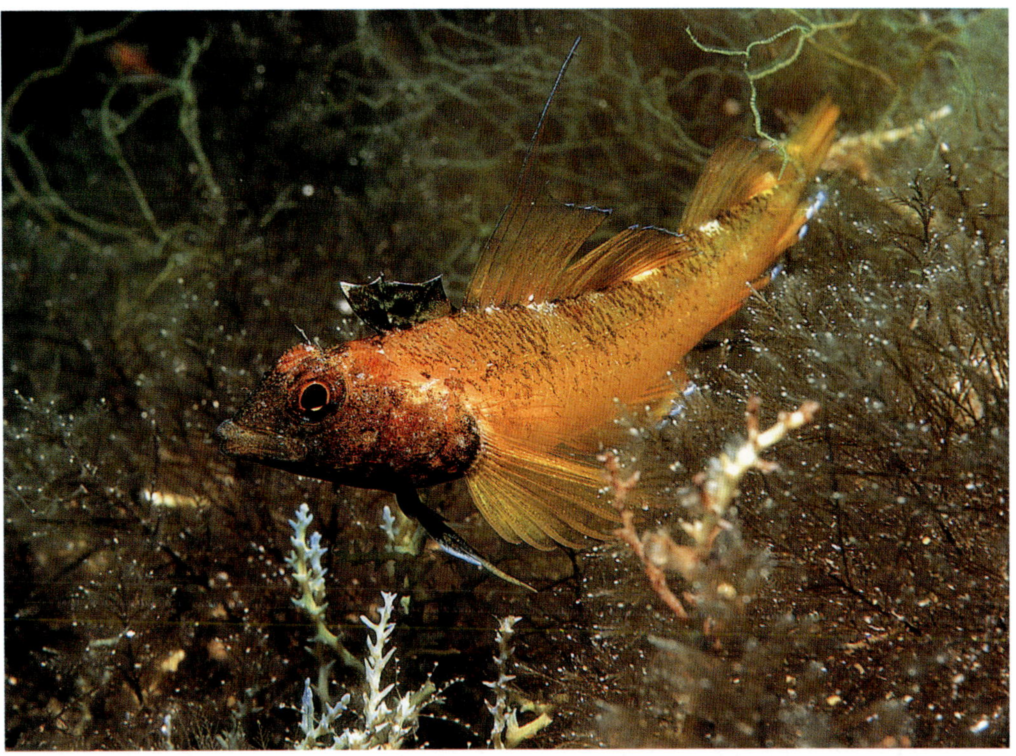

Small fish are full of fascinating fine detail. This Delais' triplefin (*Tripterygion delaisi*) has been photographed with the single flash quite close, giving a very even illumination. This relies on differential focus to throw the background out of focus and delineate the fish from it. Using illumination that is too soft can result in inadequate differentiation, so that the subject merges into the background.
Subal-housed Nikon F100 and 60mm micro-Nikkor, with a Nikon SB105 flash unit. 1/60s at f/16 on Fuji Velvia 50 ISO

Autofocus is an absolute dream underwater. Unlike photographers on land, divers often have to operate in a weightless mode, when nothing is held firmly on stable ground. Water movement and minute adjustments to buoyancy provide sufficient motion to ensure that manual focusing is always tricky. This affected manual-focus reflex cameras as much as non-reflex cameras. However, the viewfinders of existing reflex cameras tended to be significantly duller than those incorporated into cameras like the F801. This, combined with the low light levels and contrast found underwater, made focusing difficult and meant that they had never challenged the popularity of the Nikonos.

Autofocus was available with lenses such as the 60mm micro-Nikkor, which allowed continuous autofocusing from infinity right down to life-size (1:1). This fitted straight onto the F801 and sat snugly behind a compact flat port. Wide-angle lenses were usable too, including the superb 20mm autofocus Nikkor, a lens with a similar field of view to the legendary Nikonos 15mm underwater lens. This performs superbly when placed behind a purpose-designed dome port and stopped down to f/11 or smaller, although it is

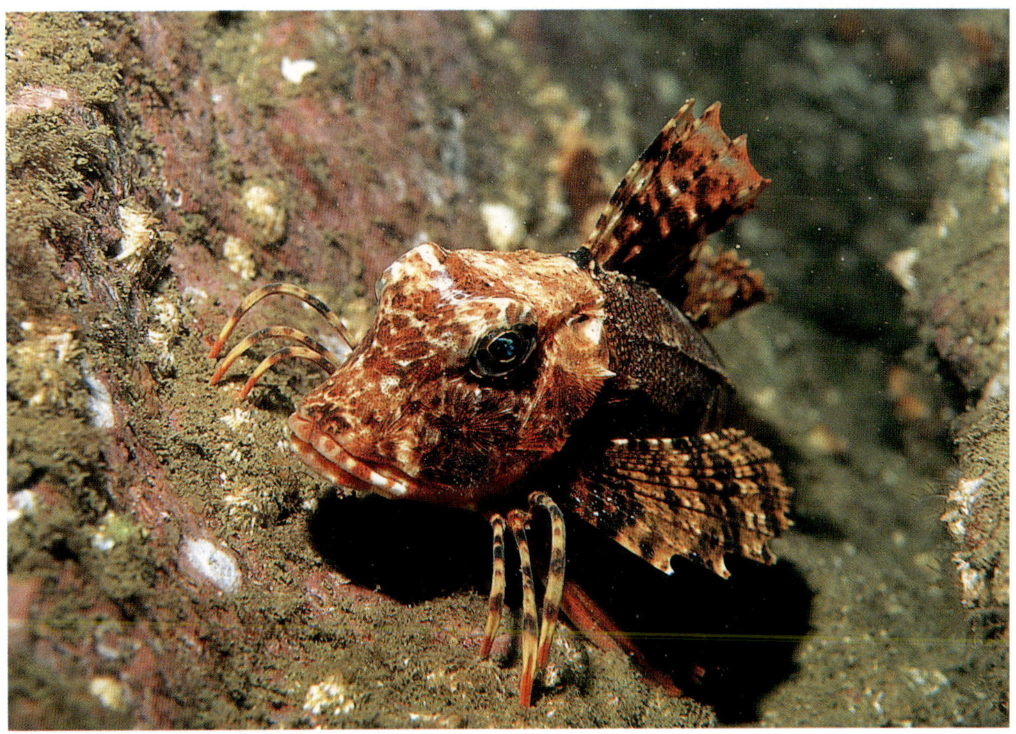

The tub gurnard (*Trigla lucerna*) is a strange fish that 'walks' across the seabed on modified feeler fins, looking for food. Correct lighting is critical to produce a useful image of such creatures, especially in areas where visibility is not always good.
Subal-housed Nikon F801 and 60mm micro-Nikkor, with a Nikon SB105 flash unit. 1/60s at f/16 on Fuji Velvia 50 ISO

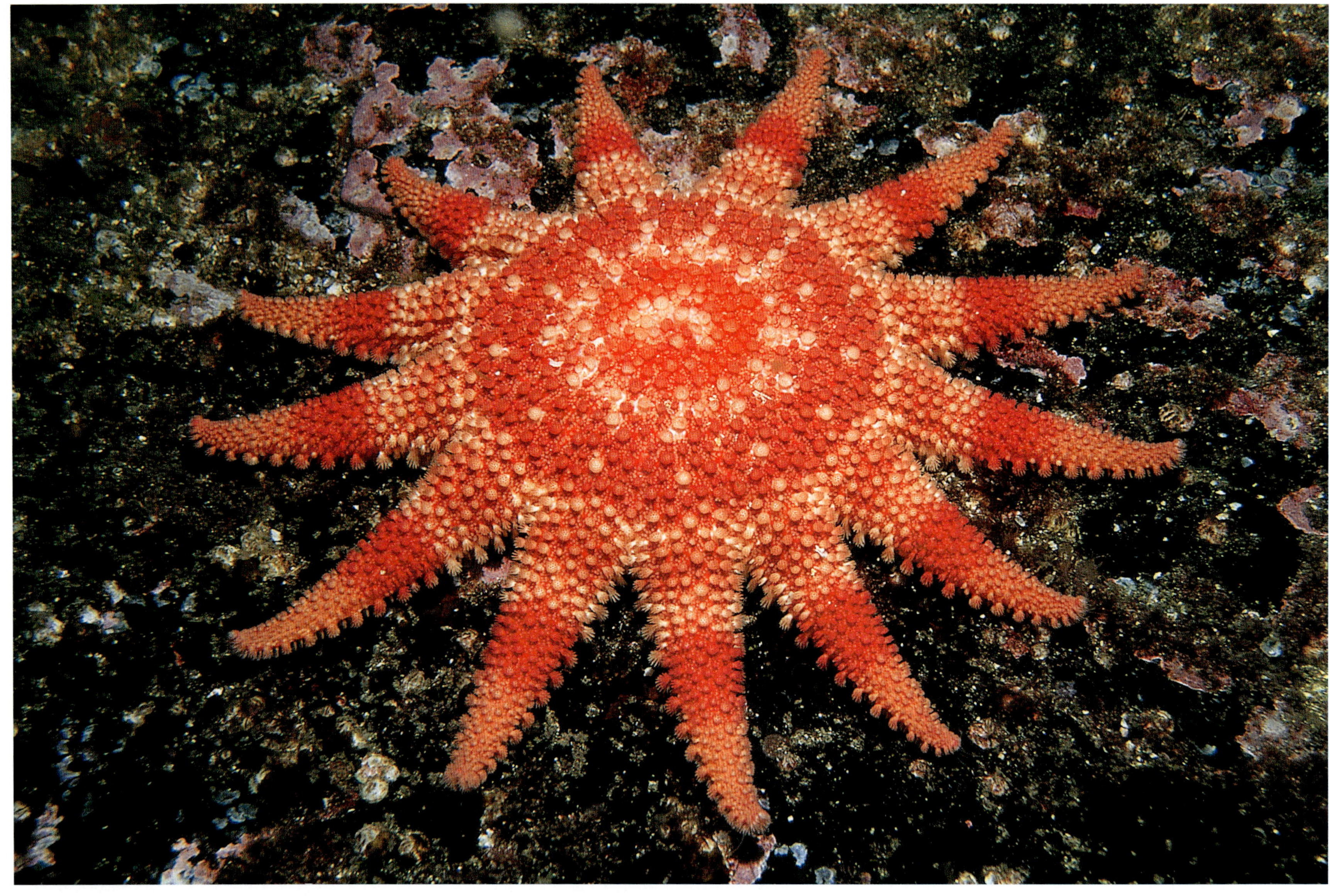

This vividly coloured and intricately patterned sunstar (*Crossaster papposus*) stands out from a dark bedrock background, enhancing the overall shot. Backgrounds can make or break photographs and should be chosen with care where possible. Taken in the Orkney Islands, north Scotland, by flash alone.
Subal-housed Nikon F100 and 60mm micro-Nikkor, with a Nikon SB105 flash unit. 1/60s at f/22 on Fuji Velvia 50 ISO

probably still not quite as good optically as the Nikonos lens when used underwater.

Another advantage of the F801 was its compatibility with the widely available flash units designed to work in TTL mode with the Nikonos V. This feature should not be underestimated – it is primarily why Nikon cameras remain the dominant housed camera. (Indeed, the Nikonos-V, or Nik-5, flash socket is so common that some manufacturers place additional circuitry in their housings in order to enable non-Nikon cameras to operate with Nikonos-type flashes and still provide TTL control.)

TTL flash control enables the photographer to take many flash-lit macro photographs without having to worry too much about exposure. It is an extremely efficient method of automating flash exposure, and is covered in detail in the chapter on flash techniques (see page 108).

So the Nikon F801 camera started a trend which has proved to be versatile, effective and very popular. There was a down side, and that was the cost. The initial outlay for a housed camera was – and remains – relatively high. However, if viewed as a replacement for an entire Nikonos outfit it was considerably cheaper, as well as significantly more useful. Housing a Nikon F801 also remained cheaper than buying the costly reflex Nikonos RS.

Today, housed reflex cameras are used by the vast majority of photographers who want to take high-quality, carefully composed images underwater. While other underwater camera systems do exist and can be used to take some stunning images, none can rival the precision and versatility of housed autofocus reflex cameras.

Currently, few camera housings are built for lower-cost models. Most are designed for the more expensive 'professional' or 'semi-professional' cameras, which bristle with features (although many of these are used rarely,

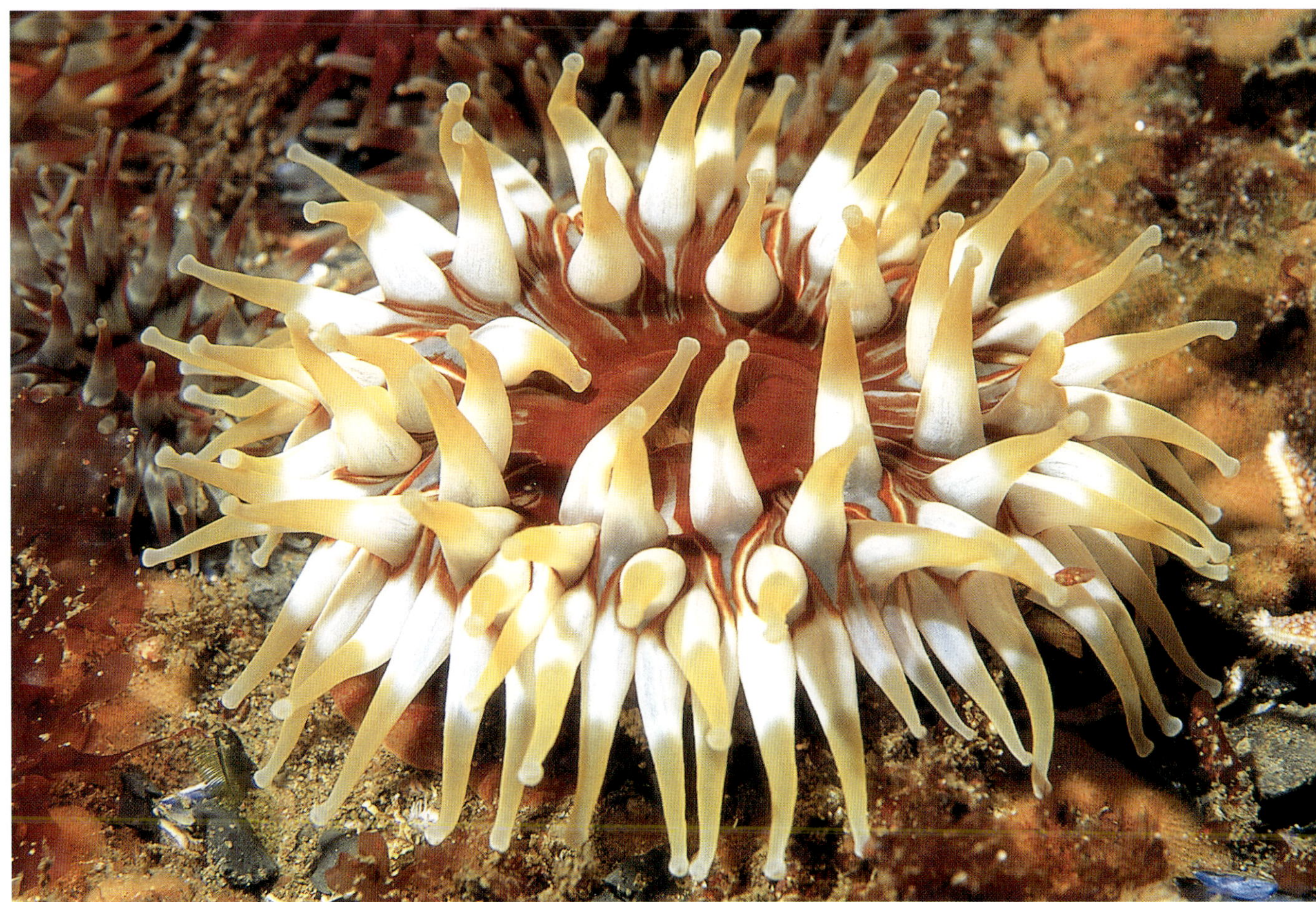

Dahlia anemones (*Urticina felina*) can be stunningly beautiful, but as with many subjects some are better than others. This glorious, vividly coloured specimen is from the Aran Islands in Galway Bay, Ireland. Taken by flash alone. ***Subal-housed Nikon F801 and 60mm micro-Nikkor lens, with a single Nikon SB105 flash unit. 1/60s at f/22 on Fuji Velvia 50 ISO***

if ever, underwater). If you are serious about wanting to take up underwater photography, it is unlikely to be cheap. There are some good second-hand housings available, including many for the Nikon F801, even now, some years after production has been discontinued.

Automation

Generally, only two exposure modes are of real use to the underwater photographer: aperture-priority automation (shown as A on mode dials or displays) and manual exposure (shown as M). Shutter priority (S) is not very useful underwater as depth of field, and hence aperture, is a much more important consideration most of the time. Nor are programme modes (P), as they allow the photographer little control over what is going on and will accordingly fail to deliver good photographs in many situations.

Flash exposure can be automated by using TTL automatic flash control. Full details of how this works can be found on page 114. The alternative is to use manual flash settings (see page 112), which again rely on estimates of distance underwater and so can be problematic.

The current Nikon range of cameras, and many other underwater systems, have features that automate the mixing of available light and flash illumination, and the adjustment of flash synchronization speeds. This is covered in more detail in the chapter on balanced light (see page 135).

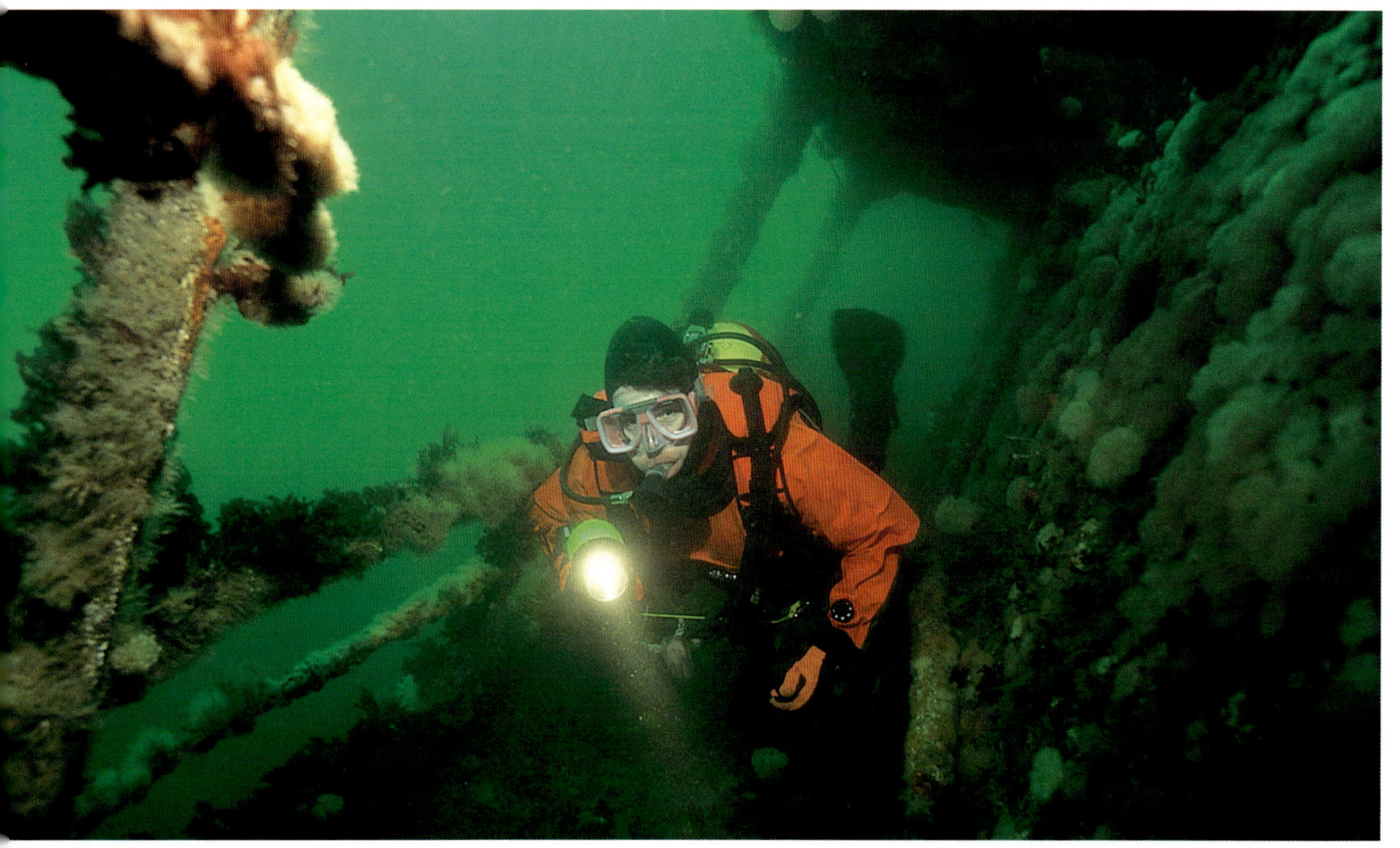

Few wrecks are as intact as the Hispania, in the Sound of Mull, west Scotland. Adding flash to an available-light shot captures the moment as a diver swims along a passageway, producing an interesting and evocative image.
Subal-housed Nikon F801 and 20mm Nikkor lens, with a diffused Nikon SB105 flash unit. 1/15s at f/11 on Fuji Provia 100 ISO

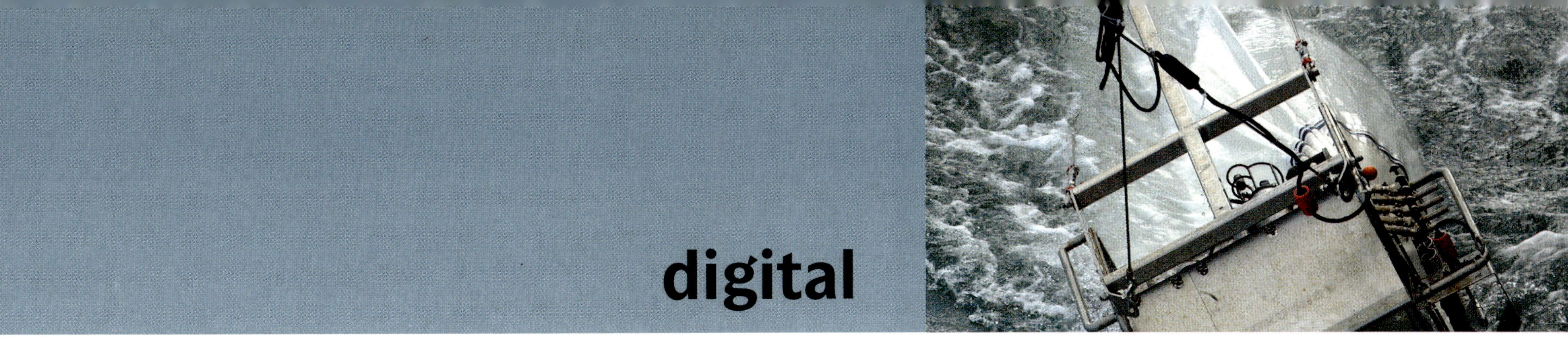

digital

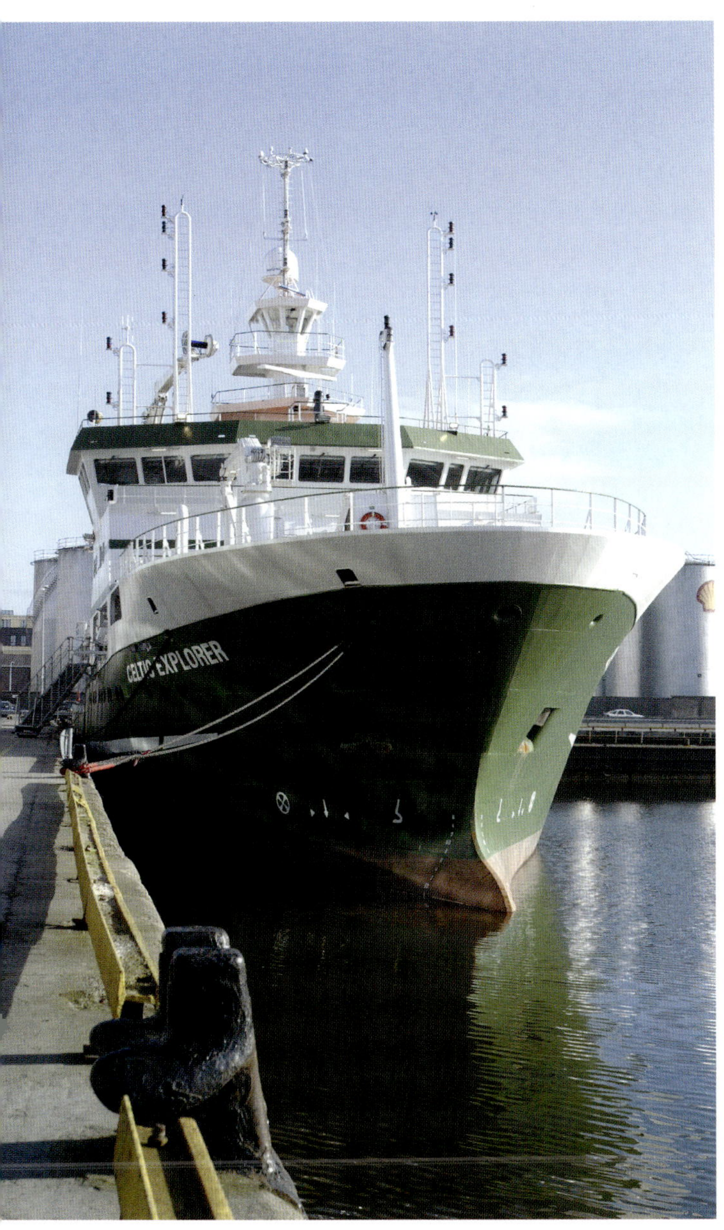

Photography is facing its biggest revolution since it was created. The electronics of the computer age have not only affected the way camera controls operate, but are also starting to redefine the way the photographic image is actually produced.

Digital equipment utilizes an electronic component to capture the photograph itself. There is no requirement for film, and the resulting digital files can be stored in the camera (possibly on a removable storage medium) before being downloaded onto a computer's hard drive. Using image-editing software, the files can then be viewed on a monitor, the image adjusted or manipulated, and copies made. It is even possible to make genuine photographic prints from digital image files that are indistinguishable from conventionally produced photographs. Alternatively, high-quality inkjet and other types of printer can make copies that are starting to rival conventional prints in terms of both quality and permanence. Digital images can also be projected using a digital projector.

The output quality of digital cameras is increasing in leaps and bounds, and manufacturers are now starting to build underwater housings for some of these cameras. While it is unlikely that the absolute quality of the 35mm film camera will be challenged for some time, the use of digital cameras will increase rapidly.

Digital cameras cope very well with varied lighting conditions and can challenge film in terms of quality, provided they are not used beyond their specifications. Shot taken in Galway Harbour, Ireland.
Digital image by Paul Kay and courtesy of the Marine Institute, Ireland. Nikon D1X, 17–35mm f/2.8 AFS Lens. 1/160s at f/8 using ISO equivalent 125

Non-reflex

Most of the digital cameras available now are relatively simple non-reflex models. Although focus is usually fully automated, it is important to realize that these retain many of the limitations of non-reflex cameras, and as such do not have the versatility of reflex systems.

Perhaps the most exciting aspect of digital cameras is the ability to use the viewing screen to compose an image, and/or to check it immediately after exposure.

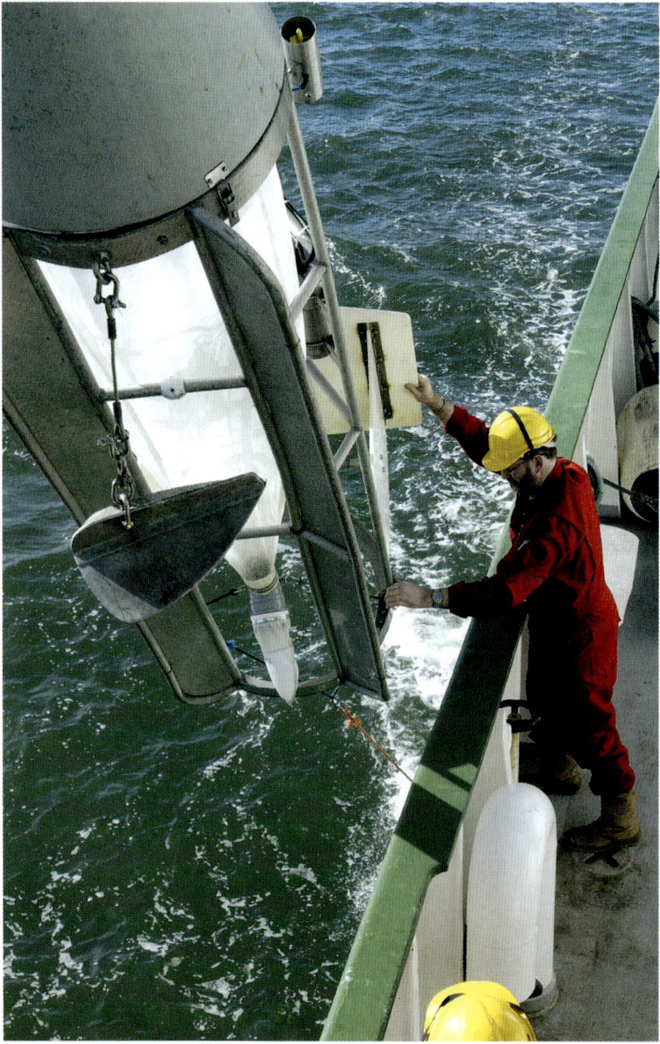

Unfortunately, the small display screen on the back of the camera is not ideal for either purpose. As yet, the screens are of insufficient quality to determine how good the digitally captured image really is, and they can be very difficult to see in bright light. Only when the image is viewed on a good computer screen can a real assessment be made. Despite this, it is possible to ensure that an image has been captured and to retake the shot if it looks as though it may not be acceptable.

Such cameras may well pose a serious threat to non-reflex 35mm cameras before too long, although neither have the sophistication nor the quality associated with housed reflex cameras. Costs are becoming comparable to non-reflex cameras, and the immediacy of results can be very useful, especially for identifying subjects seen while underwater. Digital cameras also offer the option of using powerful video-type lights. Currently, there are some technical problems associated with doing so, but these should be overcome before long.

Reflex

A growing number of reflex digital cameras are becoming available. Some yield relatively large (17MB), high-quality digital files that can be used for many of the applications normally covered by a 35mm reflex camera. Nikon and Fuji both produce cameras utilizing Nikon AF lenses, several of which have been housed (production housings are now available too).

Digital cameras are very versatile above water, but currently have limited flash systems for underwater use.

Digital image by Paul Kay and courtesy of the Marine Institute, Ireland. Nikon D1X, 17–35mm f/2.8 AFS Lens. 1/400s at f/8 using ISO equivalent 200

At present, these cameras do have drawbacks for underwater use. Their power requirement can be heavy and most use rechargeable battery packs, which require associated chargers. This can be problematic if a power supply is not readily available, or if batteries go flat in an open boat where opening a camera housing is not to be encouraged. Additionally, all digital cameras need to have their image files downloaded into some sort of additional storage device. While this may not be a problem for a dive or two, it can be more problematic and time consuming over a longer period.

A further fundamental drawback, which will limit their use underwater for now, is that they only operate TTL flash control using specific digital flash units, and they will only operate a single flash. Currently, there is no way of utilizing more than one unit using TTL control.

While digital cameras will eventually change photography, it remains unlikely that this will affect quality underwater photography dramatically in the short term due to the high cost of quality digital equipment and the technical problems that must still be overcome.

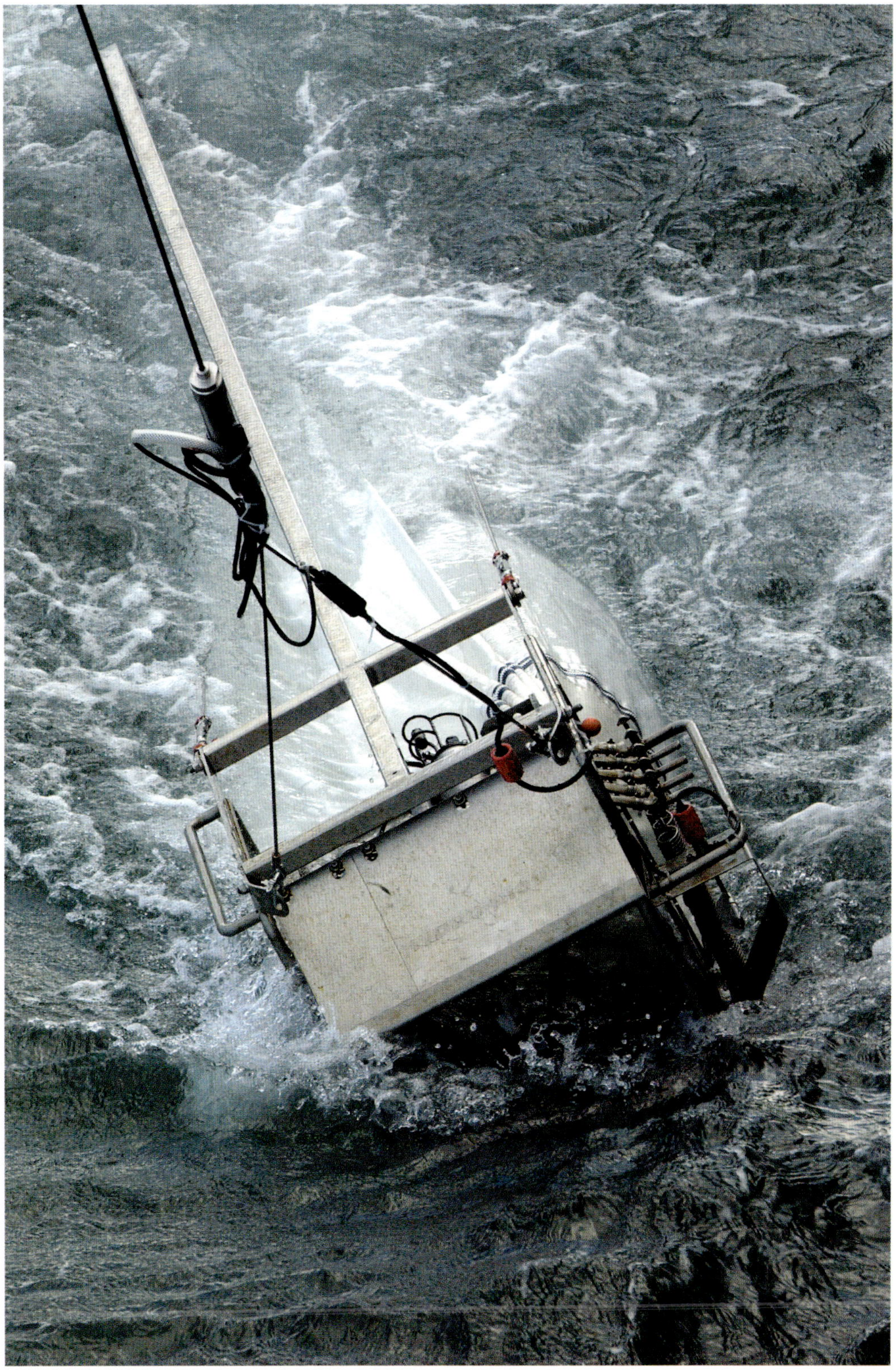

The ability to change the sensitivity of ISO equivalence is of great use when utilizing a digital camera, and all three of the digital shots used in this chapter employed a different setting.
Digital image by Paul Kay and courtesy of the Marine Institute, Ireland. Nikon D1X, 17–35mm f/2.8 AFS Lens. 1/1250s at f/8 using ISO equivalent 800

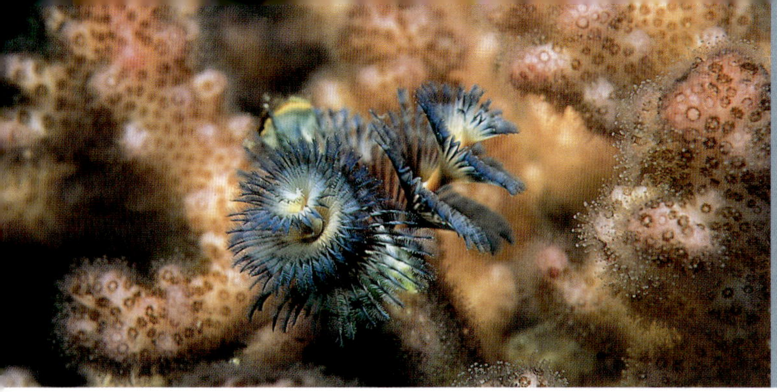

lenses

The lens controls the content of an image, its perspective, how much is of it is sharp and what the out of focus areas look like. In short, it is vital to choose and use the appropriate lens in order to produce a picture in the way that is desired.

Photographic lenses are usually referred to in terms of their focal length (in mm). This measurement is used to indicate the way in which a lens produces an image. A standard lens is generally regarded as having a focal length of about 50mm, and is called 'standard' because it produces an image of similar perspective to that seen by the human eye.

Some lenses suffer from optical problems when used underwater. For example, due to the far lower visibility encountered underwater, lenses with focal lengths of over 200mm are virtually useless. This means that fewer lenses are workable underwater than on land. In general terms, the focal lengths of lenses commonly used underwater (excluding the fisheye lens) vary from 17mm to 105mm.

Field of view

The term 'focal length' encompasses a number of attributes. For the 35mm format it determines both the field of view and the relative magnification of a lens. Field of view (FoV) refers to the angle that a lens 'sees', while relative magnification is how magnified or reduced an image appears to be, relative to a standard lens. As focal length is reduced, so relative magnification also reduces, but the FoV is increased. The net effect is that more is seen in the viewfinder, and the subject appears to be both smaller and further away. On the other hand, increasing the focal length of a lens reduces the FoV – and hence the amount seen – but the subject appears larger and closer. Lenses that increase the FoV are known as wide-angle lenses, while lenses that reduce the FoV are known as long, or, sometimes inaccurately, telephoto lenses.

At the end of a dive off La Gomera in the Canaries, I came across what appeared to be an empty shell. Two eyes then peered out from a peephole, revealing that it was actually home to a hermit crab.
Subal-housed Nikon F80, and 28–105mm lens set at 50mm. 1/125s at f/16 on Fuji Provia 100 ISO

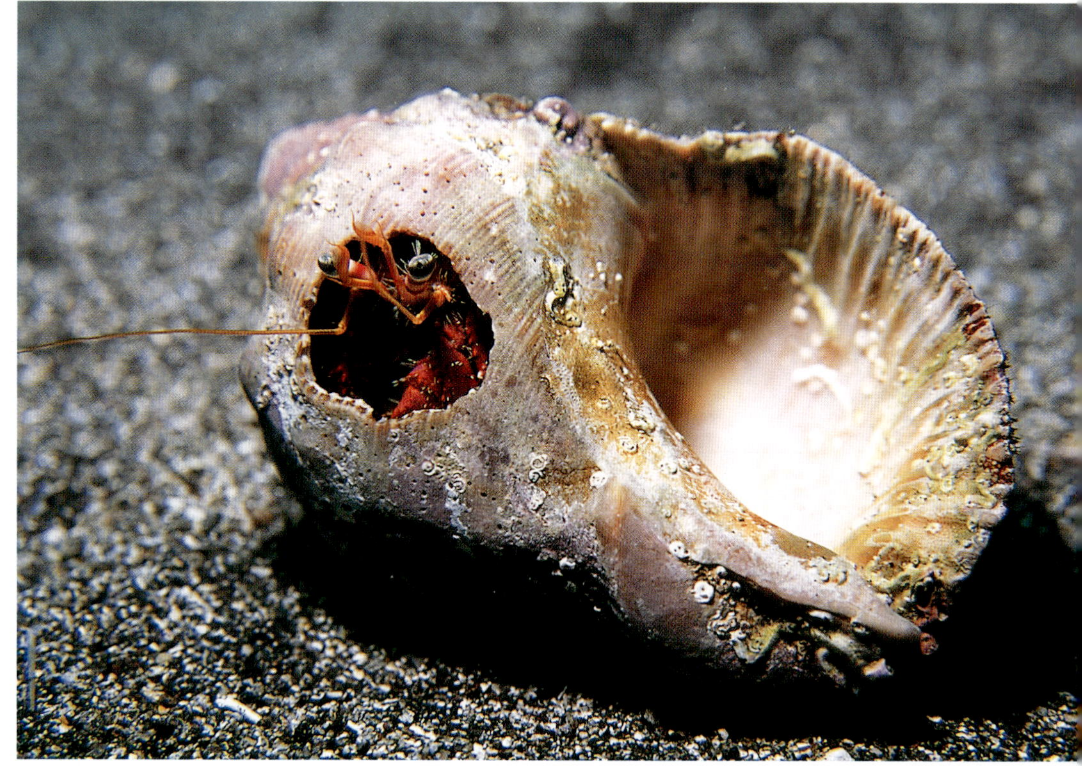

Using a partially wide-angle lens, such as a 35mm lens behind a flat port, can produce interesting marine-life studies. Here, a red cushion star (*Porania pulvillus*) has been photographed against a backdrop of plumose anemones.
Subal-housed Nikon F801 and 35mm Nikkor lens, with a Nikon SB105 flash unit. 1/30s at f/16 on Fuji Provia 100 ISO

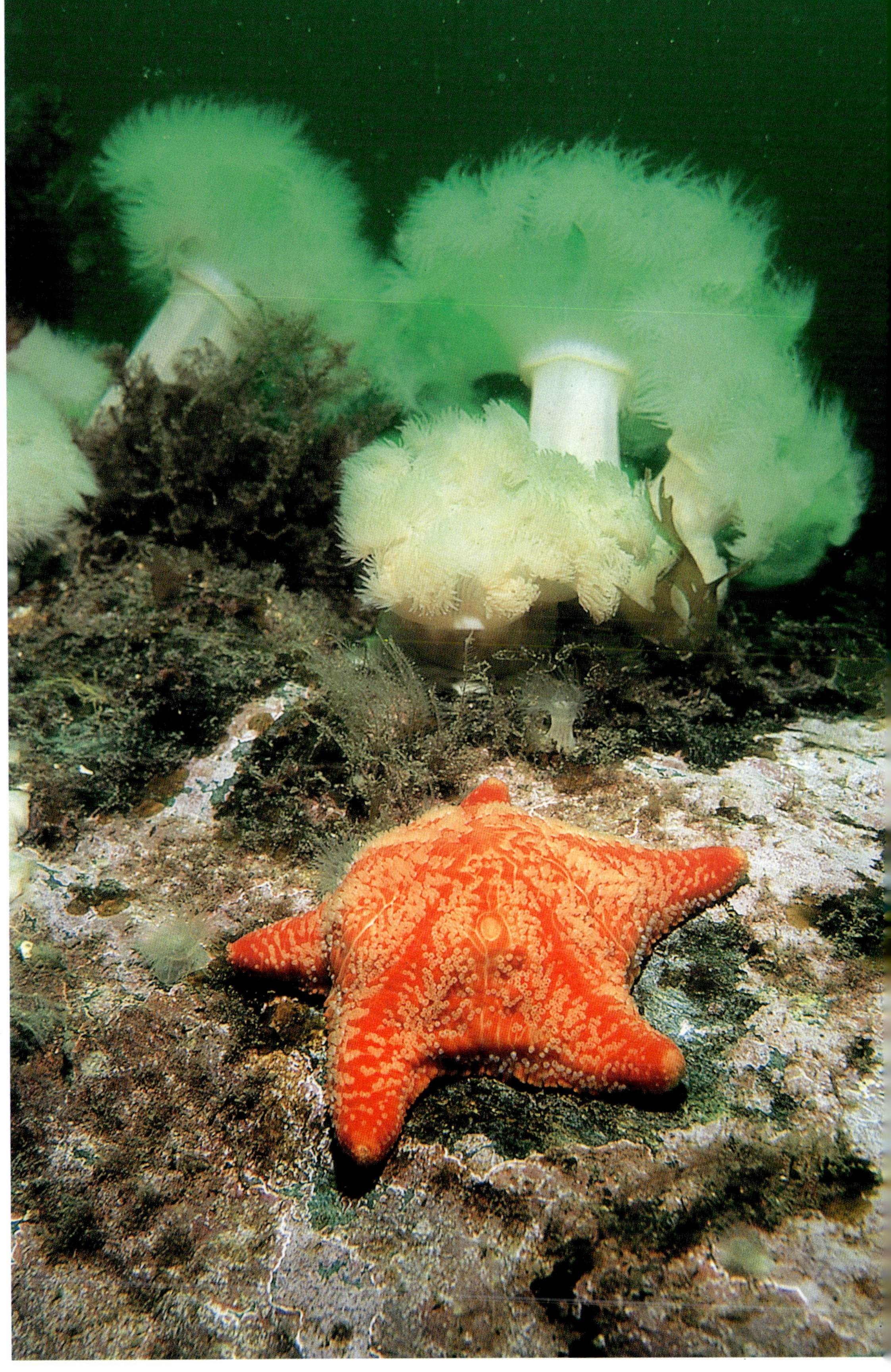

There are two categories of lens used underwater: wide angle and macro. These cannot be defined simply in terms of focal length; the FoV that the lenses cover and the way that they are used are just as important. Furthermore, it is important to realize that the FoV of a lens below water may not be the same as that found above water. This is because the FoV can change depending on whether a lens is used behind a flat or a curved piece of glass. This glass, which is placed between the lens and the water, and its mount are known as a lens port.

Flat ports

Using a flat piece of glass in front of a lens underwater leads to refraction of the light passing through it at both glass surfaces. As a result the effective FoV of the lens is reduced by approximately one third. (A similar effect occurs when using a flat diving mask, which is why everything appears bigger when underwater.) For example, a 60mm macro lens used underwater behind a flat port will see (i.e. have a similar FoV) as a 90mm macro lens would above water, and a 35mm lens operates underwater similarly to a standard 50mm lens above water. In effect, the lens will appear to increase its focal length by one half.

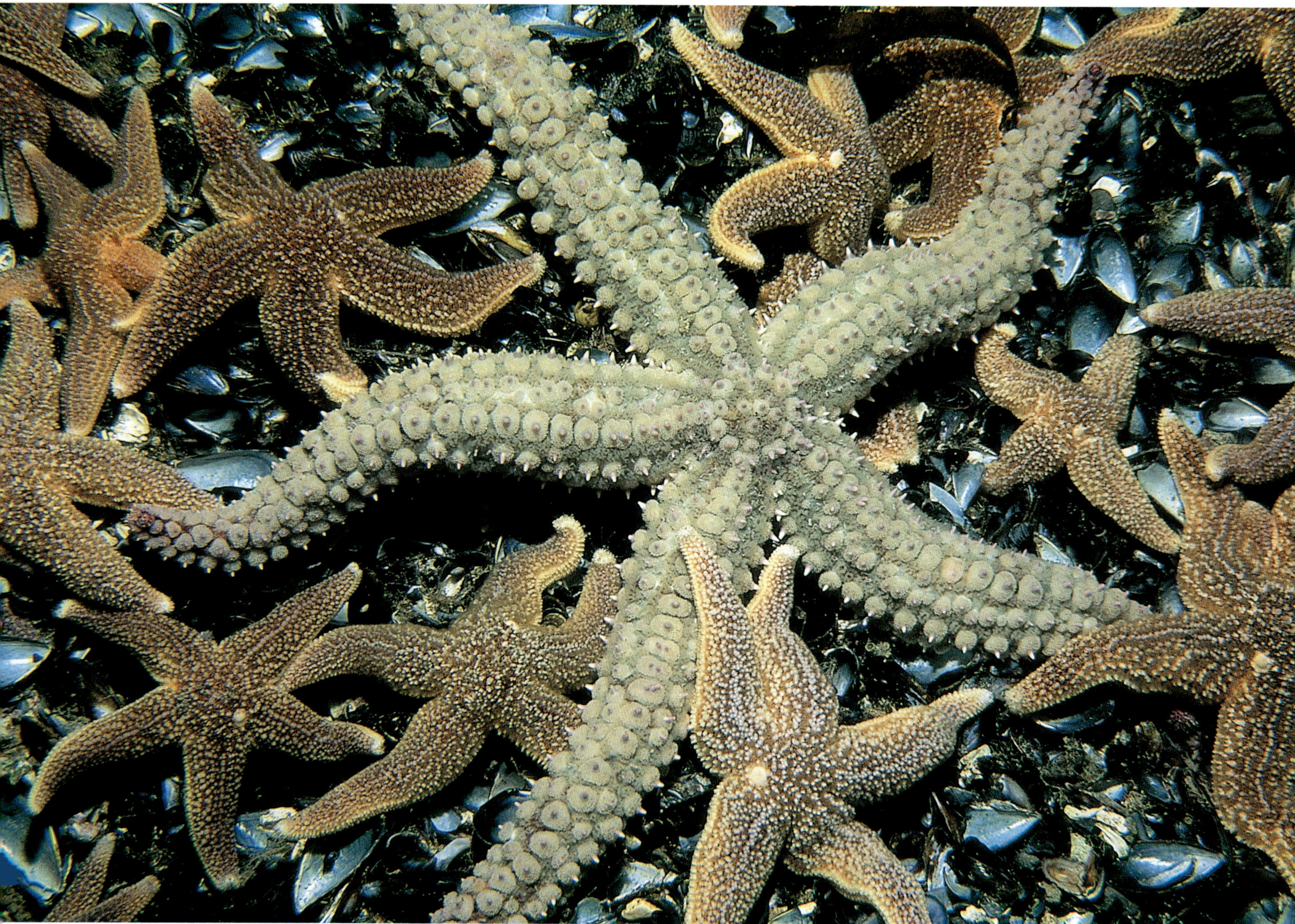

There are optical constraints to further complicate matters, and these make it impractical to use a flat piece of glass in front of lenses that are much less than 35mm in focal length without drastically reducing picture quality. Accordingly, flat ports are usually used for lenses with focal lengths greater than 35mm, as well as macro lenses.

Edible sea urchins (*Echinus esculentus*) are common in the waters around the UK and Ireland (although, oddly, not off North Wales, where this photo was taken). They make an excellent subject, and are helped by adding a balanced background.
Subal-housed Nikon F801and 35mm Nikkor lens, with a Nikon SB105 flash unit. 1/15s at f/16 on Fuji Velvia 50 ISO

Dome ports

To widen the FoV and restore a lens to its normal, above-water perspective, a curved (or dome) port is required. These are lenses in their own right and therefore need to be set up correctly for the relevant lens. Dome ports are generally used with lenses that are 35mm or less in focal length.

The dome creates an optical distortion known as a 'virtual image', in which the subject appears closer to the camera than it actually is. The lens being used requires a supplementary (or close-up) lens to be fitted in front of it, which enables the lens to focus on the (closer) virtual image. This might sound complex, but actually all it means is screwing a thin, positive, close-up lens into the filter thread of the main lens. Once attached, the above-water FoV is restored and the lens appears to focus normally.

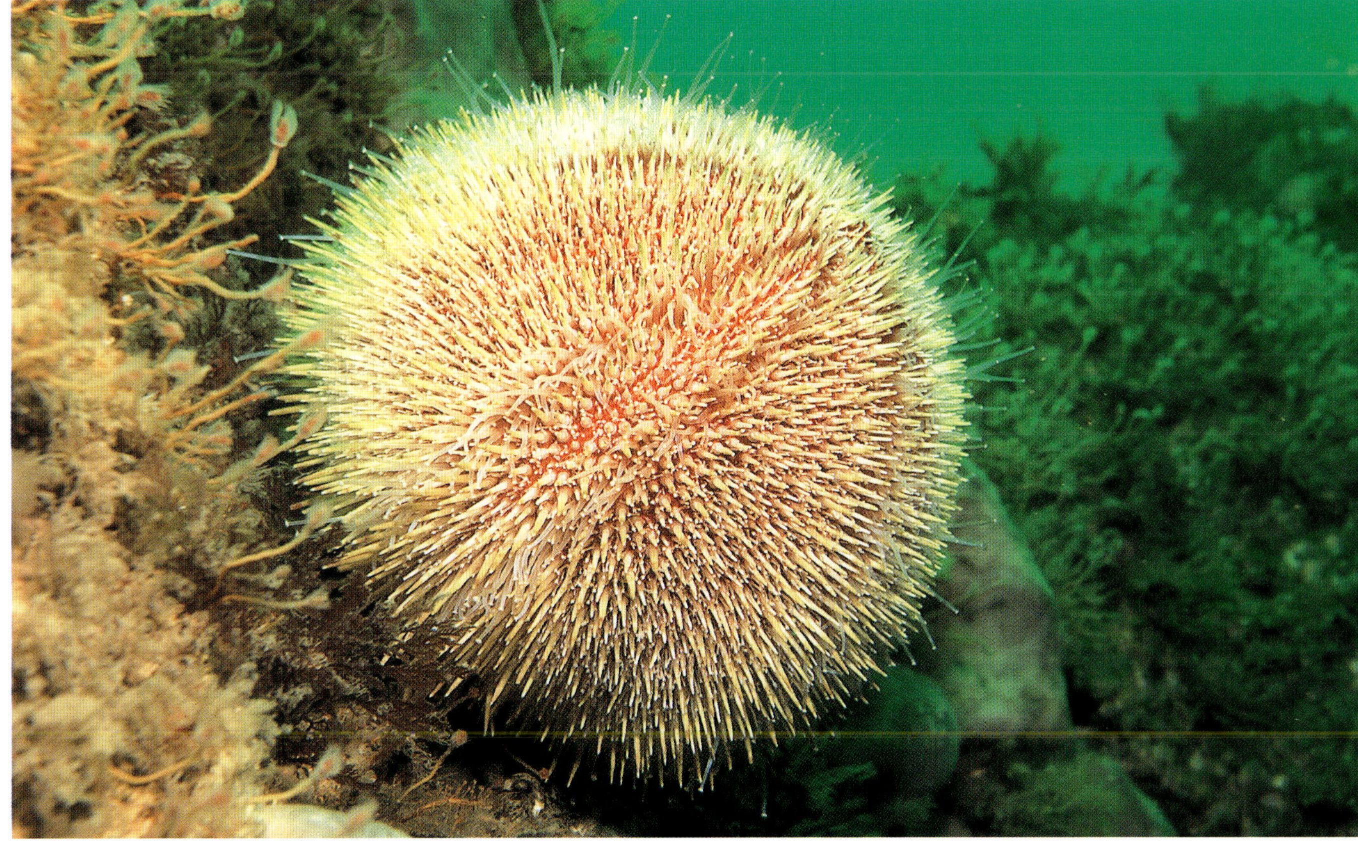

Left: A very simple photograph of a spiny starfish (*Marthasterias glacialis*) hunting common starfish (*Asterias rubens*), which are themselves eating mussels.
Shot by flash light using a 17–35mm lens, set at 35mm, on a Subal-housed Nikon F100 with two diffused strobes. 1/60s at f/16 on Fuji Provia 100 ISO

Wide-angle lenses

Above water, wide-angle lenses are generally regarded as lenses with focal lengths below that of a standard 50mm lens. As a 50mm lens covers an angle of 45 degrees, a wide angle may be considered as a lens with a FoV greater than this. A 35mm lens behind a dome port has a FoV of 60 degrees, and so is considered to be a wide-angle lens underwater (behind a flat port it functions as a macro lens, with a FoV of 45 degrees). Lenses of shorter than 35mm focal length should always be used behind domes.

As focal lengths decrease, FoV increases. A 28mm lens 'sees' 75 degrees, a 20mm lens over 90 degrees, and focal lengths lower than 20mm can achieve a FoV of up to 110 degrees. After this, the whole lens design changes and fisheye lenses are used. These have a FoV of 180 degrees.

Any lens 'seeing' more than 90 degrees may be considered a super wide-angle lens. Those with a FoV of over 100 degrees are referred to as ultra wide-angle lenses, if they preserve a normal perspective, or fisheye if they are designed to produce curved representations of straight lines.

Optical problems

A significant problem in the use of dome ports and wide-angle lenses is that of lens aberration. Many underwater photographs taken using this combination exhibit poor

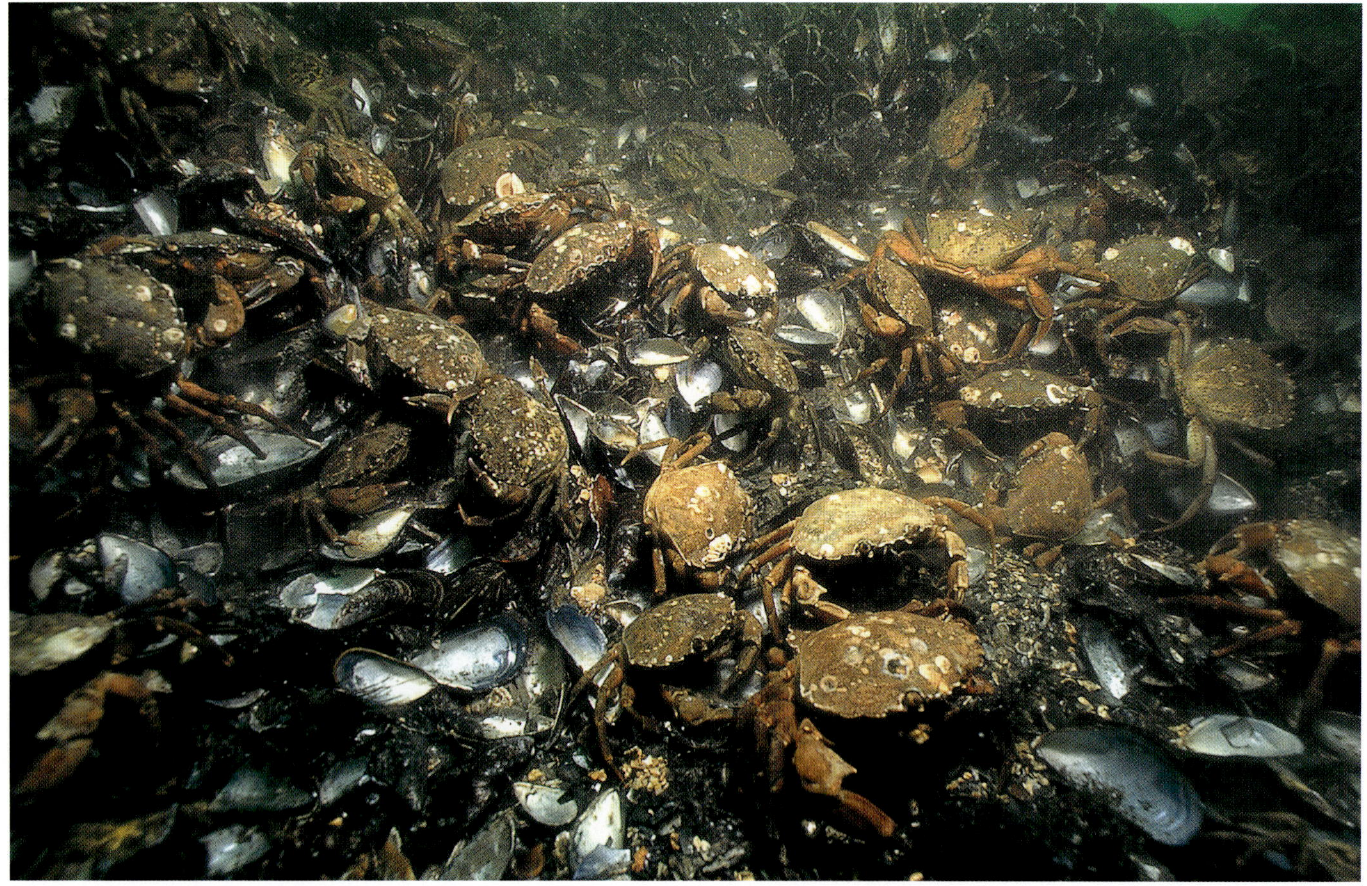

Sometimes a photograph is taken under strange conditions or of an unusual event. Here, something has damaged part of a mussel bed in the Menai Strait, and large numbers of shore crabs (*Carcinus maenas*) have moved in for an easy meal. To photograph such numbers (perhaps 30–40 crabs in a single picture), a Sigma 14mm rectilinear lens was used set to f/8 for 1/15s. The optical failings of this lens behind a dome are secondary to the interest of the subject matter. ***Subal-housed Nikon F801 and 14mm Sigma lens, with a diffused Nikon SB105 flash unit. Provia 100 ISO***

corner, and sometimes edge, sharpness. This is because of lens aberrations that occur when a large dome port is placed in front of the camera lens. These produce a virtual image (as discussed on page 57), which is not planar (i.e. flat). As a consequence the camera (which has a flat film plane carefully engineered to ensure that the film remains even) is focused on the centre of this curved virtual image, and the corners tend to remain out of focus.

This can be resolved to some extent by careful selection of the supplementary lens used to readjust the focus of the wide-angle lens. A simply designed supplementary lens, with a curved front surface and a flat back, will introduce a degree of field curvature into the image that will oppose the curvature produced by the port.

This is not an exact science as lens/port/supplementary combinations vary. For lenses with a FoV exceeding 90 degrees, it may be that full corner correction is not feasible and soft corners just have to be accepted. Port manufacturers usually make their own recommendations and sometimes supply appropriate supplementary lenses for their ports. Additionally, using the smallest aperture possible will help to reduce problems caused by field curvature, due to the greater depth of field achieved.

With many ultra wide-angle and fisheye lenses the situation is further complicated as there is no provision for a supplementary lens to be mounted in front of them. Some have filters that sit in an internal rear holder. Removing such holders, which often use an optical 'flat' when no filter is installed, has been thought to make useful adjustments.

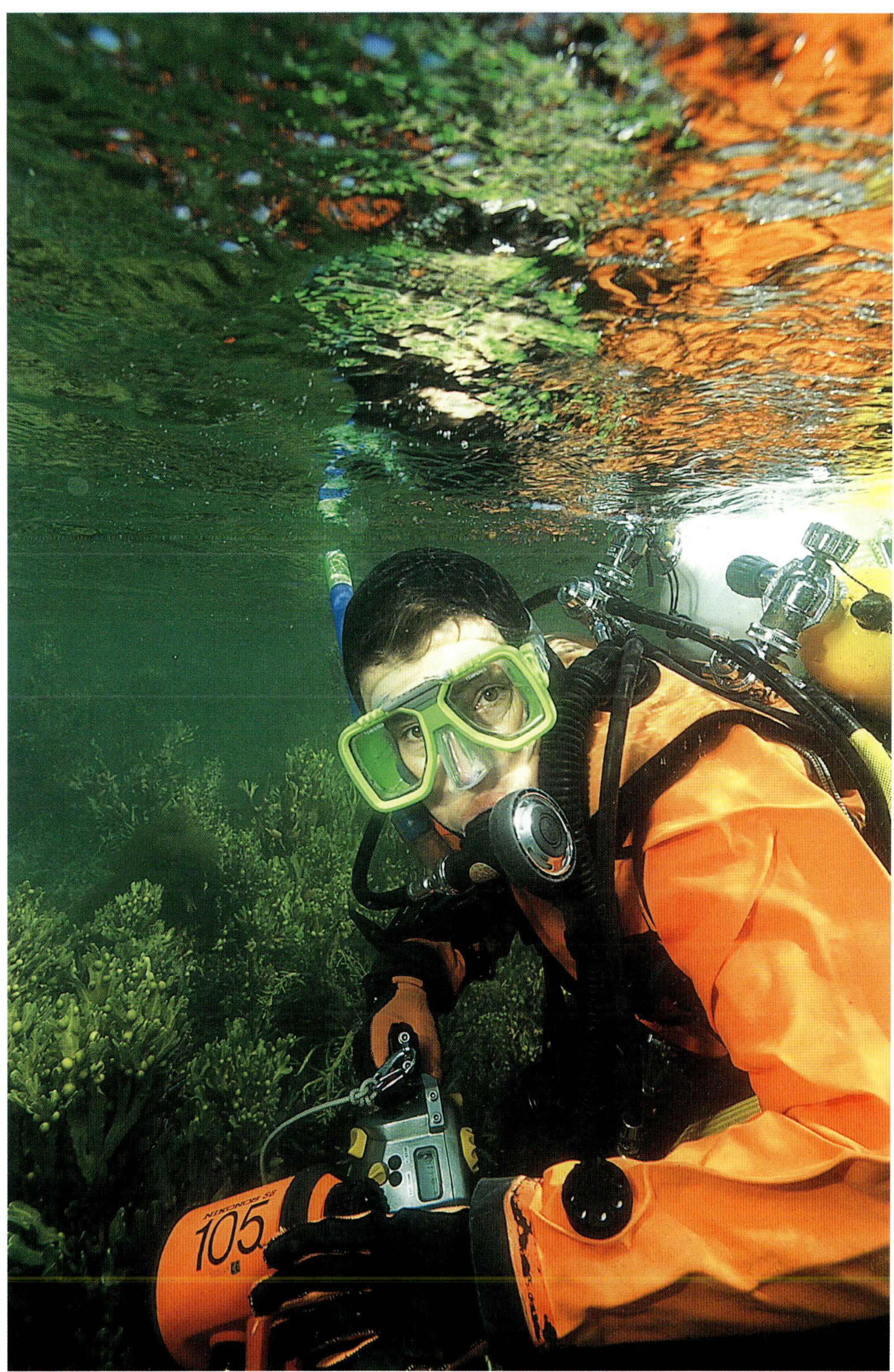

Shallow-water photography benefits from good light levels (especially on sunny days) and this, combined with flash, can produce bright, effective pictures. Wide-angle distortion is noticeable in this shot, but it has still been used on the cover of a diving publication.
Subal-housed Nikon F801 and 20mm Nikkor lens, with a diffused Nikon SB105 flash unit. 1/30s at f/11 on Fuji Velvia 50 ISO

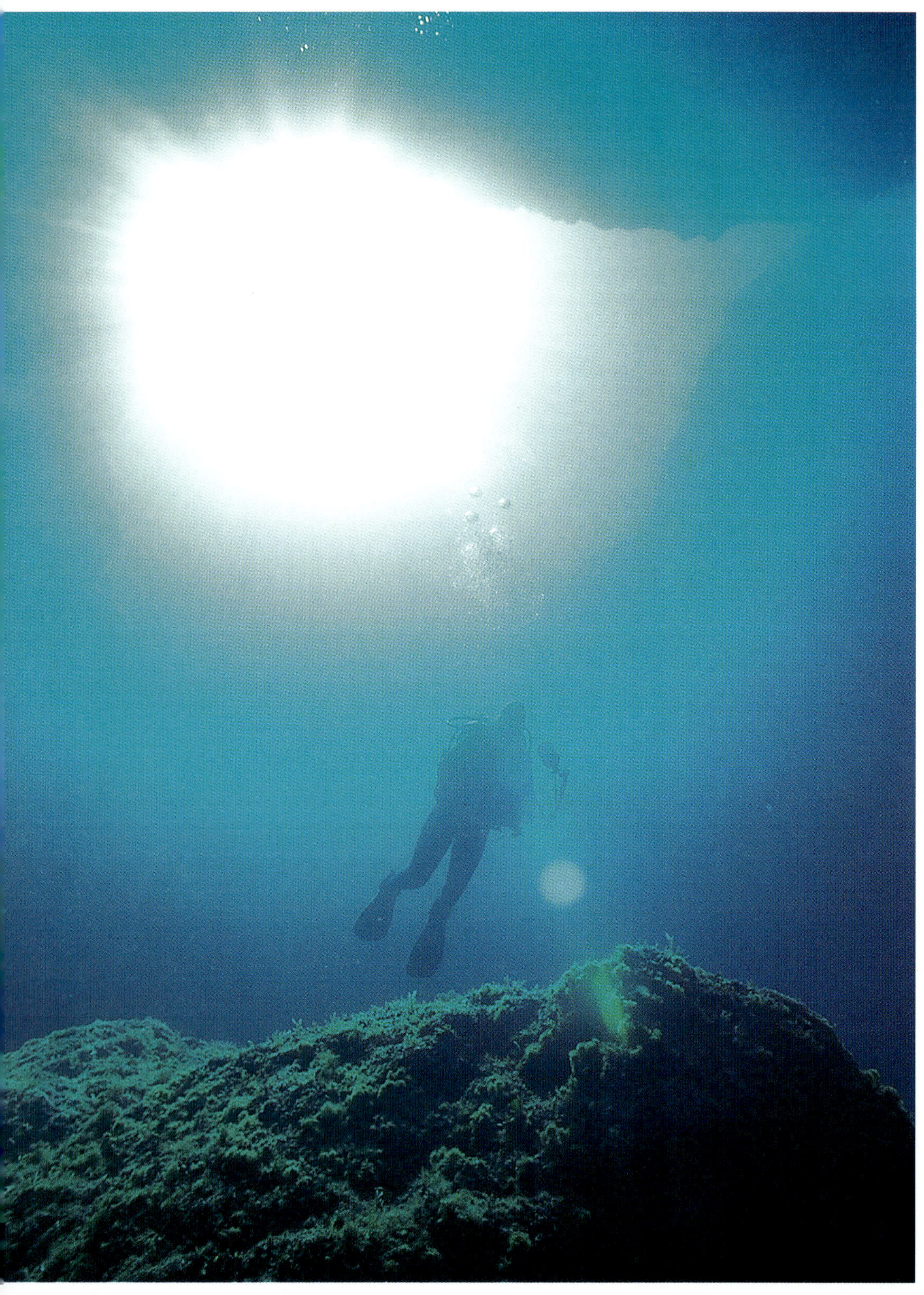

With sufficient effort, this space could even be used to install further lenses to provide optical corrections. However, this is something within the realm of lens designers, and cannot be covered here without an extensive explanation of optical theory well beyond the scope of this book.

It is worth pointing out, though, that the ultra wide-angle 15mm lens produced by Nikon for their non-reflex Nikonos camera is a purpose-designed underwater lens. It equates to a 20mm lens behind a dome port in terms of its FoV, but it lacks the edge and corner problems usually encountered when using dome ports as it is designed specifically for underwater use. As a result it has the reputation of being a superb wide-angle lens in terms of its optical quality underwater.

Wide-angle lenses can introduce significant distortions into pictures, both in terms of the 'barrel' or 'pincushion' effect (which makes straight edges, such as those found on wrecks, look curved) and stretching effects in the corners of a picture. Careful subject selection and composition can help alleviate the most noticeable of these.

Flare

Flare is caused by unwanted reflections of light entering the optical system (lens and/or lens port) and manifests itself as areas of lightness. This is sometimes coloured, and may be more sharply defined on some occasions than others. At its extreme, it can degrade the whole image, reducing contrast dramatically and even obscuring elements within the photograph. It can be a big problem when using the large

Flare is a relatively rare occurrence underwater, but under the Azure Window on Gozo, sufficient sunlight can penetrate to produce it. Whether or not this enhances or detracts from the photograph is a matter of opinion.
Subal-housed Nikon F801 and 20mm Nikkor lens. 1/60s at f/11 on Fuji Velvia 50 ISO

domes required for ultra wide-angle photography. Some manufacturers offer lens coating on their ports, but the sheer size of such domes means that they remain very prone to flaring.

There is little that can be done to avoid flare, other than shielding the port from its cause (usually a bright area of light). When flare can be seen through the camera viewfinder, photography should be avoided – unless it is caused by an inadvertently close flash unit. However, the flare seen on a photograph is not always visible through the viewfinder, as it may be aperture dependent (i.e. not actually visible until the aperture at which the photograph is taken is formed during an exposure).

Applications

In general, wide-angle lenses have similar applications underwater as they do above, but there are fundamental differences in the way in which wide-angle lenses are employed above and below water. Obviously, they are used to photograph large subjects (sea animals such as whales, dolphins and seals, or underwater scenery like coral reefs, wrecks and habitats), but they also have another role.

While wide-angle lens photography on land usually increases the FoV in order to include more of a scene in a picture, underwater wide-angle lenses are often used to allow a photographer to get closer to a subject. By reducing the distance between camera and subject, the problems inherent in shooting through water are reduced, and the potential for back scatter and colour shifts is

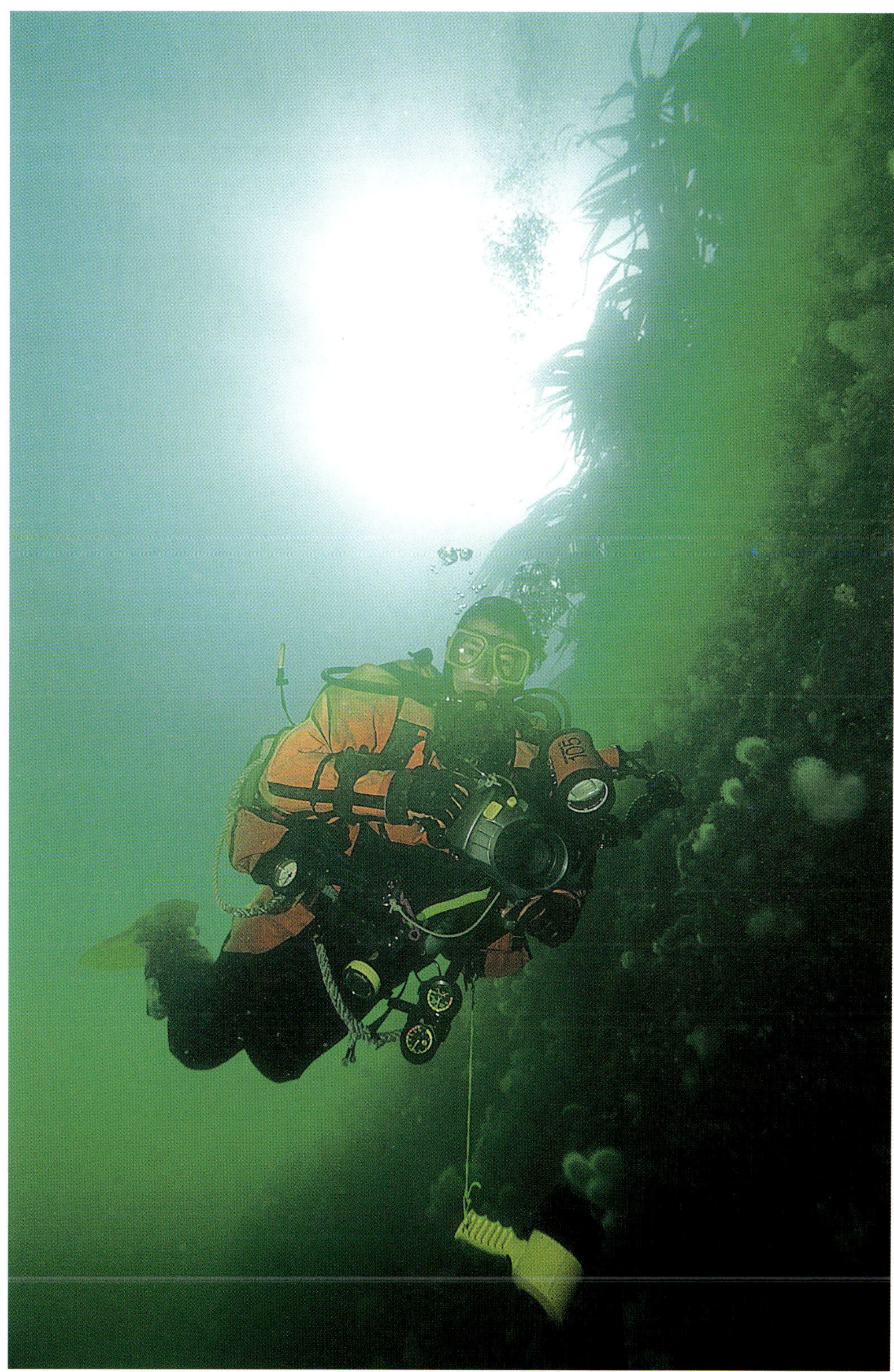

This Manx gully is one of my favourite images. I saw the shot one year while taking macro photos and returned a year later with a wide-angle lens, specifically for this shot – it was worth it.
Subal-housed Nikon F100 and 17–35mm lens set to 17mm, with two diffused Nikon SB105 flash units. 1/4s at f/16 on Fuji Provia 100 ISO

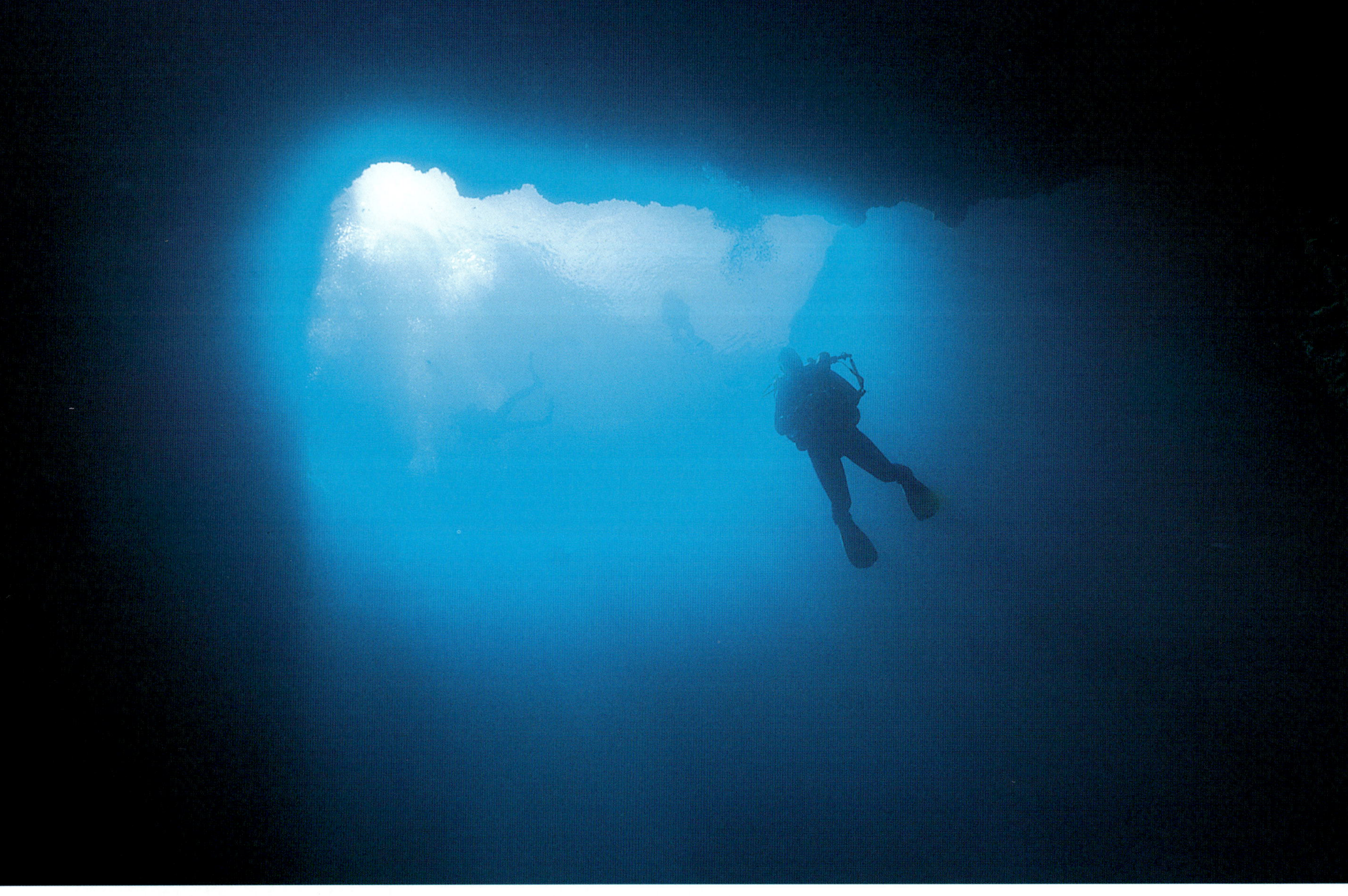

Gozo's Blue Hole is a famous dive site. On sunny days it can provide many opportunities for available-light photography, although the number of divers can be a real problem. ***Subal-housed Nikon F801 and 20mm Nikkor lens. 1/60s at f/8 on Fuji Velvia 50 ISO***

reduced (although problems with perspective and illuminating the subject can occur).

Many photos are taken using wide-angle lenses in a sort of macro mode – a close-up, wide-angle shot in which the subject is large and the background recedes in an exaggerated way. This helps to compensate for less than ideal underwater visibility, and still places the subject in its context. While this technique has significant lighting problems, can result in flare from the flash gun(s), and can give a very wrong impression of scale or perspective, it remains a popular and useful way of producing images underwater.

Underwater wide-angle photography is usually considered to be more problematic than macro photography. The main reason for this is that wide-angle subjects can be difficult to light and to expose correctly. Use of flash illumination only, while sometimes inevitable, has a tendency to produce photographs with hard shadowing because of the flash angle used to minimize back scatter, or with a dark background to the subject because it is distant and receives little flash illumination.

Available-light photography is also possible with wide-angle lenses, and in shallow, well-lit water, results

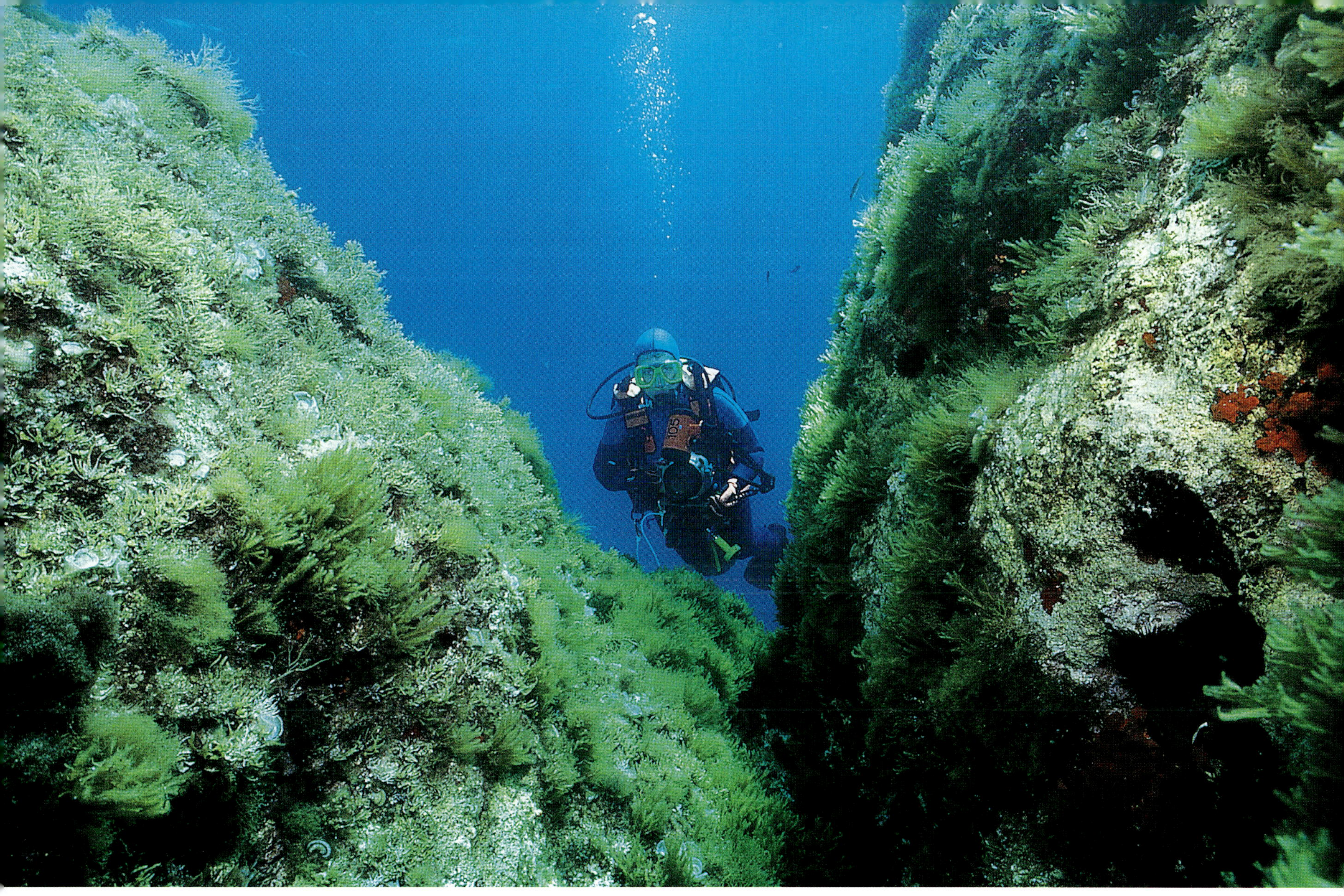

Clear, shallow water allows straightforward pictures to be taken. Here, in the bright Mediterranean Sea off Gozo, just a little high-placed fill-flash brightens both the foreground and the diver.
Subal-housed Nikon F801 and 20mm Nikkor lens, with a Nikon SB105 flash unit. 1/60s at f/8 on Fuji Velvia 50 ISO

can be very good. In deeper water, loss of light and colour limits apertures (unless a stabilizing platform, such as a tripod, is used) and pictures lose definition, becoming blue or greenish.

The answer is to mix available and flash light, or use a fill-flash technique. Many modern cameras utilize very sophisticated electronics to enable automated fill-flash, but the results are not always good. Their programming and sensors are not really designed for the underwater environment (with its low light levels and poor contrast) or for wide-angle subject matter.

To execute precise control of the fill-flash technique underwater, some knowledge of the way the two sources of light interact is needed (see page 137 for details on balancing flash and available light sources). While this can produce excellent results, it is not the easiest technique to master. Add depth, a degree of nitrogen narcosis, and a difficult, potentially hazardous environment, and it is clear why fill-flash techniques using wide-angle lenses are still regarded sceptically by many.

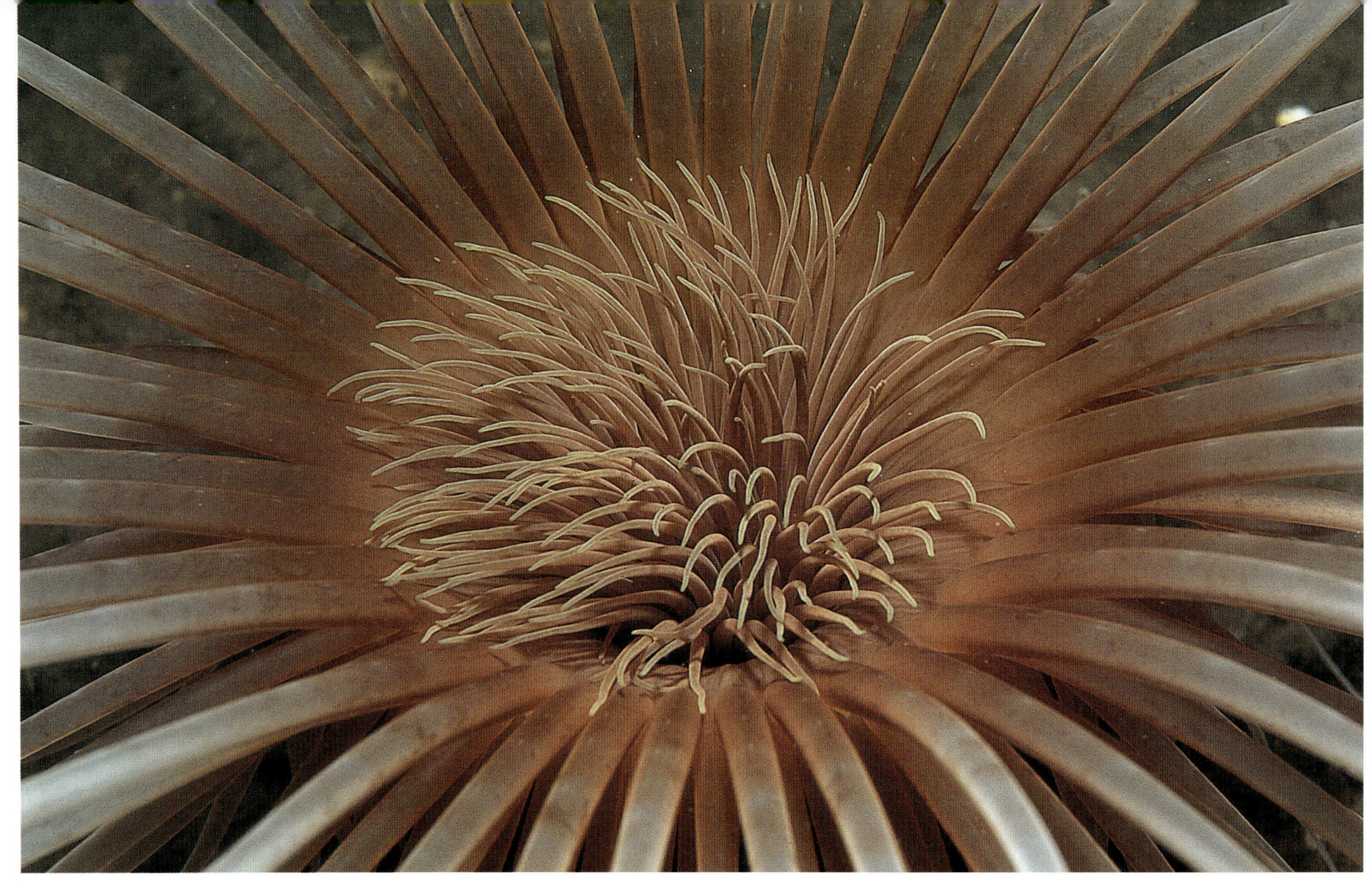

Fireworks anemones (*Pachycerianthus multiplicatus*) are large creatures, but can make effective close-up subjects. Taken, using flash alone, in the dark and dull waters of Loch Fyne on an overcast October day.
Subal-housed Nikon F80 and 60mm micro-Nikkor lens. 1/60s at f/22 on Fuji Velvia 50 ISO

Macro lenses

The basic definition of a macro lens is that it should be capable of reproducing an image of a subject at between one-tenth scale and life-size on film (expressed as from 0.1x to 1x magnification or from 1:10 to 1:1). Clearly not all lenses used as macro lenses can achieve this full range, but most will work to somewhere within it. Given that the vast majority of photographs taken underwater on lenses with a FoV of 45 degrees or less fall into this category, it makes sense that such lenses should be regarded as macro lenses when used underwater.

Lenses used for macro photography underwater vary in focal length from 35mm (behind a flat port), through to the more popular 50–105mm true macro lenses, and up to some longer lenses with focal lengths of as much as 200mm. Anything of above 105mm in focal length is a rather specialized lens and may be of limited use.

In contrast with wide-angle lenses, where the important technical feature is FoV, with macro lenses the important consideration is working distance. This is a measure of the distance between the subject and the lens for any given

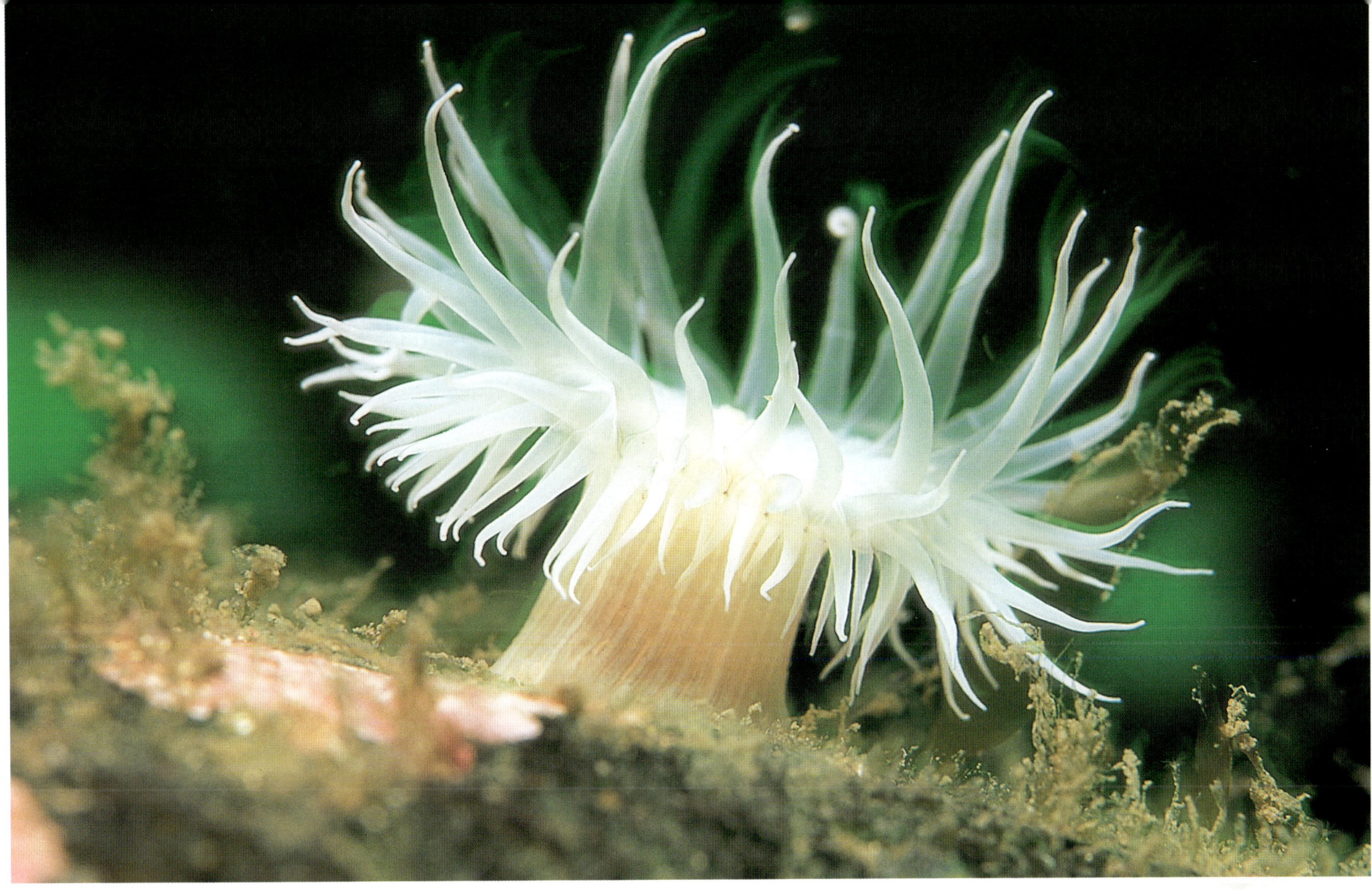

When macro photographs are taken, the exposure required increases so that four times the normal exposure is needed when imaging a subject like this anemone (*Actinothöe sphyrodeta*) off the Isle of Man. By setting a slow shutter speed, it is possible to provide some background, which creates valuable context.
Subal-housed Nikon F100 and 60mm micro-Nikkor lens, with SB105 flash. 1/2s at f/22 on Fuji Velvia 50 ISO

magnification; a distance that becomes greater as the focal length increases.

Many purpose-designed macro lenses are available in focal lengths of between 50mm and 105mm, and will focus from infinity right down to life-size on film. Many produce high-quality images, and the significant differences are usually in mechanical design. When housed, many require additional controls to allow full use of their capabilities. For example, some housed lenses may need a control on the lens itself to be operated in order to switch between manual and autofocus. This may or may not be available, depending on the lens/housing/port combination used.

Optical problems

Most macro lenses operate through a flat port and so have a narrower FoV than they would above water. Unlike wide-angle lenses, using a flat port does not significantly compromise their optical quality. They can also be used with dome ports if desired, but may not work well at large apertures and a macro-lens/dome-port combination should be tested thoroughly to see if any problems occur.

Macro lenses have an extremely narrow depth of field and are generally used at small apertures (i.e. f/16–32). Even when using such apertures, focusing is still critical and it is often necessary to use a spotting torch to help if light levels

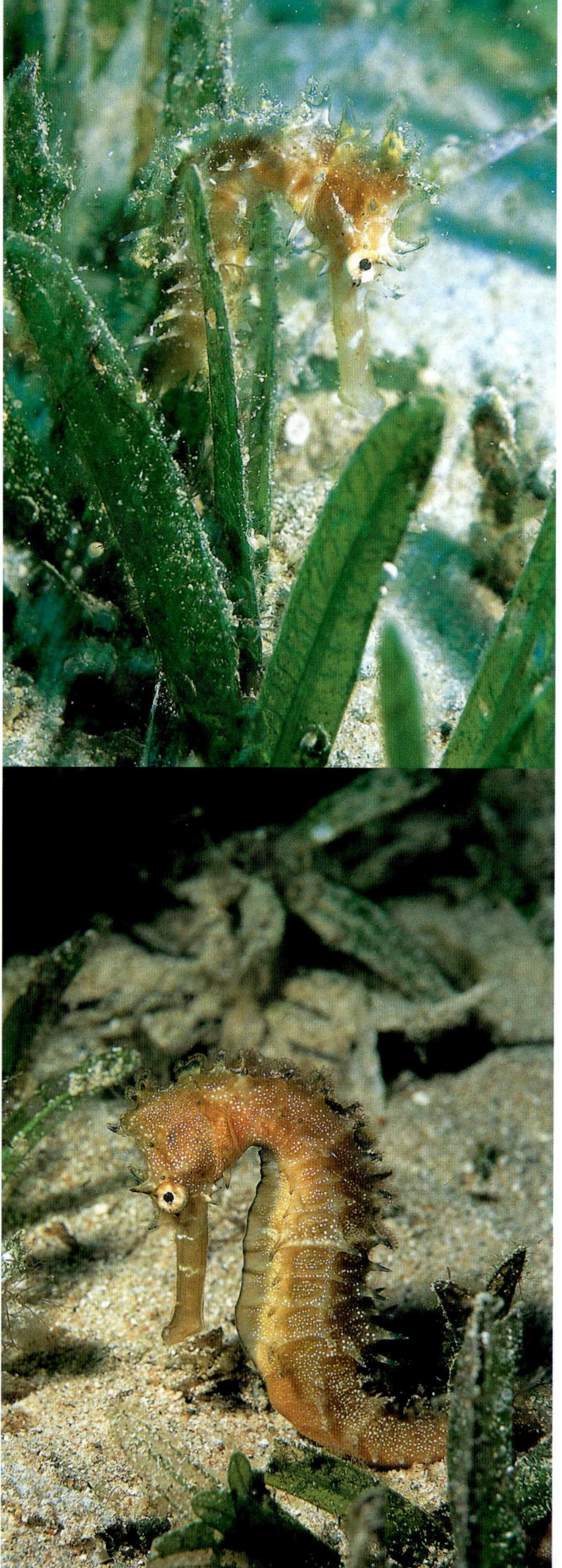

Allowing an available-light component to expose this macro shot of a Red Sea seahorse (*Hippocampus histrix*) produces a light picture that illustrates this tiny creature's ability to blend into the seagrass background.
Subal-housed Nikon F100 and 60mm micro-Nikkor lens, with a Nikon SB105 flash unit. 1/15s at f/16 on Fuji Velvia 50 ISO

An alternative macro shot of a Red Sea seahorse (*Hippocampus histrix*) uses flash alone to produce a crisp, punchy picture with lots of fine detail.
Subal-housed Nikon F100 and 60mm micro-Nikkor lens, with a Nikon SB105 flash unit. 1/60s at f/16 on Fuji Velvia 50 ISO

are low. This is less of a problem with non-reflex cameras, but the framers used in macro photography are easily bent. Full attention has to be paid to the instructions accompanying non-reflex close-up devices, as the lens settings vary depending on the manufacturer.

Applications

As explained earlier, macro lenses are designed to operate within a short distance of the subject and to produce close-up photographs. They are often used at small apertures to maximize the amount of the subject that is sharp, and are normally operated in conjunction with flash. While some fill-flash photography is possible using macro lenses, this can only be achieved when both conditions and subject positioning enable it. Usually, macro photographs are taken by flash illumination alone.

The most popular route into underwater photography is to start by shooting macro photographs using TTL flash, as this is perceived as being the easiest type of photograph to take underwater.

Zoom lenses

Zoom lenses have some characteristics that would appear to make them ideal for underwater use, but they also have drawbacks. The most obvious of these is that a dome port must be used if the lowest focal length is below 35mm. Optical constraints placed on the lens designers mean that the dome can rarely be placed in its 'ideal' position in front of a zoom, as a shift in focal length will usually necessitate an adjustment in location of the dome port. This is not practical and, as a result, only a few zooms can be used behind dome ports (these retain certain optical characteristics at all focal lengths). Also, although many zooms operate inside the macro range suitable for underwater photography, they might only do so at certain focal lengths, or the relevant controls might be inaccessible underwater.

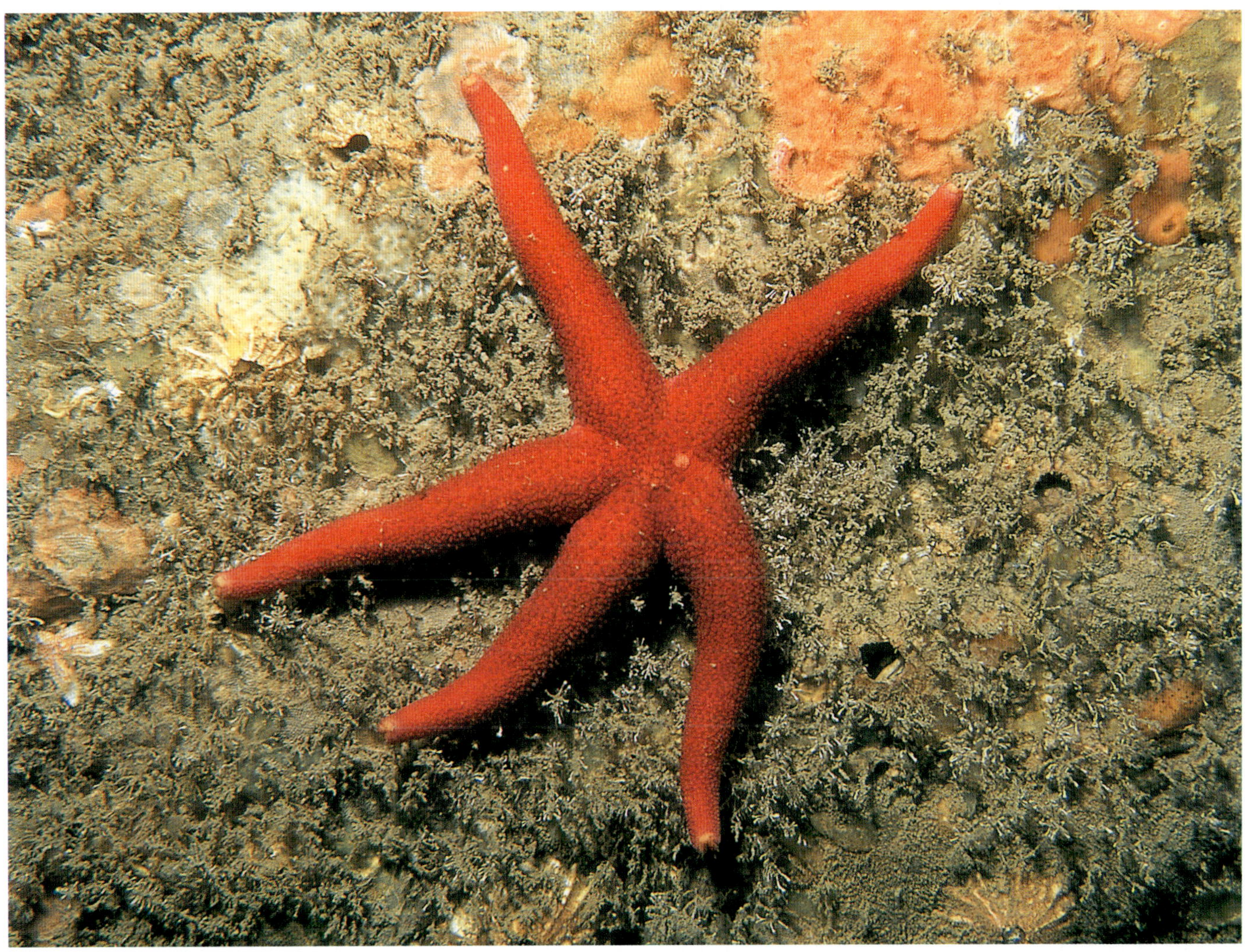

A simple subject, such as this bloody Henry starfish (*Henricia* sp.) from Hell's Mouth in North Wales, can be very striking. Selecting a particularly colourful specimen can make a huge difference, as many are much drabber.
Subal-housed Nikon F100 and 28–105mm lens set at 50mm, with a single flash. 1/125s at f/16 on Fuji Provia 100 ISO

The advantages of zoom lenses are obvious: a single lens offering range of focal lengths, the possibility of taking wide-angle and macro photographs without changing lenses, and their compactness. There are also some specialized zoom lenses available that may prove to be both versatile and very usable. These include a few wide-angle zoom lenses featuring both internal focusing and internal zooming, and some macro zooms in the 80–200mm range, which can work well through a flat port. However, prime lenses (i.e. those with a single, fixed focal length) still provide better results, and the range of prime lenses available includes lenses that are able to focus closer than zoom lenses.

Zooms remain, in general, a compromise if used underwater and are viable only when the concessions they entail are justified by the photography undertaken. The ideal zoom/port combination remains elusive.

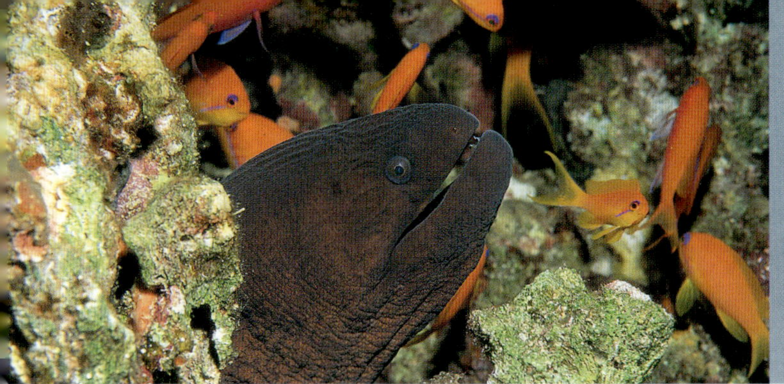

flash units

Underwater, flash is virtually indispensable. While there are some photographers who shoot only natural light, they are relatively few and far between. For the vast majority of underwater photographers, the use of flash is an essential part of their photography.

In its most basic form, a flash (or strobe) unit is designed to emit a very bright light for a very short duration. Today, electronic flash units are the standard for illuminating most underwater subjects. With the advent of electronic microprocessor control, some flash units are extremely sophisticated and capable of automating a great deal of the exposure. Underwater flash units can be divided into two types, manual and automatic:

- Manual flash units are fairly basic, and rely on the photographer to adjust the lens aperture in order to ensure that the correct amount of flash illumination exposes the film.
- Automatic units now operate using TTL flash control almost exclusively. This makes use of sensors within the camera body to tell a flash unit when it has provided sufficient light to expose the film correctly. It relies on having the flash connected to the camera by a suitable lead and, in the case of a housed camera, this usually means using a Nik-5 flash socket as discussed earlier (see page 48). Generally speaking, a good TTL flash unit is preferable, provided the camera to which it will be fitted offers this option.

Housed flash units

Housed flash units tend to be a compromise, as few powerful land units seem to be a size or shape that fits conveniently into a housing. Often, land flashes offer high degrees of electronic sophistication and compatibility when used with housed cameras, but, to counter this, a large number of controls need to be operated and housings do not always permit access to these.

Housed flashes can convey significant advantages when used for macro photography. Many allow the flash head to zoom and deliver a very powerful, narrow flash beam giving high-quality illumination. They offer very high power outputs when the beam is narrowed down, and this can be very useful for close-up photographs as it allows small apertures and maximizes depth of field.

For wide-angle photography, few housed units have sufficiently high power outputs relative to those offered by purpose-built underwater flashes. Some of the more sophisticated land flashes give an indication of whether a 'correct' exposure has been made or, if not, by how much the photograph was underexposed, although viewing such data may be a problem when the unit is housed.

For non-Nikon housed cameras, a housed flash unit is a relatively straightforward way of obtaining a TTL flash. Sometimes the flash socket used on such housed cameras remains the Nik-5 form, but it is wired for a specific housed flash. Although this appears to be a good solution, such sockets should not have Nikonos-type flash units fitted as they may cause problems due to incompatibility (see page 70).

Lastly, it is worth noting that housed land-based flash units may be far more difficult to use manually than their purpose-built counterparts. There are so many ways of adjusting them that their power outputs can vary dramatically, depending on the focal length and power output selected. This makes tables (which are not supplied for underwater use) difficult to determine and complex to use. Such units are not ideal for manual exposure use and should probably be regarded more as automated units.

Use of flash here has helped to add a little interest to the foreground. The wreck of the Tulamben off Bali, Indonesia, is a photographer's paradise with numerous fish and lots of swim-throughs.
Subal-housed Nikon F801 and 20mm Nikkor lens, with a diffused Nikon SB105 flash unit. 1/30s at f/11 on Fuji Provia 100 ISO

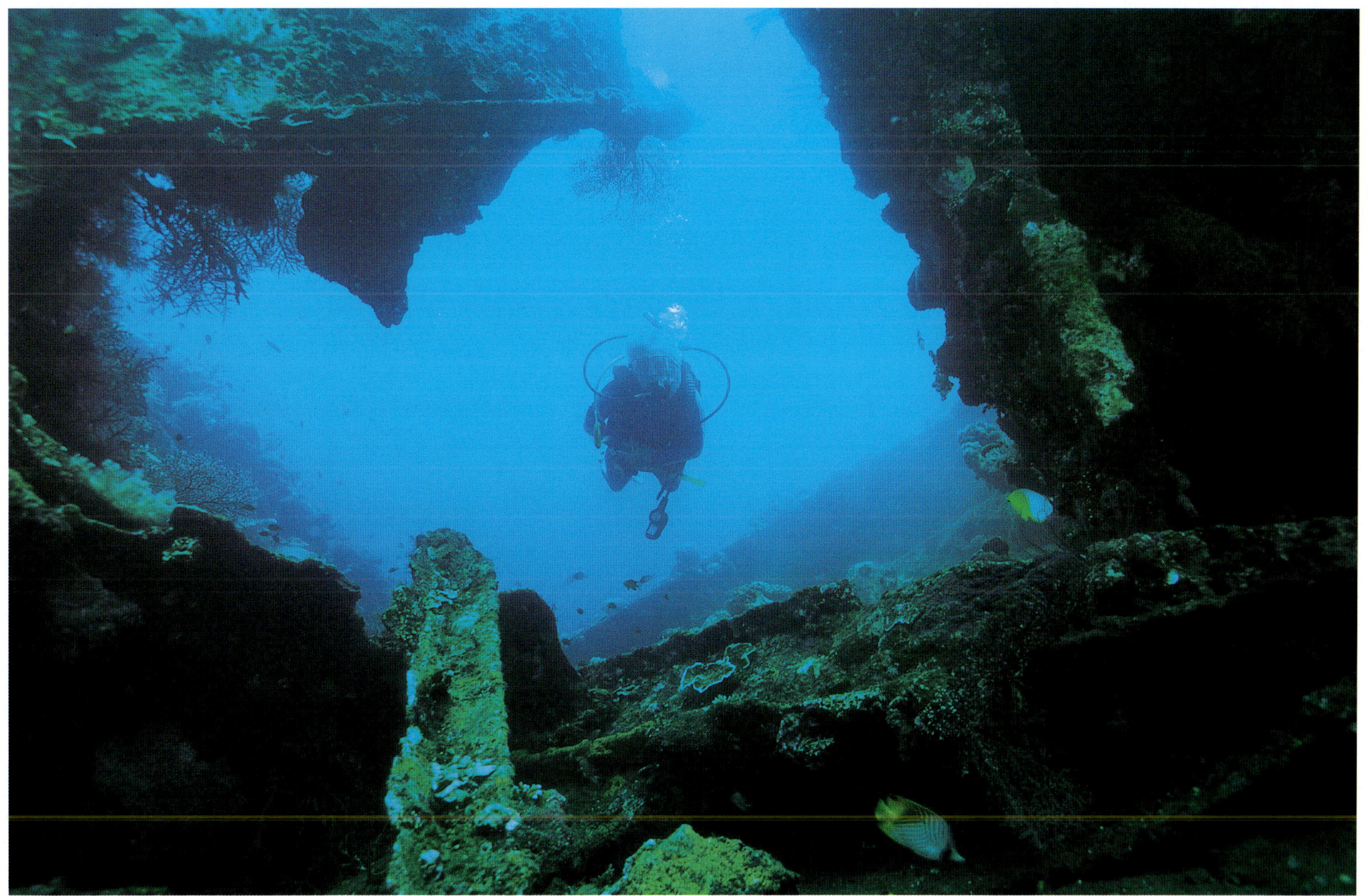

Purpose-built flash units

Purpose-built units can offer high power output, a wide beam angle (essential for wide-angle photography), and a considerable number of flashes from their batteries (whether rechargeable or otherwise). Prices are usually high compared with their sophisticated counterparts designed for use above water, and powerful, wide-beam-angle units designed to provide even illumination for lenses with a FoV of around 100 degrees are especially expensive.

There are also physical advantages to purpose-built units. Most are easy to carry, store, and mount on appropriate flash arms. They are generally robust and quite reliable, especially those from well-known manufacturers. Many are designed to be fully compatible with the electronics of both Nikonos and housed Nikon cameras.

Most units can be switched into a manual mode (or modes giving various power outputs), and are usually supplied with comprehensive tables for underwater use. If only a few film speeds are used, it can be very helpful to transcribe the parts of the table most likely to be used onto an underwater 'slate', rather than use the whole thing.

Compatibility

Some modern SLR cameras – especially the cheaper models – are not designed to cope with the high voltages used in older flash units. Although these may couple to housings via the Nik-5 socket, there is a real risk that damage to the camera electronics may occur in use. If any doubt exists, check with manufacturers or importers for any potential problems before coupling and using older flash units with a new camera. I know of at least one underwater photographer who 'fried' the flash circuit on a Nikon by trying out an early Nikonos-V compatible flash unit, completely destroying the camera as the damage was too expensive to repair.

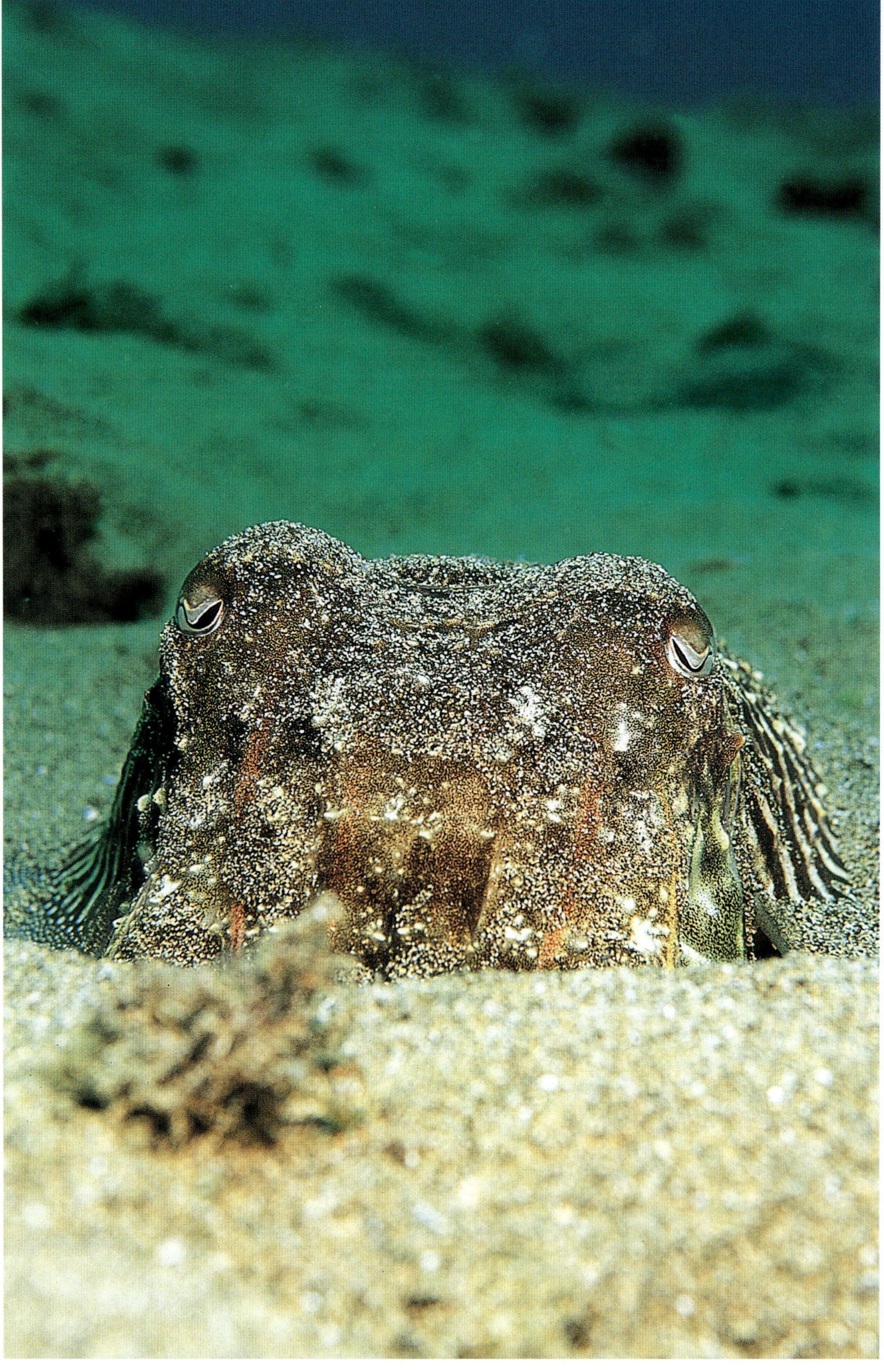

This cuttlefish (*Sepia officinalis*) did not mind being photographed. Although these creatures are sensitive to light, this one was in shallow, well-illuminated water and seemed happy to tolerate the flash bursts. ***Subal-housed Nikon F100 and 60mm micro-Nikkor, with a Nikon SB105 flash unit. 1/30s at f/16 on Fuji Velvia 50 ISO***

Quality of light

Although the actual amount of light produced by a particular flash is measured in terms of power output, there are other variations. Two flash units might have similar power outputs, but one may cover a wider angle than the other and so be more suited to wide-angle photography. Narrow-beam flash units (especially housed land flashes) can be very effective for macro photography and give relatively high outputs over an acute angle. Some can even change their angle, either manually or automatically, as a zoom lens is moved through its range of focal lengths.

Each flash unit has its own distinctive characteristics. Precisely how each one provides its cone of illumination is determined by the design of the actual area that produces the burst of light and the associated reflector system (sometimes these 'flash-tube characteristics' are adjustable). One aim of the designer is to provide even illumination throughout the cone of flash illumination, as failure to do so would produce uneven exposure across the subject. Reflector size, shape and texture all play a part in the final quality of light output and affect the way that shadows are formed in the final photograph.

Add to this specific techniques favoured by each photographer, and the whole question of light quality becomes both complex and subjective. In fact, initially there are so many other difficulties to contend with that the choice of flash unit is largely irrelevant in terms of

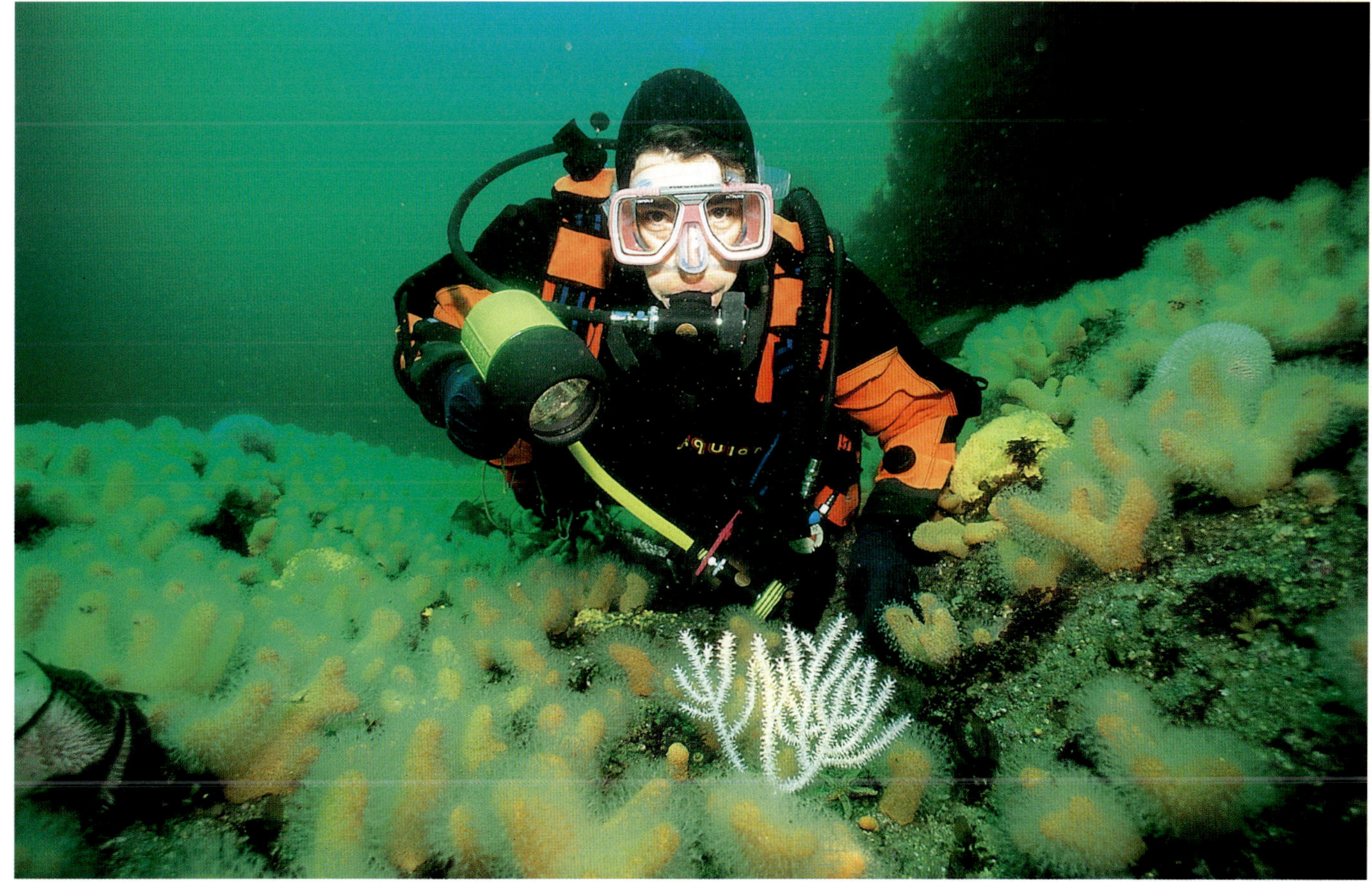

My dive buddy (my wife Lucy), looking at a sea fan (*Eunicella verrucosa*) off the Aran Islands in Ireland. Skin rapidly overexposes and can take on a hint of cyan, which is often removed by using a 'warm' flash. ***Subal-housed Nikon F801 and 20mm Nikkor lens, with a single diffused flash unit. 1/15s at f/11 on Fuji Provia 100 ISO***

light quality. A newcomer to underwater photography may find looking at the work of other underwater photographers worthwhile, and then basing their purchase of flash unit on preferences within such photos (providing details of units used can be obtained). Any choice should be well though out, as flash units are expensive items.

The 'colour temperature' of a flash unit provides yet another variable. This term is used to describe the colour of a flash unit's light output. The standard colour temperature for flash illumination is generally 5500–6000°K (degrees Kelvin), which equates to light similar to daylight.

Underwater there is a tendency for colours to cool (i.e. to shift towards blue or green) due to the differential absorbency of light (see page 98). To counter this, many underwater flash units output light at a lower colour temperature – at times as low as 4600°K – and some even feature variable colour temperature. Mired shift filters do exactly the same thing, and are available in sheets of thin acetate or polyester. These can be cut to shape and fitted over any flash unit, making them a highly affordable option.

Flash arms

Flash arms are an important part of an underwater photographer's kit. Often they are thought of as an add-on extra, but should actually be seen as an essential. Versatile flash arms can really help when it comes to accurate and useful flash positioning, and should be given careful consideration before buying.

Manufacturers offer a variety of arms, but the most common consist of either rigid lengths linked by adjustable ball joints, or flexible plastic connectors. Both have their exponents and arm choice is a personal matter, but here are some points to bear in mind when choosing an arm:

- Articulated flash arms are relatively easy to lock into position when underwater, but they may flop about once out of water. While they do not need to be locked solid above water, they do need to be fairly rigid. Inevitably, someone will try to pick a camera up by the flash arm, and it does need to be able to bear the camera's weight without coming apart.
- Many flash arms are designed so that they can be used with a variety of flash units and cameras. Articulated arms also come in various configurations allowing longer or shorter sections to be inserted for wide-angle or macro photography. They can be locked rigid, or slackened so that they can be moved with ease while underwater. Sections from some can even be interchanged with parts from other manufacturers' arms. Such arms are a long-term investment as they can probably be upgraded and used with new cameras and flash units.
- Flexible plastic arms (often made from machine-tool lubricant hoses) are very versatile and can also be lengthened or shortened. The weight of flash they can hold is limited, and they should have a cord through them so that they cannot snap apart and deposit camera or flash on the ground if lifted by the arm.
- Flash arms should be easy to maintain and corrosion resistant. They should also be light and easy to dismantle for transportation. Fortunately, many companies make flash arms and most fulfil these requirements.

Whichever type of arm is used, it must be capable of satisfying the requirements of the photographer who uses it. Therefore, it is essential to determine the techniques most likely to be employed while underwater before obtaining one. It is also well worth looking at the arms used by other underwater photographers before deciding what to go for, as this may provide some useful hints.

Moray eels (*Gymnothorax* sp.) are a common subject for underwater photographs. Standard shots like this can be successful when used with acceptably positioned flash to provide a sharp portrait. ***Subal-housed Nikon F801 and 60mm micro-Nikkor lens, with a Nikon SB105 flash unit. 1/60s at f/11 on Fuji Velvia 50 ISO.***

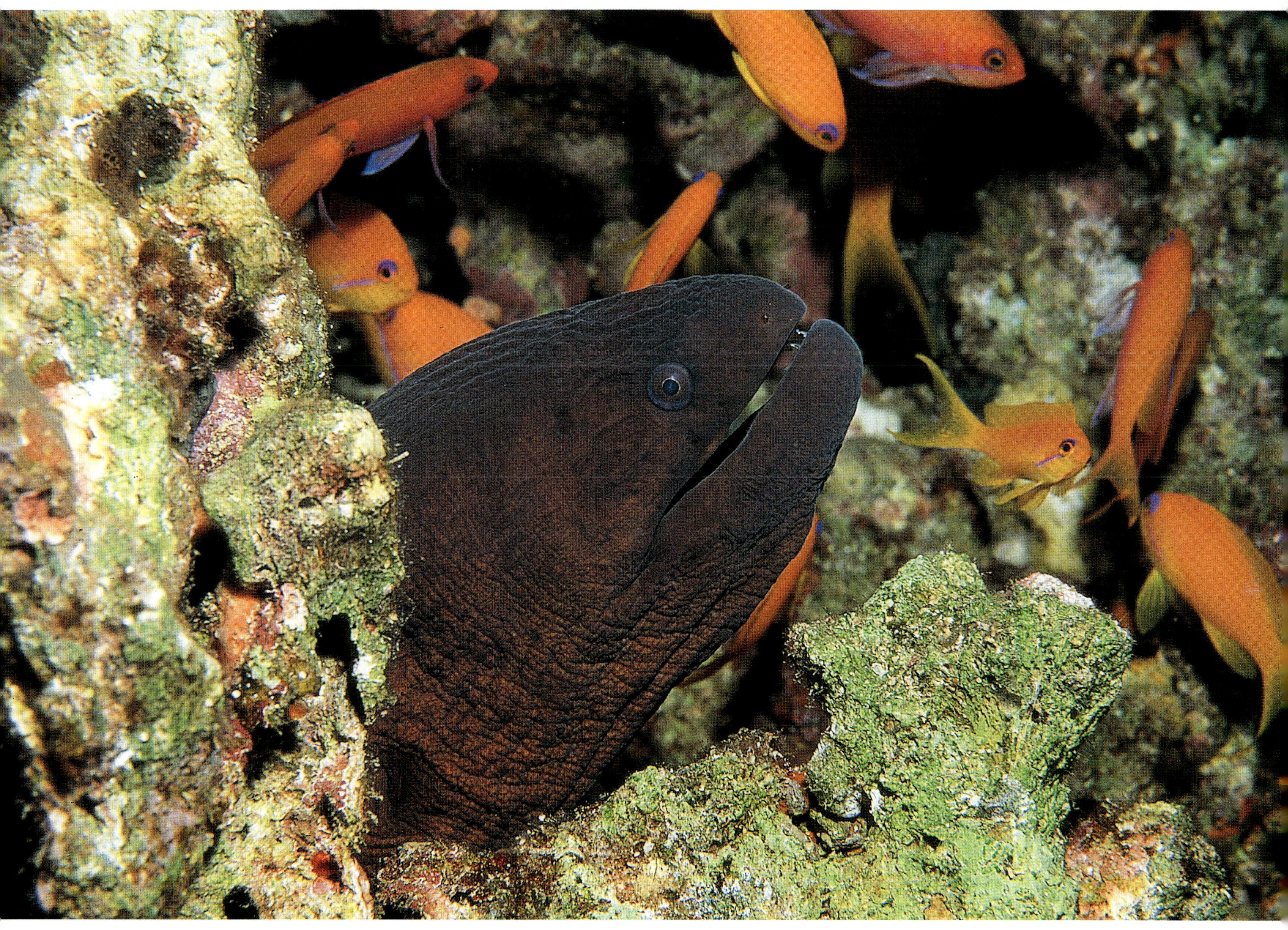

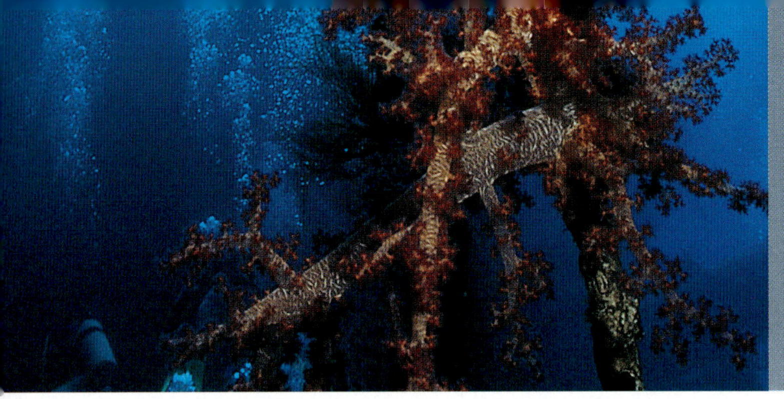

equipment maintenance

As the internals of amphibious cameras, camera housings, amphibious flash units, flash housings and flash leads are easily damaged by damp (let alone water ingress), their design must enable them to remain waterproof (to specified depth limits) for their whole working life.

To do so they must also be corrosion resistant, as corrosion may damage sealing surfaces and this will lead to leaks. While most equipment is built to be corrosion resistant, in order to maintain this resistance it is essential to carry out routine maintenance. This should take into account the fact that salt water is a far worse medium in which to operate cameras than fresh water – water encourages corrosion, but salt water is corrosive.

The underwater environment

While fresh water is a safe medium for using underwater photographic equipment, it can be somewhat corrosive if equipment is not left to dry out after immersion. In general, however, there should be few problems with quality equipment.

Salt water is an entirely different prospect in terms of its corrosive effects. The damage that occurs to metal objects used in salt water is due to 'electrolytic' corrosion. Basically, this corrosion takes place due to electrical differences created between different metals that are in contact with each other when immersed in sea water. It can also be caused by electrical differences within the same metal if poorly designed, and especially if the metal incorporates sharp edges.

Corrosion is at its worst when two metals that create a high electrical difference are used. Compatible (those which produce little electrical difference and so lower corrosion when used together) and incompatible metals are well known to designers, who try to avoid the latter. Marine-grade alloys and stainless steel are reasonably compatible, and are often used together. Even so, they can corrode if not maintained correctly.

Further items (such as bolts to hold base plates or flash arms in place) should be added with care; only marine-grade stainless steel fittings should be used. If the bolt will be used in a static (i.e. not regularly removed) position – holding a flash adapter onto the camera housing, for example – it should be fitted using a special thread filling and sealing compound. This will help prevent electrolysis by stopping salt water from penetrating down the thread, and will also often allow the bolt to be undone easily when needed.

Materials

A designer of underwater photographic equipment has several decisions to make when selecting materials. Where viable, plastics are frequently used and can work very well, requiring relatively low maintenance. However, plastics are more prone to physical damage than metal items, and this means that they have to be used with reasonable care; damage to a plastic sealing surface, for example, could be very difficult to repair. They also tend to have more inherent flexibility, which can lead to seal failures if one part of an item is subject to flexing and another part is not.

Some lower-cost amphibious cameras, many flash housings and some flash arms are built from appropriate, hard-wearing, tough plastics. These require little maintenance other than a good wash, and servicing according to the manufacturer's recommendations.

The two metals most often used for underwater cameras are aluminium alloy and stainless steel. Some aluminium alloys (referred to as marine-grade alloys) and some (marine-grade) stainless steels are very resistant to saltwater corrosion. Not all manufacturers make the right decisions though, and incorrect or poor alloys can lead to corrosion, pitting and reduced equipment life. Stainless steel is available in two common grades: A2 and A4. A2 is a freshwater-grade stainless steel that is not suitable for use in salt water, where it will corrode; A4 is marine grade. If equipment is to be used in salt water, anything bolted onto it should have A4 stainless-steel fittings to help prevent corrosion.

Aluminium alloys can be further protected from corrosion if they are anodized (a specialized process that oxidizes the outer surface). Unfortunately, anodizing is only an exterior treatment and if the surface is damaged by abrasion, the affected area can start to corrode. Large areas of alloy such as cast housings are often painted with durable undercoats and epoxy topcoats, as well as being hard anodized.

Other specialized processes can be used on alloys, including oil impregnation and surface 'polish hardening'. Such treatments can create extremely durable materials, depending on the manufacturer's selection and care.

Unfortunately, few underwater photographers are able to keep their equipment looking new; operating in a hostile, alien environment ensures that a few knocks and bumps are inevitable. Any surface finish that becomes damaged should be cleaned and re-coated with waterproof paint and lacquer to make sure that the damaged area does not start to corrode.

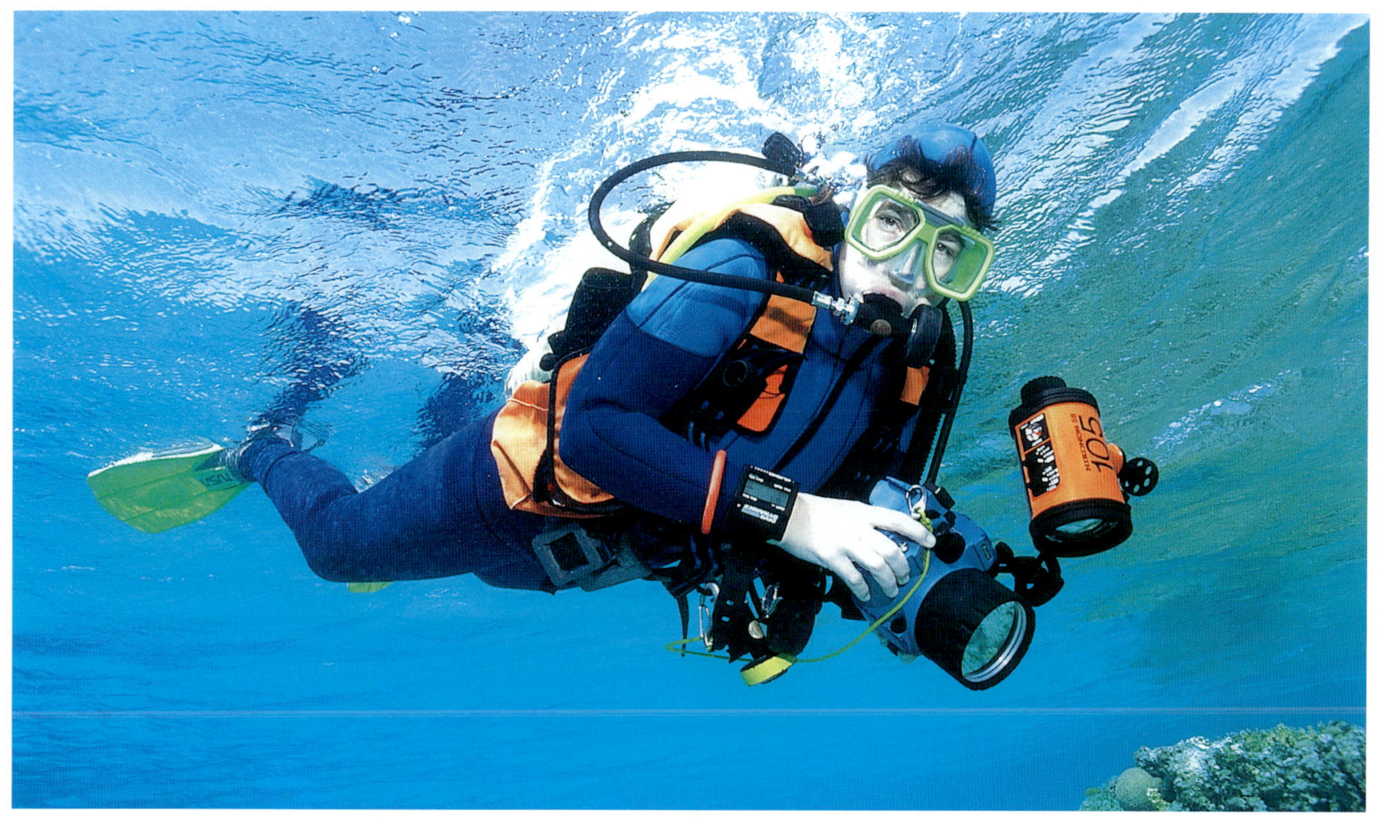

Clear water and an obviously happy subject make for a pleasant photograph. Lucy (my wife) is carrying a Subal housing for a Nikon F801 camera, fitted with a macro lens and port, a TLC flash arm and a Nikonos SB105 flash unit. The flash is set in a standard compromise position (see page 125) so that only minor adjustments will be needed to optimize the set-up for the sort of subjects she intends to take.

Subal-housed Nikon F801 and 20mm Nikkor, with a diffused Nikon SB105 flash unit. 1/60s at f/11 on Fuji Velvia 50 ISO

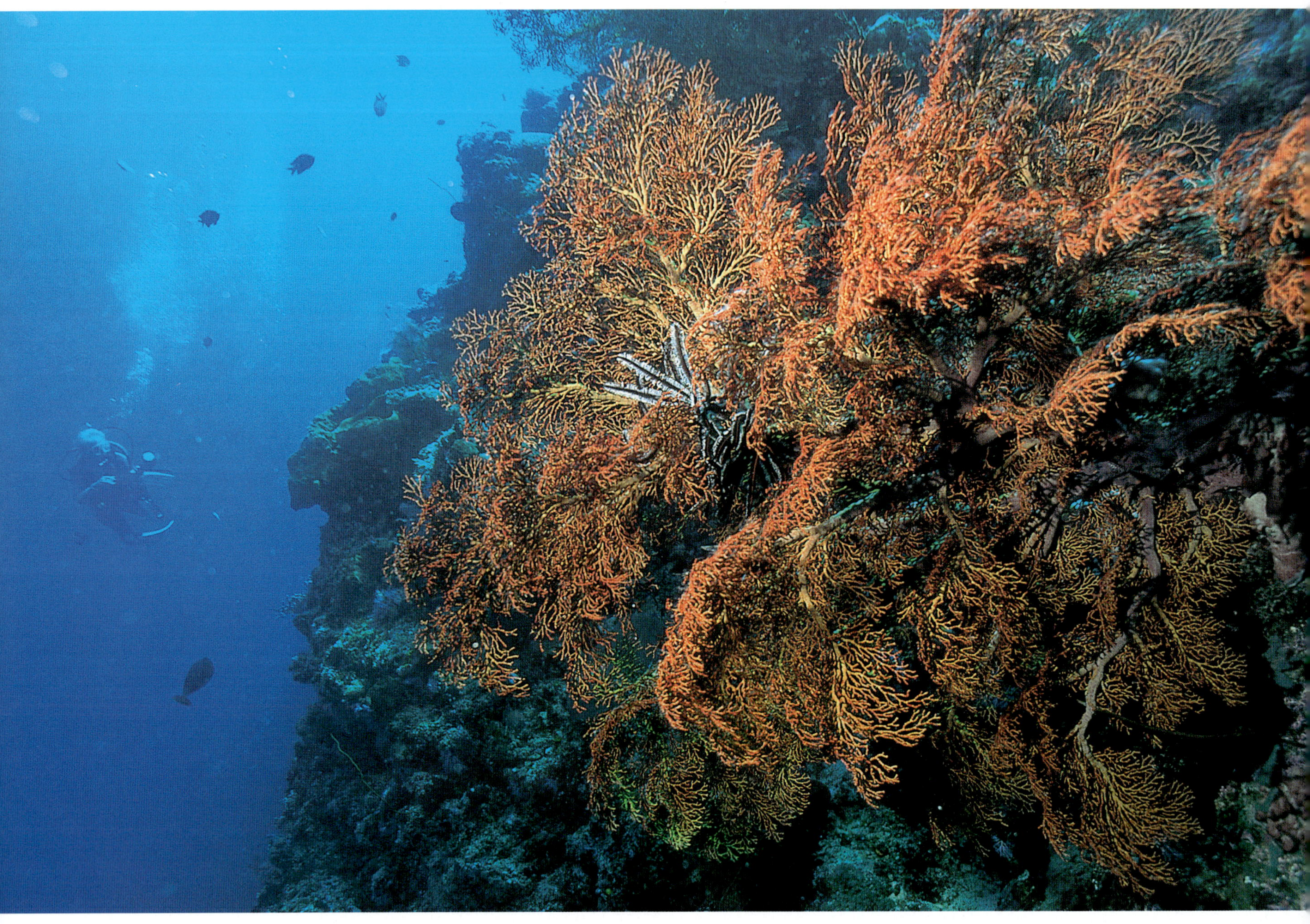

Preventative maintenance

It is much better to ensure that equipment is checked and maintained continuously so that it works all the time, rather than risk erratic electronic connections, stiff controls, slight leaks, or – worst of all – a total flood. Preventative maintenance is an essential part of owning underwater photographic equipment that operates properly, but it can be time consuming.

Pressure testing

Whenever a new (or indeed second-hand) item is obtained, it needs to be pressure tested. The best way of doing this is to take the new piece of equipment to a depth of 10–20 metres on a freshwater dive. This is especially true for housings and their ports, which should be taken underwater without their contents (camera, flash or lenses), and have all controls tested several times at various depths. Only by doing so can the soundness, in terms of water resistance and smooth operation, of equipment be established. This is also a good way of boosting confidence in your ability to set up a new piece of kit.

If a leak occurs in these circumstances, the water that has entered the housing should be washed out and the housing dried thoroughly. Little damage should occur, providing the housing itself contains no electronics. Clearly, the cause of the water ingress has to be found before the equipment is tested again. The source of a leak is usually obvious, but if not, lightly coating the inside of the housing with talcum powder should make the problem become clear on the next test dive.

Left: The coral walls at Bunaken Marine Reserve in North Sulawesi, Indonesia, are spectacular. Including a diver in this shot helps to give a sense of the scale involved when diving these walls.
Subal-housed Nikon F801 and 20mm Nikkor lens, with a diffused Nikon SB105 flash unit. 1/15s at f/11 on Fuji Provia 100 ISO

A pressure test can be considered as the first preventative piece of maintenance carried out on an item, and should be repeated after servicing, replacement of seals or even following a long period of disuse.

Assembly sequence

Most underwater cameras consist of a camera (and its housing, if appropriate), a flash unit or units (and housing, if appropriate), a flash arm or arms (and possibly base plate) and a flash lead. All of these need to be assembled so that they are fully operational and waterproof. As equipment is disassembled and reassembled, seals will be disturbed and will require cleaning, checking and re-lubricating. It makes a great deal of sense to adopt an assembly sequence, which ensures that all the disturbed seals are reassembled correctly, that nothing is missed, and that everything is

Surreal inhabitants of the underwater world, such as this little cuttlefish in Cardigan Bay, Wales, are the equals of any imaginings of science-fiction writers and film makers.
Subal-housed Nikon F801 and 60mm micro Nikkor lens, with a Nikon SB105 flash unit. 1/30s at f/11 on Fuji Velvia 50 ISO

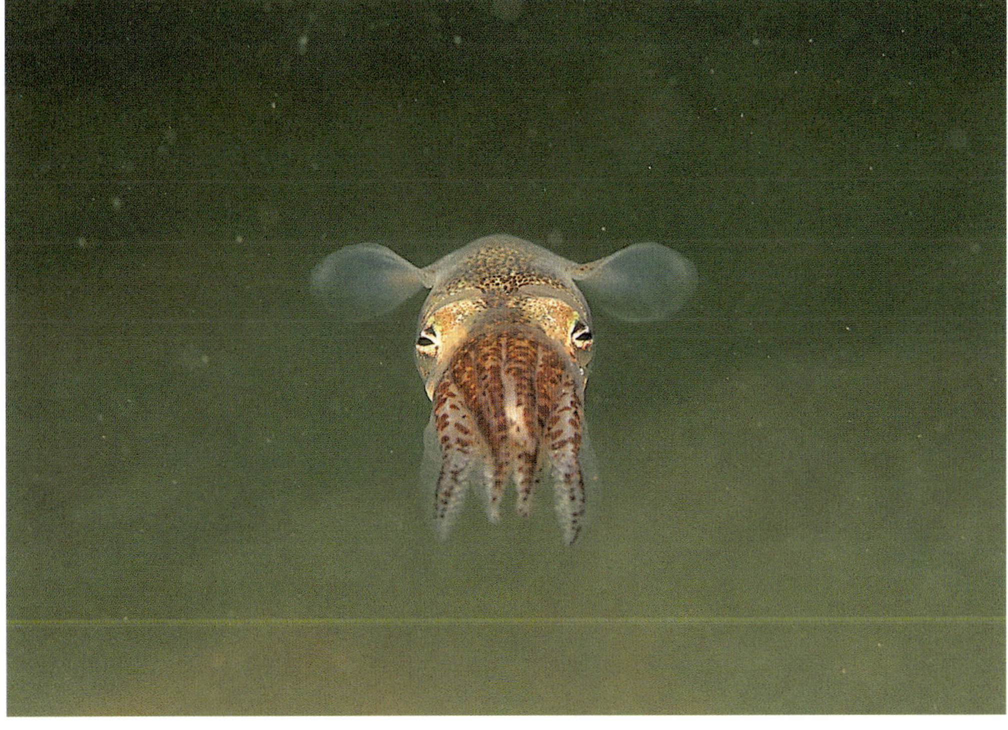

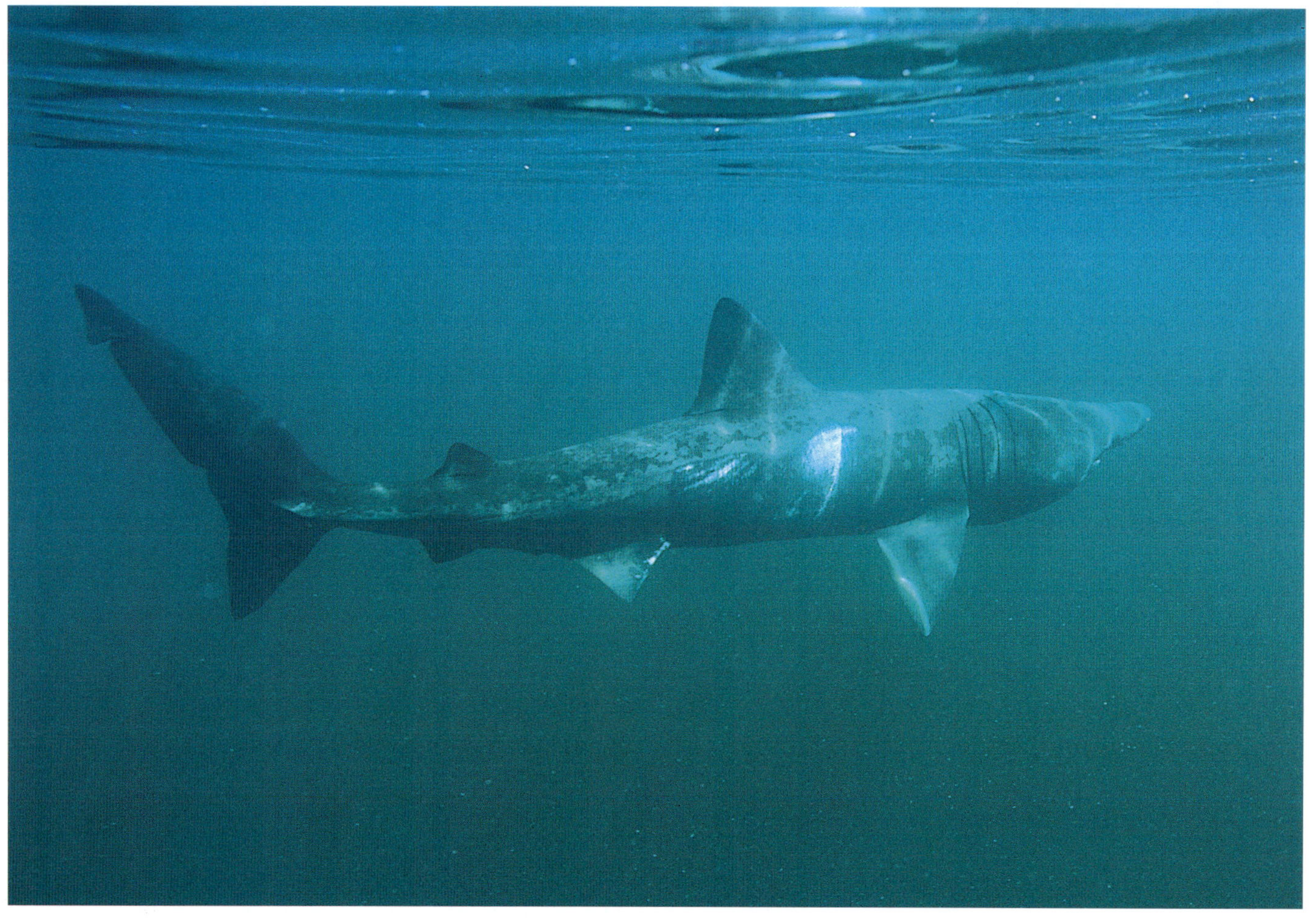

Encounters with basking sharks (*Cetorhinus maximus*) are rare events. These creatures are protected by law and so should not be interfered with, but snorkelling with them may enable a few shots to be taken. This magnificent creature had its mouth closed and looked at its most 'shark-like', when pictured off the Isle of Man.
Subal-housed Nikon F100 and 17–35mm Nikkor AFS lens. Aperture priority 1/60s at f/5.6 on Fuji Provia 100 ISO

working correctly. Once this sequence has been modified so that it works efficiently, it can be used every time the equipment is assembled, and should reduce the risk of missing anything out.

The sequence chosen is largely a matter of personal choice, but should be a logical one and easy to repeat. Generally, it is best to work through the camera (and housing), before moving onto the flash, then the flash lead. All of these can then be assembled, and the flash arm(s) and base plate fitted last. At each stage, the correct operation of the item should be checked before moving on. Finally, when flash and camera are attached, their correct connection should be established (see page 82).

O-rings

O-rings are circular rubber rings with a round cross section. They are designed to seal in various ways depending on their function.

Main O-rings, which are required to seal large areas such as camera backs and housings, are often placed under compression by clamping them before external water pressure is applied. They operate by being squeezed into their groove and also against a sealing surface above the groove. The design of this seal will depend on how the initial pressure is applied.

Many systems use a spring-loaded latch of some kind, which will apply the same initial pressure whenever it is operated. Others require the use of a screw system to push

This curious-looking frogfish (*Antennarius* sp.) was found on a very small coral outcrop in 6 metres of water off Aqaba, Jordan, where it remained during the whole of a week's stay there. Repeated visits made it possible to try out various different techniques.
Subal-housed Nikon F100 and 60mm micro-Nikkor lens, with a Nikon SB105 flash unit. 1/30s at f/16 on Fuji Velvia 50 ISO

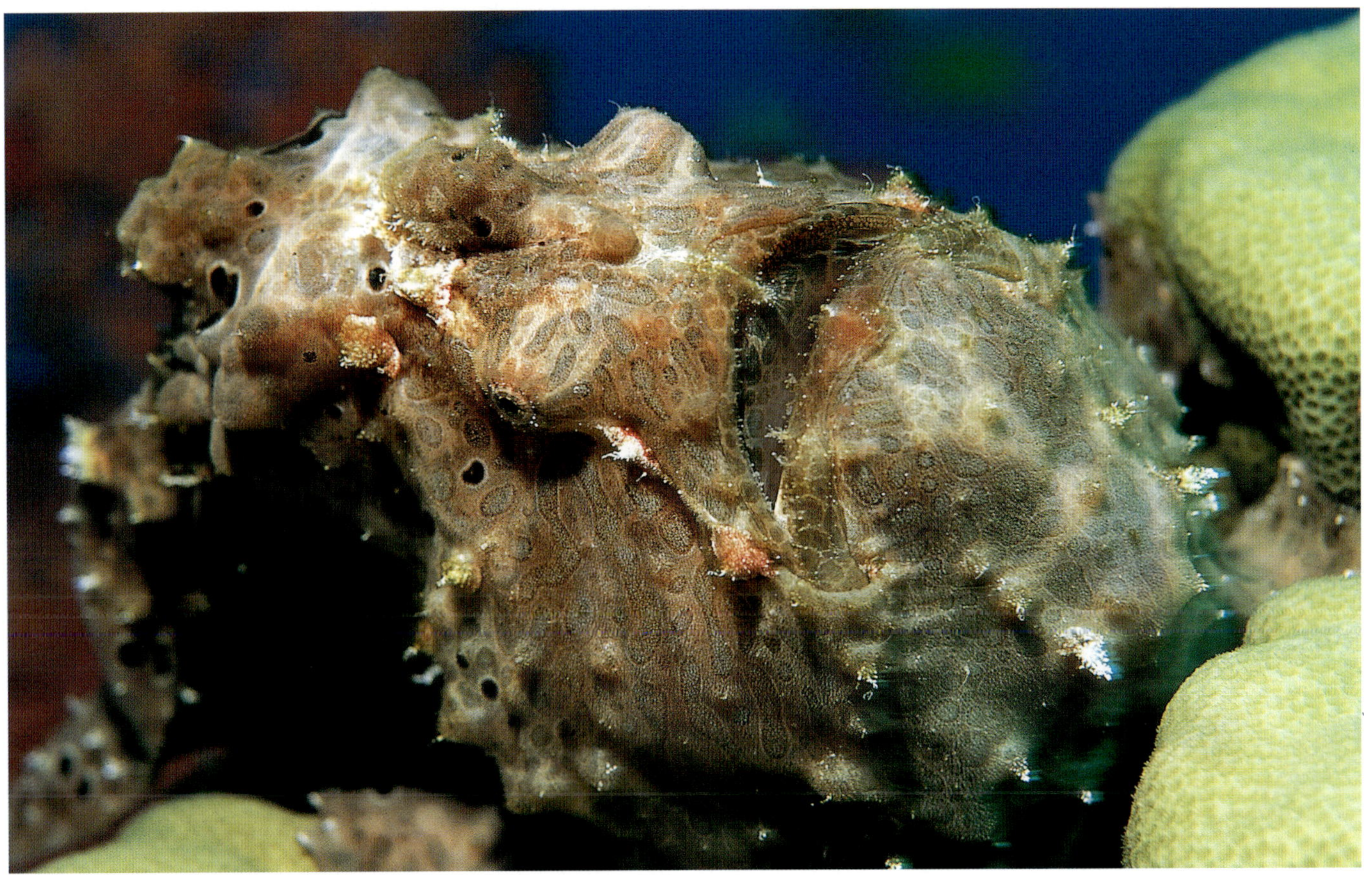

down the sealing surface. In this case, sufficient pressure must be applied to prevent the screws from slackening at depth underwater; otherwise they could come undone during an ascent, when water pressure can no longer hold the sealing surface in place.

The basic idea of such a seal is that the initially applied pressure maintains the seal until a higher water pressure is reached, at which point the seal is maintained by water pressure. As water pressure increases the sealing ability is increased (up to a cut-off point, which will be specified as the item's maximum working depth). With such seals, failure is most likely to occur just below the surface if the initially applied pressure is, for some reason, insufficient.

O-rings are also used to seal rotating controls. They are pushed against the rear of the groove in which they sit, and onto the outside of the control rod, and thus form a seal when under pressure. The whole assembly, consisting of a tube, rod and O-ring(s), is often referred to as a gland.

There is also a static version of this seal, known as a piston seal. These are sometimes used on large-diameter circular openings, and again rely on a degree of inherent pressure (caused by the physical fit of the O-ring between its groove and the tolerance of the gap in which it fits), followed by external pressure.

Lastly, there are O-rings that appear to operate in much the same way as those surrounding rotating control rods, but which allow the rod to be pushed up and down rather than rotated. This is the least safe option, as debris or salt crystals (formed if salt water has been allowed to dry out around the rod) can be pushed down into the seal and may damage it.

O-rings are used extensively, and are a well-proven, reliable seal. However, all O-ring systems rely on three factors to ensure that they operate correctly:

- First, O-rings must be clean. Any foreign matter, especially hairs, but also dust and other particles, can impair their efficiency and allow water past the seal. Cleaning an O-ring is easy enough; just wash it in pure soap and water, dry it, and then re-grease it.
- Second, O-rings must be undamaged. Scratches or other flaws can impair efficiency in much the same way as stray hairs and dirt. Replacement is the only solution for a damaged O-ring.
- Third, they need to be able to move (if only a very little) in the groove and against the sealing surface. To do so, they require lubrication in the form of grease (usually silicone). The grease itself does not act as a seal, and only enough to cover the ring surface with a thin film should be applied.

Most O-rings are made from nitrile rubber, and it is these that require a silicone-based grease lubricant. Some O-rings are made from silicone rubber, which should have different lubricants applied (usually Vaseline). It is important to make the distinction and follow manufacturer's recommendations, as using the wrong lubricant or washing such O-rings with soap may lead to seal failure. If there is any doubt about the O-rings fitted to a specific product, contact the manufacturer or a well-established retailer for full details on how to clean and lubricate it.

The standard way to re-grease a clean O-ring is to place a small (pea-sized) blob of the appropriate grease onto a forefinger and rub it between finger and thumb (first ensuring that these are clean). Hold the O-ring in the other hand, and gently pull it between the greased finger and thumb until it glistens all over with a thin coat of grease. Then install it carefully. This method has an additional advantage because the sensitive finger and thumb can easily detect irregularities and/or debris on the O-ring.

Routine maintenance

Eventually, moving parts like O-rings wear out. How long they last depends on how they are treated, the conditions in which they are used, their accessibility for cleaning, how often they are cleaned, and so on. It can be very difficult to determine when O-rings should be replaced. Obviously, those removed, cleaned and re-greased by the user can be examined every time this is done. Any signs of wear or damage can be spotted and a replacement fitted. Gland-sealing O-rings, and others that are hidden from view, will also need to be re-greased and/or replaced at times.

Some subjects are better than others, and in this case a specific starfish is more colourful than most of its relations. A straight flash-lit shot of a particularly striking specimen has produced a better than average shot of this sand star (*Astropecten irregularis*) off Criccieth in North Wales.
Subal-housed Nikon F801 and 60mm micro-Nikkor lens, with a Nikon SB105 flash unit. 1/60s at f/16 on Fuji Velvia 50 ISO

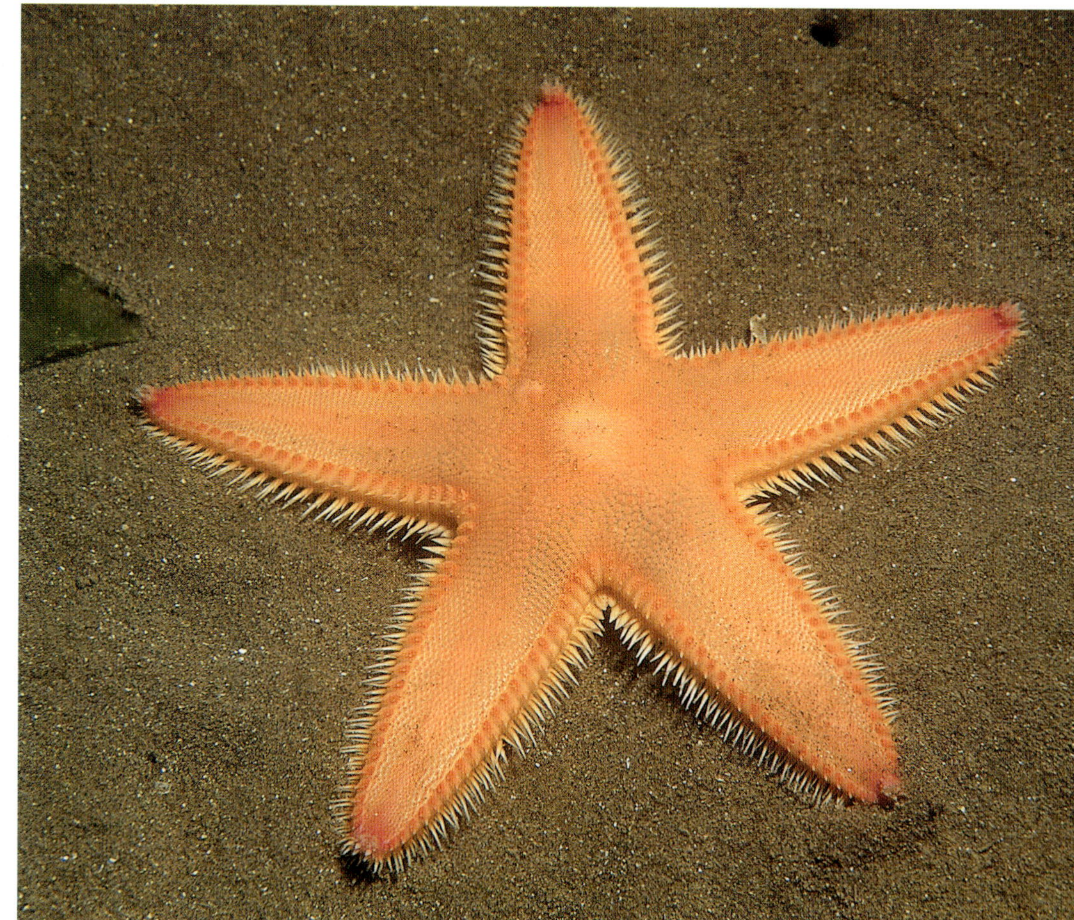

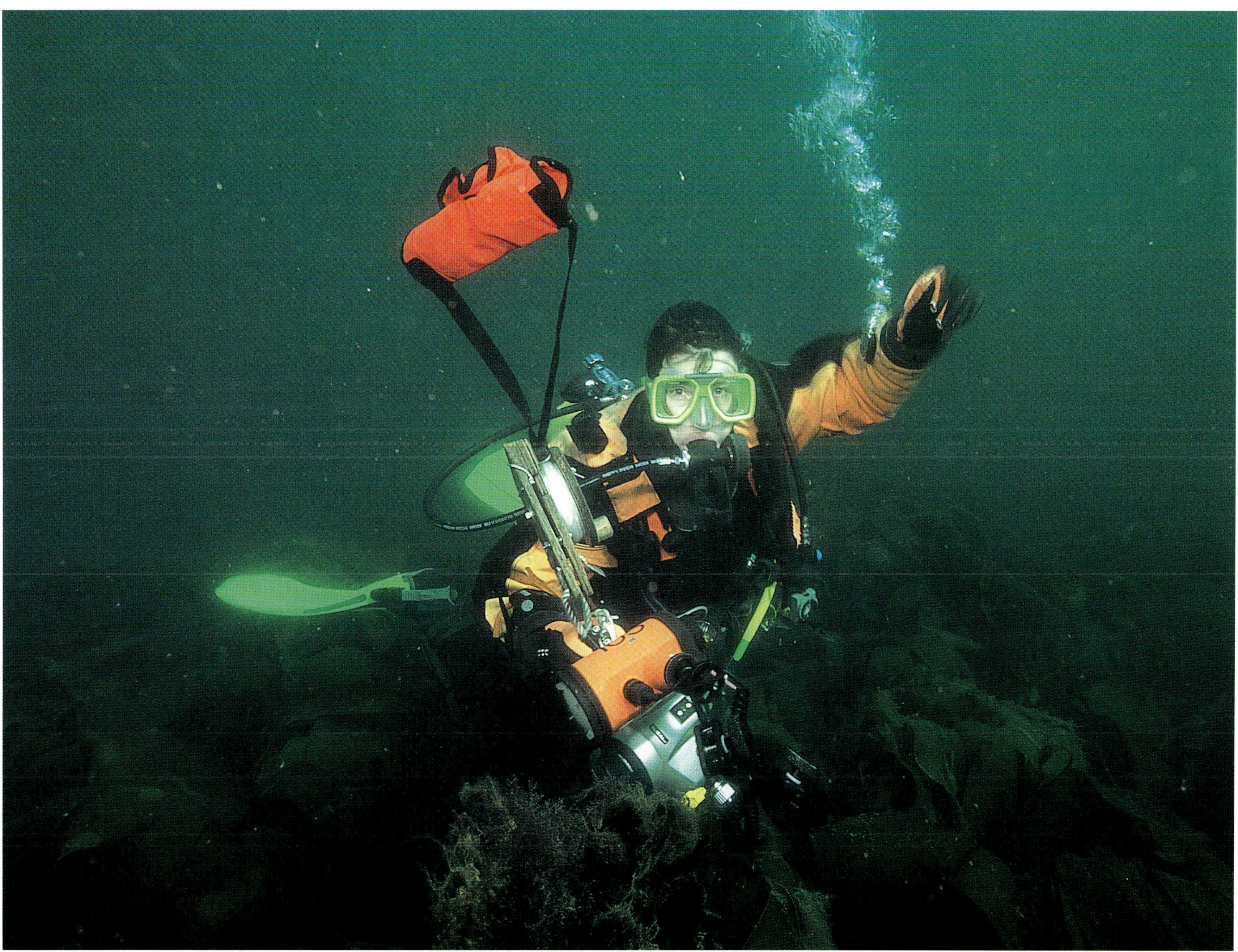

Full diver shots can rarely be taken in temperate waters, as low visibility often prevents good results. However, when conditions are right, they are well worth the effort. The subject is about to deploy a delayed surface-marker buoy.

Subal-housed Nikon F100 and 17–35mm lens set at 17mm, with two diffused Nikon SB105 flash units. 1/15s at f/8 on Fuji Provia 100 ISO

As a result, periodic servicing is required. This can be carried out either by the user or by a competent professional, and the choice will depend on the complexity of the equipment and the owner's confidence in his or her ability to undertake such a task. Most repairers or underwater photographic equipment retailers will advise on frequency of servicing, either in terms of dive numbers or time. If a control starts to feel stiff or exhibit torsional resistance (perhaps it tends to rotate back slightly when released, as if the rubber O-ring is tight or dry), maintenance is required. I tend to think that equipment should be serviced after every 100 dives or so, but I know of people who have carried out 500 dives without servicing their gear. After a service, or after O-rings have been replaced, an 'empty' dive in fresh water, should be undertaken to ensure that the replaced seals are functioning correctly.

Stainless-steel parts such as control rods and clamps can be cleaned ultrasonically to remove any corrosion or unwanted material build up. Regularly removed bolts (such as those fastening flash arms or base plates onto a camera or housing) should be fitted with a coating of O-ring (silicone) grease to prevent or reduce saltwater penetration and aid easy removal. Old grease should be cleaned off and reapplied regularly.

Electric components

The most important item to check and clean regularly is the flash socket. Failure of the flash to operate correctly is one of the most common problems associated with underwater photography. Any water, silicone grease, corrosion of the small and delicate contacts (which often contain small and very vulnerable springs), or any other interference with the connection, can easily prevent the flash from operating properly.

There are many purpose-made cleaners, which can be used in flash sockets once any build up of O-ring grease has been removed using absorbent cotton. If the cleaner fails to alleviate a flash connection problem, a resistance meter should be used to determine where the problem lies. It should be used on socket, cord and, if appropriate, the internal connections to the camera, to ensure that all are functioning correctly.

If they are not, and cleaning fails to sort out the problem, a repairer may have to be consulted. First, try the flash on another camera/housing, and another flash on the original camera housing, to try to establish where the fault lies. Flash cables are notorious for breaking wires internally. The broken wires may touch and separate repeatedly, which can manifest as intermittent breaks in connection (sometimes these only separate and cause connection failure when under pressure). They can also flood, and behave very erratically as a result. Using a meter to establish whether there are any reduced resistances between the different wires within the cable can check this.

Useful hints

On appropriate cameras, a good way to establish the electronic link between camera and flash unit is to switch the camera to aperture priority (**A**) with standard flash synchronization set (not slow or rear sync), and then turn on the flash. The camera should take note that the flash has switched on and select a designated synchronization speed. The available-light shutter speed will reappear when the flash unit is switched off. The viewfinder's flash-ready light should also be checked for correct operation by making sure that it comes on when the flash is charged.

To test the operation of TTL flash control, take a series of shots of the same subject at different apertures (without using film). The flash recycle time should vary, and the flash should fully discharge if it is pointed away from the flash-illuminated subject. This indicates that the flash and camera are 'talking' to each other, and that TTL flash control is working.

Emergency maintenance

No matter how much care is lavished on underwater photographic equipment, the worst can still happen. Whether through impact damage, failure to spot a hair on an O-ring, or some other problem, a flood can occur.

If there is to be any hope of saving the equipment after a catastrophic ingress of water, it is essential to undertake remedial action. The first priority should be to remove any batteries; doing so will reduce the risk of further destroying live circuitry through accelerated electrolytic corrosion.

A flood in fresh water is not quite as serious as a flood in salt water. Fresh water should be emptied out, the batteries removed, and equipment thoroughly dried, preferably in a warm airflow (above a radiator, for instance).

Salt water is a different matter. The first priority should always be to remove any batteries and empty out all of the salt water. It is possible for flammable gas to build up as batteries and salt water react; mixed with air this can form a potentially explosive combination. Never open up flooded equipment in the presence of a naked flame or anything that might ignite any gas build up. In very rare cases, equipment has been known to explode due to a spark igniting an explosive gas build-up, so great care should be taken when there is any likelihood of batteries and salt water having mixed.

Once batteries and salt water have been removed, any residual salt must also be removed. In the case of a serious flood, this means repeated immersions fresh water before drying the equipment out.

After a flood, equipment should be returned to a competent repairer for evaluation and repair, and the cost of restoration versus equipment value should be taken into account. Anticipate the worst, especially if power from the batteries was running through the camera, lens and/or flash at the time of the flood and there was a significant delay

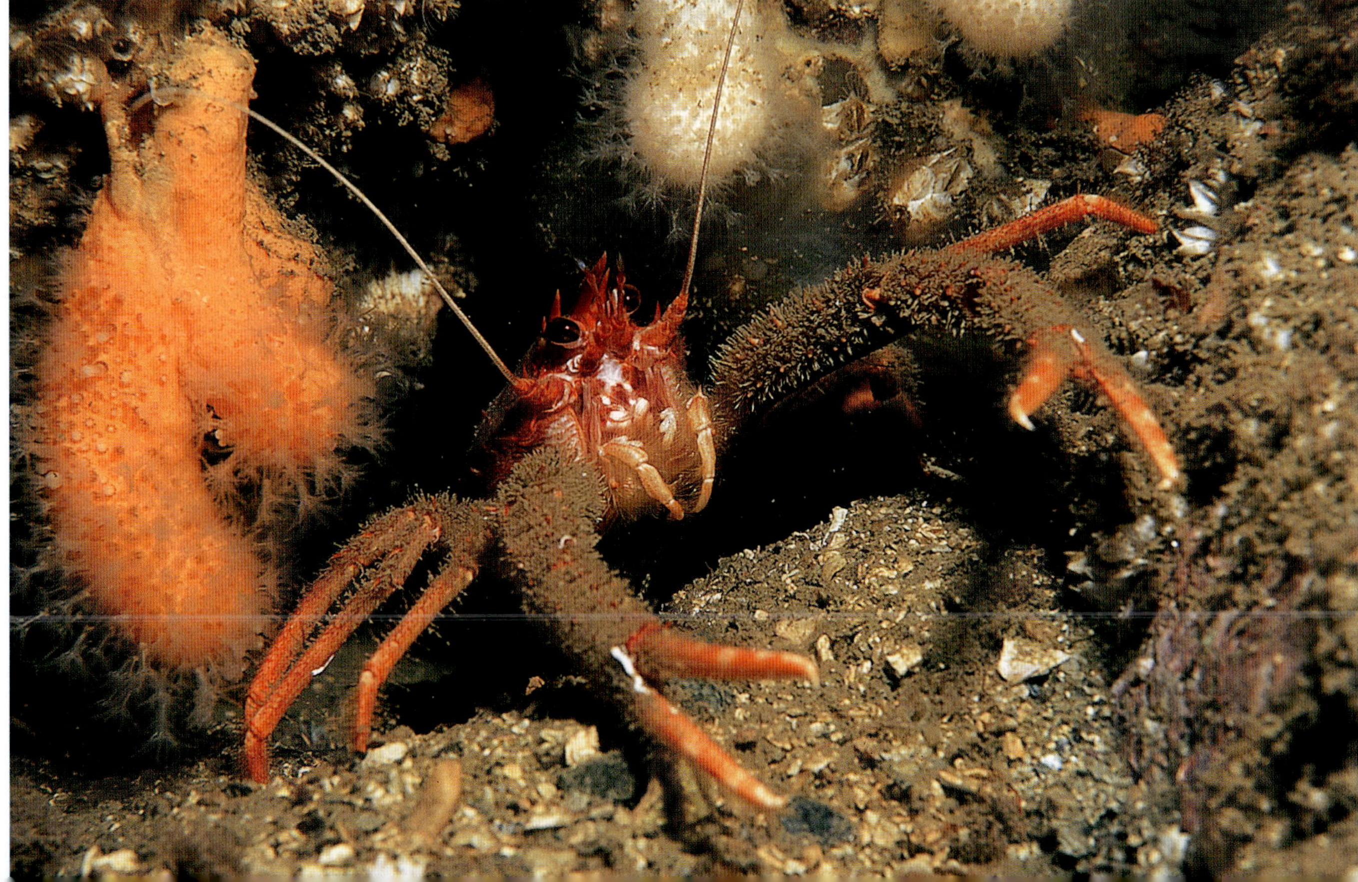

In Scottish waters, these long-clawed squat lobsters (*Munida rugosa*) make superb subjects. Taken using single flash in the Sound of Mull, west Scotland. ***Subal-housed Nikon F100 and 60mm micro-Nikkor lens. 1/60s at f/16 on Fuji Velvia 50 ISO***

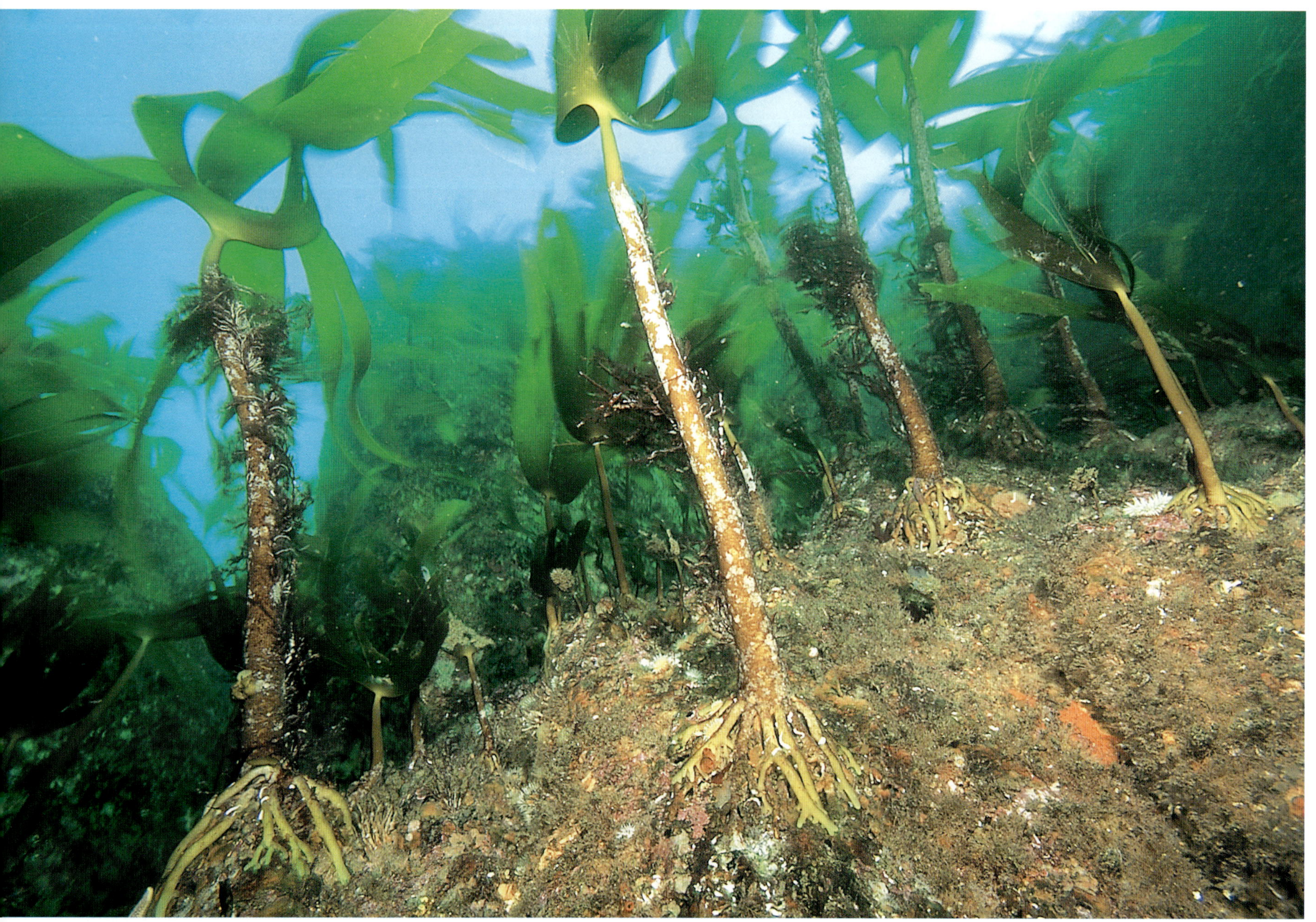

Kelp comes in differing quantities, which are given technical terms. This shot shows 'park' rather than 'forest' kelp, as it is less abundant and has larger gaps between plants. Flash is able to penetrate more easily, and so is more dominant as a source of light.
Subal-housed Nikon F100 and 17–35mm AFS Nikkor, with a Nikon SB105 flash unit. 1/8s at f/16 on Fuji Provia 100 ISO

before they were removed. Most electronics may not be salvageable after immersion in salt water, especially if items such as drive motors (for autofocus, film wind and shutter) are present. It is possible to save equipment though, so it is worth trying.

If no damage appears to have been sustained, and the equipment is absolutely dry, a decision has to be made as to whether to reinsert the batteries. If there is any residual dampness, batteries should not be replaced; the flow of power through damp circuitry can cause immense damage. Do not use solvents to dry out flooded equipment, and especially not drinks with a high alcohol content, as has apparently been tried – it doesn't work.

Be warned: insurers tend not to like unexplained flooding or other such types of damage. Always check the small print on any insurance policy covering underwater photographic equipment.

Depth limits

Most manufacturers quote safe working depths for their photographic equipment. Obviously, if exceptionally deep dives are foreseen, the choice of equipment is limited to that which will operate at the depths you expect to encounter.

Most equipment will operate below the quoted depth rating, but not without risk (not to mention the fact that using equipment below its designed maximum depth negates any insurance policy covering it).

Additional pressure places increased strain on seals, and excessive pressure may be a real problem with large dome ports – any scratches can provide a weak point where failure may occur. If the subject is deep and no other way of obtaining photographs exists, all parts of the equipment should – at the very least – be overhauled and checked thoroughly to minimize the chance of failure.

Batteries

Correct battery choice is an essential part of keeping an underwater camera running throughout a dive. Unlike on land, batteries (and film) cannot be replaced during a shoot, and little is more frustrating than finding a stunning subject only to discover that there is inadequate power to charge the flash unit or operate the camera.

Disposable batteries

Disposable batteries vary in terms of their output depending on manufacturer, type and age. For underwater use, only well-proven battery types should be used. Some have testers built into them, and this can be a very useful feature. Fresh batteries are the best to buy, as they will have the highest power output left. Always check expiry

Why some marine creatures are red is a puzzling question, and why they camouflage themselves using this colour is even more curious. Whatever the reason, this photogenic surge gully off the Isle of Islay, Scotland, provided some intriguing pictures.
Subal-housed Nikon F801 and 60mm micro-Nikkor lens, with a Nikon SB105 flash unit. 1/60s at f/16 on Fuji Velvia 50 ISO

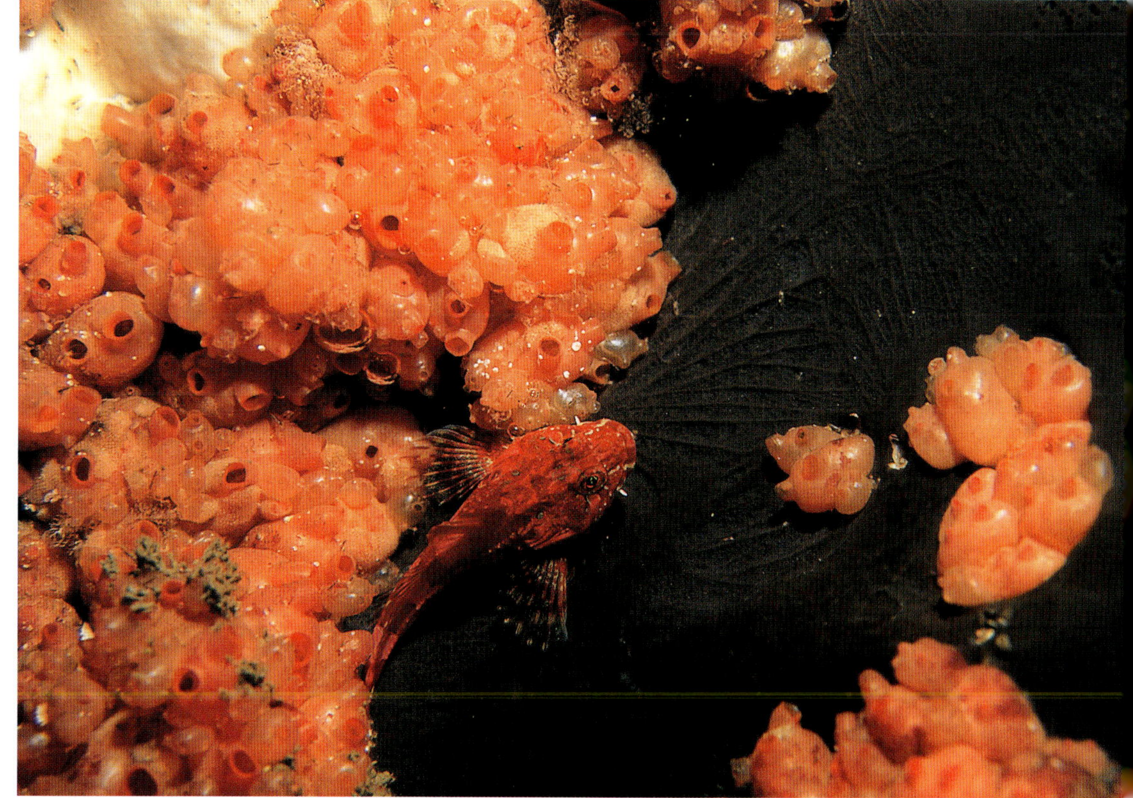

dates before purchasing new batteries, and avoid brands that don't display them.

The claims made by camera and/or flash manufacturers regarding battery life in their products are usually quoted from a strict set of parameters. In practice, batteries seem rarely to achieve the claimed figures for numbers of films used or flashes taken. Some manufacturers also recommend specific battery types or brands. While there may be commercial reasons behind this, it can be a good indication of the battery types required. Once an effective battery type has been found, it is worth sticking to, and should be used for less than the maximum number of films/flashes known to be possible.

Rechargeable batteries

Rechargeable batteries are another matter altogether. On balance they carry a higher risk of failing underwater, as there is little way of knowing how their operating characteristics vary throughout their working life. It is claimed that ni-cad batteries can be recharged up to 1000 times, but this depends on how they are used and recharged. Newer nickel-hydride batteries don't have the 'memory effects' that ni-cad batteries suffer from and which often reduce their power over time. Clearly, some types of rechargeable battery are better than others, and new types are developed frequently.

Most rechargeable batteries quote their power output in terms of milliamp hours. All recommendations in terms of charging rates, voltages, care and storage should be adhered to, as failure to do so will almost certainly result in reduced battery life and reliability.

Batteries are heavy, and when travelling it may be best simply to buy them at the destination. Rechargeable batteries not only incur the extra weight of their chargers, they also rely on the availability of a satisfactory power supply.

Digital cameras rely on batteries even more than conventional cameras. Many only use their own rechargeable units, so sufficient spare packs should be carried, as should charger adapters if travelling abroad.

Buying second hand

Buying a second-hand camera or housing can be an attractive option simply because of the high price of new equipment, but there are many pitfalls for the unwary. Buying from a reputable specialist dealer, who has serviced and tested the equipment and offers some form of guarantee, is about the best option available. Any other equipment should be examined very carefully indeed, and the cost of a full service deducted from the asking price if there are any doubts.

Most used underwater camera equipment will have been immersed in sea water. Any second-hand item needs a thorough inspection for corrosion, and if no proof of recent servicing is offered then the price should reflect this.

When buying an older housing, check the availability of cameras, lenses and other accessories to fit it. Older models may be scarce in anything but a well-used condition, and servicing may become a problem. However, a housing/camera combination that has been used exclusively underwater might have experinced relatively light use – housed cameras rarely do a tremendous amount of work compared to those used on land.

Always check housings for signs of water ingress/damage. Telltale signs include rusting, salt deposits and missing labels. The most important areas for examination are the sealing surfaces, which should be undamaged, and the glands where controls fit through the housing (any stiffness indicates that servicing is needed, before they start leaking). A saltwater-flooded housing may be in good working order generally, but the flash socket and any cabling may need to be replaced. These can be expensive parts – and the reason for the flood should be not be a mystery.

Shooting details of popular wrecks (such as the Cedar Pride off Aqaba, Jordan) can be problematic, not because of the photographic techniques required, but because it is rare to find backgrounds without other divers in them!
Subal-housed Nikon F100 and 17–35mm lens set at 17mm, with two diffused Nikon SB105 flash units. 1/15s at f/11 on Fuji Provia 100 ISO

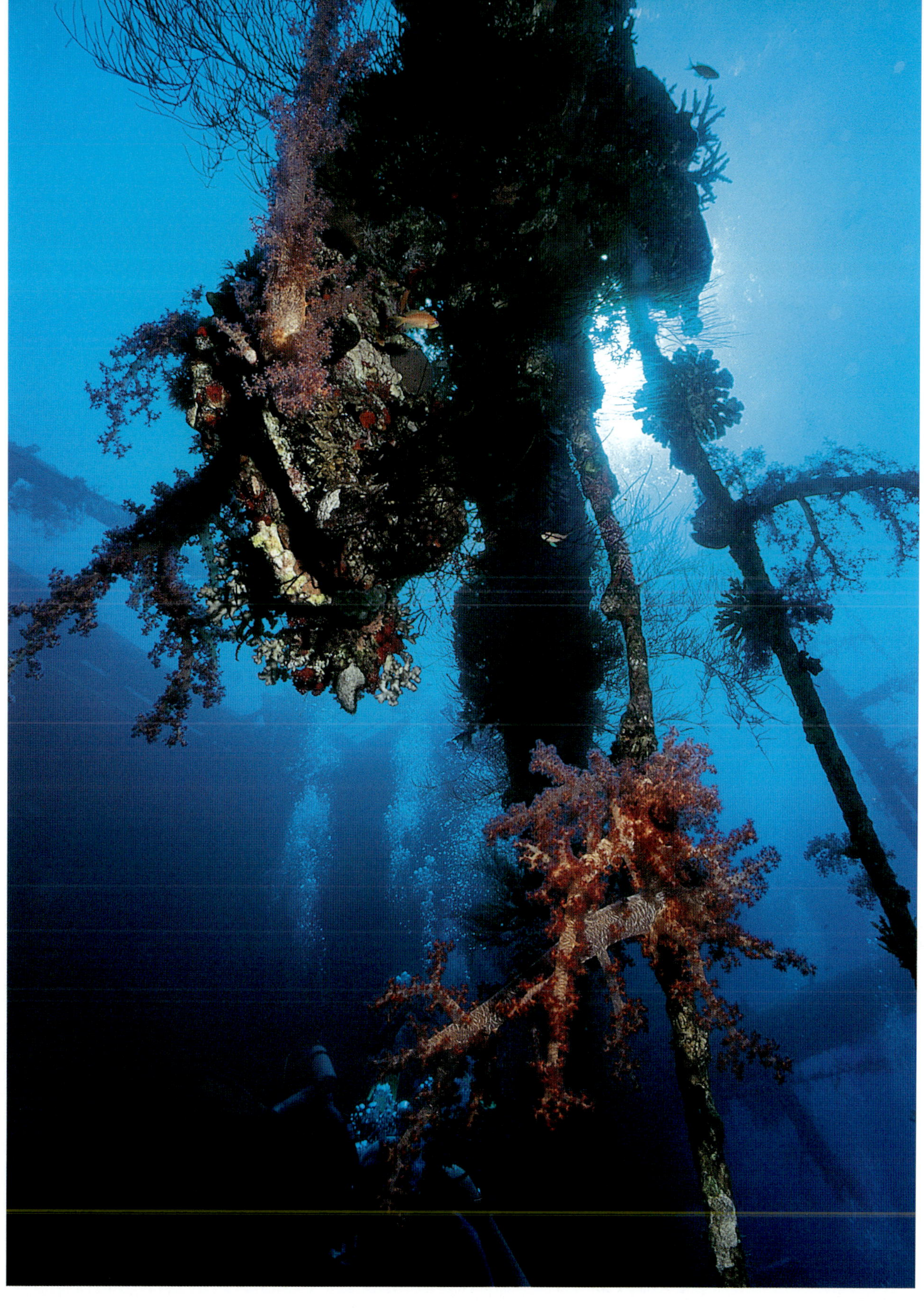

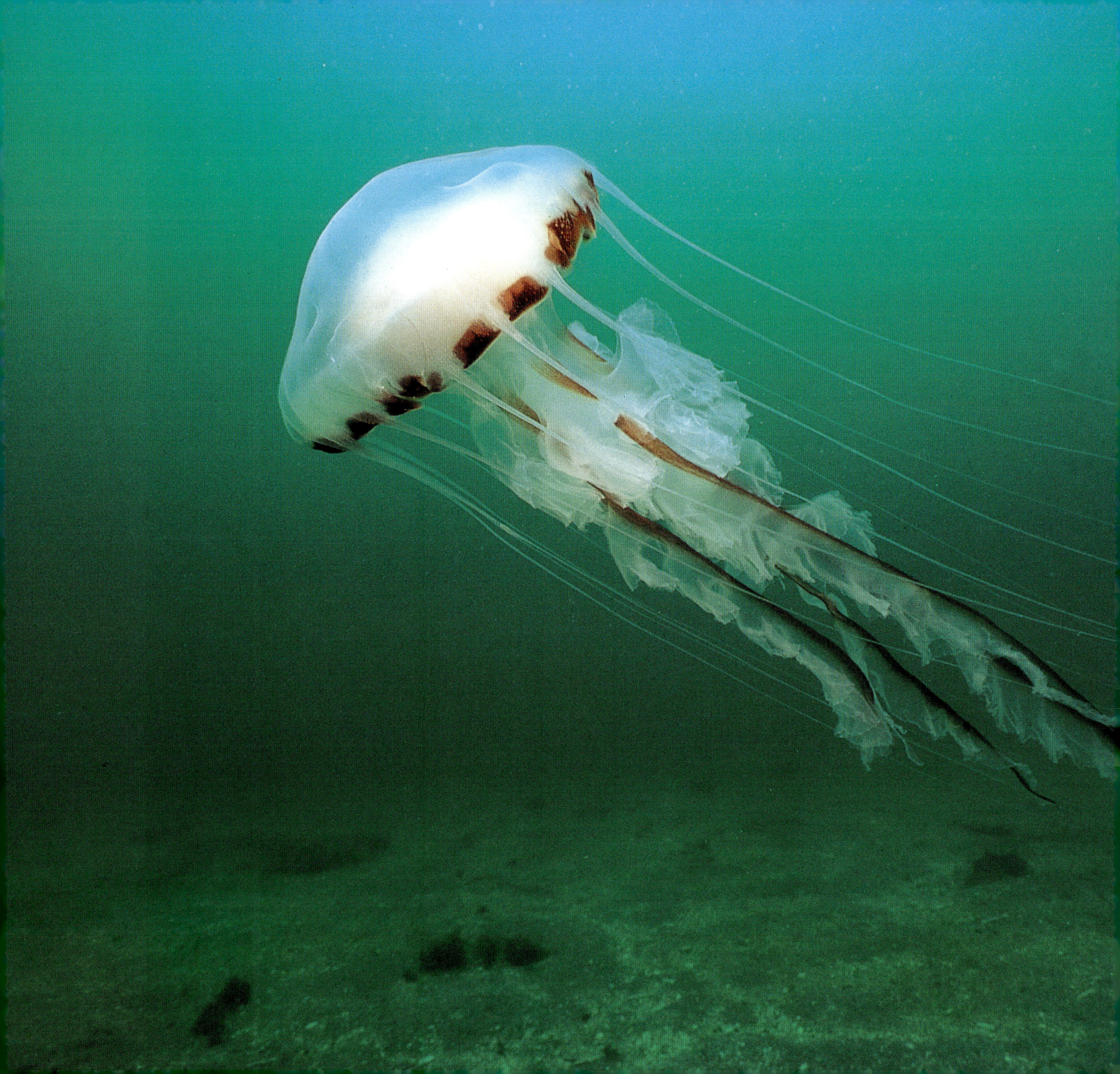

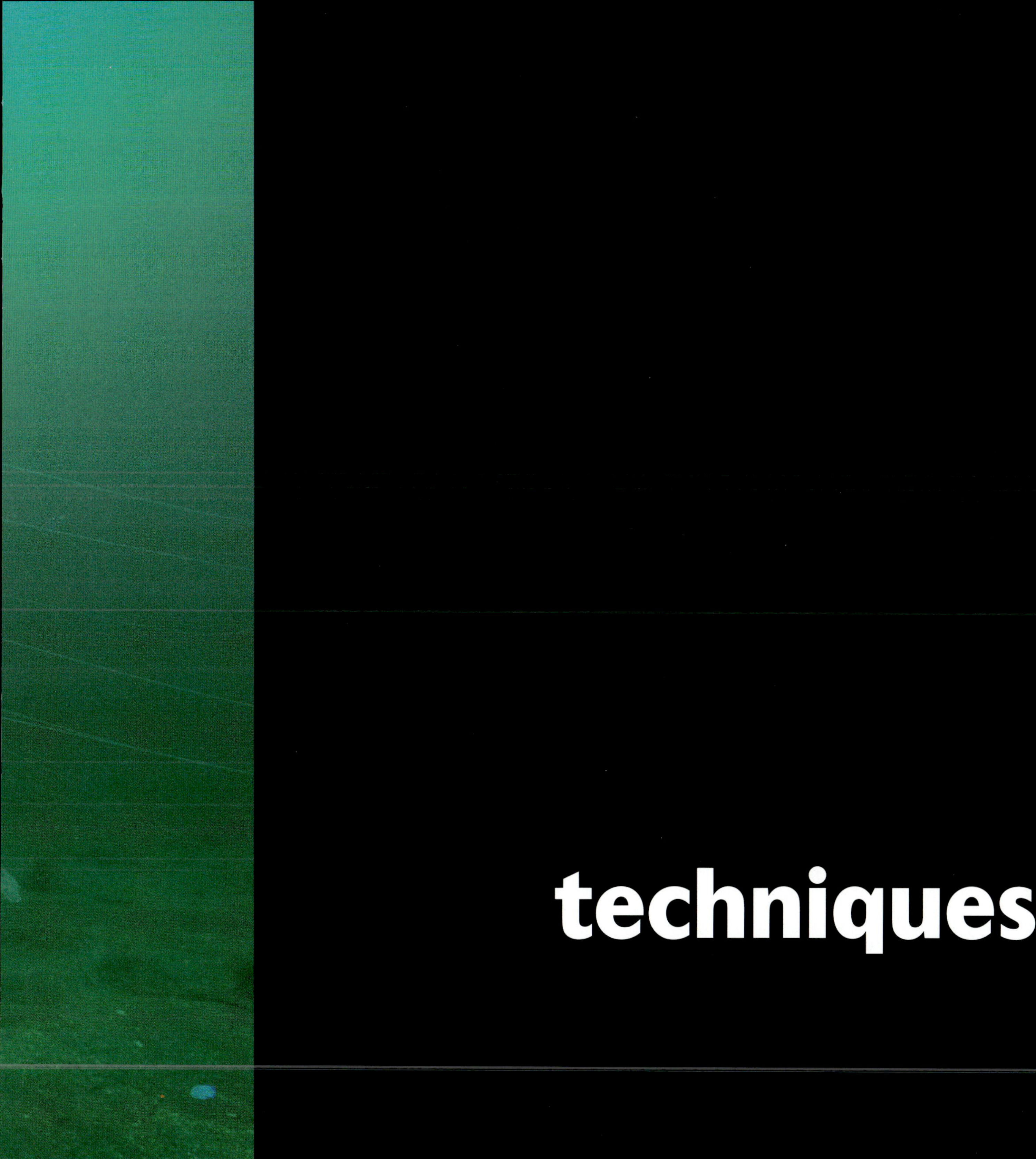

techniques

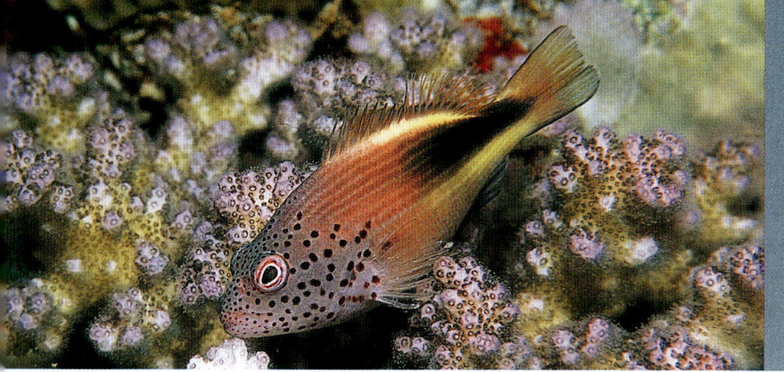

subjects

The undersea is full of fascinating photographic subject matter; so much so, that it can often be difficult to decide what actually to photograph. As with above-water photography, the secret of taking good pictures lies in appreciating the subject matter, and understanding how to show it to best effect.

As divers' interests vary, so does their choice of photographic subject. For example, divers interested in shipwrecks might want to photograph and document those dived on. Detailed records of parts of the wreck can help to identify it, and many wreck divers gain a lot of satisfaction from researching the history of a forgotten or unknown wreck. A wide-angle set-up is most likely to be useful for taking photographs of parts of a wreck's structure and, as wrecks are often deep and dark, a powerful flash may be the best (and only) lighting available.

Even within the confines of natural history, divers' interests vary. Some are interested solely in fish, and they

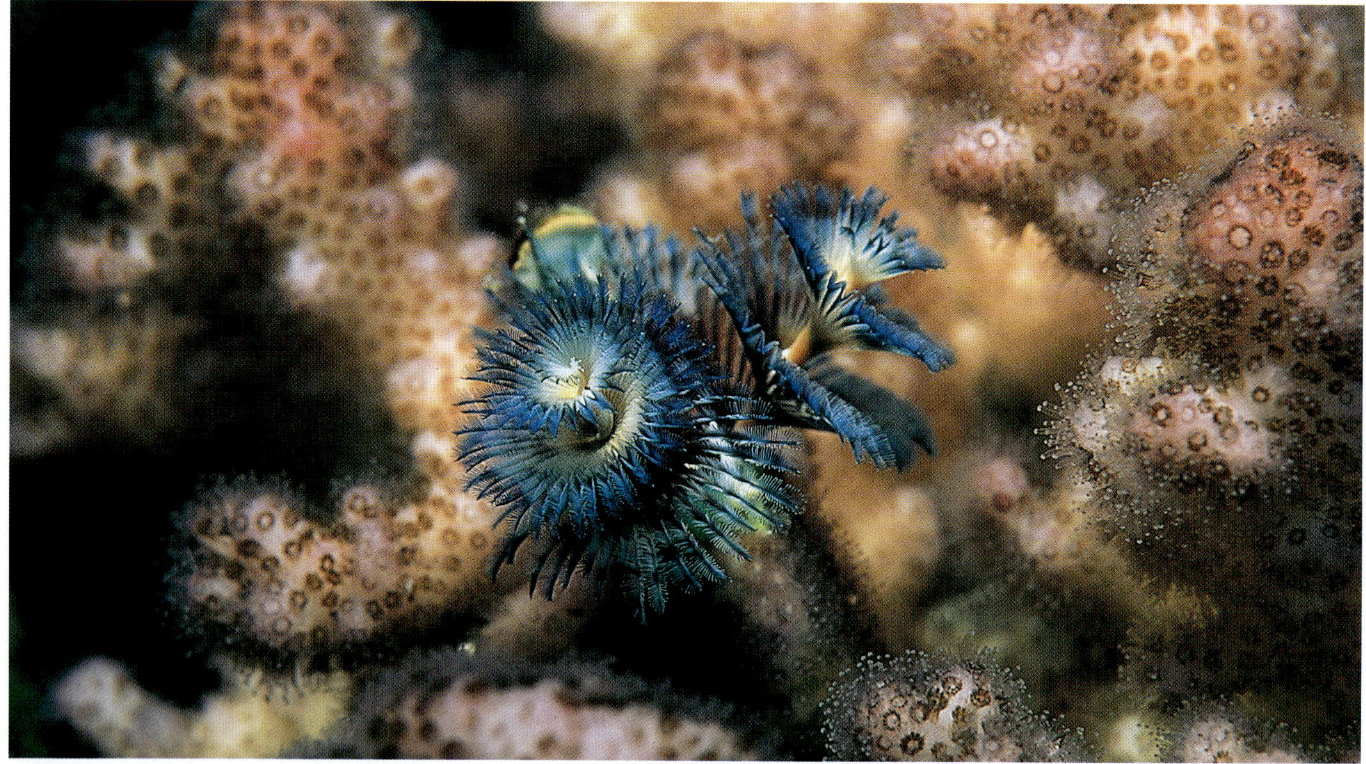

Christmas-tree worms are a favourite of macro photographers in the tropics. They have been photographed countless times and it is more than likely that they will continue to be pictured. ***Subal-housed Nikon F801 and 60mm micro-Nikkor lens, with a Nikon SB105 flash unit. 1/60s at f/16 on Fuji Provia 100 ISO***

A view inside the wreck of the Carnatic, in the Egyptian Red Sea. Some flash has succeeded in brightening the foreground, but the photograph is taken substantially by available light. Unusually, it has depth and perspective, which was helped by the strong contrast.
Subal-housed Nikon F100 and 17–35mm lens set at 17mm, with two diffused Nikon SB105 flash units. 1/8s at f/16 on Fuji Provia 100 ISO

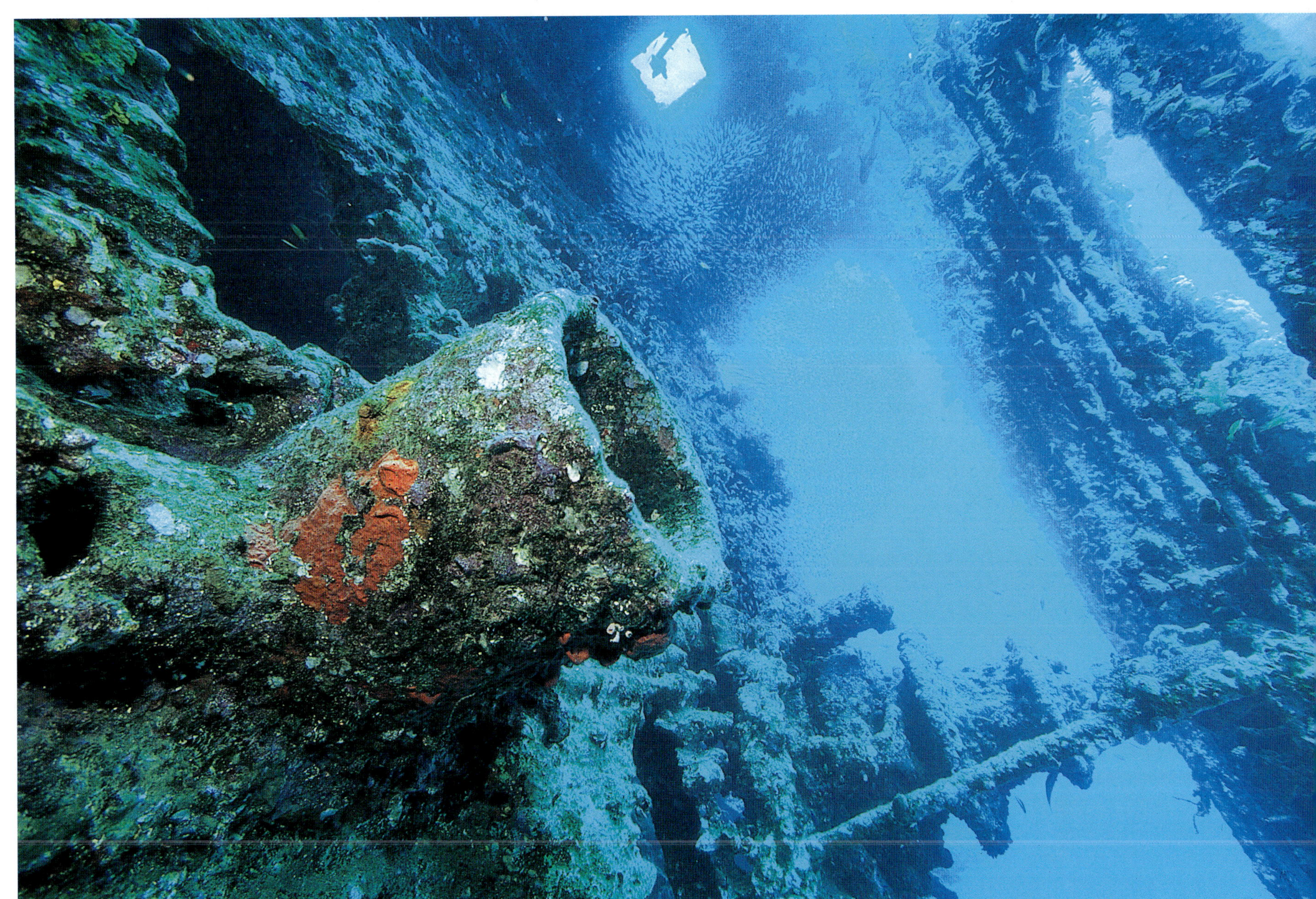

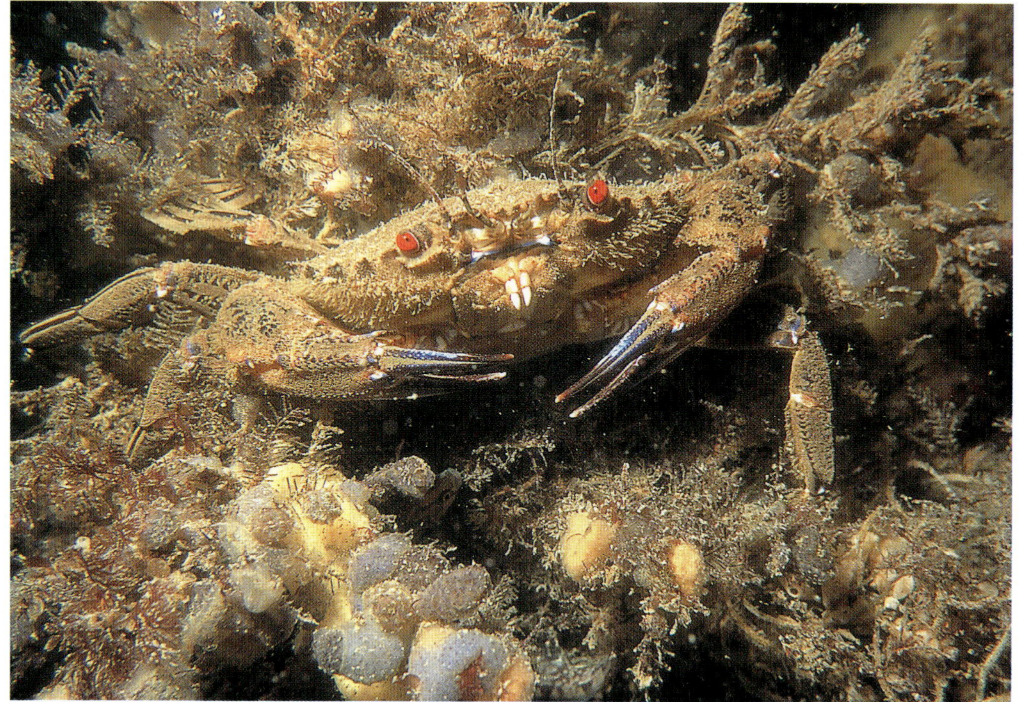

Velvet swimming crabs (*Liocarcinus puber*), like this one in the Menai Strait, Wales, make excellent subjects, with vivid red eyes to act as focal points. As with many photographs, the background here can make or break the picture. Obviously, it should enhance rather than detract from the subject.
Subal-housed Nikon F801 and 60mm micro-Nikkor lens. Single-flash illumination only. 1/60s at f/16 on Fuji Velvia 50 ISO

might choose to take photographs using a long-reach macro lens, such as a 105mm or perhaps even longer. Others might be fascinated by corals or anemones, which often require a macro lens with a shorter focal length.

Clearly, even before entering the water it is essential to have some idea of the type of subject matter that is likely to be of interest, and to choose equipment accordingly. Few underwater photographers are able to dive with two cameras, and the problem of deciding on set-up is far less difficult for these fortunate people than most. Even so, a series of decisions has to be made for every subject in order to arrive at the best way to treat it photographically.

A simple example of how a specific subject should be treated is that of a free-swimming fish. Very few fish photographs are successful if the fish is swimming away from the camera (although there are, of course, exceptions), and in general they should be lit from the side of the photograph they are moving towards, with the lighting aimed at the subject's head. Usually this will produce a well-lit portrait.

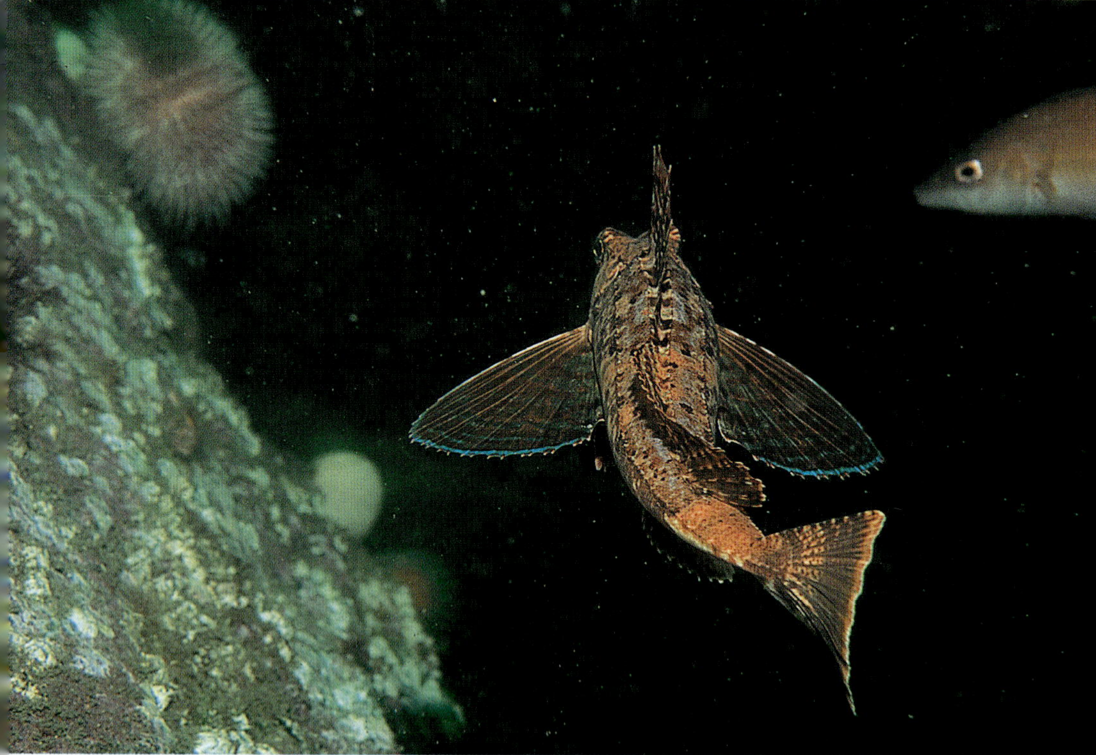

An often-quoted 'rule' of underwater photography is that fish should not be photographed swimming away from the camera. There are exceptions, and this shot identifies this fish clearly as a tub gurnard (*Trigla lucerna*) because it shows the distinctive blue coloration.
Subal-housed Nikon F100 and 60mm micro-Nikkor lens, with a Nikon SB105 flash unit. 1/60s at f/16 on Fuji Provia 100 ISO

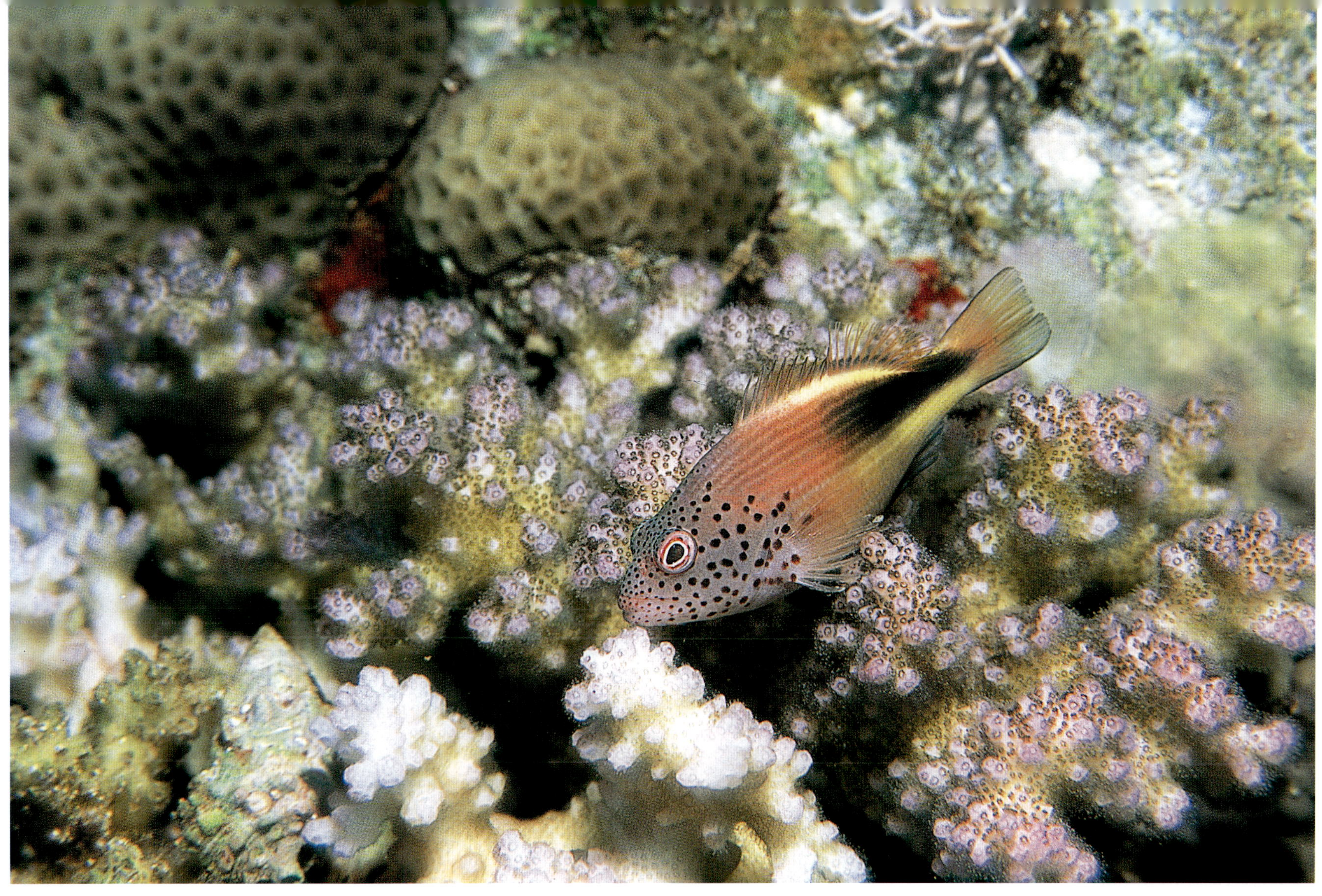

Whenever shooting animals it is important to ensure that the eye is absolutely crisp. The rest of the picture can be adjusted using depth of field, flash placement and other techniques, but it is rare for a subject to work if its eye is not in focus. Freckled hawkfish (*Paracirrhites forsteri*), Red Sea. *Subal-housed Nikon F100 and 60mm micro-Nikkor, with a Nikon SB105 flash unit. 1/60s at f/16 on Fuji Provia 100 ISO*

Other decisions to be made include whether to use a secondary flash (usually at a lower power setting than the main flash) to illuminate the rear of the fish, or whether to use some ambient light in the exposure instead. In the latter case, should the background be blurred by panning, or should rear-curtain sync (see page 143) be set?

Some subjects are simpler – taking a shot of an anemone, perhaps – but even this requires decisions like where to focus, which aperture should be used to maximize depth of field, and where best to place the flash (or flashes).

Previous chapters have dealt with camera equipment and how it can be used. The following chapters look at the other major factor that underwater photographers have to take into account when deciding how best to capture a subject: light.

First, the photographer has to decide whether the photograph should be taken by available light, by a combination of available light and flash, or by flash alone. Having made this decision, the next step is to determine how the actual exposure should be made – using automation, manually, or with a mixture of both. The majority of underwater photographs are taken either using flash alone or a mixture of flash and available light, but there are many options and each has its own considerations.

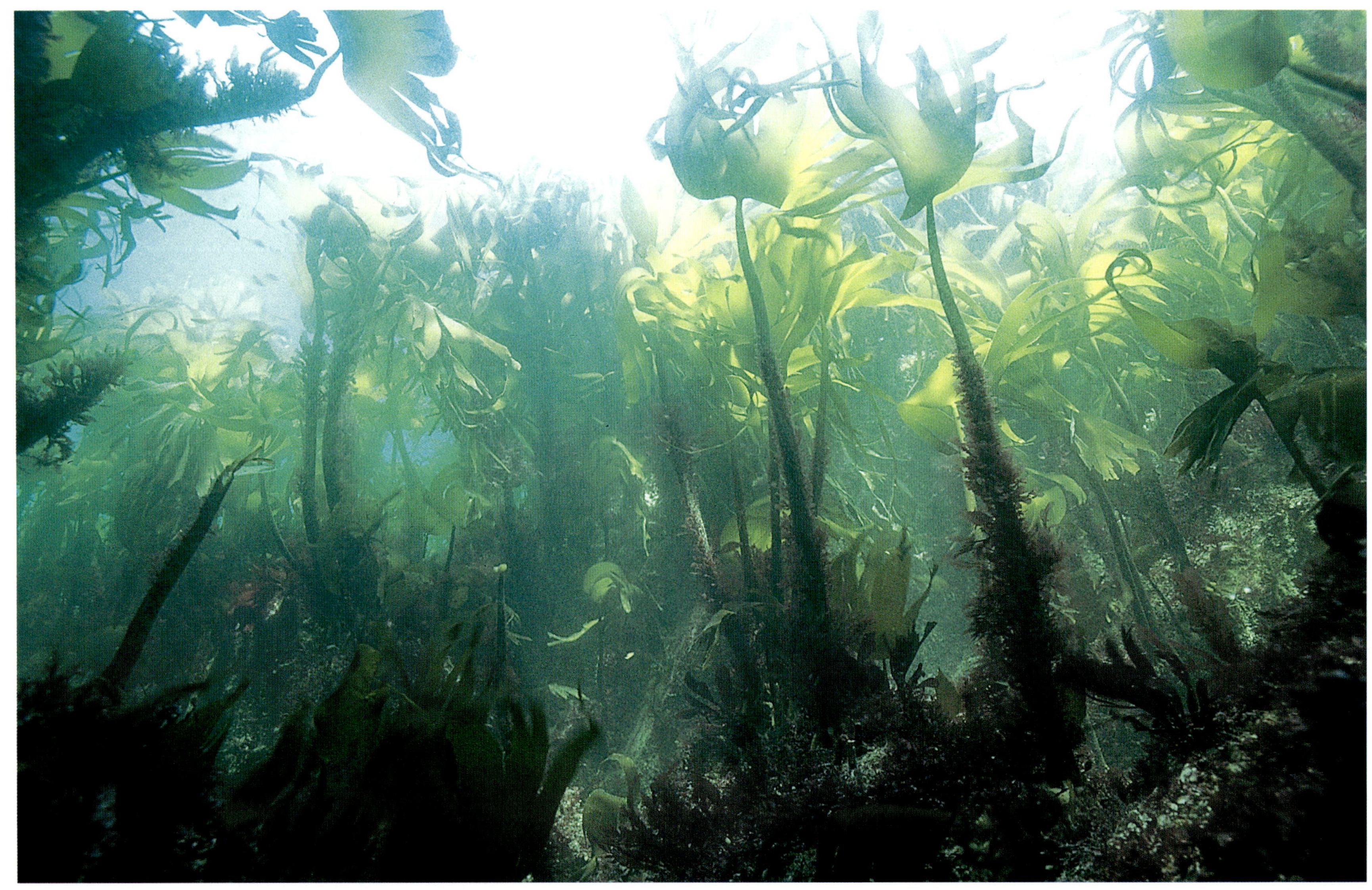

Shooting subjects like this kelp forest from below emphasizes the brightness of the overhead light and produces a dramatic picture of a straightforward subject. Taken off Sherkin Island in County Cork, Ireland, by available light.
Subal-housed Nikon F801 and 20mm Nikkor lens. 1/60s at f/8 on Fuji Velvia 50 ISO

available light

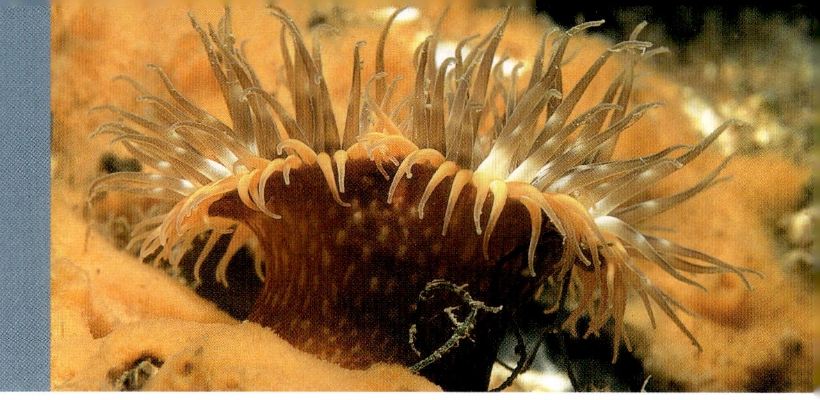

All water alters the light passing through it, but bodies of water like seas and lakes contain extraneous particulate matter that can cause additional unwanted effects (for an underwater photographer at least). Furthermore, even before light actually enters water it has another barrier to penetrate: the water's surface. Whether or not direct sunlight succeeds in entering the water depends on the angle at which it strikes the surface. When conditions are ideal, water is absolutely still and its surface perfectly flat. In these circumstances, any light from the sun that hits the surface at an angle of greater than 48.6 degrees (which is known as the 'critical angle') will penetrate through it; any light that strikes the surface at less than the critical angle will be reflected.

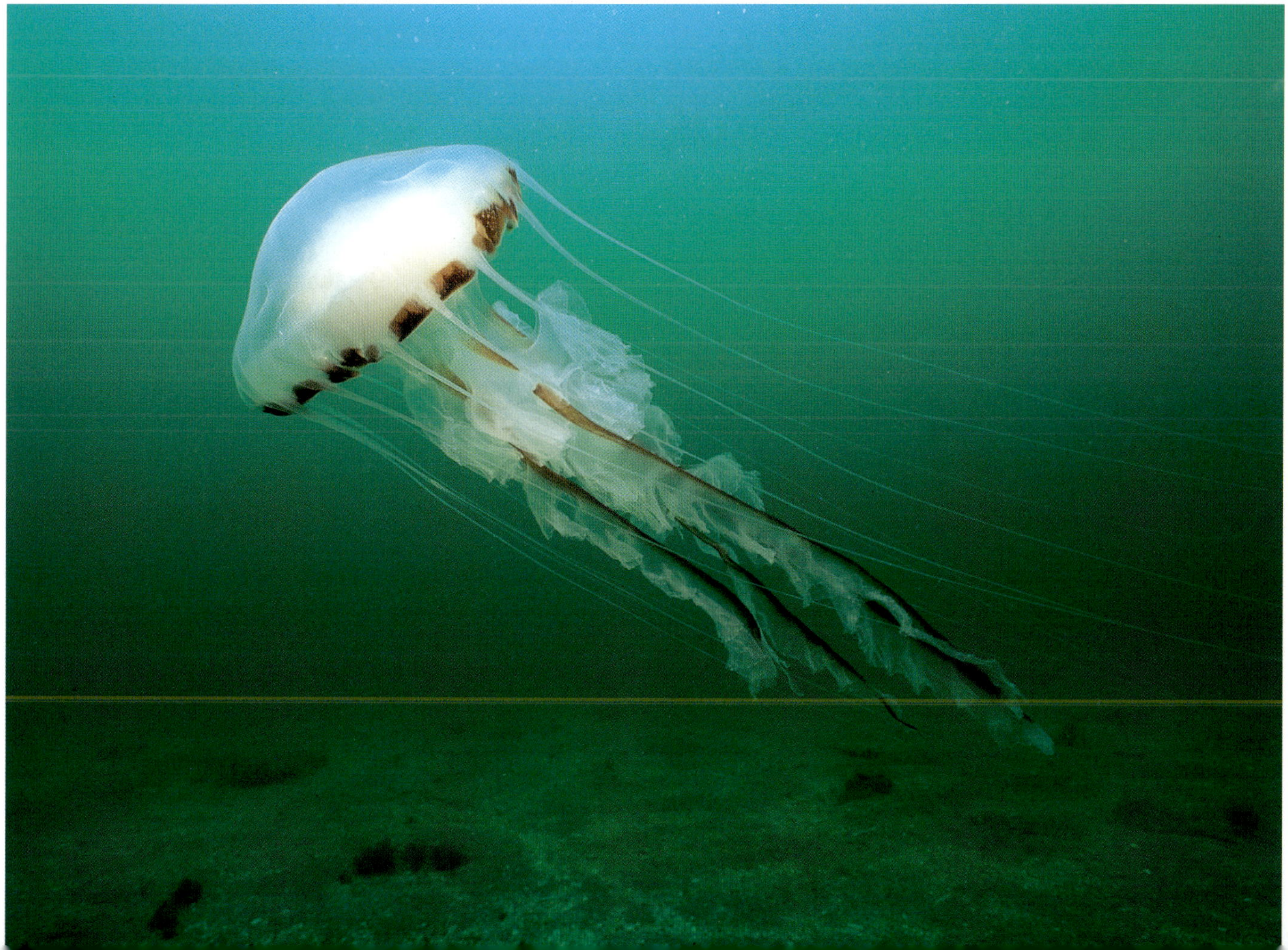

The sea is rarely absolutely calm, with little surface movement and no discernible current, but that was the situation here. This compass jellyfish (*Chrysaora hysoscella*) was photographed off the Aran Islands, Ireland, using a balanced mix of available and diffused flash lighting.
Subal-housed Nikon F801 and 20mm Nikkor lens, with a diffused Nikon SB105 flash unit. 1/15s at f/11 on Fuji Provia 100 ISO

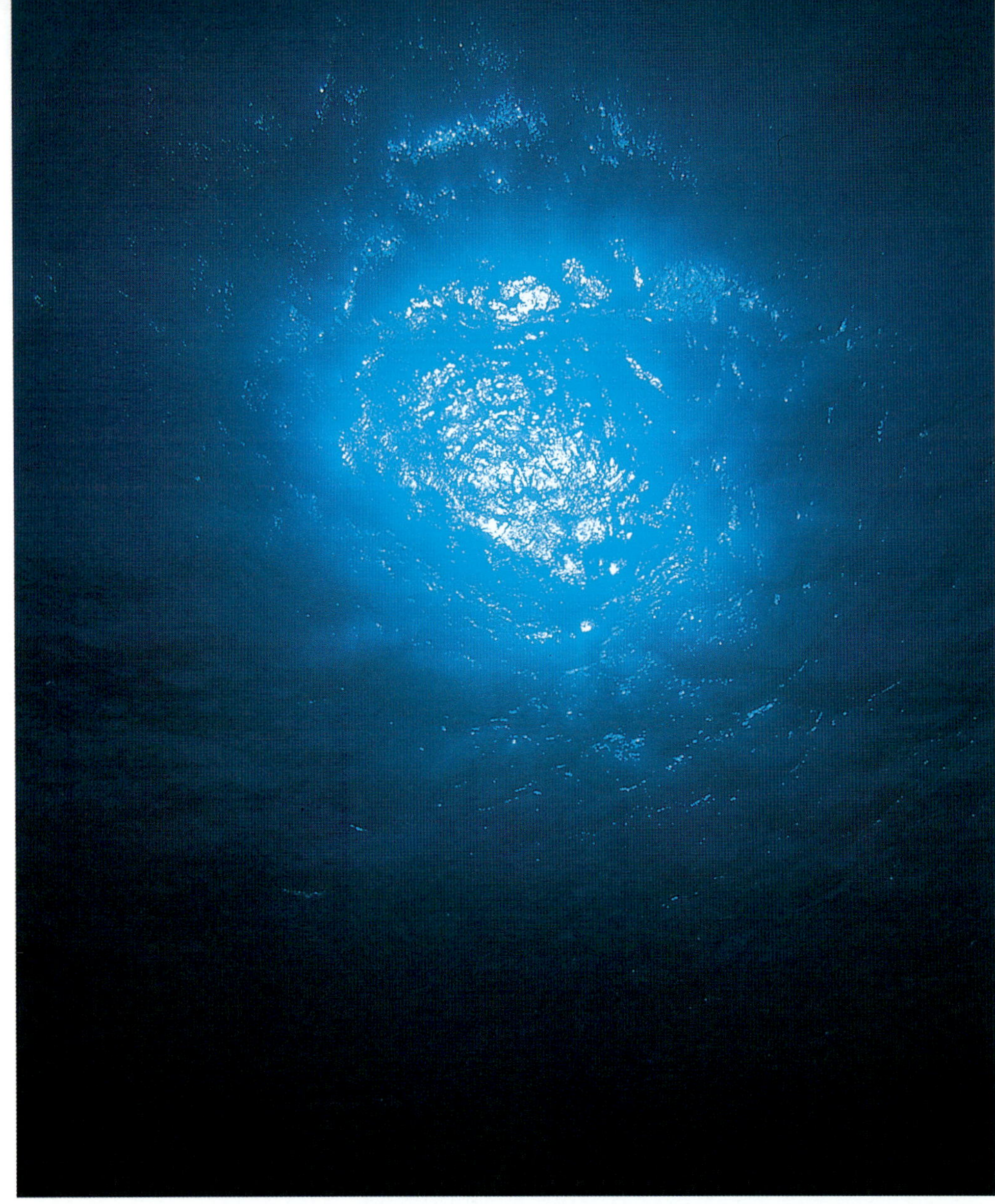

This is an available-light shot of the sun filtering through into the Red Sea. Looking up at the sun shows just how different the quality of light illuminating the undersea world actually is.
Subal-housed Nikon F100 and 20mm Nikkor lens. 1/125s at f/16 on Fuji Velvia 50 ISO

If, under perfect conditions, you look up at the water's surface from below, you will only see out of the water through a circle known as Snell's Window (named after the Dutch physicist who worked out the principle behind the phenomenon). In the right conditions this creates a circle of sunlight, which can be photographed using a very wide-angle lens. Snell's Window is responsible for much of the sunlight that penetrates through the water's surface. It will not be a perfect circle because the water will not be absolutely still, and the area around the circle will not be black (as it would be if no light were penetrating), but blue. This is because sky light, which is not the same thing as direct sunlight, does penetrate the water's surface.

As this implies, the undersea can be lit either by a combination of diffuse daylight and sunlight or by diffuse daylight alone. The change between the two is often more rapid than expected – as the sun sets, its rays will fall below the critical angle and be totally reflected by the water's surface. Without any sunlight, the undersea scene is very flat and lacks contrast.

As some light is always reflected, the level of illumination below the surface is inevitably lower than above. Furthermore, once it has penetrated the surface, light starts to be absorbed by the water itself. Light levels diminish continually as the water gets deeper, until it is completely absorbed. Consequently, light does not penetrate to the deepest parts of the oceans.

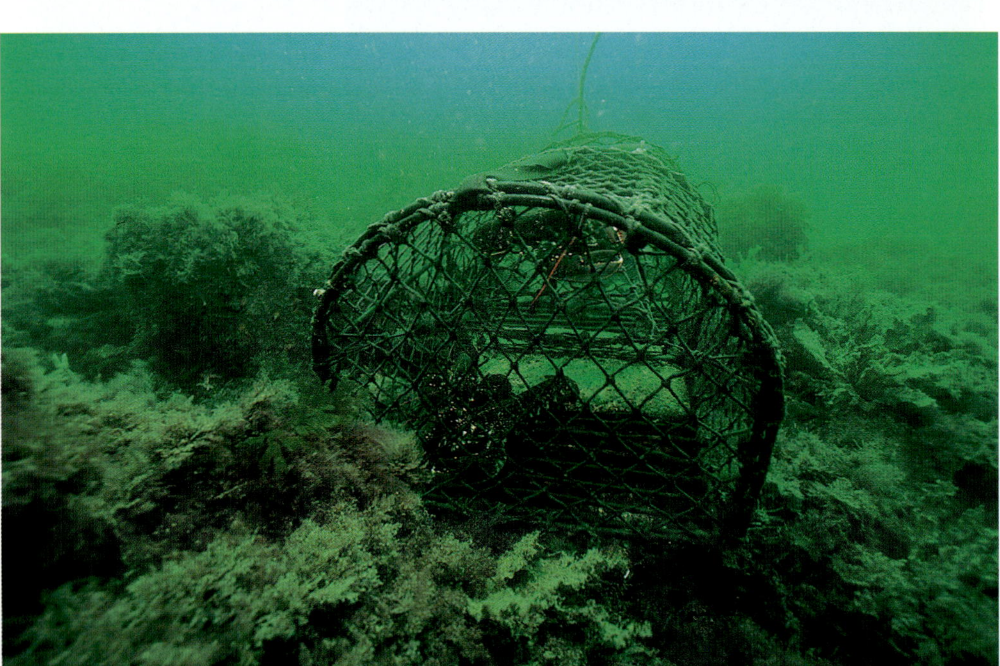

At a depth of around 10 metres, available light alone was insufficient to expose this photo of a lobster pot off St Tudwal's Islands, in the north of Cardigan Bay, North Wales.
Subal-housed Nikon F801 and 20mm Nikkor lens, with a single, diffused flash unit. 1/15s at f/11 with Fuji Provia 100 ISO

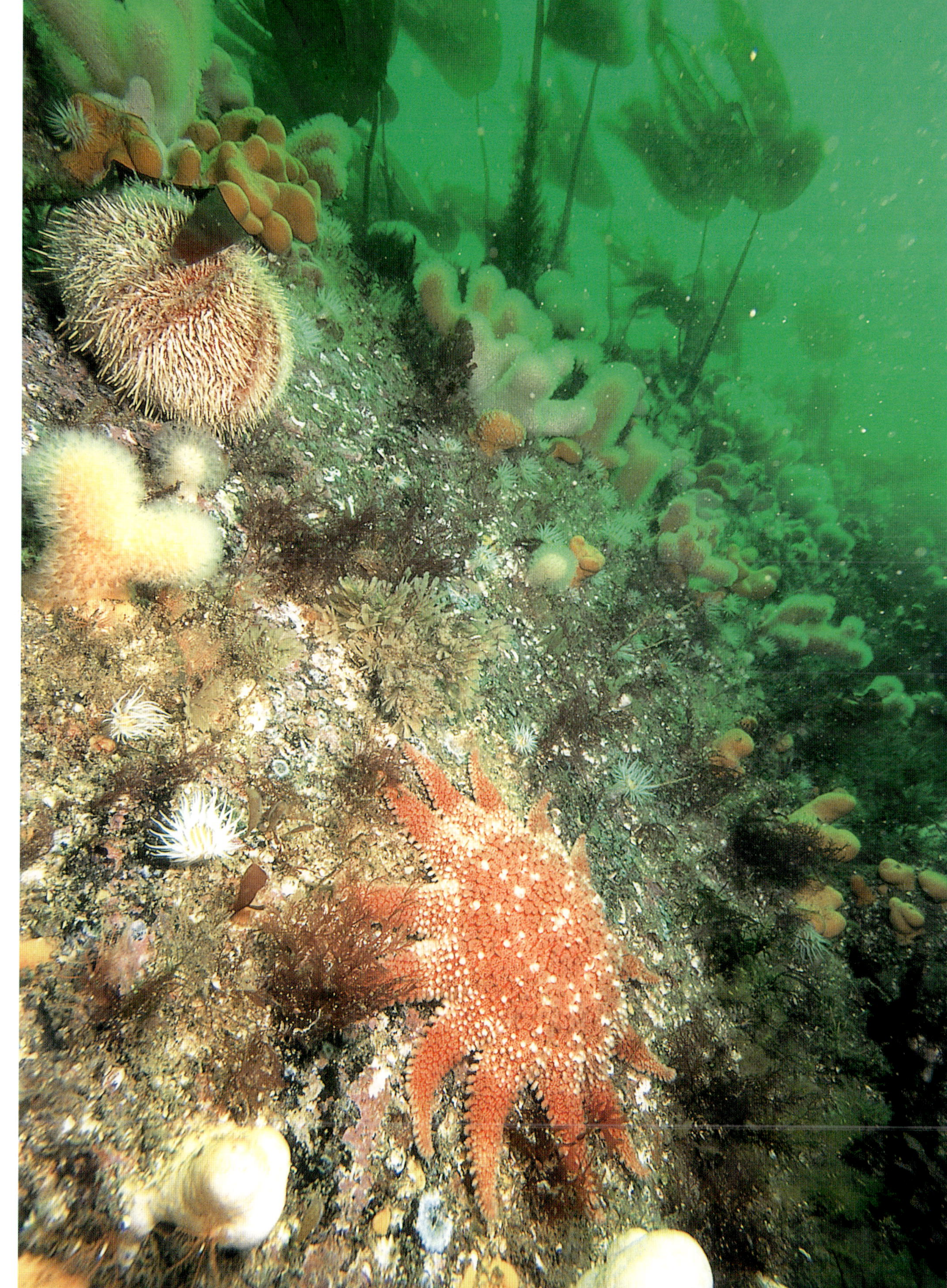

A careful balance of flash and available light results in even density throughout this photograph, at the expense of realism in the final picture. Taken in the Torrans Rocks off south-west Mull, this shot shows how colourful the seabed can be.
Subal-housed Nikon F100 and 17–35mm lens set at 35mm, with two diffused strobes. 1/15s at f/16 on Fuji Provia 100 ISO

Colour

White light is made up from a spectrum of colours, and these are removed gradually as they pass through water. First to be absorbed is red light, then orange, yellow, and so on through the spectrum to violet, after which all colour has been absorbed. So at any given depth there will not only be a reduced amount of light (compared with above water), but also a reduced range of colours.

To counter these effects, corrections have to be made for both exposure (as light diminishes) and colour (as the colours available are reduced). Exposure can be adjusted by altering aperture and shutter speed, but colour presents more of a problem, as it can only be compensated to a limited degree through the use of colour-correcting filters.

Pure water absorbs light in a well-documented way, but sea water and fresh water usually contain some (and sometimes lots of) dissolved and suspended material. This absorbs colour variably as well as selectively, depending on the amount of particulate matter it contains. In the tropics there is little suspended matter, and water tends to be blue. In temperate areas containing significant amounts of suspended material, the dominant colour is green. This is true near the surface as well as at depth, and it will be apparent in any photographs taken.

Conditions

The more particulate matter in the water the murkier it will become, and visibility will be lower as a result. When taking photographs underwater using available light, poor visibility and low light penetration will give pictures a soft, flat appearance. Available-light photography relies on reasonable light levels, good contrast and adequate visibility, so is difficult under anything other than good conditions, when these factors are available. Just how 'good' the conditions need to be depends on the photographer and the subject.

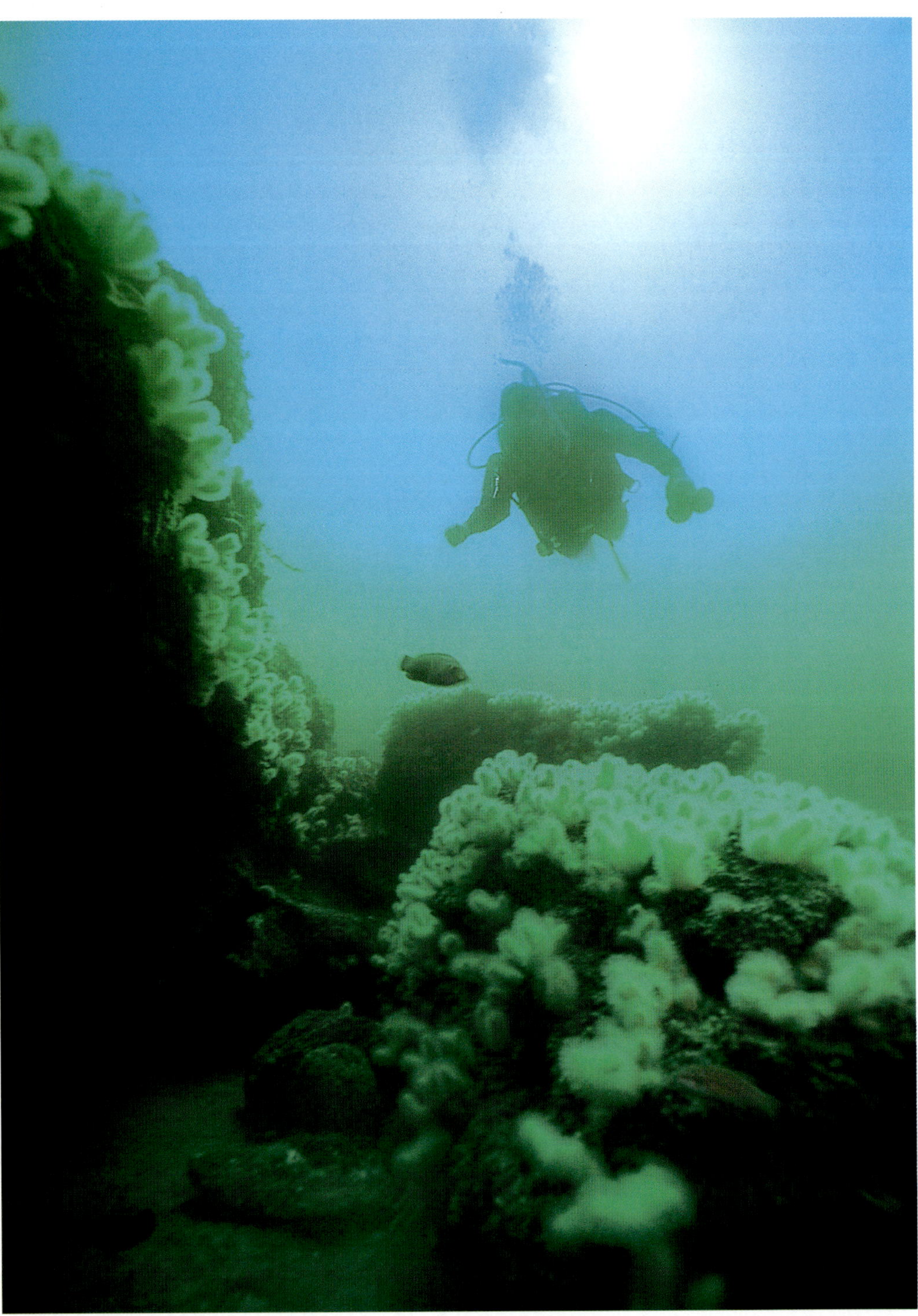

An available-light shot from the Aran Islands in west Ireland. Even at a depth of 20 metres there is plenty of light, although colour is reduced to a green-blue.
Subal-housed Nikon F801 and 20mm Nikon lens. 1/30s at f/5.6 on Fuji Provia 100 ISO

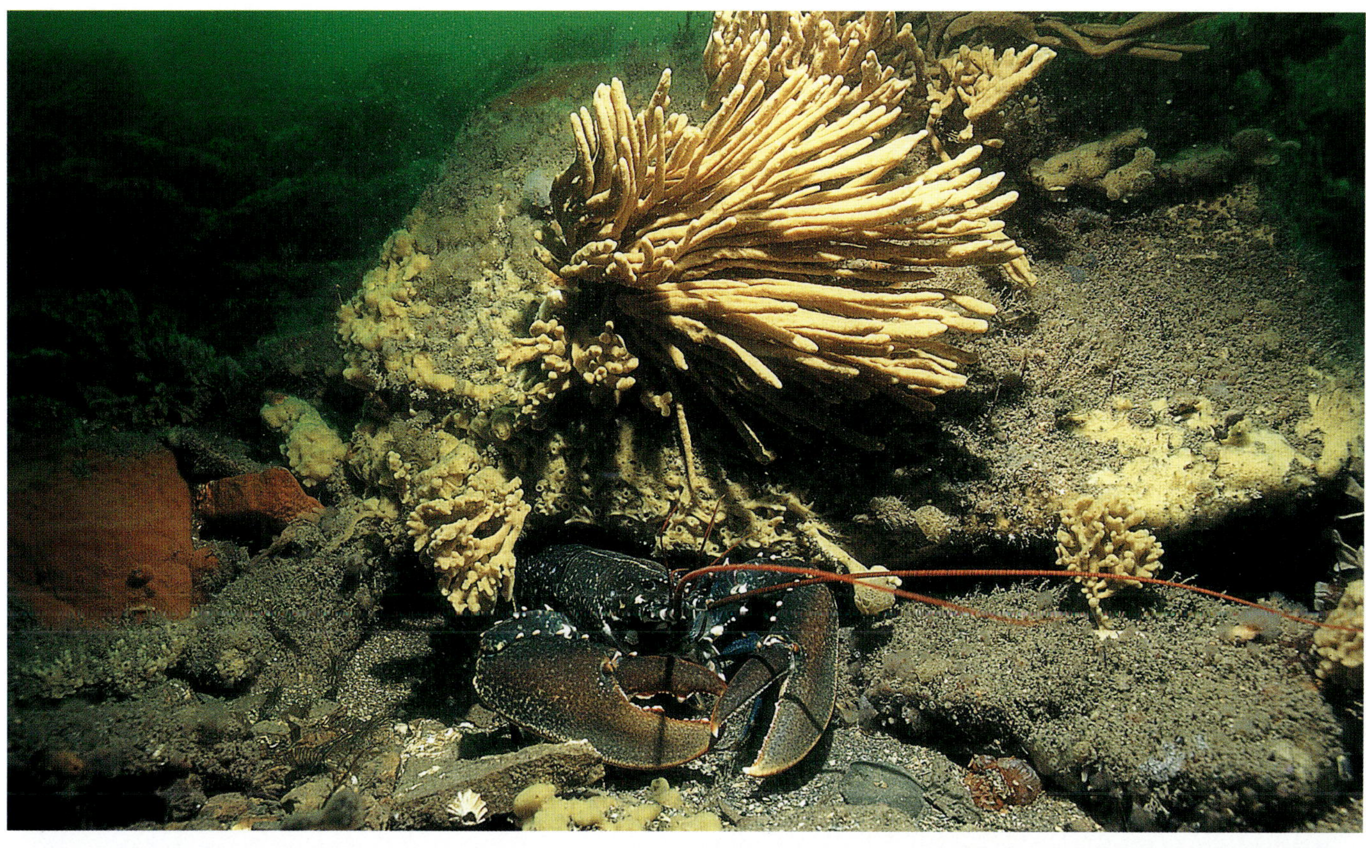

Some dive sites never experience good visibility. For this hand-held shot, taken in the Menai Strait in North Wales, visibility was reduced to just 5 metres.
Subal-housed Nikon F801 and 20mm Nikkor lens, with a single diffused flash unit. 1/2s at f/11 Fuji Provia 100 ISO

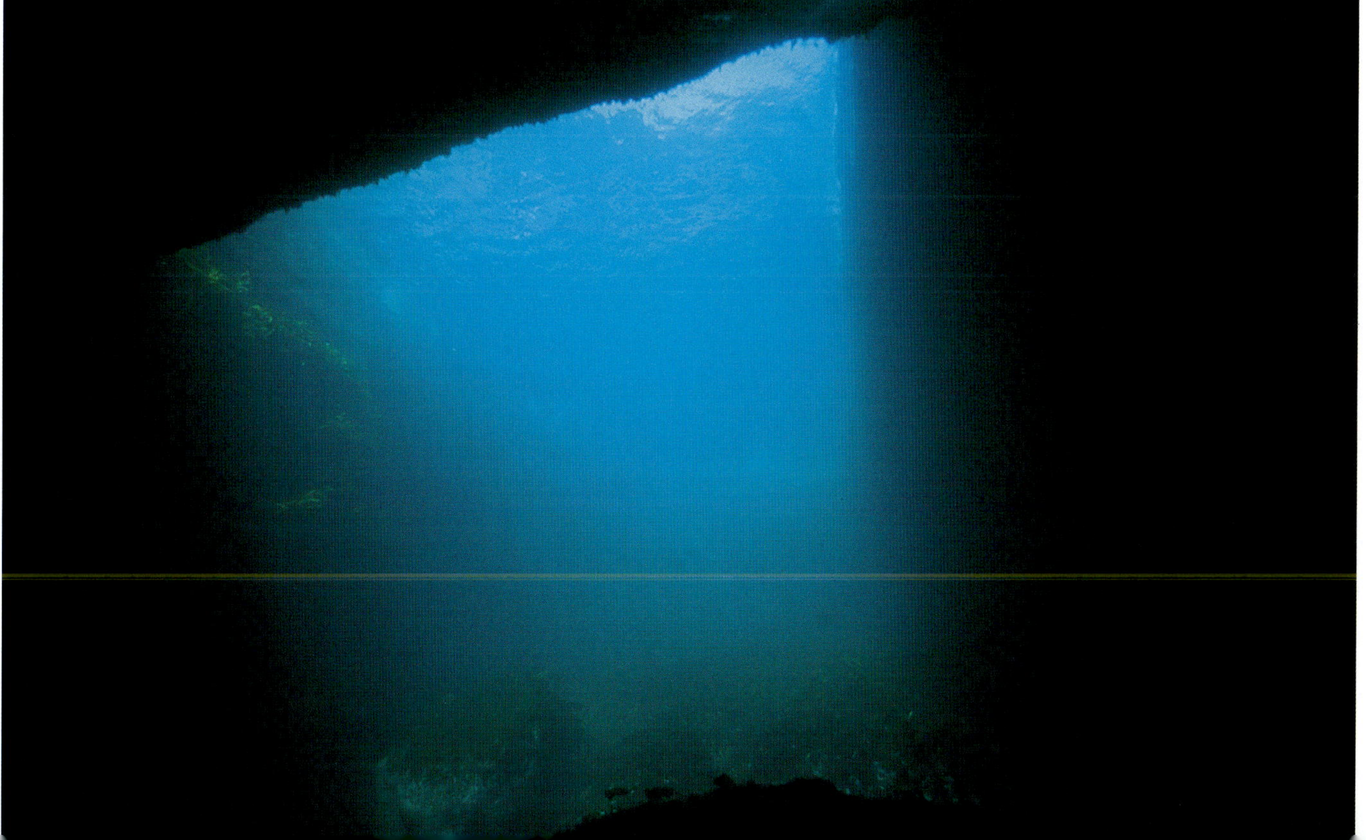

The Worm's Hole, a strange geological formation on the west of the largest of the Aran Islands. Superb water clarity and brilliant sunlight have allowed this photograph to be shot by available light alone.
Subal-housed Nikon F801 and 20mm Nikkor lens. 1/15s at f/8 on Fuji Provia 100 ISO

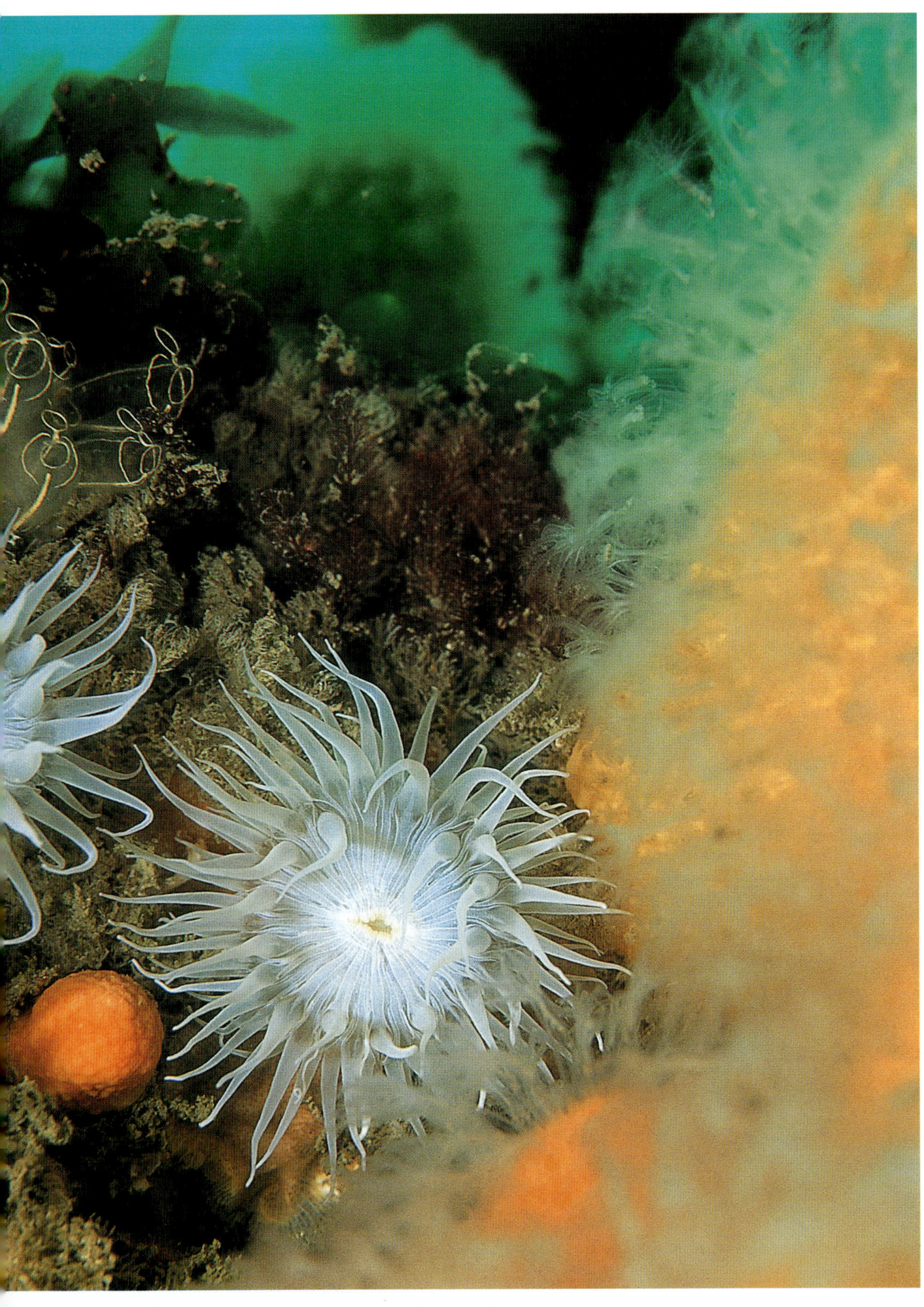

In ideal conditions (i.e. calm, sunny, shallow waters), photographs exhibiting both good contrast and colour can be taken by available light alone, but only reasonably close to the surface, where light levels are relatively high and much colour is still retained. At depth, photographs can be taken by available light using long exposures, which may mean that some form of mounting is needed to stabilize the camera. Such photographs usually exhibit quite low contrast due to the diffuseness of the light penetrating to depth, and are predominantly green or blue. Employing specific processing and/or enhancement techniques can yield useful photographs, depending on the subject and the reason for taking it.

Focus illumination

Another problem that may be encountered on dull, overcast days is that of accurate focusing. Focusing through a reflex camera, either manually or by using autofocus, can be tricky in the dull light conditions encountered underwater. In such conditions it is useful to have an additional light source to enhance contrast and assist focus assessment.

Some flash units have built-in focus-assist lamps. Alternatively, it is possible to fit an underwater torch to the side of a flash unit (there are even some holders built specifically for this), or onto the flash arm or housing. A final option is to hold a torch using your spare hand.

A few housings enable this to be pushed one stage further. As the shutter is fired, the light from a torch is switched off to ensure that it does not affect photographs taken at slow shutter speeds. A bright, concentrated light beam can show up on shots, even when taken at a relatively high shutter speed, so it is worth testing beforehand if this is the sort of light you intend to use.

This photograph, taken off the Kerry coast in Ireland, would have no depth without the available-light exposure, which provides a rich turquoise backdrop and significantly enhances what would otherwise have been a very mediocre shot.
Subal-housed Nikon F100 and 60mm micro-Nikkor, with a Nikon SB105 flash unit. 1/30s at f/16 on Fuji Velvia 50 ISO

This view down onto a canopy of a dense kelp forest located to the west of the Aran Islands, west of Ireland, gives little indication of what lies below. Such subjects are very low in contrast, and flash has been added to improve the situation.
Subal-housed Nikon F801 and 20mm Nikkor lens, with a diffused Nikon SB105 flash unit. 1/60s at f/8 on Fuji Provia 100 ISO

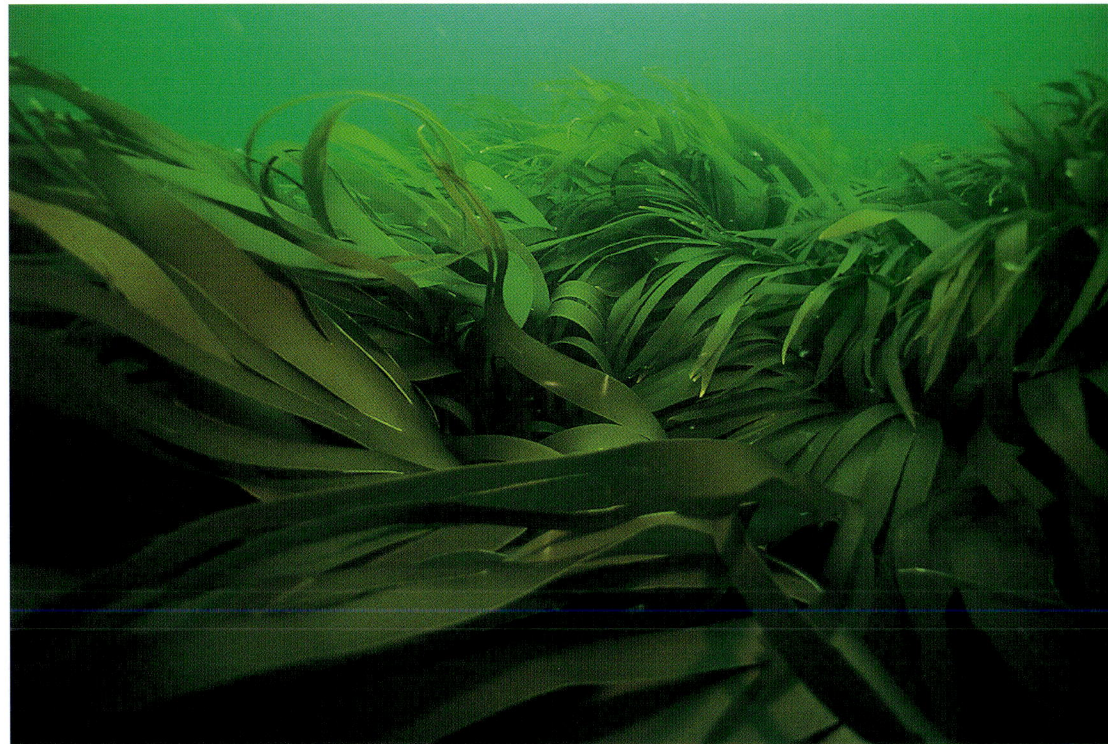

Direction of view

As contrast is very much lower below water than above, the direction in which a scene is viewed becomes significant when taking photographs by available light.

The lowest contrast of all occurs when looking directly downwards. The problem is caused by the diffuseness of the light, and only when conditions are extremely good are these shots effective. They will work if there is sufficient inherent contrast in the scene, perhaps a dark wreck sitting on light sand or brightly coloured divers against deep blue water, but photographs of this type are very much the exception.

Viewing sideways (i.e. horizontally) offers higher contrast. Careful choice of subject and composition can produce excellent underwater photographs; for example, reefs or wrecks lit by the sun against a blue or green watery background. As we prefer to look at most scenes with the sun behind us, it often makes sense to take a picture lit in this way, and consequently such photographs are common. The addition of some flash illumination can help considerably.

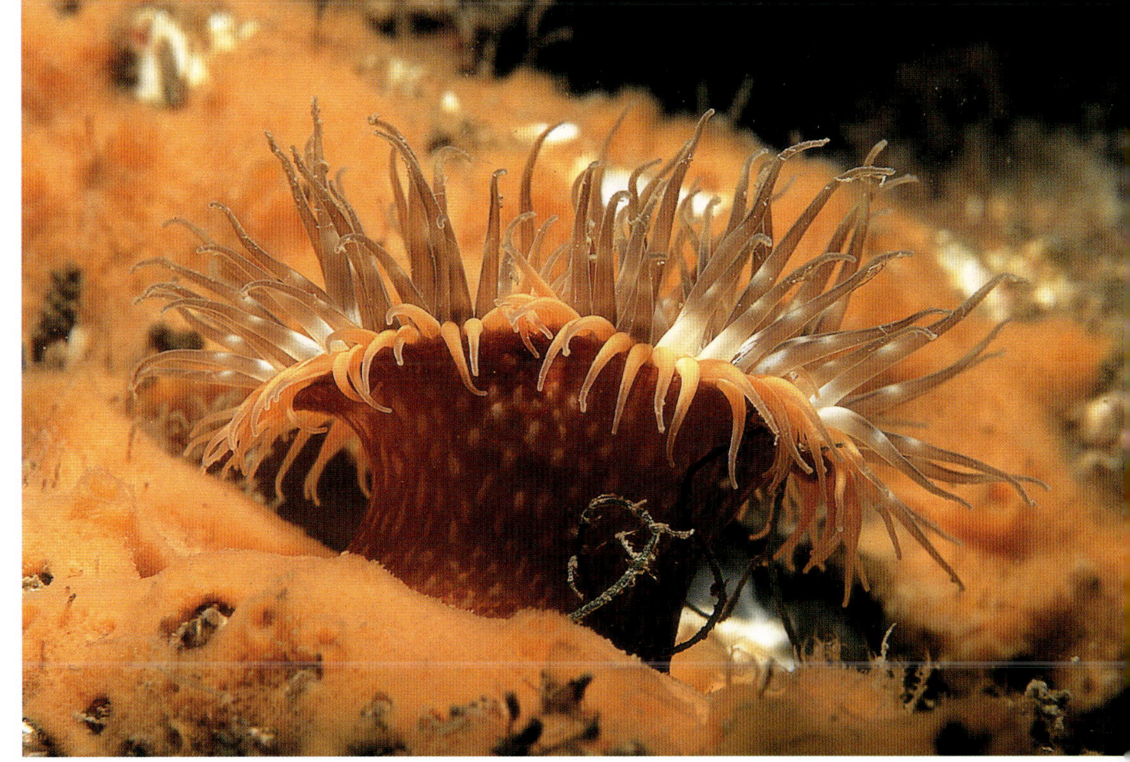

Anemones are often photographed from above, but a side-on shot of an appropriate creature can produce a simple and striking composition. This one is *Sagartia elegans*, and is pictured amid orange sponge on the wreck of the HMS *Conway* in the Menai Strait.
Subal-housed Nikon F801 and 60mm micro-Nikkor lens. Single-flash illumination only. 1/60s at f/16 on Fuji Velvia 50 ISO

A picture of kelp stipes and holdfasts from the Inner Hebrides, taken using a Nikon 17–35mm zoom on a Subal-housed Nikon F100 and twin diffused flash units. Shooting into good sunlight has boosted contrast.
Zoom set at 17mm. 1/60s at f/16 using Fuji Provia III 100 ISO

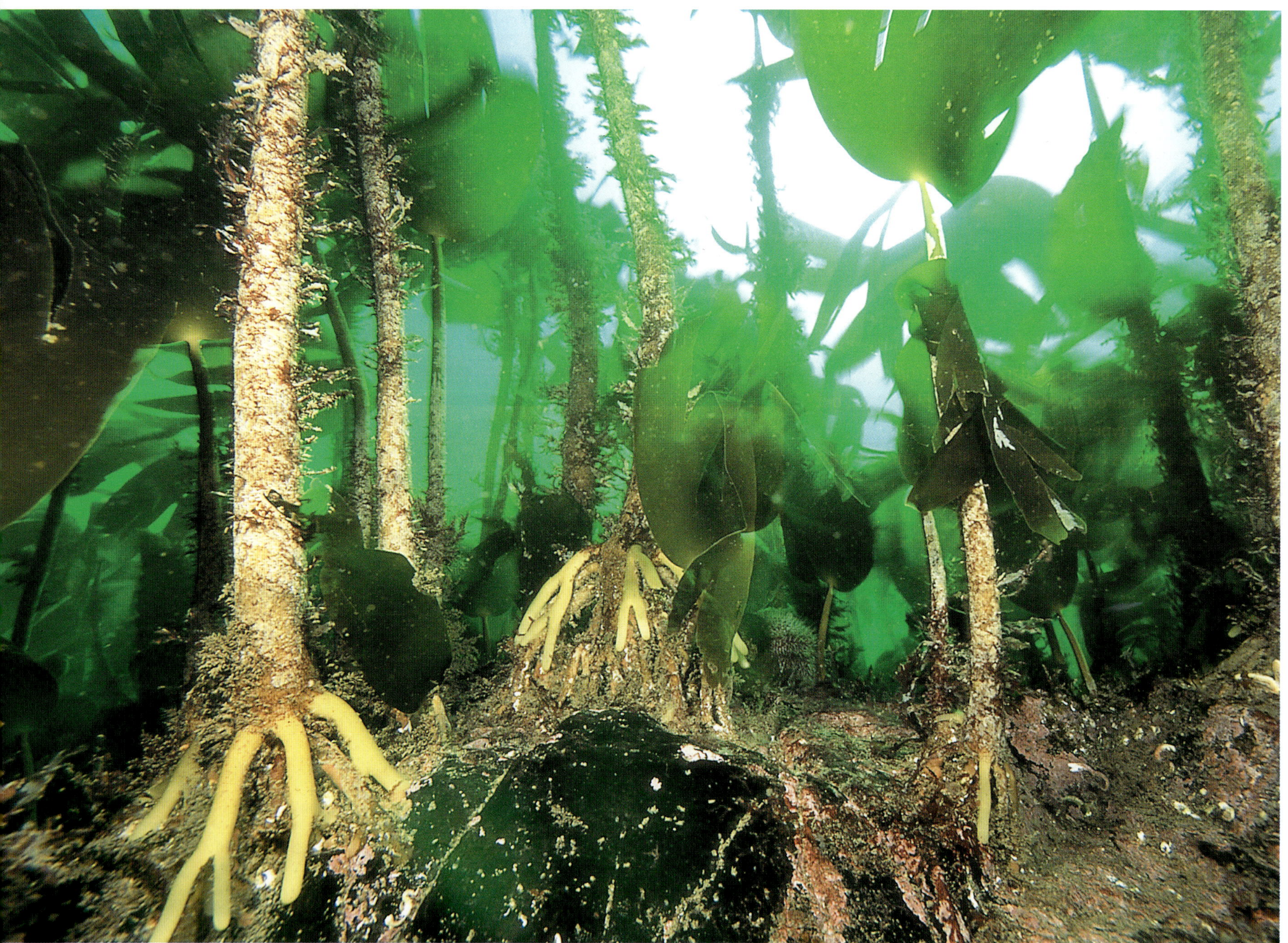

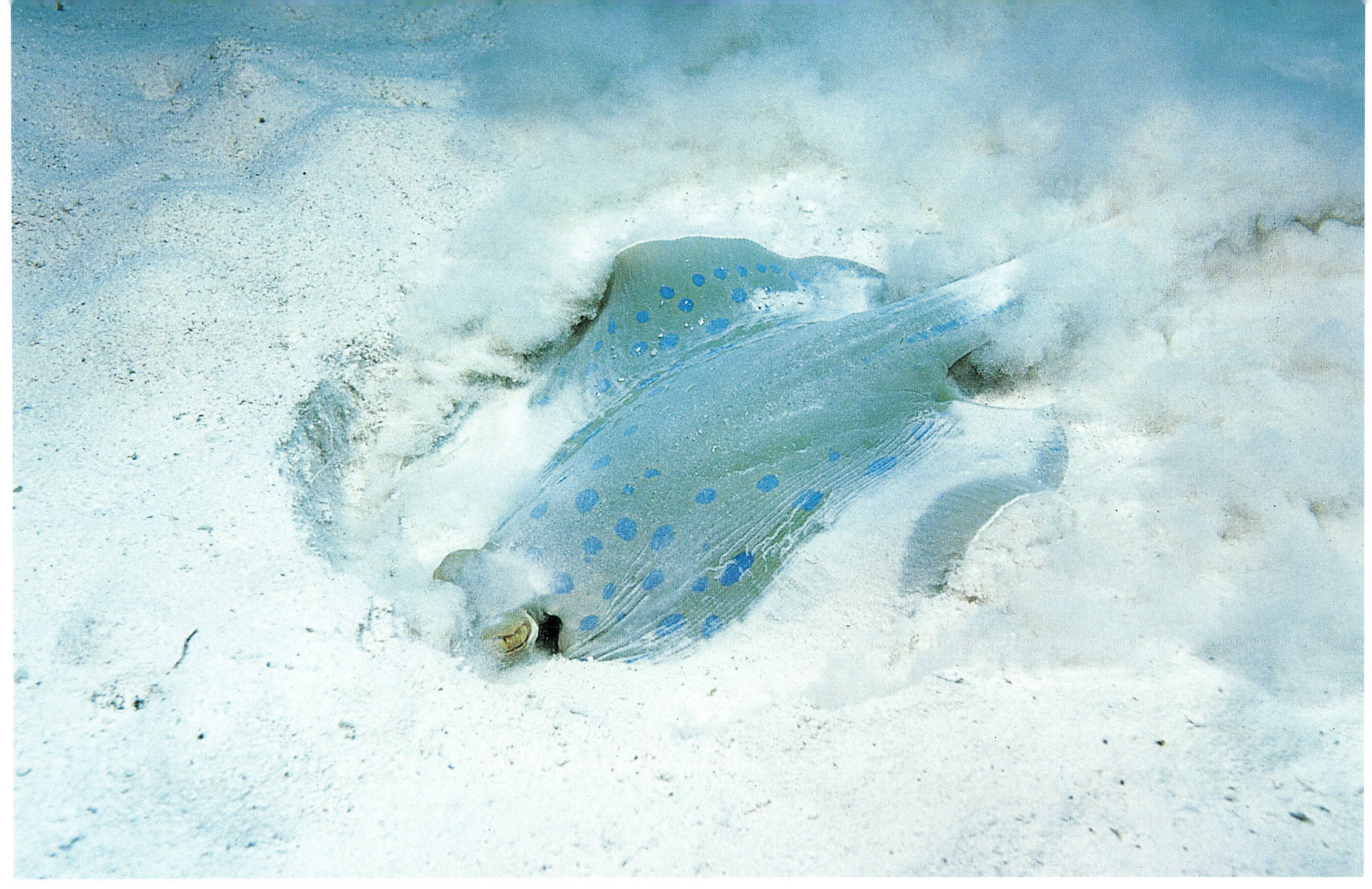

Shooting light subjects, such as this Red Sea-dwelling blue-spotted stingray (*Taeniura lymma*) against light sand, requires some exposure compensation (in this case +1 stop) in order to avoid underexposure.
Subal-housed Nikon F100 and 60mm micro-Nikkor, with a Nikon SB105 flash unit. 1/60s at f/11 on Fuji Provia 100 ISO

Viewing scenes against the light will increase contrast, but this is usually at the expense of shadow detail and only edges that are part silhouetted against the sunlit water may have much detail in them.

Maximum contrast is obtained when looking upwards towards the surface, the lightest part of the undersea scene. This is especially true in clear water, and when the sun is both bright and high in the sky. At such times, the sun's rays can become subjects in themselves, or they can be used as a backdrop to turn another subject, such as a diver, into a silhouette. In these cases, care needs to be taken when working out exposures to ensure a good silhouette without overexposing any other parts of the picture.

Exposure metering

Many underwater photographers try various methods for calculating exposure until they find the system that they feel is best for them. The various methods all require some way of assessing the amount of light available to make an exposure with, and all use some form of meter, which is usually built into the camera. The meter will give exposure details in terms of the required aperture and shutter speeds, and these can be set automatically (by the camera) or manually (by the photographer).

By far the most common method of taking a light reading underwater is to use a camera's built-in meter.

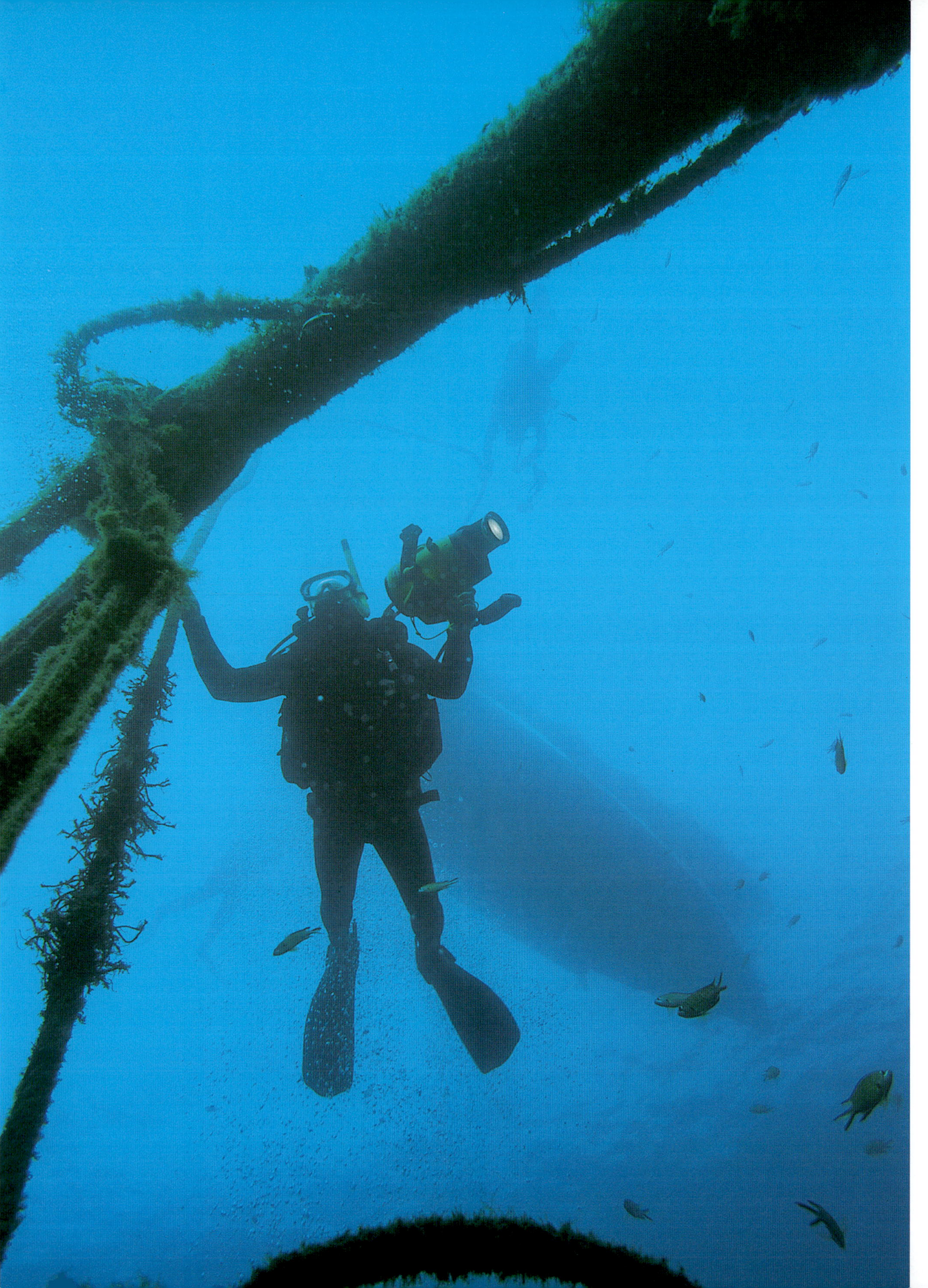

Looking up from the mast of a sunken vessel during a precautionary decompression stop allowed a silhouette of the videographer to be obtained while still showing the dive boat moored above. Shot in Lanzarotte, using available light. ***Subal-housed Nikon F100 and 17–35mm lens. 1/30s at f/11 on Fuji Provia 100 ISO***

Many 35mm cameras now have very accurate and highly capable meters fitted within them, which measure light through the lens. These analyse a scene in one of several ways. Some use the older and more conventional 'centre-weighted' system, which assess a scene by giving more regard to the light in the centre of the composition. Others use sophisticated 'matrix' meters that use a variety of parameters to determine exposure.

Conventional metering systems measure the amount of light entering the camera assuming that 18% of the light falling on a 'normal' subject will be reflected back from it. As discussed earlier (see page 17), this is because the meter is designed to read from a mid-tone grey. On this basis, pointing a camera towards a 'normal' subject and setting the aperture and shutter speed as indicated by a centre-weighted meter should yield a technically 'correct' exposure.

Matrix meters, on the other hand, look at the overall light, contrast and even colour distributions within a picture. Microprocessors then use this data, in conjunction with pre-programmed algorithms and database information, to calculate the exposure.

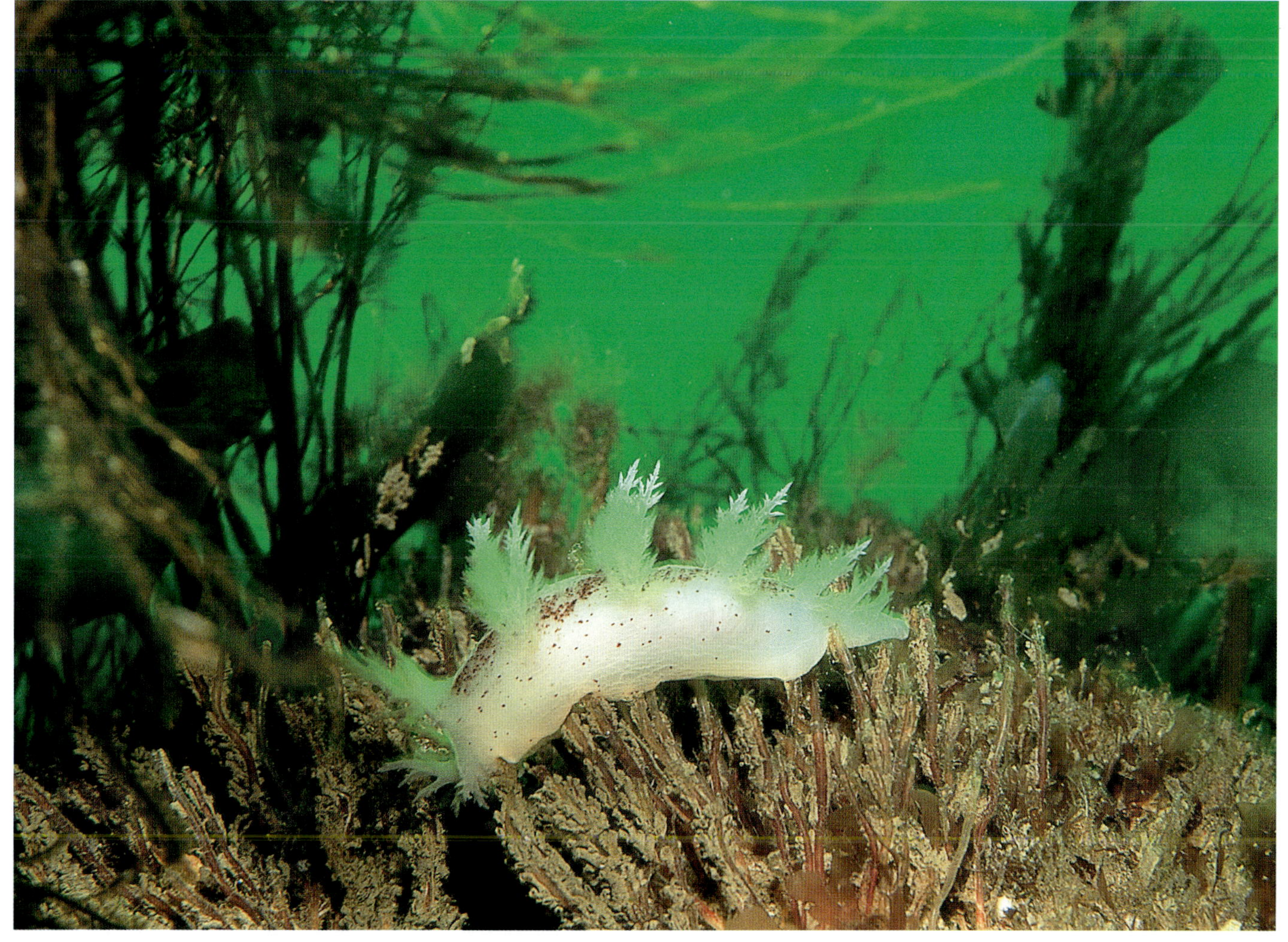

This picture of a small seaslug is an example of how balancing background light can place a subject in its context.
Subal-housed Nikon F100 and 60mm micro-Nikkor, with a Nikon SB105 flash unit. 1/4s at f/16 on Fuji Velvia 50 ISO

Assessing available-light exposure

Due to the limitations of using ambient light for photography underwater (as discussed above), only a relatively low proportion of photographs is taken using available light alone. Fortunately, many are of static subjects, such as wrecks or scenery, and often a straightforward meter reading will produce an excellent exposure. Such shots can always be bracketed, either by setting the camera manually and deliberately overexposing and underexposing several shots either side of the indicated reading, or by using exposure compensation to introduce the desired degree of adjustment when using an automatic exposure mode.

If a silhouette or similar shot is required, the meter is best used in either centre-weighted or 'spot' setting. The camera can then take a reading from an area that is to be reproduced as a mid-tone. Photos such as this can be problematic when using matrix metering, as the indicated setting may not yield the desired result but rather a 'standard' shot based on the meter's reading of the overall light and contrast distribution.

In mixed-light underwater photography, the element of the composition that requires available-light exposure is often the background. The technique for taking an exposure reading to expose the part of the photograph under consideration correctly is similar to that required for available-light photographs – the camera should be pointed at the relevant area, and the indicated levels set manually. However, the background to a flash-lit foreground may well be a lot darker than that required for an exposure lit by available light alone. The only area required to be mid-tone might be the open water behind the subject. Again, it is very important to realize that when a camera's internal meter is used, it should be set to centre-weighted (or preferably spot) metering, not used in the more sophisticated matrix or multi-sensor mode, and that the settings should be adjusted manually.

When the background is clear water, the mid-tone is that part of the water which will look best as a mid-colour (blue or green). If there is an illuminated foreground element – perhaps a diver – then it is important not to allow the clear water to become too light, so the mid-tone may be quite high up in the frame. A method for ensuring appropriate exposure is to meter from the background water and expose to keep this at a reasonably dark level.

As water colour and visibility both vary, so does their effect on a photograph of a specific subject. Here, both factors result in a colder, almost ghostly effect when the sun is photographed through a kelp forest.
Subal-housed Nikon F100 and 17–35mm lens set at 17mm, with two diffused Nikon SB105 flash units. 1/4s at f/16 on Fuji Provia 100 ISO

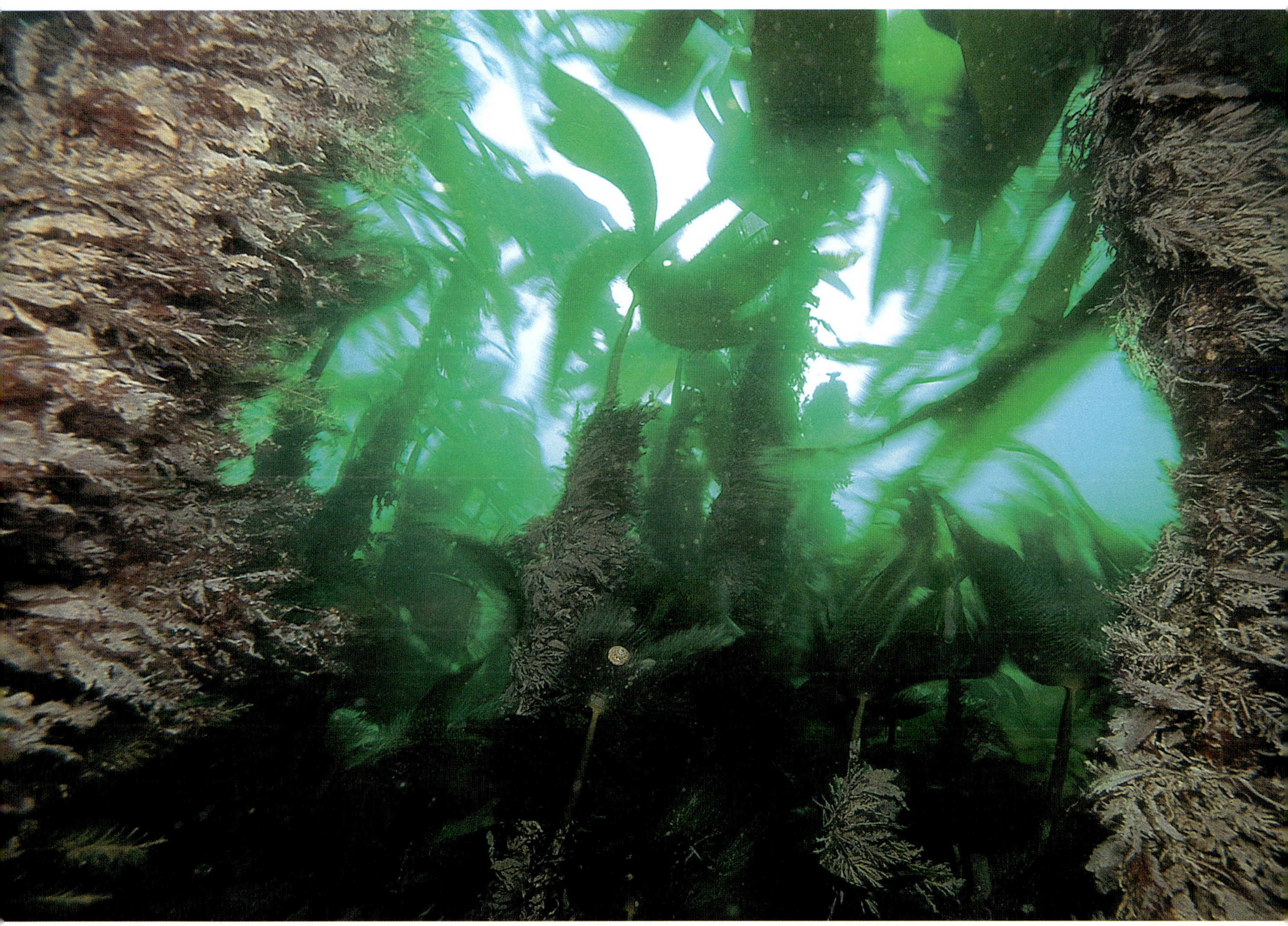

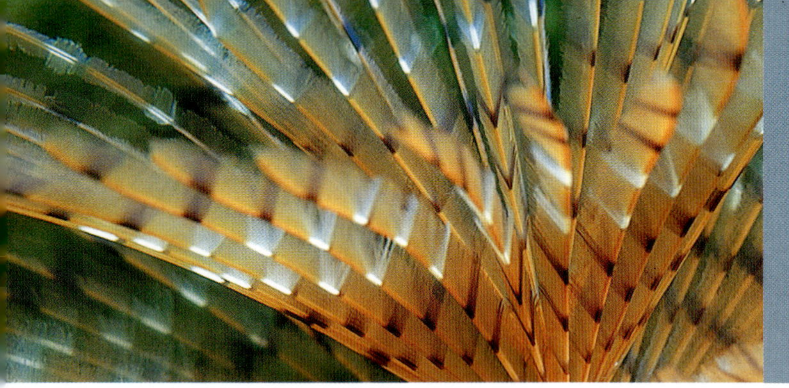

flash photography

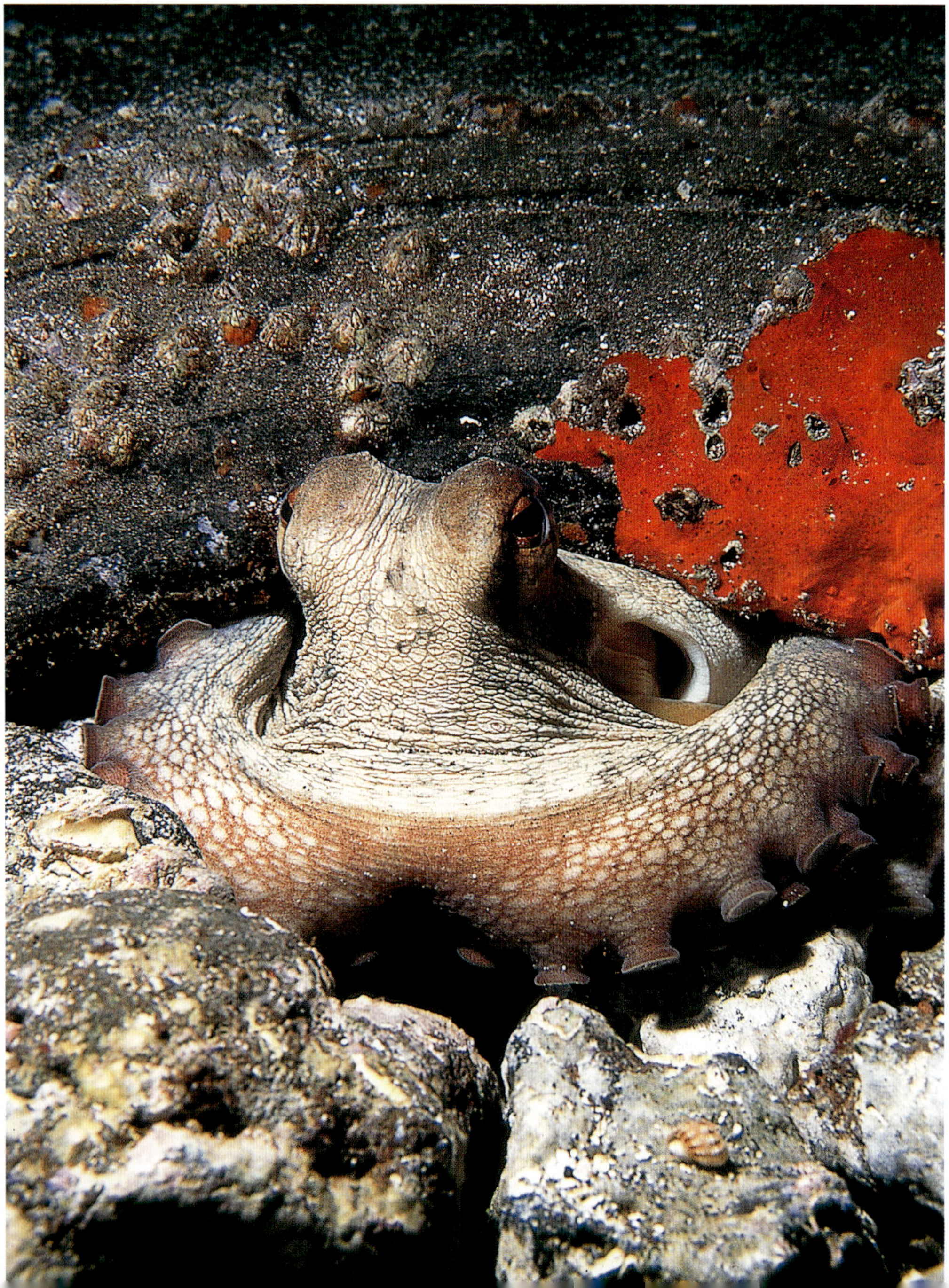

Both light and colour levels diminish quickly as water depth increases, and it is essential to compensate for these problems in order to be able to take photographs. The accepted solution is to carry a convenient portable light source – a flash unit.

Few lamps are capable of effective continuous light output, and those that are tend either to be very expensive or require massive amounts of power (or both). As a result, this type of lighting is impractical for the vast majority of underwater photographers, and (at the moment) the most readily available alternative is flash illumination.

Flash units have considerable advantages over continuous light sources, such as lower weight, cost and power requirements. Their one major drawback is that it is

Right: Sea anthias are frequently found on Red Sea reefs, and photographs of these fish are very common. This example is slightly different as it isolates one fish from the rest by using differential focus and fill-flash.
Subal-housed Nikon F100 and 60mm micro-Nikkor, with a Nikon SB105 flash unit. 1/60s at f/5.6 on Fuji Velvia 50 ISO

A common octopus (*Octopus vulgaris*) living in an old tyre in 30 metres of water off La Gomera in the Canaries. No available light could be used on a dull day, so a single flash was used as illumination.
Subal-housed Nikon F100 and 28–105mm lens set at 50mm. 1/125s at f/16 on Fuji Provia 100 ISO

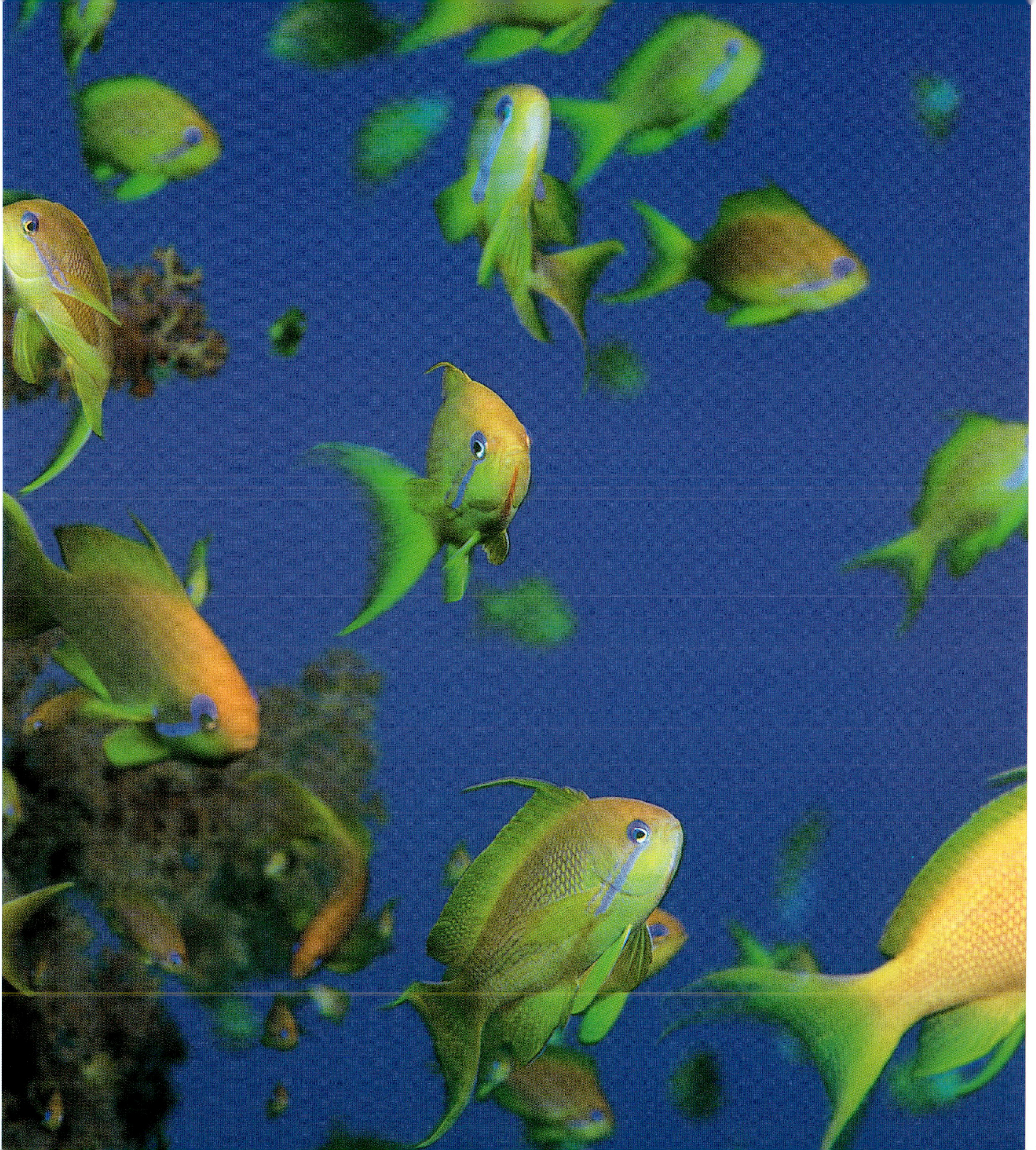

impossible to see exactly how they illuminate the subject; this has to be visualized by the photographer before an exposure is made. For any given type of flash unit, the exact light quality is unique. Accordingly, the only way in which its output can be anticipated accurately is by using it and looking at the resulting pictures. (For more details on flash units, see page 68.)

Panning the camera as this Turkish wrasse swam upwards has produced a motion-blurred background, while flash has frozen the movement of the fish.
Subal-housed Nikon F80, and 28–105mm lens set at 70mm. 1/30s at f/16 on Fuji Provia 100 ISO

Flash synchronization

The burst of light produced by the flash has to be able to expose the film within the camera correctly, and in order to do so it has to be synchronized with the shutter mechanism. In essence, this means that the shutter has to be fully open when the flash fires. If it is not, part of the image will be covered by part of the shutter, and so it will not be exposed to the flash illumination. To explain this, it is useful to understand how the shutter mechanism works.

Many, but not all, cameras use a focal plane shutter. This sits immediately in front of the film, protecting it from

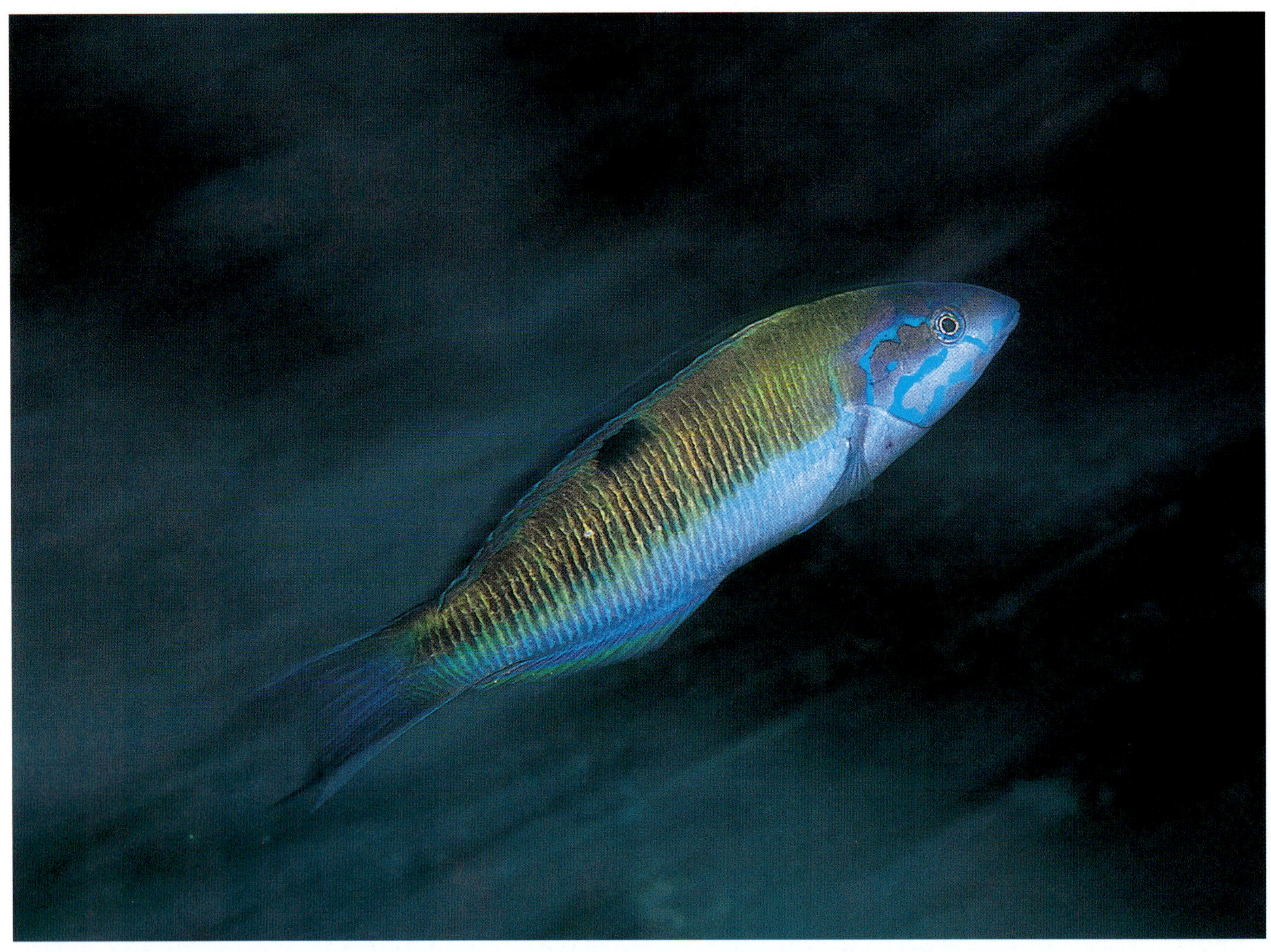

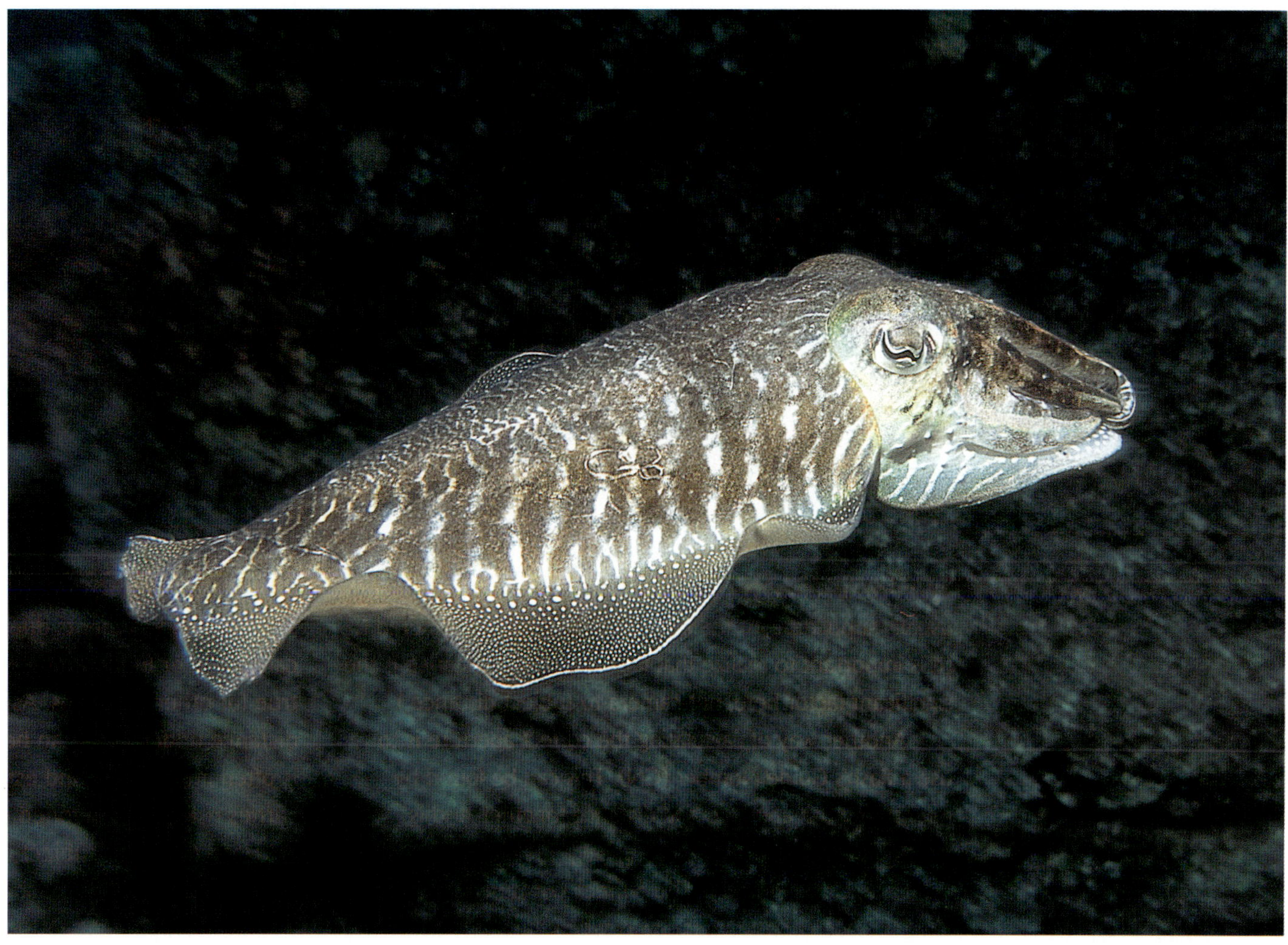

Dark backgrounds can be effective in isolating a subject but are easily overused. This common cuttlefish (*Sepia officinalis*) looks quite surreal and mysterious shot in this way, with flash providing most of the illumination. Taken off La Gomera, Canary Islands.
Subal-housed Nikon F80 and 28–105mm Nikkor lens set at 70mm. 1/60s at f/16 on Fuji Provia 100 ISO

the light entering the lens. Such shutters consist of two lightproof 'curtains'. At the point at which a photograph is taken, the first of these curtains starts to move out of the way. The time it takes for this shutter to move out of the way until the second curtain starts to cover the film is the shutter speed.

At low shutter speeds there is a delay between the movement of the two curtains. For a period of time the film is completely uncovered, and if the flash fires during this time the whole of the film frame will be exposed to the flash illumination. At high shutter speeds, the second curtain will start to cover the film before the first has uncovered it fully. The resulting gap between the moving curtains exposes the film for the very brief period of time required.

As mentioned, for a flash to expose the film properly, neither curtain can be in front of the film. Therefore, the fastest shutter speed at which the flash can operate, is the highest one that allows the film to be fully uncovered.

A variation on this is referred to as 'rear-curtain sync'. This can be used in various ways, but it is most commonly employed in conjunction with ambient light and slow shutter speeds to produce an impression of movement (see page 135 for details on combining flash and ambient light).

Slow sync flash

On some cameras, when a flash unit is turned on in aperture-priority mode, the shutter is synchronized automatically. Generally, this means that the camera sets a shutter speed of between 1/60 and 1/250 of a second. Some cameras allow photographers to override this by selecting a slow sync setting, which enables a slow shutter speed to be retained even when the camera is still working in an automatic mode.

Manual flash control

The simplest flash units and the easiest to operate – in theory – are manual ones that emit a single burst of light set to a specific and repeatable power output. Different flash-to-subject distances (for films of a given ISO rating) require the use of specific apertures to expose a film correctly. A table featuring distances, ISO ratings and the correct apertures is usually supplied with the flash, and this must be adhered to. (It is important to realize that flash-to-subject distance is the significant factor here, not camera-to-subject distance.)

Another way of calculating the correct aperture is to use a flash's Guide Number (GN). This can be found by multiplying the aperture and distance together, and is quoted for a given ISO rating – usually 100 ISO . For example, if a flash produces a correct exposure on 100 ISO film for a subject one metre away when the aperture is set at f/11, the GN is 11. The same flash unit would give a correct exposure for a subject 0.5 metres away if the aperture is set to f/22 (22 x 0.5 = GN of 11).

Unfortunately, various difficulties encountered underwater make manual flash control using guide numbers difficult. Close-up photographs that are taken using extension tubes or a true macro lens, for example, require an exposure adjustment when the level of magnification approaches life-size. The formula for this is:

$$\mathbf{E}_{\text{Corrected}} = \mathbf{E}_{\text{Indicated}} \times (1 + \mathbf{m})^2$$

where **E** is exposure and **m** is the magnification of the subject (measured on the film). This can cause problems in practice, especially at depth where narcosis can make any mathematical exercises difficult.

While adjustments due to magnification can be either calculated or found empirically, the same is not always true for other problems. Assessing flash-to-subject distance underwater can be difficult – accurate measuring is often impractical, and estimating distances underwater carries risks, as mentioned earlier. Also, as the distance between flash and subject increases, more light is absorbed by the water and the flash burst loses power.

The best solution to the problems encountered when using manual flash might be simply to work out correct exposures by trial and error. Experience can then be combined with predetermined settings written on an underwater slate. Alternatively, many divers use a unit featuring some form of automated flash control.

This club-tipped anemone (*Telmatactis crinoides*) off Lanzarotte, has been shot with flash only in order to ensure that its true colours can be seen. It was a very straightforward shot using TTL flash.
Subal-housed Nikon F100 and 60mm micro-Nikkor lens, with one Nikon SB105 flash unit. 1/60s at f/22 on Fuji Provia 100 ISO

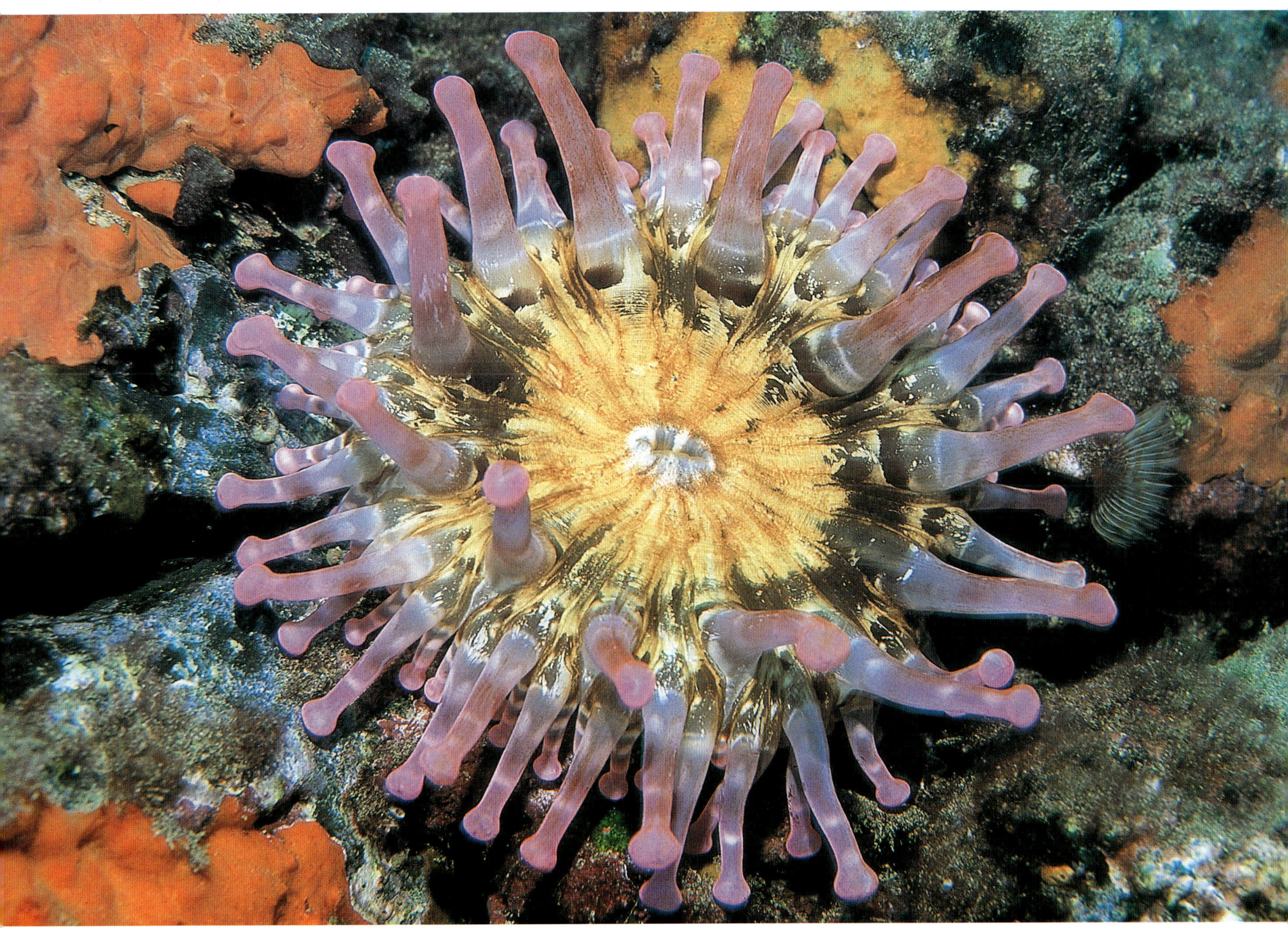

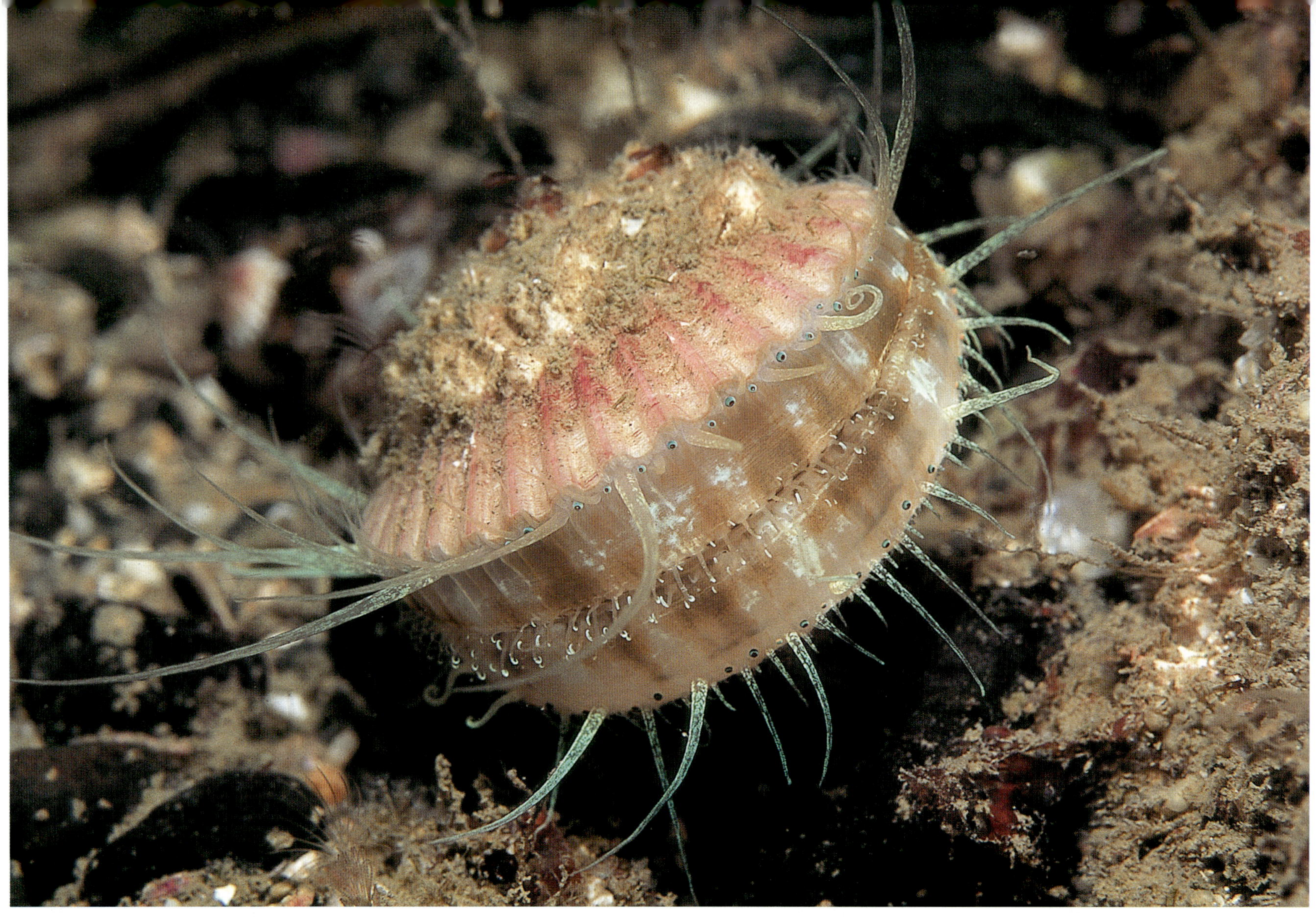

Some might prefer to see this 'queenie' or queen scallop (*Aequipecten opercularis*) on a plate, but even these animals can produce striking pictures when carefully lit by flash. ***Subal-housed Nikon F801 and 60mm micro-Nikkor, with a Nikon SB105 flash unit. 1/60s at f/22 on Fuji Velvia 50 ISO***

Automatic flash control

Broadly speaking, there are two types of automatic flash control available for underwater use. One relies on a remote sensor outside the camera body to control the exposure, but the most popular form uses an internal camera sensor that operates through the lens (TTL).

TTL flash control works by linking flash and camera with a cable that carries information from one to the other. Once an initial signal triggers the flash, a sensor inside the camera records the light (from the flash) that is reflected by the film during the exposure. When the film has received sufficient light to produce a correct exposure, a second signal is sent from the camera to tell the flash to shut off (this process is known as 'quenching').

TTL flash control offers a very elegant and, within limits, an extremely effective solution to many of the problems faced by underwater photographers when using flash. It is not influenced by flash-to-subject distance, and one particular advantage that it has over the less commonly used alternative is that the latter cannot compensate for magnification effects.

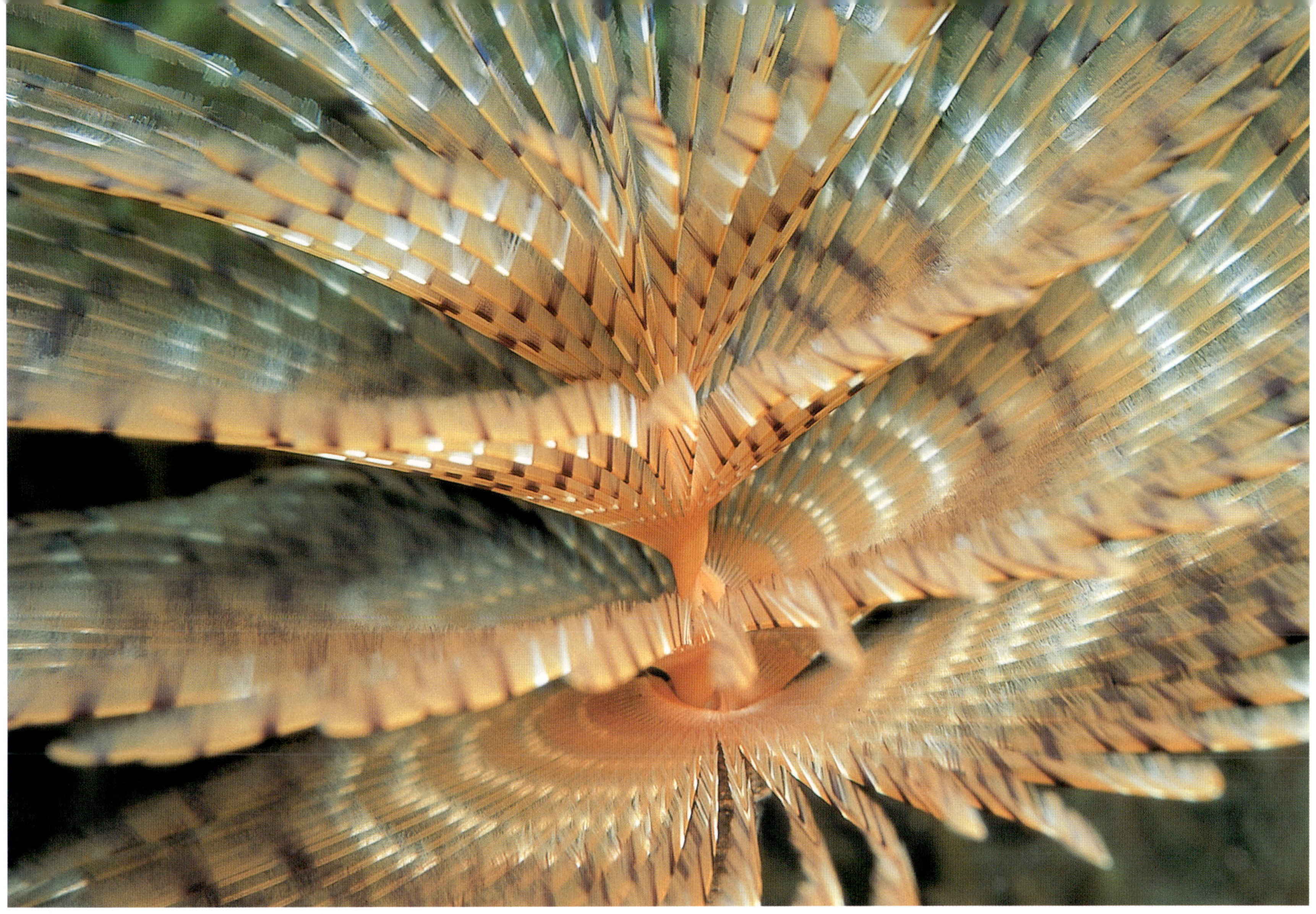

Fan worms are tricky little creatures to photograph, as they withdraw their photogenic filtering fans at the slightest provocation. This near life-size image of a fan (of *Sabella spellanzani*) was difficult not photographically (it was taken using TTL flash), but for practical reasons. Precise buoyancy control and great care are needed for such shots. ***Subal-housed Nikon F801 and 60mm micro-Nikkor lens, with a Nikon SB105 flash unit. 1/60s at f/16 on Fuji Provia 100 ISO***

However, TTL flash control has its limitations. In order to quench the flash, the electronics within the camera and flash have to operate extremely quickly, and there are limits to their capabilities. Many flashes cannot quench the flash if its output is below around 1/16 or 1/32 of its full output (although this does vary). As each halving of a flash's power output is equivalent to a reduction of one stop (i.e. full to half power = one stop, half to quarter = one stop, etc), this means that they can operate within four or five stops of full output when used on TTL mode. If an aperture that requires an output outside this range is set, the flash unit will either run out of power (if the aperture is too small) or will be unable to 'quench' the light in time (if the aperture is too wide).

Modern TTL automated flash control can be a very effective way of taking close-ups underwater, and will produce highly acceptable results in a wide range of circumstances. However, it should not be seen as a substitute for understanding the principles behind flash photography – situations can occur in which an automated system is fooled and will yield an unacceptable exposure.

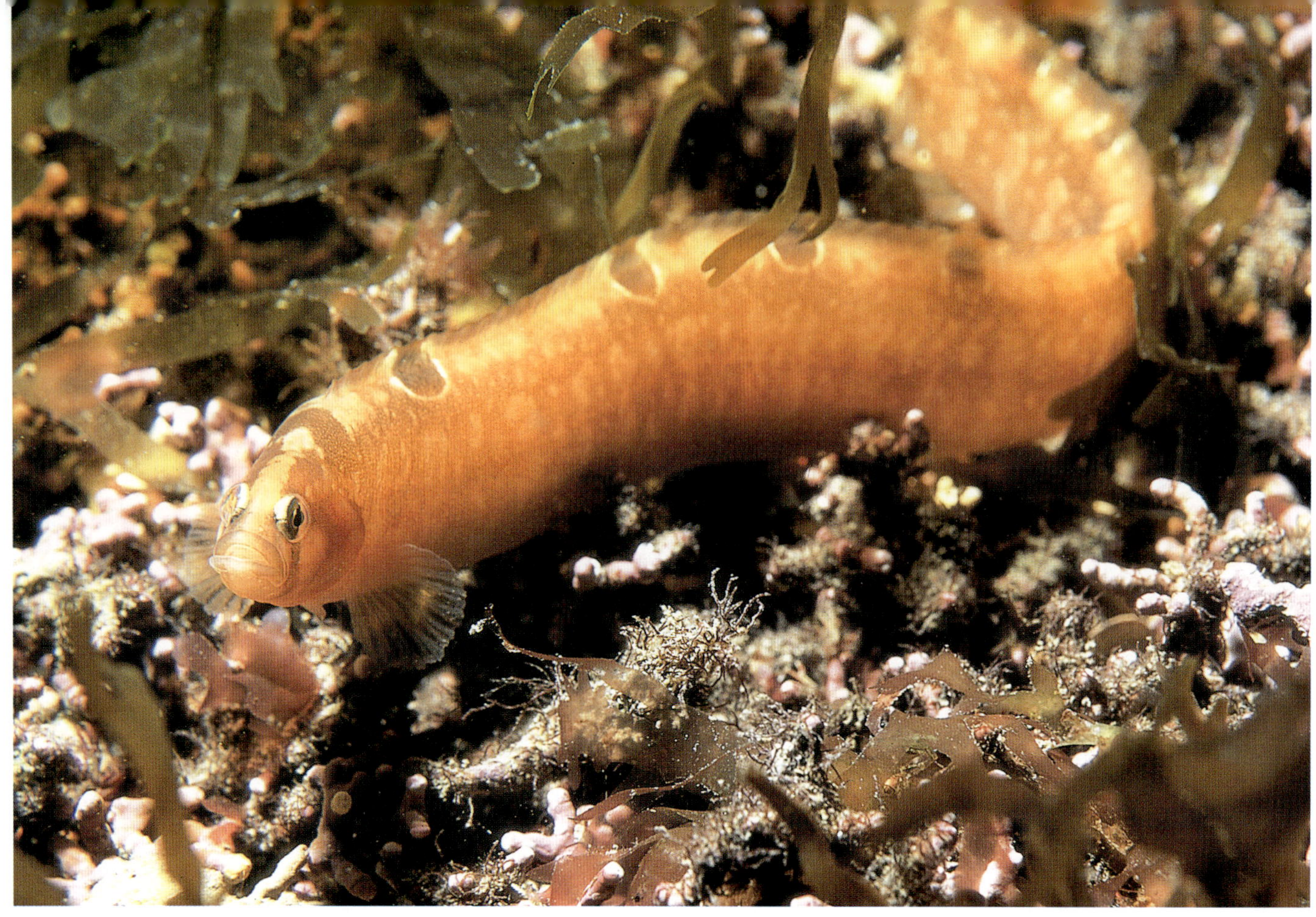

Despite being partially side lit, this butterfish (*Pholis gunnelus*) is translucent enough to allow some illumination to pass through it, resulting in a rich colour. Taken on a maerl bed off Connemara, Ireland. ***Subal-housed Nikon F801 and 60mm micro-Nikkor lens, with a Nikon SB105 flash unit. 1/60s at f/16 on Fuji Velvia 50 ISO***

Using TTL flash

Using flash illumination only and utilizing TTL automation will cope with many, if not all, macro subjects – unless they are very bright or very dark. Under these circumstances exposure compensation may be needed. (Compensation is used to produce deliberate over- or underexposure; to lighten a photograph additional exposure has to be applied, while reduced exposure will darken a photograph.)

Until the late 1990s, few options were available for applying exposure compensation when using flash only. Most relied on setting a general adjustment on the camera, which would then be applied to the flash. Only some land flash units had exposure-compensation controls built in, and not all housings enabled these to be accessed underwater.

This does not matter when using flash as the only illumination, since the compensation system used on the camera can be used to adjust flash output power. As no available light is being used for the exposure, compensation will be applied solely to the TTL flash output. However, there can be problems if more than one flash unit is being used or when available light makes up a part of the exposure.

The way that TTL flash metering operates varies; it depends on the specific camera manufacturer and model of camera being used. As reflex cameras have increased in sophistication, multiple sensors have replaced their single TTL sensor. These operate similarly to the matrix or multi-sensor metering systems used by the cameras to measure available light, and are similarly intended to offer enhanced exposure accuracy by considering more than the standard 18% reflectance from the subject. On some cameras, either a matrix or a centre-weighted (which is older and less sophisticated, but possibly more predictable) system can be selected. On others there is only one option.

It is worth remembering that any matrix or multi-sensor metering system may behave unpredictably, as it is an automated way of interpreting the brightness, contrast and colour of a scene. Often, the use of such metering systems with flash-only illumination will work very well, but there are occasions when even the most sophisticated systems fail to produce the required result. It may well be worth taking the same picture using both centre-weighted and matrix options if possible, to see what difference (if any) occurs.

TTL flash control is very effective for macro photographs, but is often far less accurate when shooting wide-angle photographs. Again, if the only method of illuminating a subject (such as part of a deep wreck) is going to be flash, and if the flash unit being used gives sufficient power and wide enough coverage, then TTL may be adequate.

Clearly, the flash must be able to illuminate the whole subject, and this is not always possible, especially on large, three-dimensional subjects like shipwrecks. In this case, TTL flash control tends to produce overexposed images, as the sensors in the camera struggle to cope with the very dark, recessed areas of the subject, which reflect no light at all.

Many wide-angle scenes also tend to be ones in which the area of interest is seen at an angle (relative to the film plane). For even illumination, the light from the flash should hit such surfaces at 90 degrees, and so the axis of the flash needs to be perpendicular to them. Again, for this scenario to work, suitable, photogenic subjects have to be found, and they may not be plentiful.

Highly reflective subjects like these glassfish in the Egyptian Red Sea can overexpose very easily. Flash power should be reduced or compensated to underexpose them slightly.
Subal-housed Nikon F100 and 20mm Nikkor lens, with a Nikon SB105 flash unit. 1/60s at f/16 on Fuji Provia 100 ISO

Back scatter

Even when some of the technicalities of flash exposure are being taken care of by the camera's automatic systems, controlling flash underwater is not easy and there are various problems to be appreciated and overcome. Many of these are purely physical factors that arise from operating underwater. Obviously, it is important to position and aim the flash units correctly, but, given the magnifying effects of water, it is easy to misalign the flash head.

One of the best-known problems – and one that ruins many underwater photographs – is that of back scatter. Back scatter occurs when flash illumination is reflected by particles suspended in the water. These small particles are illuminated by light from the flash, and are recorded on film as bright or light highlights, the size and intensity of which depend on whether they are in focus or how out of focus they are. Those that are in focus are seen as light-coloured specks, while out-of-focus particles may appear in the shape of the aperture diaphragm. In either case, back scatter is an unacceptable distraction that detracts from the overall quality of a picture.

The degree to which back scatter occurs depends on various factors. Obviously, the amount of suspended particulate material in the water is a major factor. In extremely clear tropical or near-freezing water there is very little particulate matter, but in most other water there will be some suspended material that can create problems. (Indeed, sometimes there is so much suspended material in water that underwater visibility is reduced to zero.) Therefore, the most obvious way to reduce back scatter is to take underwater photographs in water that is as clear as possible. Where practical, this might mean waiting for better weather and sea conditions, or diving in another location that offers similar subject matter.

In very murky (or 'turbid') water, there is more potential for illuminating particles, and so there is more likelihood of back scatter. As the amount of water between the camera lens and the photographic subject increases, so does the

In temperate waters, visibility is rarely perfect enough to prevent at least some back scatter. Despite this, a dramatic subject such as this stinging jellyfish against a sunburst – taken off the south coast of Mull in the Inner Hebrides, Scotland – reduces the impact of such reflective particulate matter in the cool water.
Subal-housed Nikon F100 and 17–35mm lens set at 17mm, with two diffused Nikon SB105 flash units. 1/15s at f/16 on Fuji Provia 100 ISO

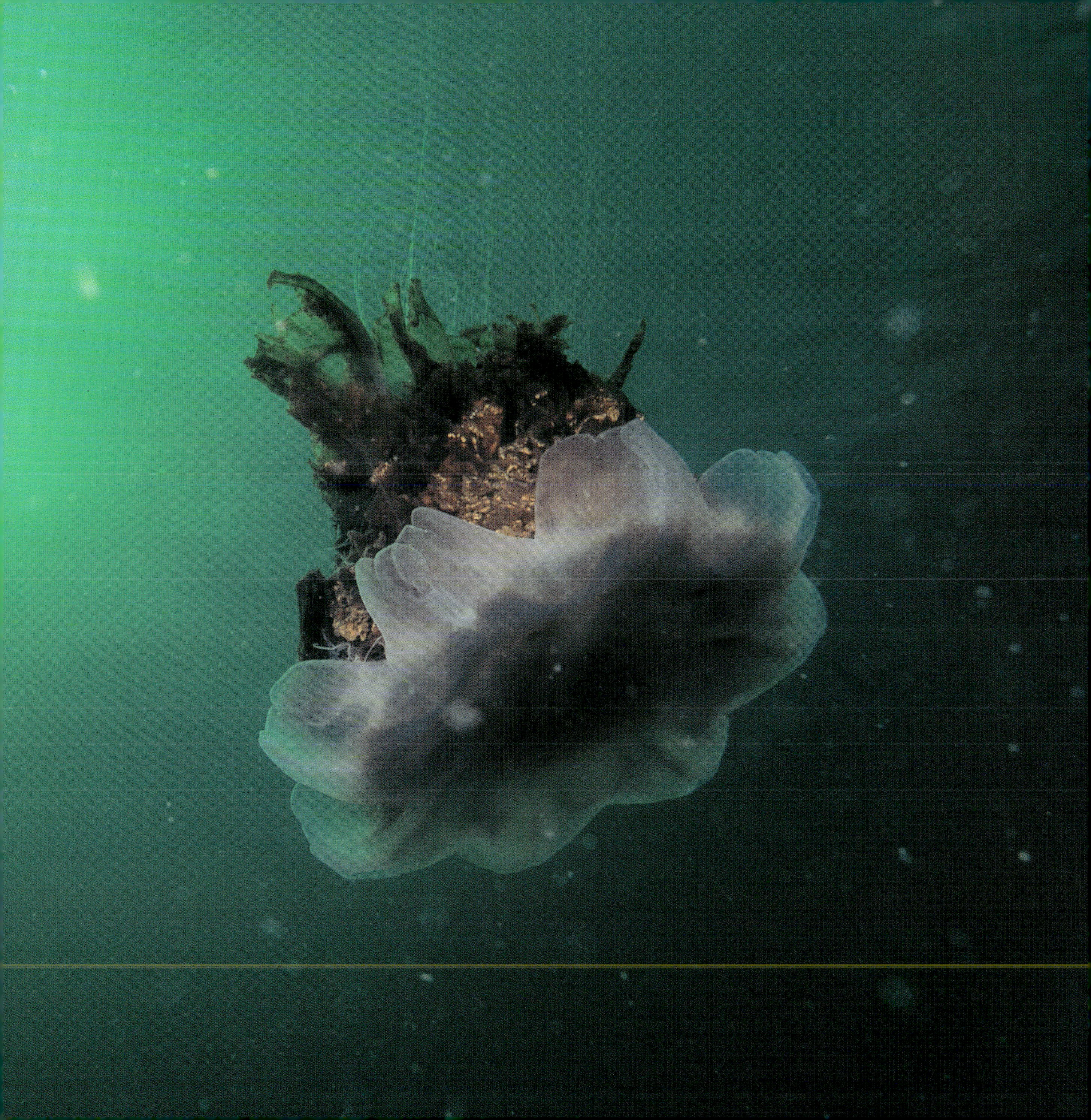

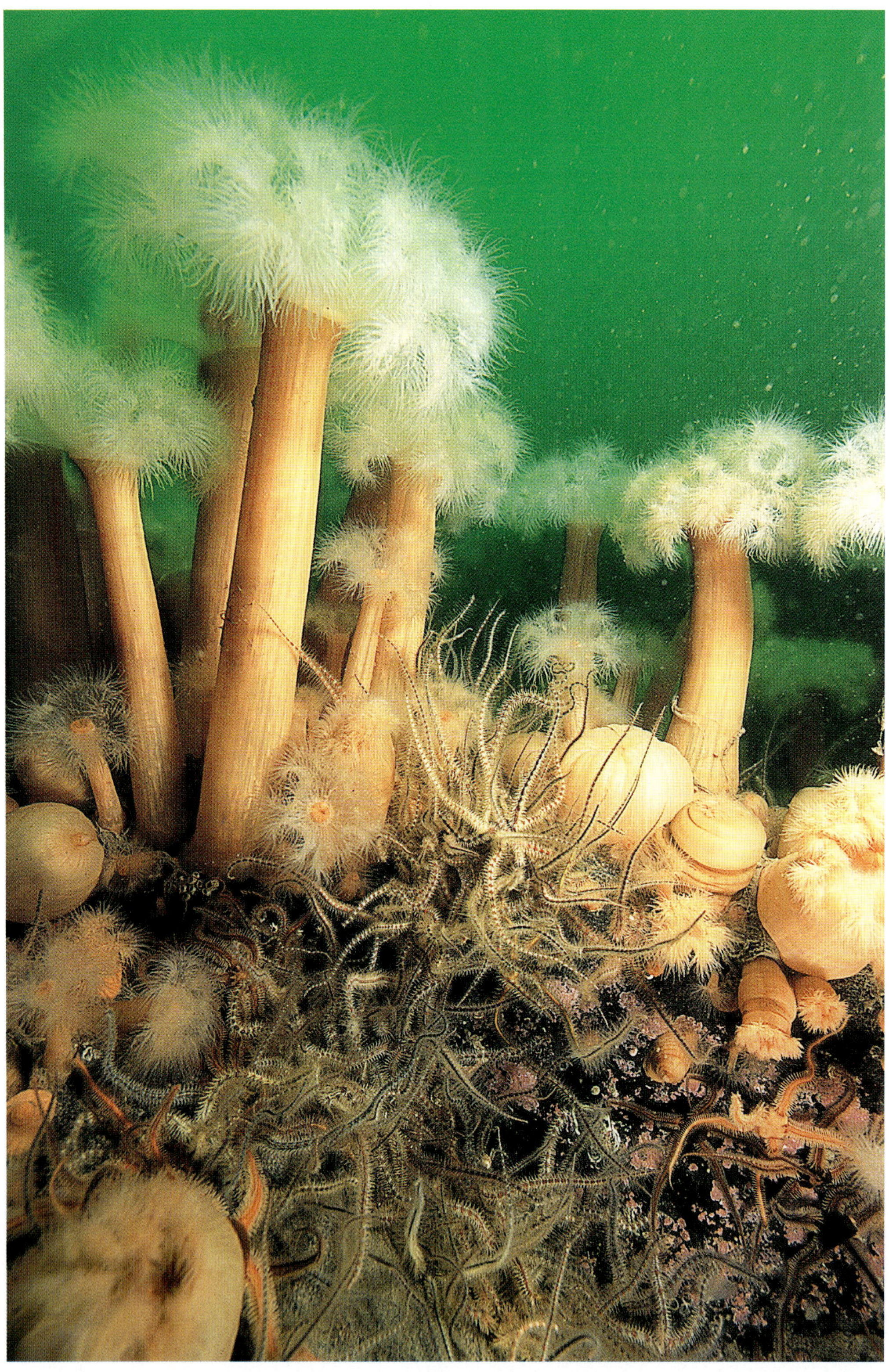

quantity of suspended particles, and, subsequently, minimizing subject-to-camera distance will reduce back scatter. Using a lens with a shorter focal length will help reduce the amount of water between the lens and subject. For example, replacing a 105mm macro lens with a 60mm lens will allow a photographer nearly to halve the distance to the subject, thus significantly reducing the amount of murky water between it and the lens. (This is one reason for the domination of wide-angle and macro lenses in underwater photography.)

In water that contains particulate matter, the closer that the flash is placed to the lens axis, the greater will be the effects of back scatter. Therefore, the angle and direction from which the flash illuminates the particles is also important. Put simply, the effects of back scatter can be minimized by positioning the flash away from the camera. Not only will this result in less light being reflected directly back into the lens, it will also help to reduce the amount of water in front of the lens that receives flash illumination, which is why articulated flash arms are so important in underwater photography.

While this can work extremely well, it often involves some form of compromise in the way that the subject is lit. The most desirable way of producing 'good' lighting may also result in high levels of back scatter, and, similarly, reducing back scatter can mean having a less than perfectly illuminated subject.

Scottish sea lochs are challenging marine environments photographically. Dark, often with poor visibility, and containing much particulate matter, they are also crammed with life. Some back scatter is almost inevitable.

Subal-housed Nikon F100 and 17–35mm lens set at 17mm, with two diffused Nikon SB105 flash units. 1/8s at f/16 on Fuji Provia 100 ISO

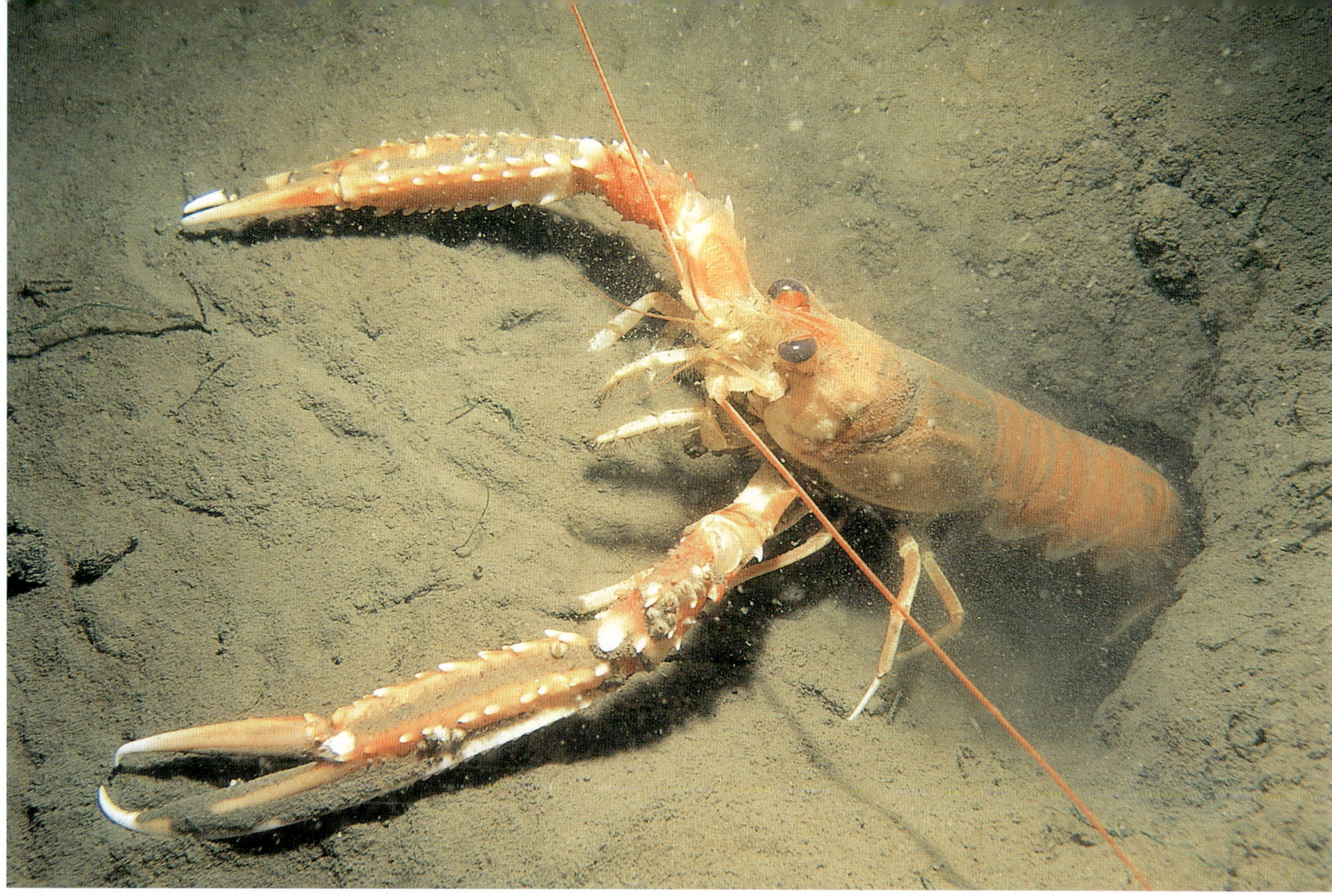

Some subjects, like scampi (*Nephrops norvegicus*), live in notoriously low-visibility habitats such as mud burrows. Placing flash (the only light source) almost above the animal results in acceptable lighting with minimal back scatter. Luiung Island, west Scotland. *Subal-housed Nikon F801 and 60mm micro-Nikkor lens, with two Nikon SB105 flash units. 1/60s at f/16 on Fuji Velvia 50 ISO*

A smack of moon jellyfish (*Aurelia aurita*) greeted us as we surfaced from a fabulous dive off the Aran Islands in Galway Bay, Ireland. I used just a little flash to boost contrast and accepted that there might be a little back scatter. *Subal-housed Nikon F100 and 17–35mm lens set at 17mm, with two diffused Nikon SB105 flash units. 1/60s at f/11 on Fuji Provia 100 ISO*

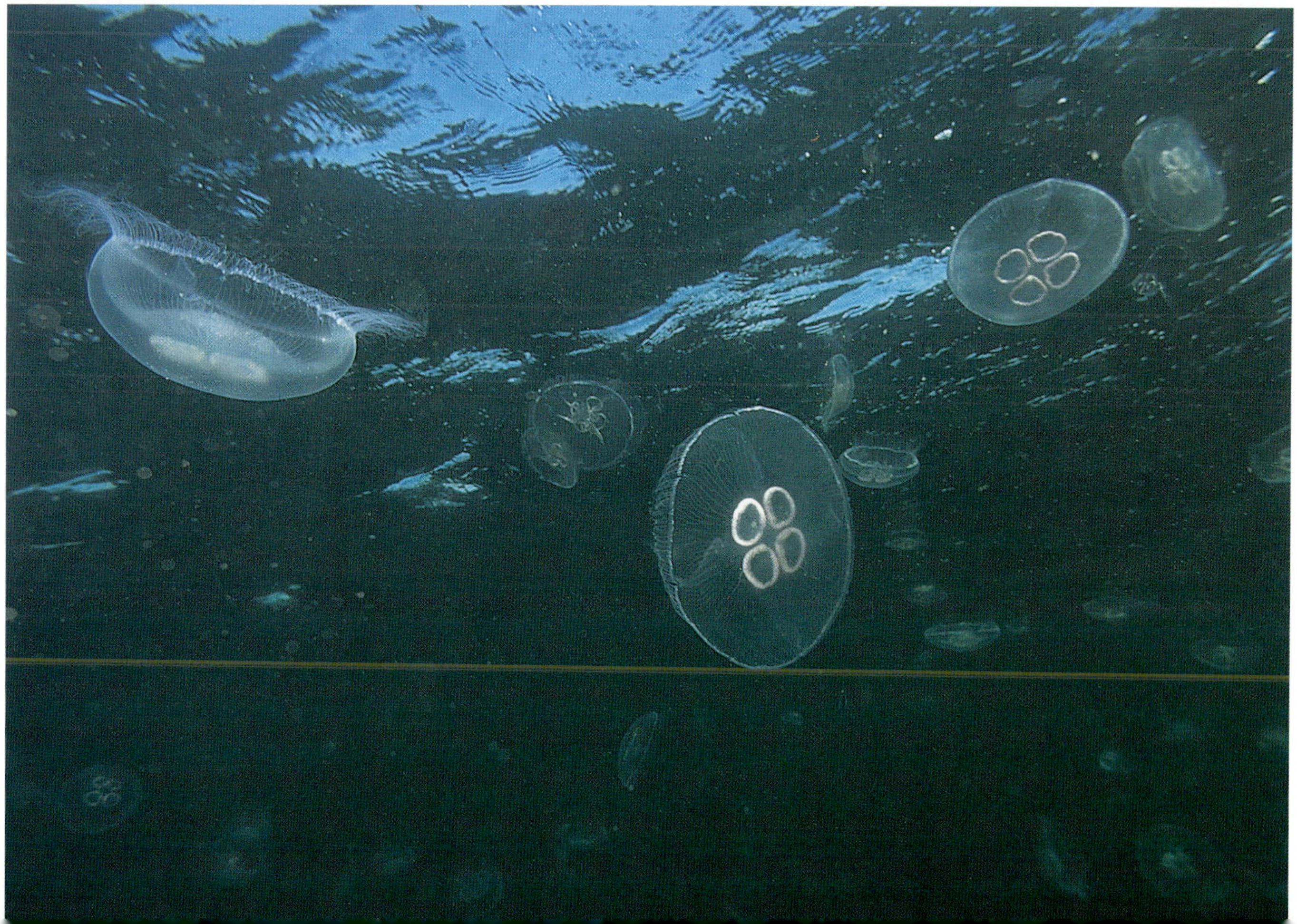

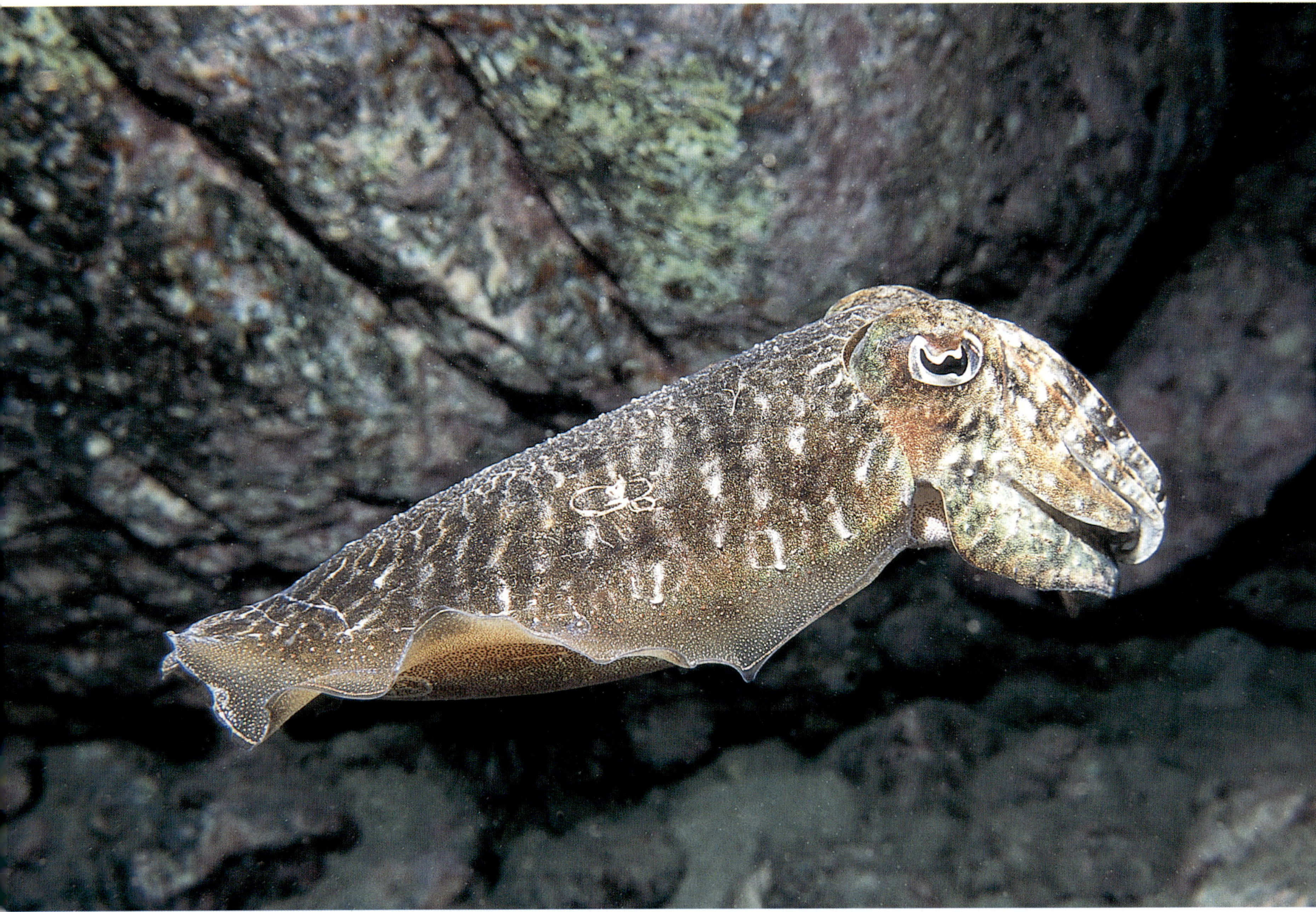

This cuttlefish (*Sepia officinalis*), off La Gomera, swam sedately around in the shallow water over tumbling bedrock and showed little concern while being photographed. Differential focus allowed the background to blur acceptably, but even in the relatively clear water some particulate matter is still evident.
Subal-housed Nikon F80, and 28–105mm lens set at 50mm. 1/60s at f/11 on Fuji Provia 100 ISO

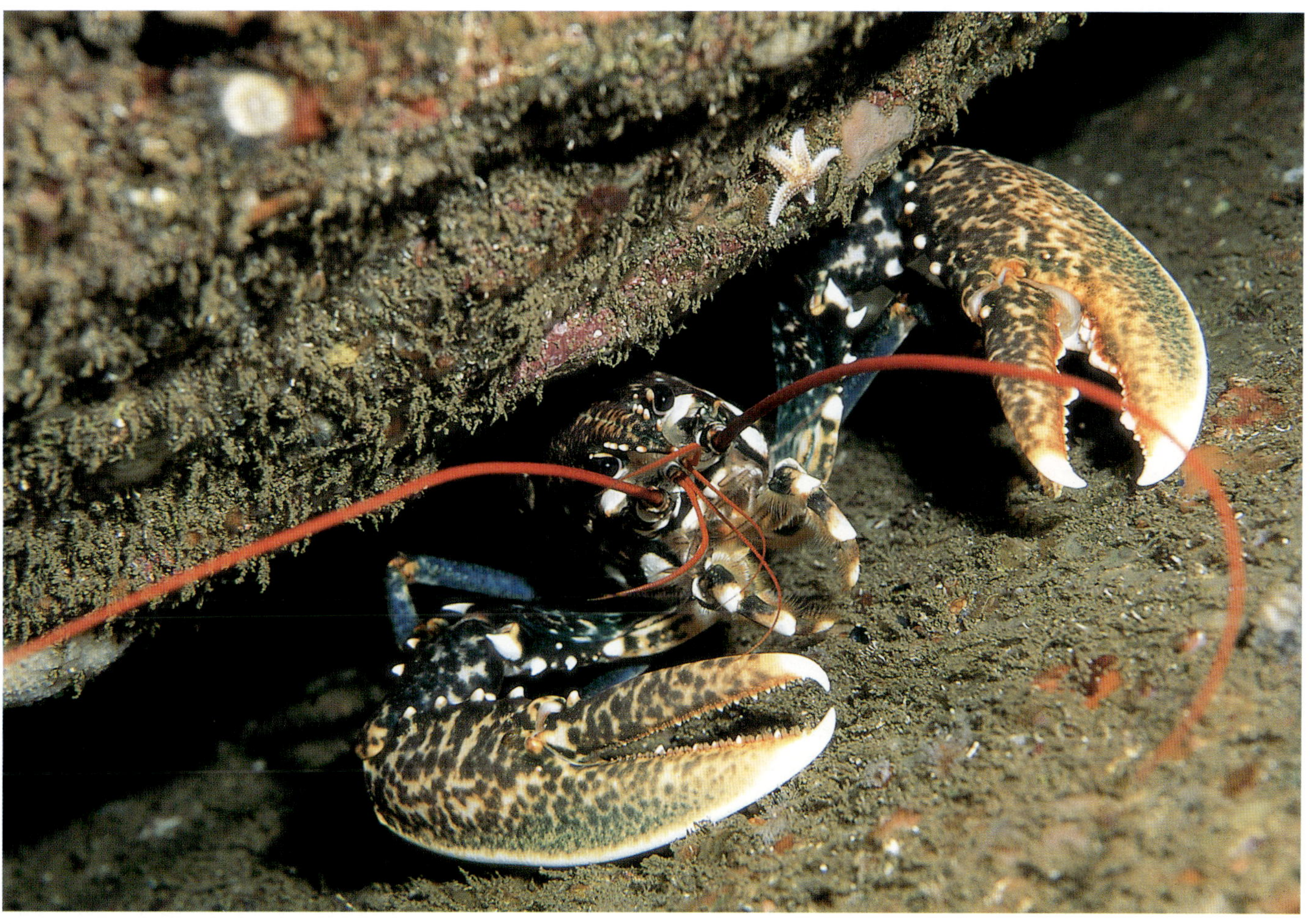

A very clean common lobster (*Homarus gammarus*) from south-west Kerry in Ireland.
Subal-housed Nikon F801 and 60mm micro-Nikkor lens. Taken by single flash illumination alone. 1/60s at f/16 on Fuji Velvia 50 ISO

Flash illumination and field of view

Many underwater cameras are supplied with a flash set-up that can be regarded as a standard, quite effective compromise. This is when the flash unit is mounted on a simple arm that sits to the photographer's left (when the camera is pointing away from the photographer), usually with the flash on about the same plane as the camera. The lighting that this gives is excellent for some subjects, adequate for many more, and only becomes poor when wide-angle lenses or increased subject-to-camera distance force further compromise.

If a simple flash arm is supplied with a flash unit, it will almost certainly be designed to give this type of lighting. As mentioned previously, whatever flash unit is used, it will be improved immeasurably by adding a sturdy articulated flash arm. However, to further improve the effectiveness of a flash unit, it is worth trying to perceive how light from a flash operates, and how it interacts with the field of view of a lens. (A diagram illustrating this can be found in the Appendix, on page 172.)

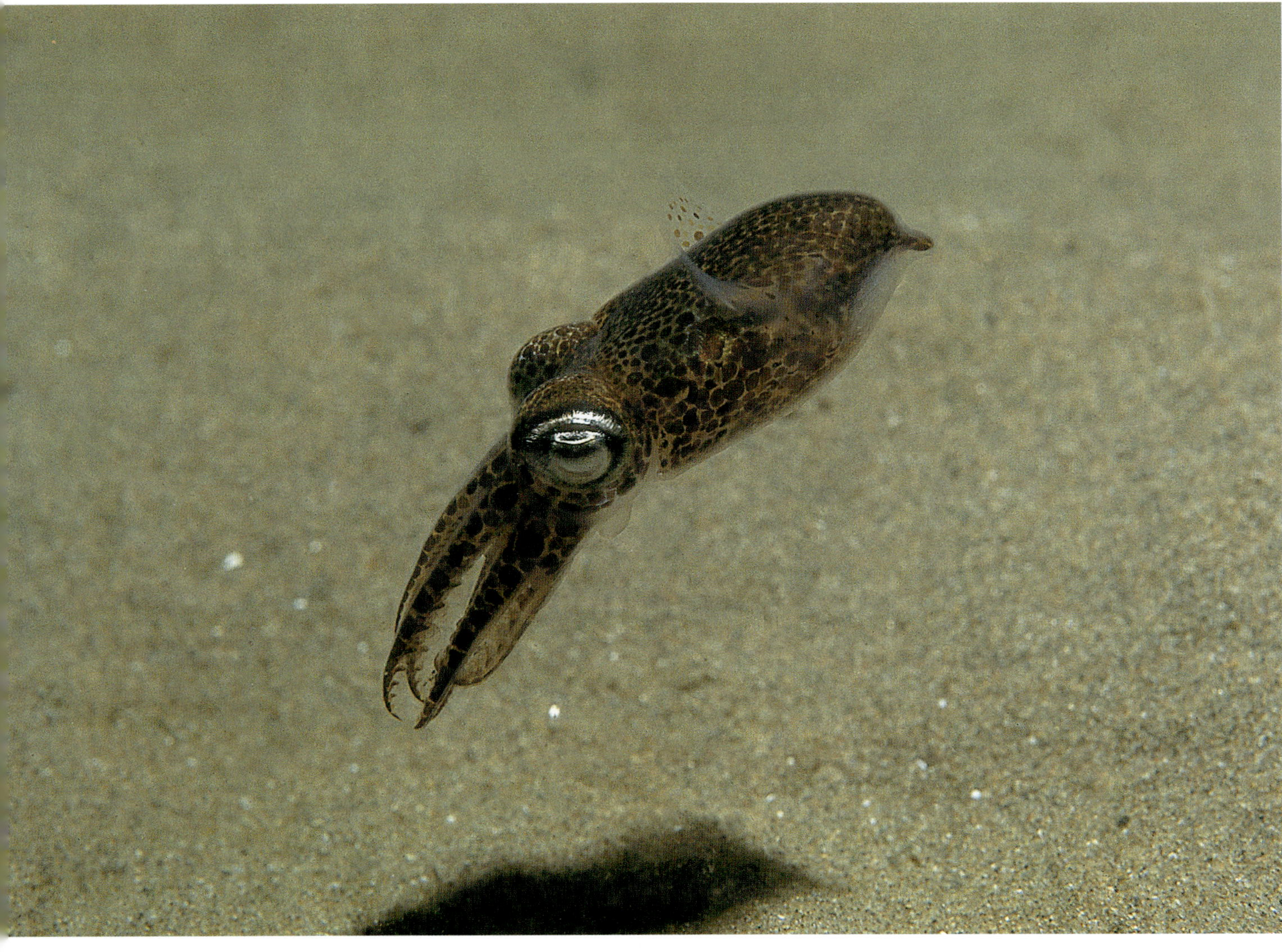

By using the flash almost overhead to photograph this little cuttlefish (*Sepia atlantica*), it is possible to reduce back scatter to an absolute minimum, even over the sandy seabed of Cardigan Bay in North Wales. ***Subal-housed Nikon F801 and 60mm micro-Nikkor, with a Nikon SB105 flash unit. 1/60s at f/16 on Fuji Velvia 50 ISO***

A camera lens will 'see' a rectangular picture, and the water seen within this picture is shaped like an elongated pyramid. The length and shape of this pyramid will depend on the focal length of the lens in use, the type of port that it is viewing through, and the lens-to-subject distance. Most flash units, on the other hand, operate by producing a circle of light, and the water illuminated within this circle is cone-shaped. Again, the exact length and shape of this cone will depend on the angular coverage of the flash and the flash-to-subject distance.

Clearly, the interaction between these two shapes needs to be adjusted to meet various conditions. These include minimizing back scatter, enabling even illumination to fall on the subject and its surroundings, and providing the subject with acceptable lighting. The interaction between flash light and available light (if any) must also be taken into account when assessing a scene.

This might sound complex, but in practice the positioning of a flash unit is restricted for obvious and straightforward reasons. The flash unit should not be placed too near the lens axis to help reduce back scatter. Nor should it be placed too far away from the subject, as there will always be a limit on how far away the flash can be used and still remain effective (due to its power output and the area of illumination that it can provide). Also, if the unit is placed too close to the subject, it may not be possible to quench the flash if used in TTL mode, and the cone of illumination may no longer cover the area seen by the lens.

As a flash unit is moved away from the camera lens axis, the illumination becomes more oblique, the lighting becomes 'harder' and shadows deeper. As a result, the lighting ceases to be effective and produces images that are unacceptable. This could be expressed in terms of an 'illuminating angle' – a shallow illuminating angle can provide better lighting but tends to increase back scatter, while a steep illuminating angle reduces back scatter but may provide poor lighting. The 'standard' illumination provided by a simple flash set-up is designed to operate at a medium illuminating angle, and is a compromise between the two. Given a reasonably close subject, it can work very well and provide acceptable lighting. Ultimately, despite its limitations, it is a good position for new underwater photographers to start from.

By understanding and visualizing the interaction between the cone of illumination from the flash and the pyramid of view of the lens, it becomes clear that the effects of back scatter are reduced the less the two overlap. While the number of particles between camera and subject matter does not change when the overlap is reduced, fewer of them can be illuminated. This is a very effective way of considering flash illumination and its effects, and quickly shows that variables such as flash-to-subject distance can be used to alter the overlap of the cones while still maintaining a reasonable illumination angle.

Only physical constraints and the flexibility of the flash arm limit the potential for varied flash positioning. Some underwater photographers prefer to use a hand-held flash unit, so providing even more versatility.

Illuminating angles for macro subjects

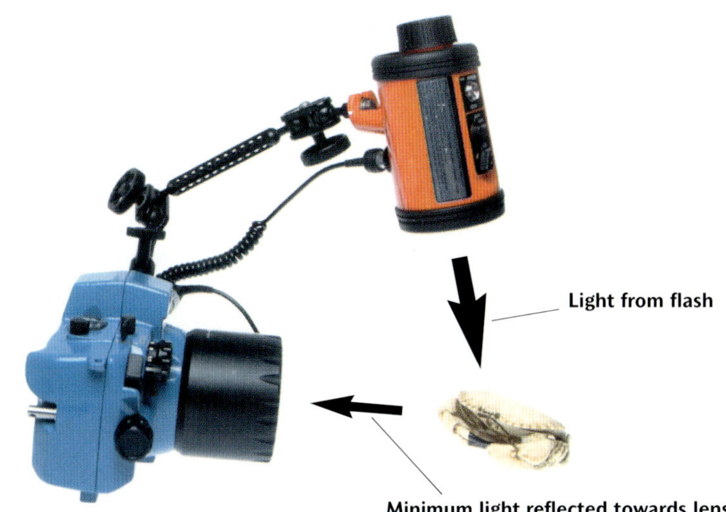

Least backscatter but flash too far overhead, creating severe shadowing

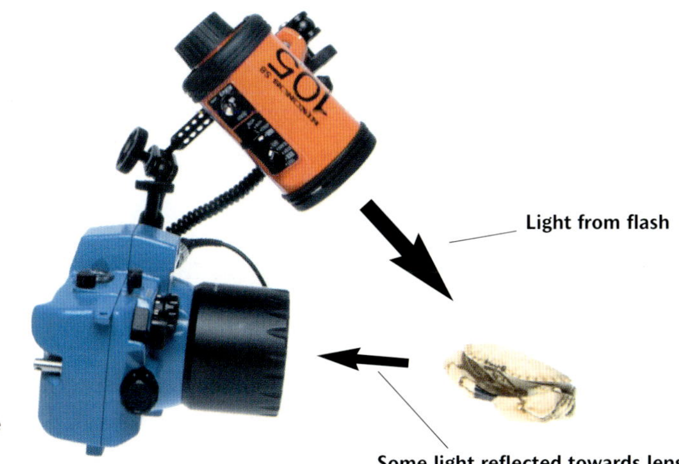

Best compromise: not too much backscatter and lighting acceptable

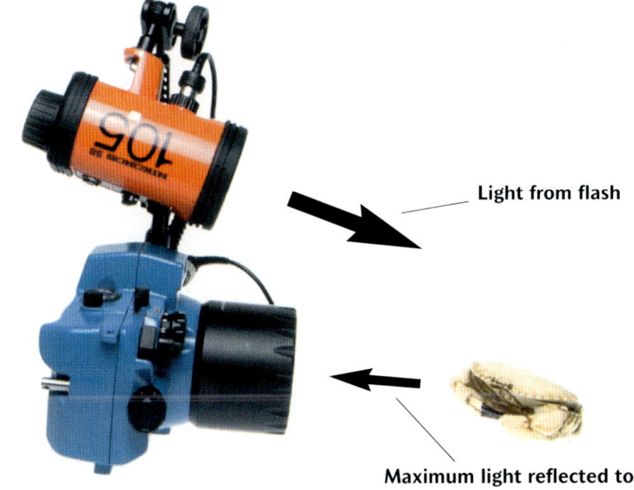

Lighting good but flash too close to lens axis, creating most backscatter

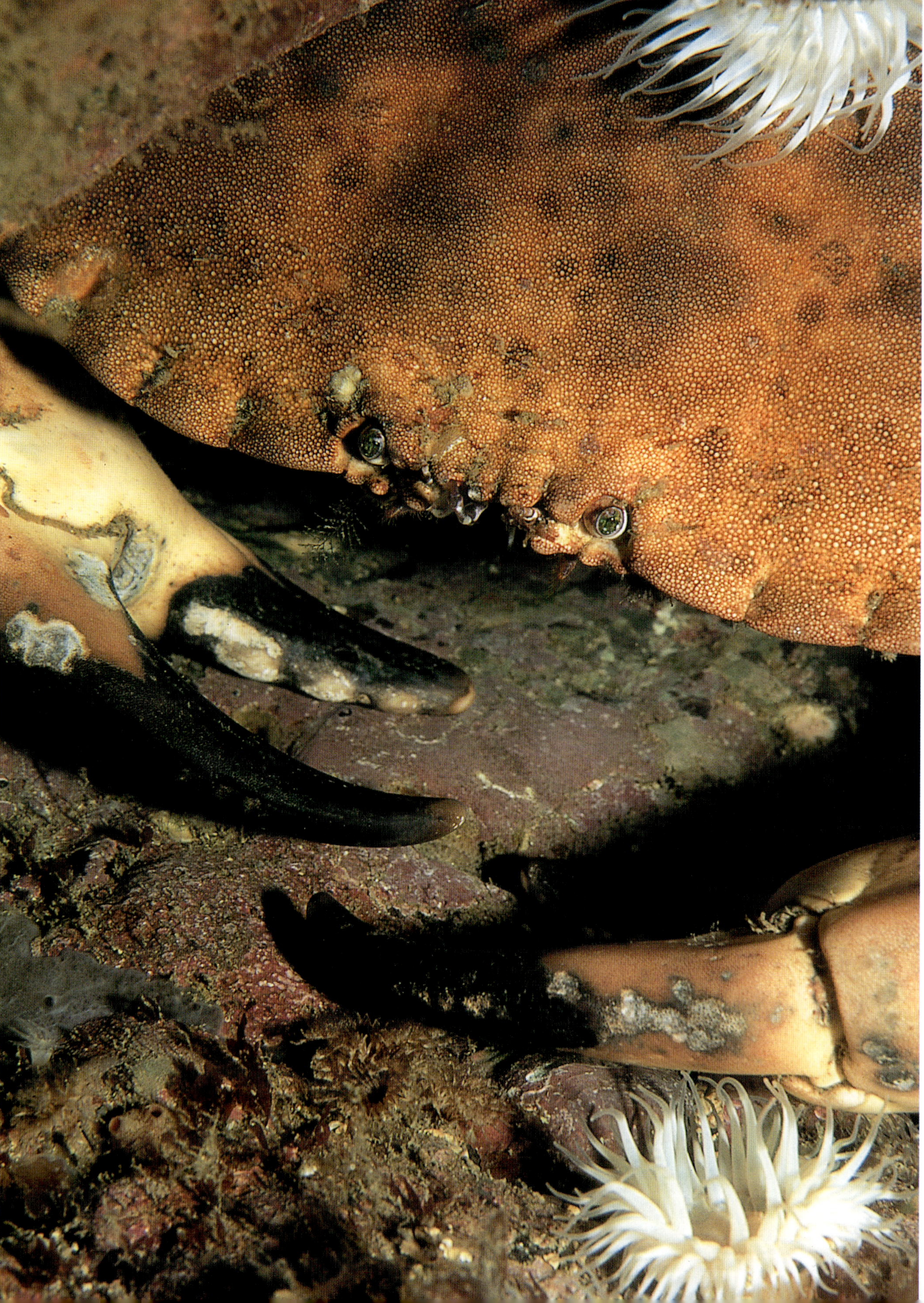

This rather gnarled edible crab (*Cancer pagurus*) has been photographed to make a symbolic composition. Harsh lighting has resulted in deep shadows, but the overall effect is one of a harsh creature living in a difficult environment. Shot off the Isle of Man, UK, using flash alone.
Subal-housed Nikon F100 and 60mm micro-Nikkor lens, with a Nikon SB105 flash unit. 1/60s at f/22 on Fuji Velvia 50 ISO

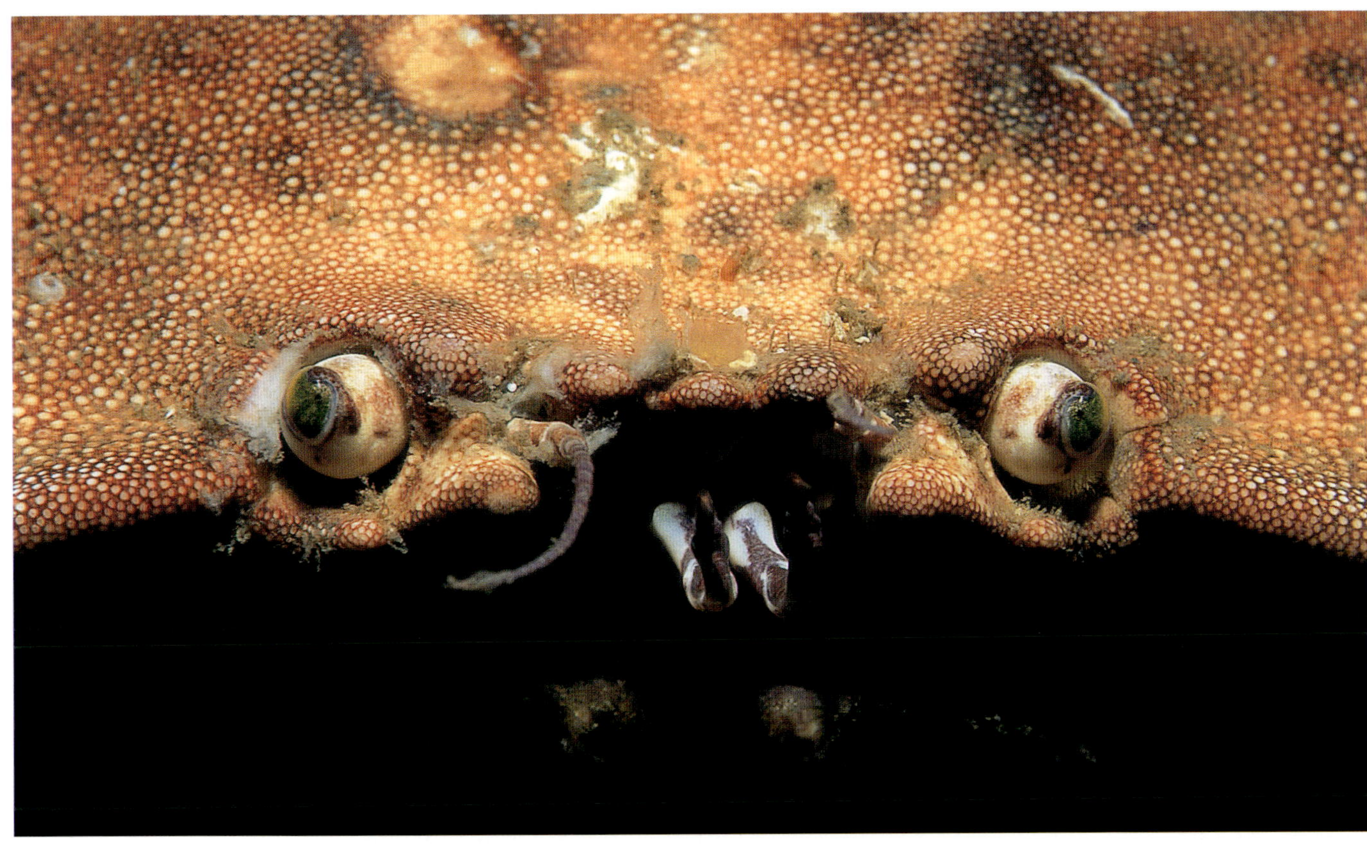

Extreme close-up views of creatures, such as this edible crab (*Cancer pagurus*) off the Isle of Man, reveals textural and other fine detail. Lighting can become difficult and care needs to be taken to ensure that harsh shadows do not detract from the overall image.
Subal-housed Nikon F100 and 60mm micro-Nikkor lens, with a Nikon SB105 flash unit. 1/60s at f/22 on Fuji Velvia 50 ISO

Macro lighting

One of the problems associated with flash photography is that the use of single flash units can produce harsh and unpleasant shadowing. This can be overcome in several ways. Bringing the flash closer to the subject than normal is perhaps the simplest method and an effective technique for macro photography, providing 'softer' illumination by making the flash reflector relatively large in comparison with the subject. It also means that less of the water between the subject and the lens is illuminated, and so reduces the possibility of back scatter.

One drawback of using this method is that if the flash unit is placed too close to the subject, TTL flash control may not be able to quench it quickly enough – even if a very small aperture is used – and an image may be overexposed as a result. Another problem is that it may soften the light too much, leading to a reduction in contrast and definition. This will depend on the subject to some extent, but it is very effective in many cases and is always available as an option.

Another solution is to fit a diffuser over the flash (purpose-designed wide-angle diffusers are available for some units). Again, this softens the light and reduces shadowing, but it can also flatten the picture too much and reduce overall contrast and definition. It also diminishes the light output, and may result in insufficient flash power.

The physical size of both the camera and the flash unit can cause problems when attempting to illuminate very small macro subjects. If the camera lens/port is in

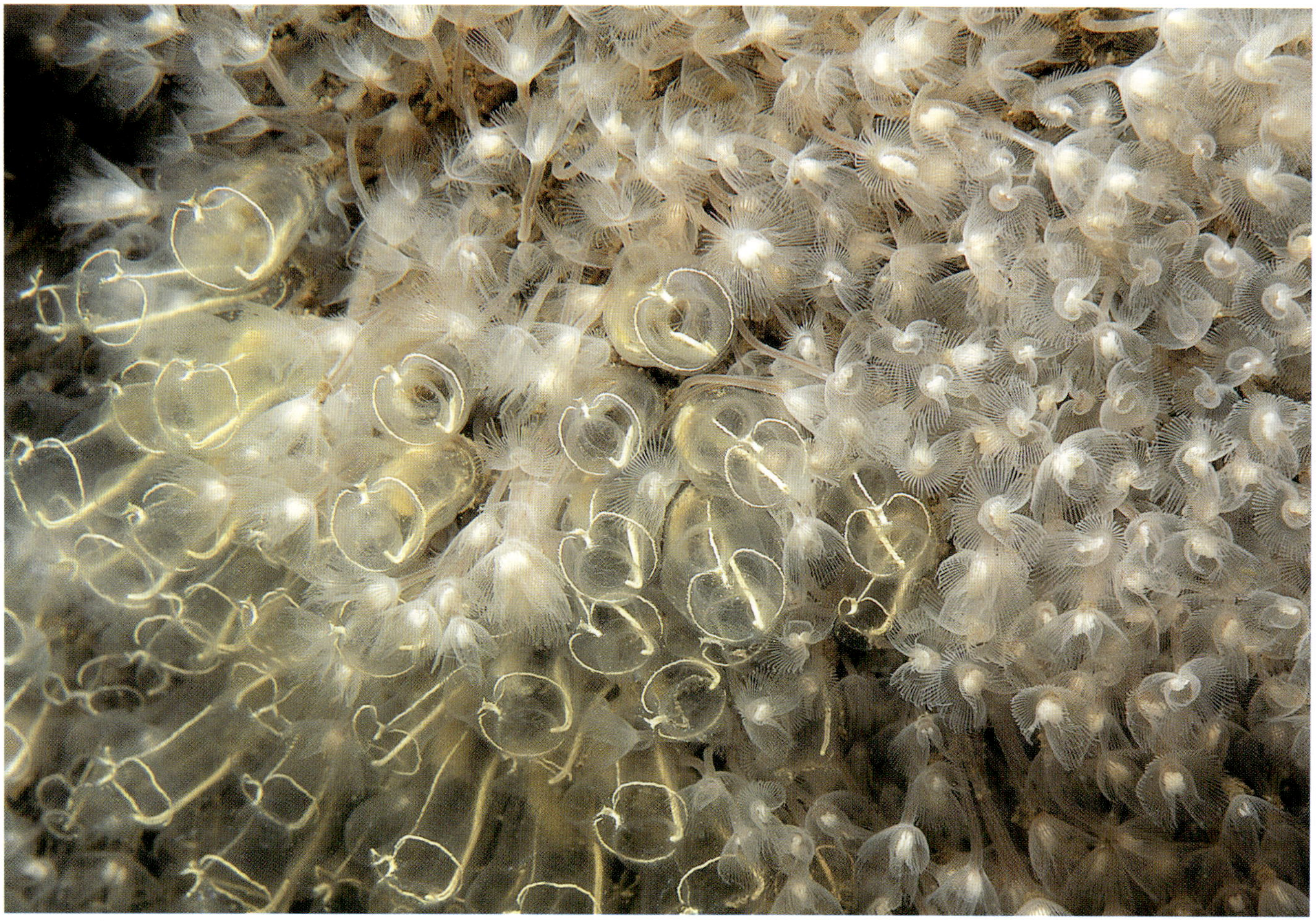

The Gower, in South Wales, contains much limestone, which attracts many rock-boring creatures underwater. This 1:1 (life-size) macro shot shows a very small area of rock covered in horseshoe worms and light-bulb sea squirts, and was taken by flash alone.
Subal-housed Nikon F801 and 60mm micro-Nikkor lens, with a Nikon SB105 flash unit. 1/60s at f/16 on Fuji Velvia 50 ISO

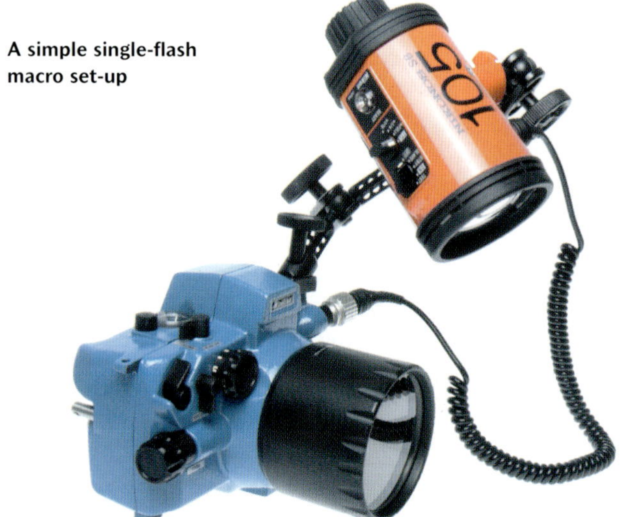

A simple single-flash macro set-up

the way, it simply may not be possible to place the flash unit in an ideal position, and the lighting may have to be quite oblique. One way around this is to use a macro lens with a longer focal length so that the working distance (i.e. the distance between lens and subject) is increased and there is more room to move the flash unit. Another alternative is to use small, narrow macro ports. It is important to be aware that this may limit the way that a lens operates (such as cutting off the corners of an image when used at a longer distance), but they can help to increase the space available for a flash unit. Such ports are not always widely produced, but many custom-built versions are available.

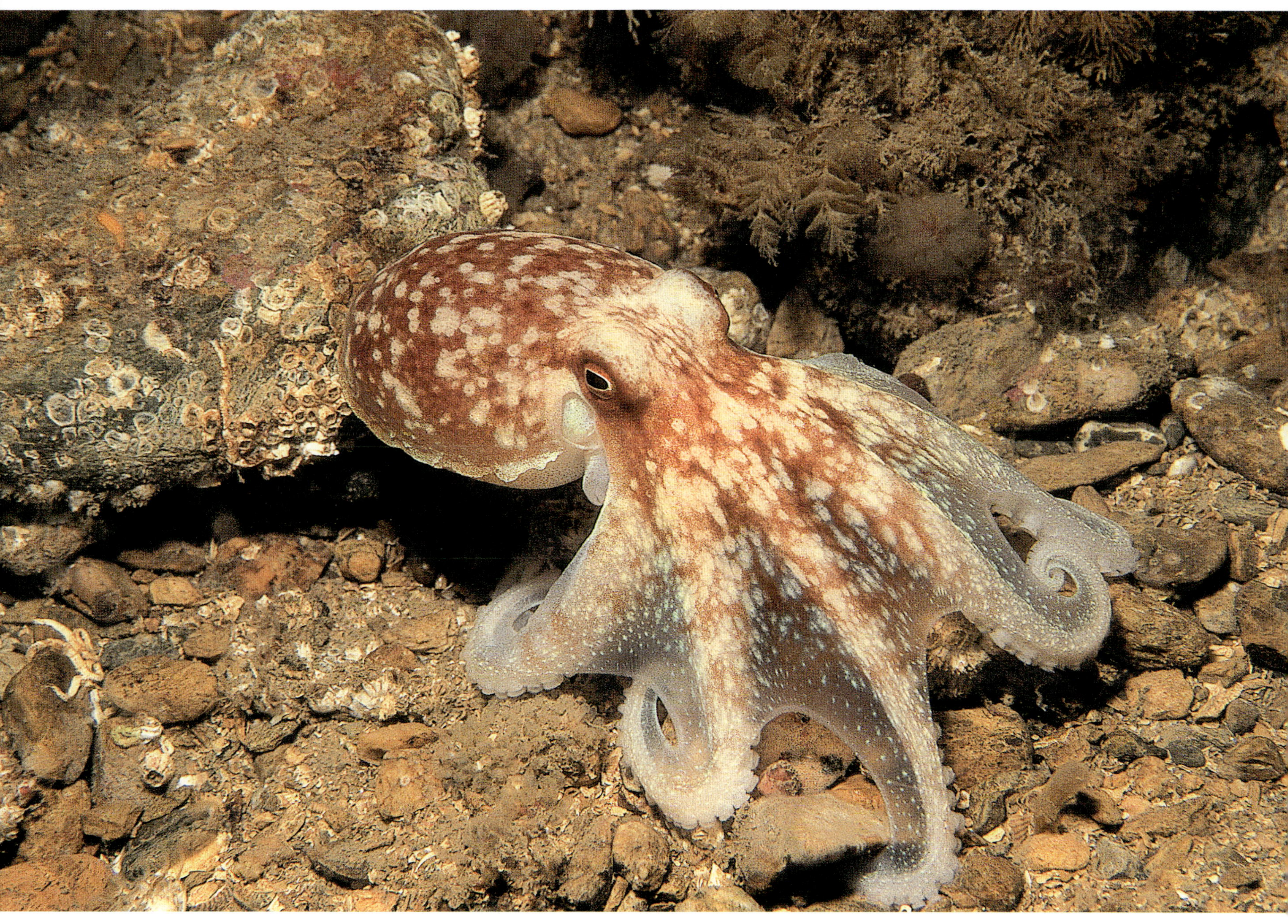

Many subjects, such as this lesser octopus (*Eledone cirrhosa*), from Bardsey Island, North Wales, require very simple single-flash lighting. Care needs to be taken to ensure that shadows do not become too harsh or elongated.
Subal-housed Nikon F801 and 60mm micro-Nikkor lens, with a Nikon SB105 flash unit. 1/30s at f/16 on Fuji Velvia 50 ISO

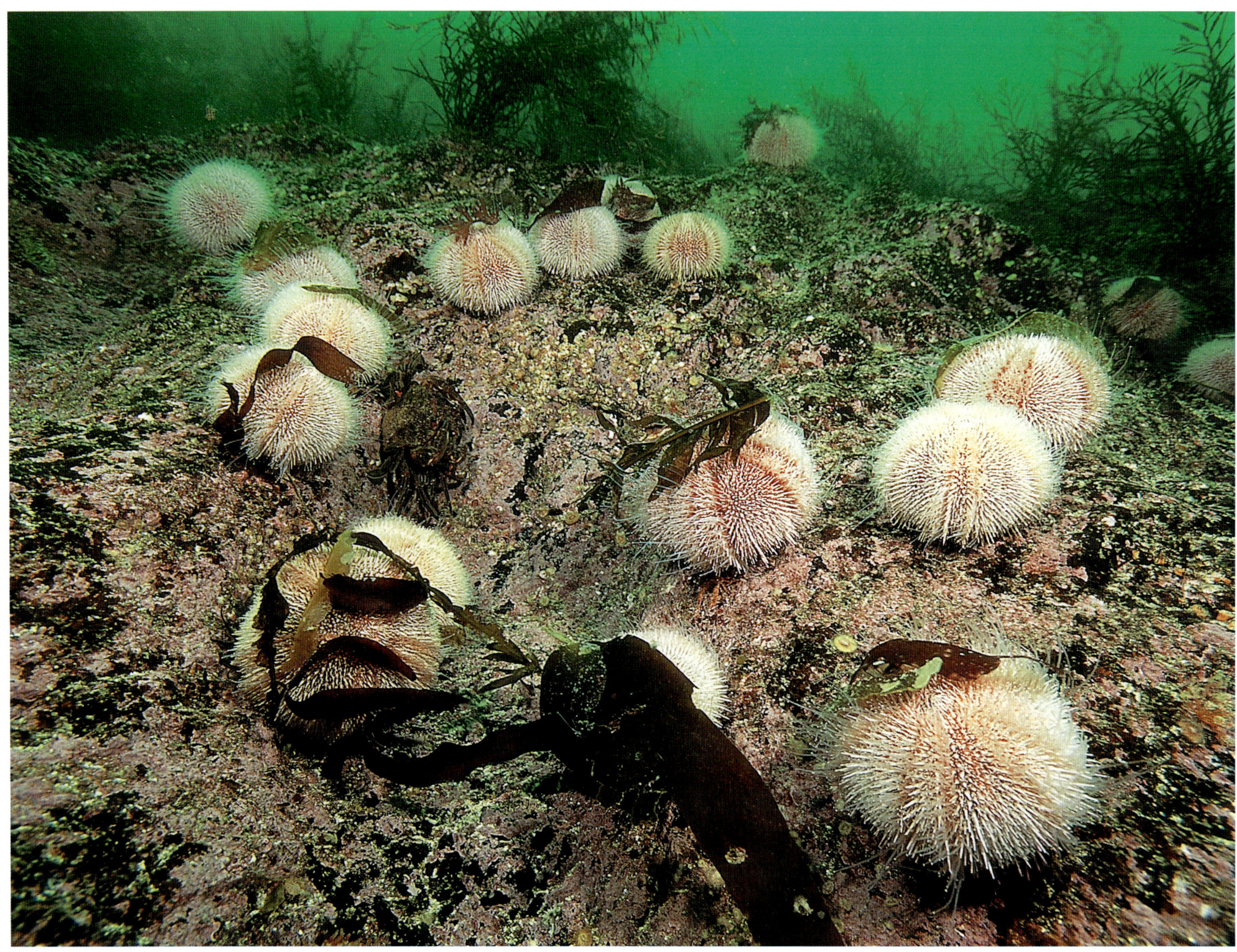

Sea urchins photographed grazing over bedrock on the western side of the Outer Hebrides. This shot was taken at 17mm using available light plus two diffused flash units, at a depth of around 20 metres.
1/15s at f/16 on Fuji Provia 100 ISO

Using multiple flash units

A popular – if more expensive – way of reducing unwanted hard shadows is to direct light onto them from a second flash unit. Any additional units are usually of reduced power compared to the main illuminating unit, although this can be achieved by fitting a diffuser or positioning it at a greater distance from the subject.

Using twin flash units does present some technical problems. Some camera housings are fitted with two flash sockets, but if not either a 'splitter' unit (which allows two flash cables to connect to one socket) or a cordless 'slave' unit can be used. Various configurations are available depending on whether precise TTL control is wanted, or whether a small manual flash unit will suffice.

Ring flash

There have been several attempts to utilize ring flash units underwater. These are, as their name indicates, flash units built as a ring that surrounds the camera lens. They can be effective, but as they are inherently close to the lens axis, they are only suitable for either very close-up photography or for use in very clear water. The 'shadowless' lighting that they produce is not to everyone's taste, although they do have their exponents. Whether they are worth considering is a matter of personal opinion.

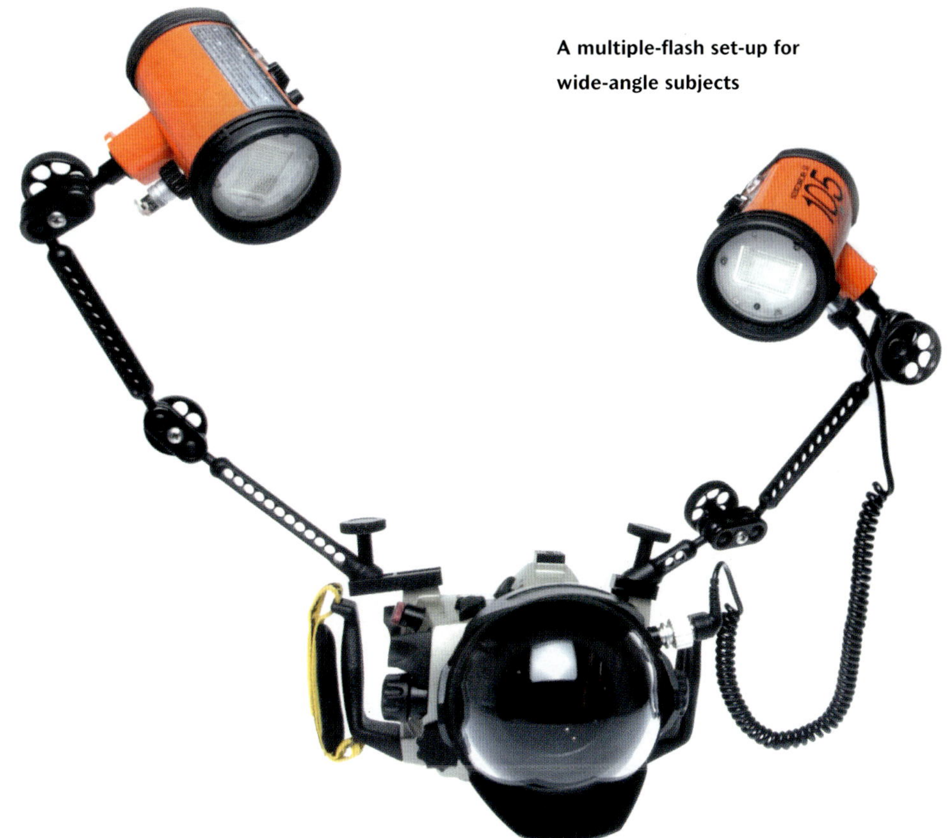

A multiple-flash set-up for wide-angle subjects

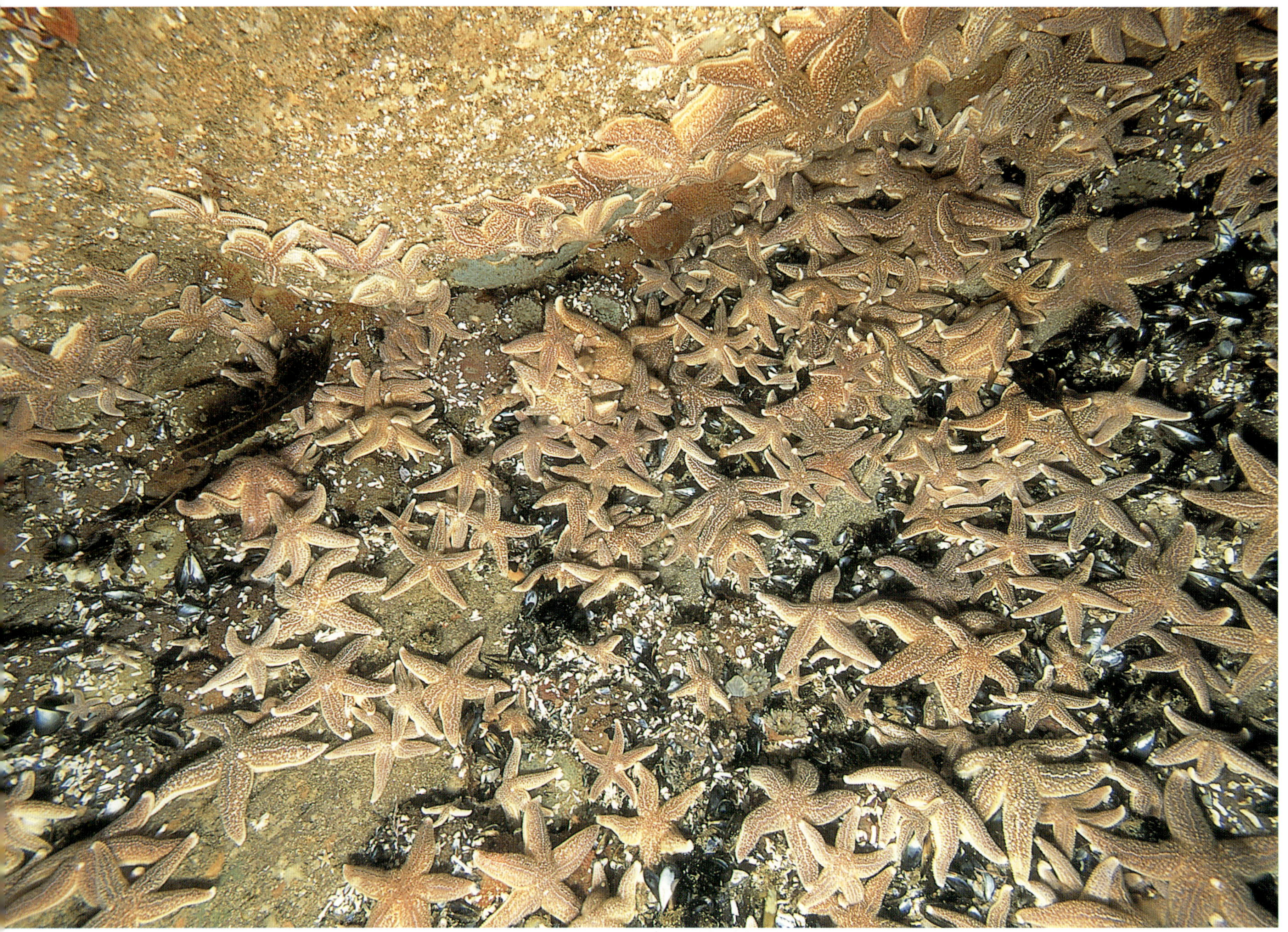

Sometimes a shot has to be taken in a less than ideal situation. Off Dursey Island in County Cork, Ireland, common starfish (*Asterias rubens*) gather in large numbers to feast off the mussels washed from the cliffs above. They are clustered in the bottom of gullies and it is difficult to squeeze into these with a camera. This shot had to be taken with two diffused flash units located where physically possible, and the lens set at 17mm to show the scale of the massed starfish.
Subal-housed Nikon F100. Fuji Provia 100 ISO

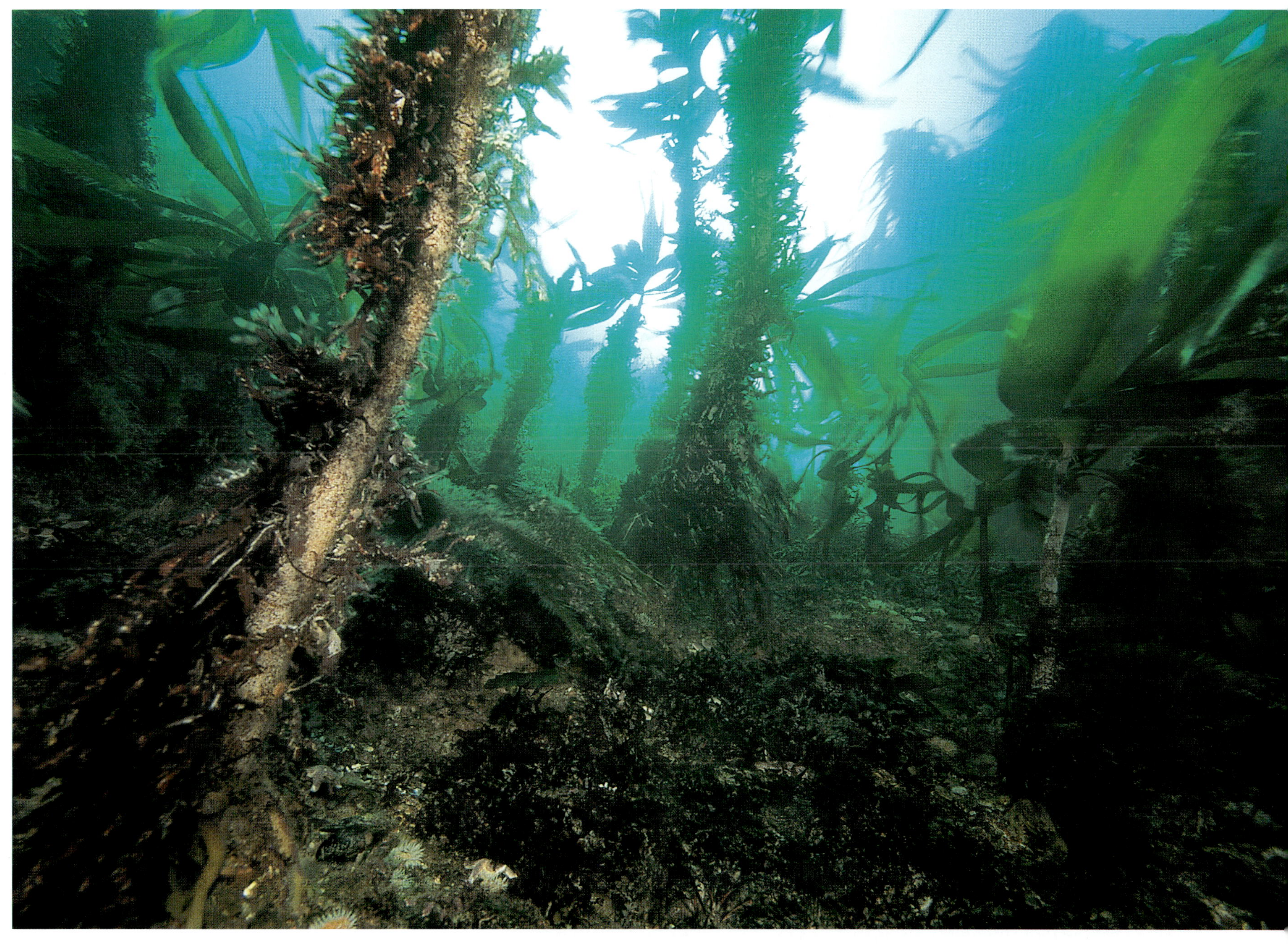

The addition of two diffused flashes at full power has provided sufficient foreground illumination to add interest to this against-the-light kelp photo. Taken in the Outer Hebrides, Scotland.
Subal-housed Nikon F100 and 17–35mm lens set at 17mm, with two diffused Nikon SB105 flash units. 1/4s at f/16 on Fuji Provia 100 ISO

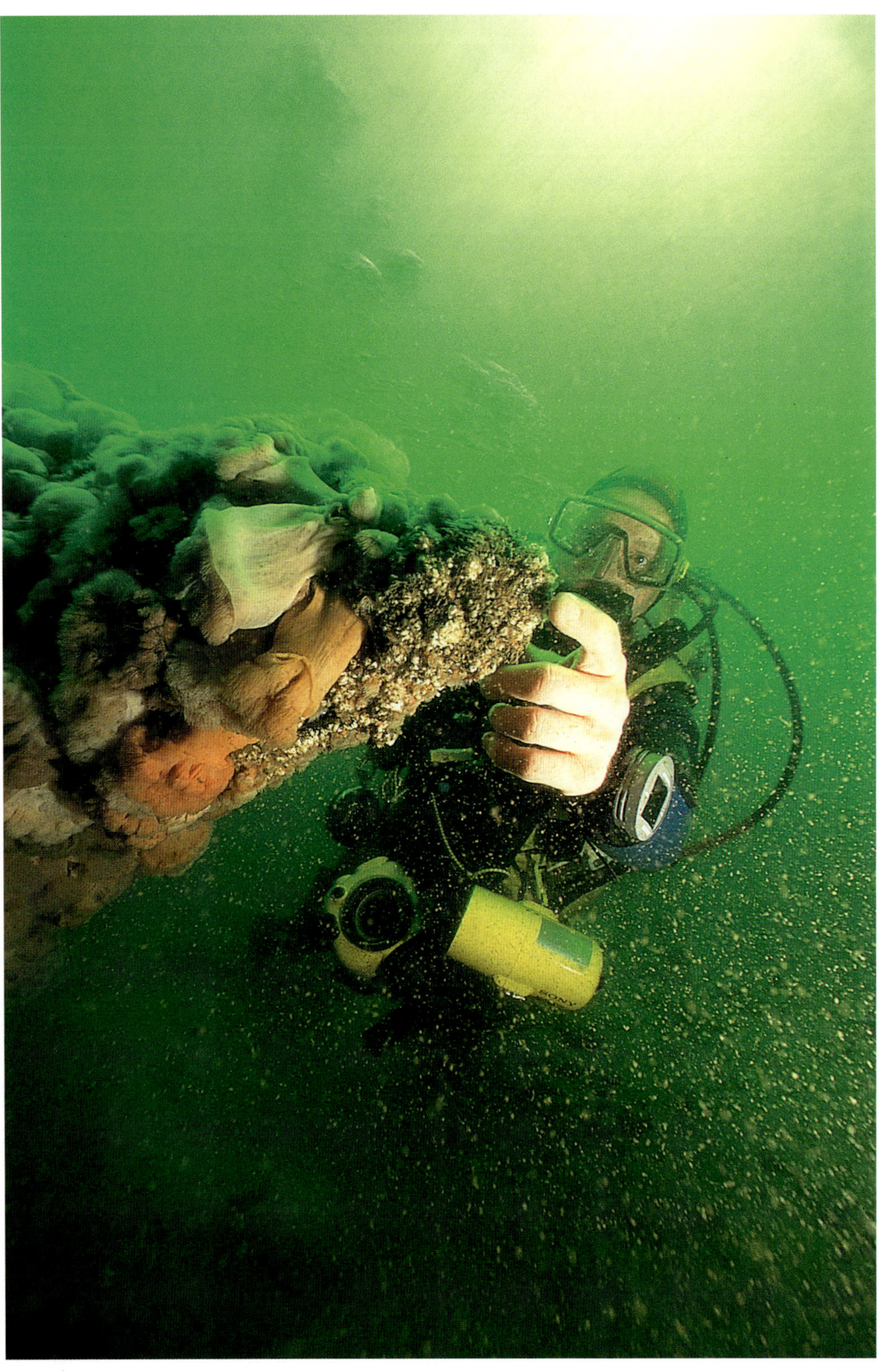

Using two flash units in TTL mode presents some additional technical problems. In general it is thought best to use two similar flash units, or at least two from the same manufacturer. This is because flash units vary in how they operate. Some have longer 'burn' times than others, and this may mean that two dissimilar units would give inconsistent results if used together in TTL mode.

Wide-angle lighting

Illuminating wide-angle subjects by flash alone is no easy task. In essence, the simplest way to light any such subject is to use a flash with a cone of illumination that provides adequate coverage, and to place it in such a way that it illuminates the subject at an angle that will minimize back scatter. However, there are a number of other factors to take into consideration.

As parts of a subject recede into the distance, the flash illumination is unable to expose them correctly, and they may become too dark. Therefore, the biggest problem is to ensure that the light covering the subject is sufficiently even to provide correct exposure.

Flash illumination can be made to fall on the subject evenly by placing the flash unit so that its illumination axis is perpendicular to the plane of the subject (see pages 117 and 141). This will give a reasonably even exposure with an appropriate subject, but means that a high percentage of the camera's field of view is illuminated. As a result, wide-angle photography by flash alone is inherently problematic.

The wreck of the world's first (steam-driven) submarine lies in the murky and current-swept waters of Liverpool Bay, UK. Both of these factors can be seen in this picture, and back scatter is inevitable under such conditions.
Subal-housed Nikon F801 and 20mm Nikkor lens, with two diffused Nikon SB105 flash units. 1/4s at f/11 on Fuji Provia 100 ISO

balanced light

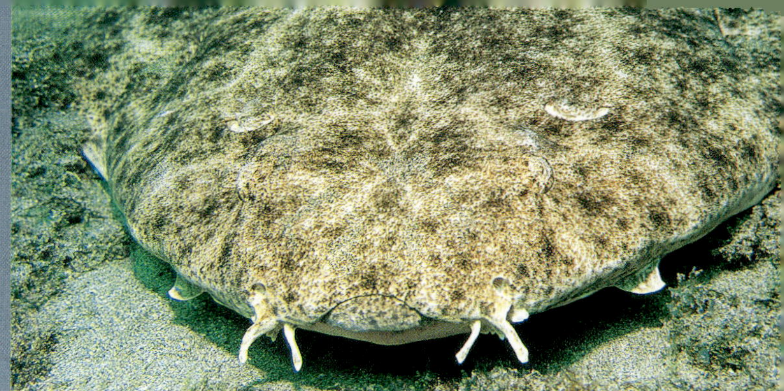

Balanced light describes the use of two different sources of light in such a way that they combine to produce an exposure that captures an image as intended by the photographer. Mixing light sources is not as difficult as it is sometimes thought to be, and the chance of success relies mainly on a photographer's appreciation and understanding of the scene under consideration.

By far the biggest problem to overcome when attempting to produce a photograph containing mixed illumination is that of visualizing the end result. Indeed, until an underwater photographer is quite familiar with how both flash and available light sources produce images independently, it is very difficult to develop an accurate appreciation of how they will work together.

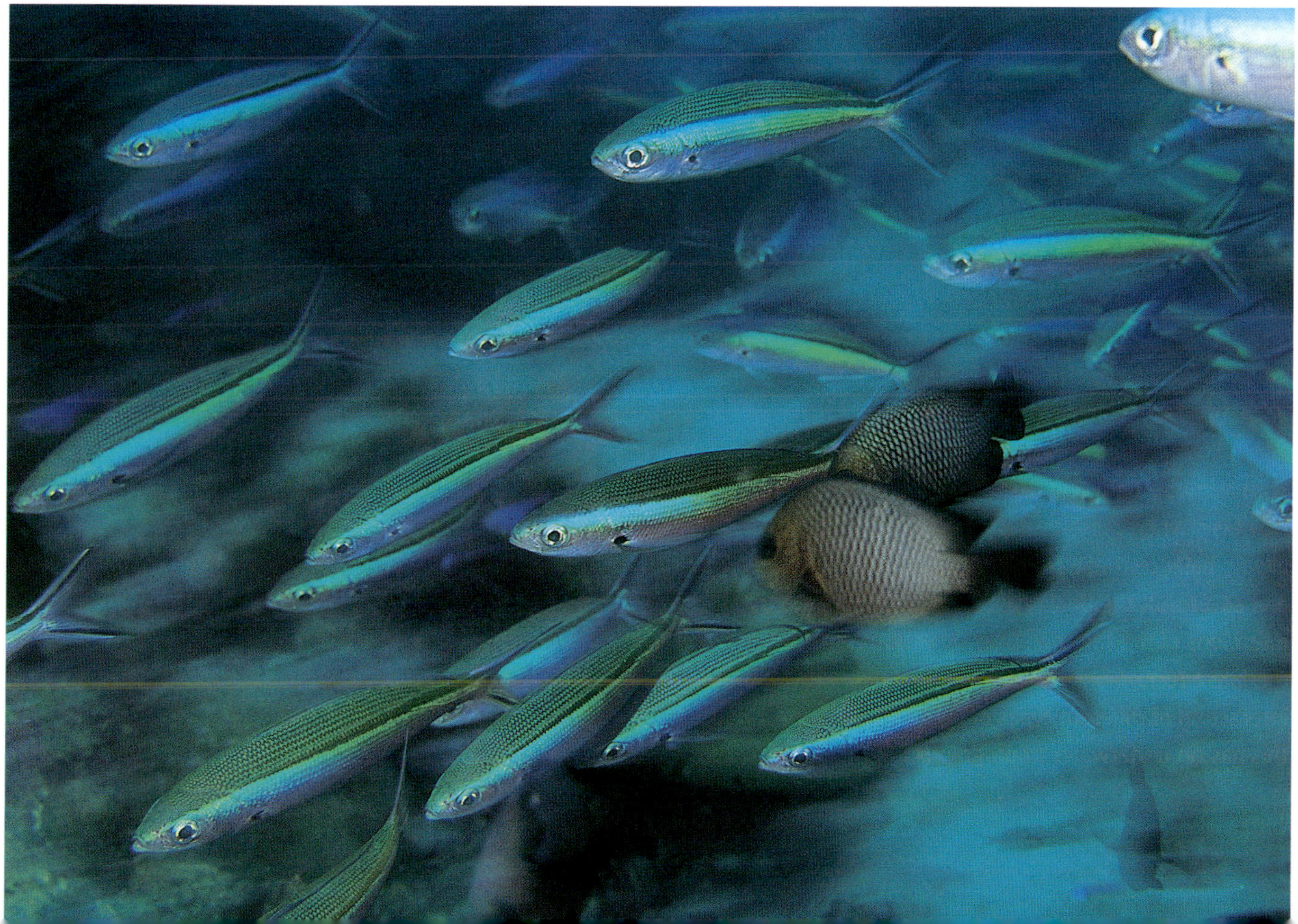

I like this shot of an undersea traffic jam off the Seychelles. Shot using an equal mix of flash and available light, it shows sufficient movement to prevent it being too clinical, but is sharp enough to satisfy technically.
Subal-housed Nikon F801 and 35mm Nikkor lens, with a diffused Nikon SB105 flash unit. 1/30s at f/11 on Fuji Velvia 50 ISO

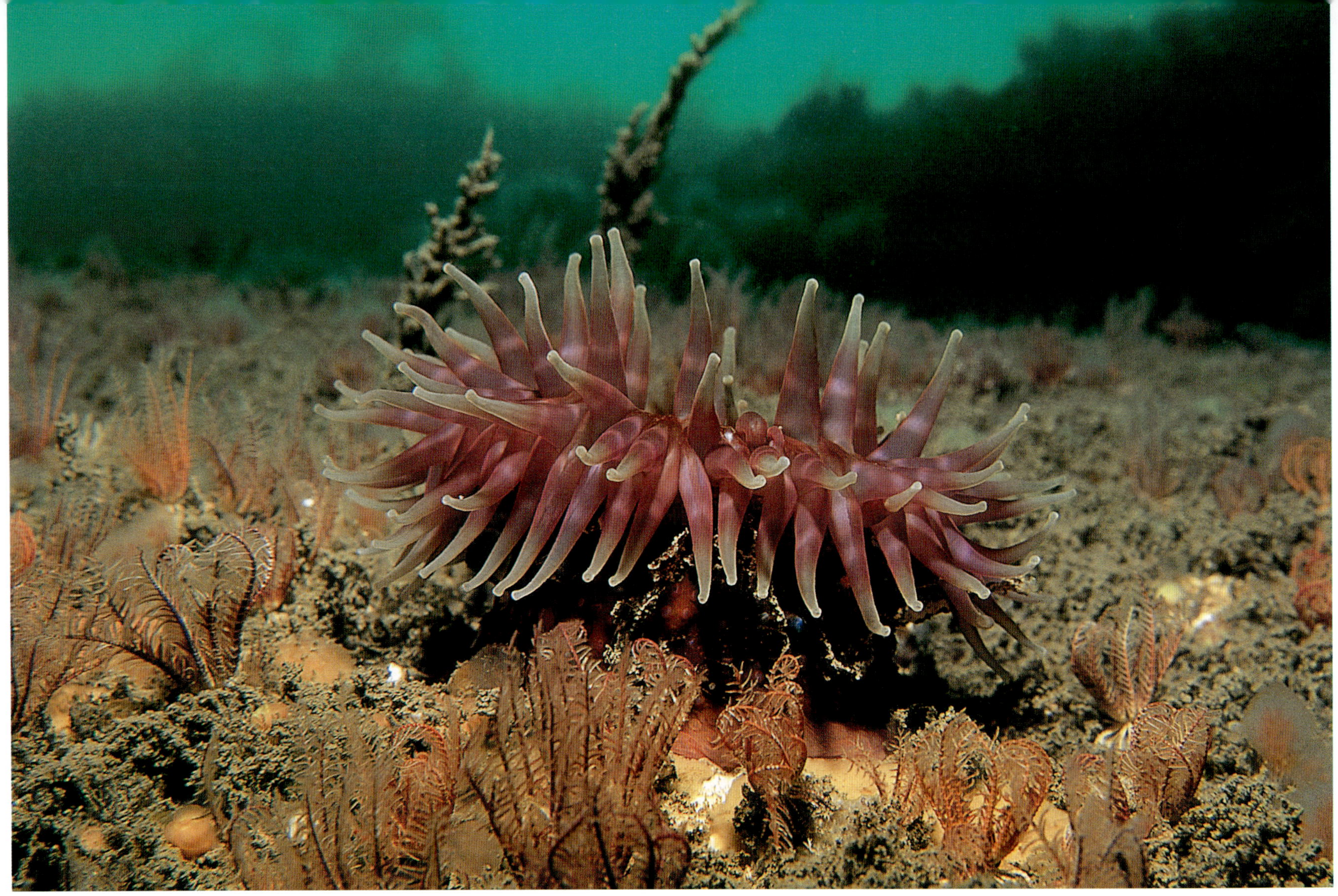

The oceanic water that washes against Ireland's west coast can be extremely clear, if cold. I looked up an underwater cliff to see this dahlia anemone (*Urticina felina*) against a turquoise sky, and just had to photograph it. This is another shot showing two light sources being used and treated independently.
Subal-housed Nikon F100 and 17–35mm lens set at 35mm, with two diffused Nikon SB105 flash units. 1/4s at f/16 on Fuji Provia 100 ISO

Many of today's more sophisticated reflex cameras are designed to take the complexity out of balancing flash and available light by automating the process. They do so by utilizing complex electronic controls and pre-programmed information, which are combined to assess and integrate both available light and flash illumination in an exposure. However, when presented with similar scenes, they will always balance these two elements in much the same way, and as a result the final image may not reflect the true intentions of the photographer. Therefore, even when using the latest technology it is still essential to understand the interaction of different types of light and the impact that this has on underwater photographs.

Balancing flash and available light

When assessing an exposure that uses a mixture of flash and available light, it is important to determine what effect each light source will have on a scene. The first step is to decide which areas of a composition will be lit by flash illumination, and which will be exposed by available light. More often than not, the foreground (or the closest subject matter) will require flash illumination, while the background needs to be exposed by available light.

Balancing light for pictures like this one is more difficult than when the subject is not well illuminated. Here, the angel shark (*Squatina squatina*) had to have sufficient flash to emphasize its head, but not so much that it overwhelmed the available light. Automatic fill-flash systems can work well in the bright conditions under which this shot was taken.
Subal-housed Nikon F100 and 17–35mm lens set at 35mm, with one diffused Nikon SB105 flash unit. 1/60s at f/16 on Fuji Provia 100 ISO

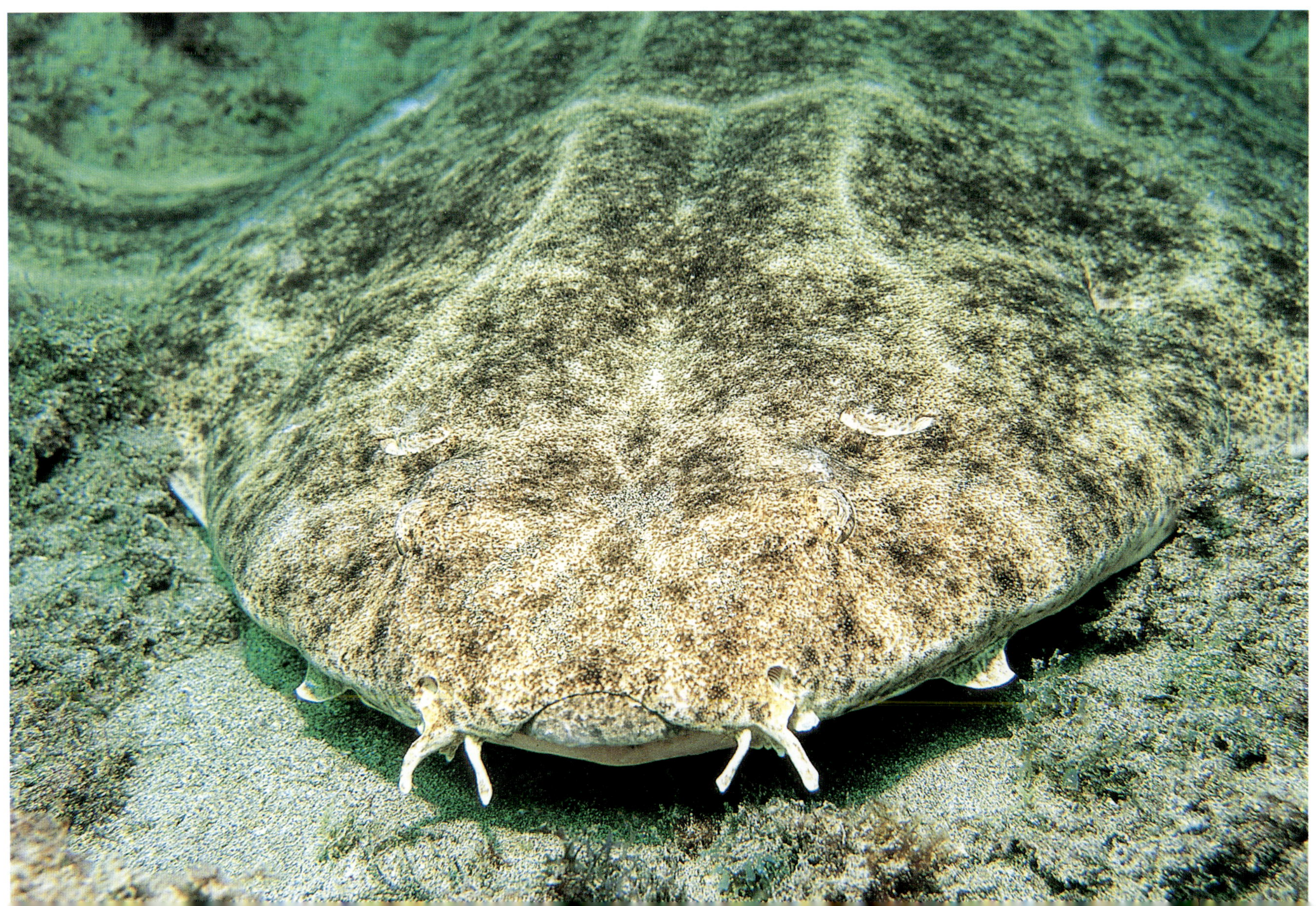

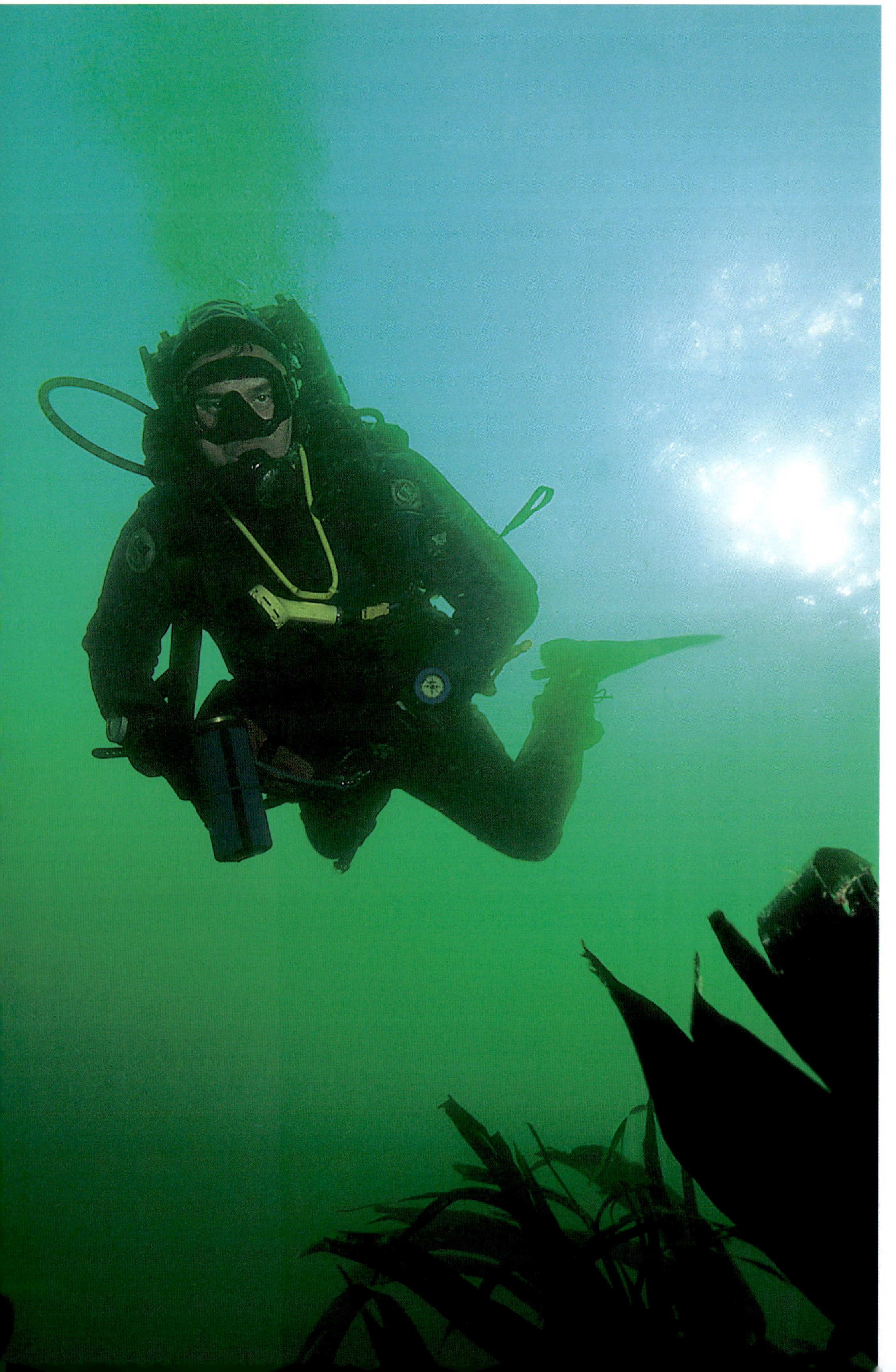

A useful way of thinking about separate light sources is to see each in terms of stops. In other words, it is possible to consider a scene in terms of the exposure required from each light source.

A good example of this is a photograph of a diver, taken from below, against a background featuring a sunburst beaming down through the water. In order to use the available light, it is necessary to take a meter reading and then set the camera so that the sun remains bright but not too 'burnt out' (i.e. overexposed). This can be achieved by taking an overall meter reading and then deliberately overexposing by a specific amount (usually around two stops, but this can vary), or better still by taking an appropriate spot-meter reading. If the reading indicates f/22 at 1/60s, setting f/11 at 1/60s will produce a light sunburst with dark water surrounding it. If a subsequent reading is taken of the diver, it may be that a setting of f/4 at 1/60s is needed. In other words, the diver will still be underexposed by three stops. The solution is to use flash illumination, so that f/11 gives a correct exposure on the diver.

A note of caution: using flash to light the diver could well produce a harsh, garish result. A bright diver shown against a sunburst may not look very pleasing, and could have an unnatural appearance. Adjusting the flash exposure to produce slight underexposure on the diver (perhaps a half to one stop) may well produce a far better balance and a more visually pleasing result.

This shot shows that only a little flash is needed to add detail to what would otherwise have been a silhouetted diver against the watery sun. Taken at Bo Fascadale pinnacle, west Scotland.
Subal-housed Nikon F100 and 17–35mm lens set at 28mm, with a Nikon SB105 flash unit. 1/30s at f/11 on Fuji Provia 100 ISO

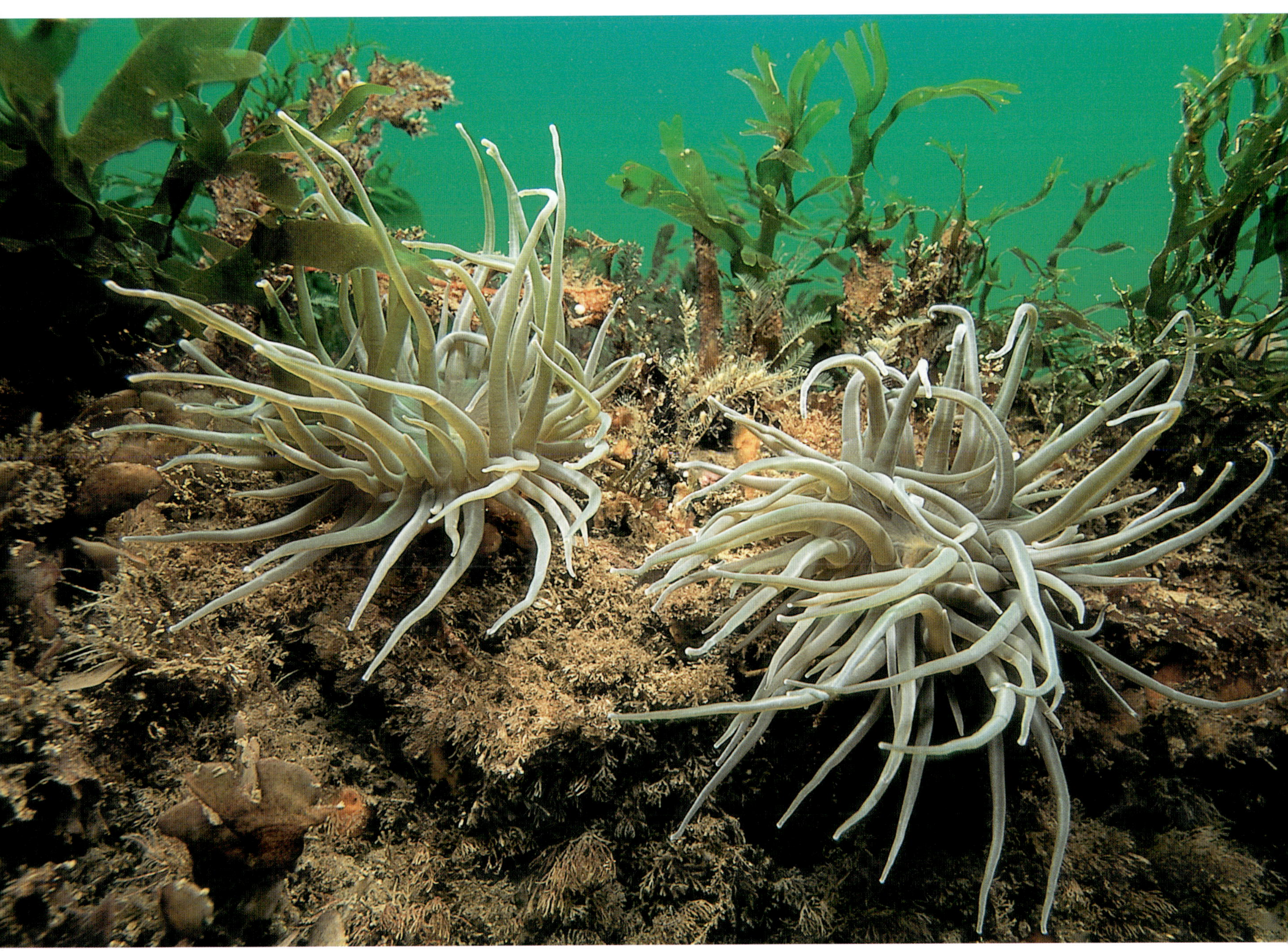

This is a classic shot using two light sources that can be treated separately. Flash was used to illuminate the subject – two snakelocks anemones (*Anemonia sulcata*) in Hell's Mouth, North Wales – by setting the aperture to f/16. Then the background water was (spot) metered and the shutter speed adjusted to 1/4s to balance the picture.
Fuji Provia 100 ISO

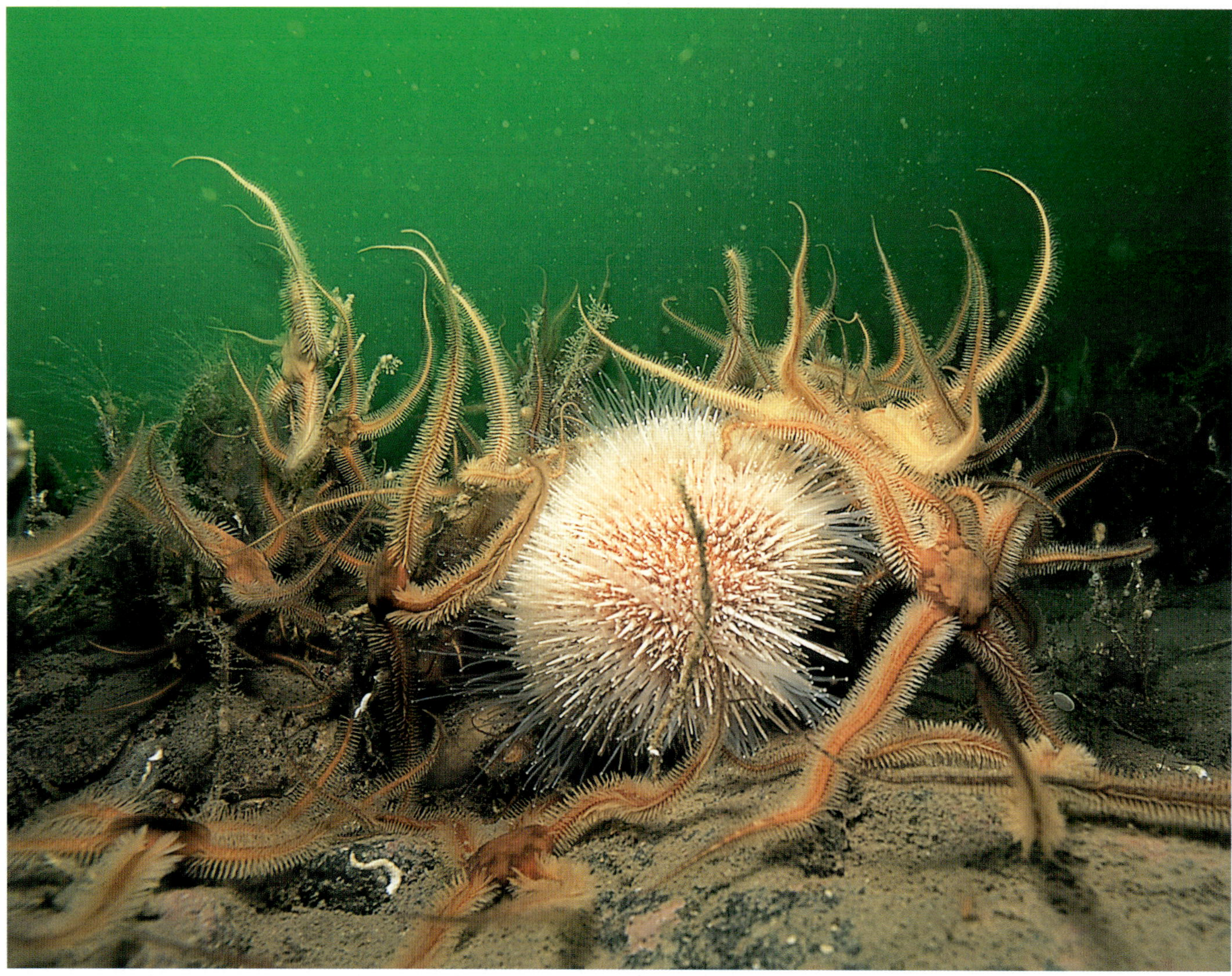

In this picture of an edible sea urchin (*Echinus esculentus*) amid brittlestars (*Ophiocomina* sp.) in a Scottish sea loch, the green background is captured using available light, while the animals are exposed by flash alone. ***Subal-housed Nikon F100 and 60mm micro-Nikkor lens. 1/8s at f/16 on Fuji Velvia 50 ISO***

This can be achieved in a number of ways. For example, by using the camera and flash in a manual setting and adjusting settings appropriately, or by applying exposure compensation to the camera while using the aperture priority mode and using the flash manually. Alternatively, exposure compensation can be applied to both camera and flash (+2 stops on the camera, and –1/2 to –1 on the flash unit), with the camera set to aperture priority and the flash set to TTL. The latter may or may not be possible, depending on the equipment used – setting at least one of these manually is probably the most likely option, as only a few systems have compensation controls for both.

This is not a complex as it might appear. Put simply, a scene should be assessed and the adjustments considered appropriate made. If only one source of light was used to make the exposure, there would only be one adjustment to make. With two sources, both need to be adjusted and their interaction taken into account. This creates three adjustments to deal with rather than just one, but the results should make the extra effort worthwhile.

Assessing a mixed-light scene

Before any decisions are made regarding the use of flash and available light, the scene under consideration needs to be assessed. Some of the variables (such as light levels, flash distances, and so on) are obvious, but others are not and each scene will have its own specific requirements. (Obviously, it is not possible to explain every possible permutation here.) The best way to understand this technique is to divide each scene into its two component parts – the flash-lit scene and the available-light scene – and to consider the effect they have on each other.

The area of a composition that needs flash illumination may or may not be obvious, although almost all photographs featuring foreground detail will benefit from the use of some flash. If a photograph incorporating an equal mixture of flash and available light (i.e. exactly half-and-half) were to be taken, the first step could be to estimate flash-to-subject distance and calculate the correct aperture. The scene could then be metered for available light, and an appropriate shutter speed set for the aperture required by the flash.

However, it is still important to consider the effect that each exposure has on the other. In this case, the film would receive twice the necessary exposure – each individual light source would expose the film correctly, and their effects would be combined. Effectively, it would be overexposed by one stop. Setting a one-stop smaller aperture than calculated would halve both the flash and available-light exposure, and should yield a correct exposure.
There are other ways of doing this (such as setting a reduced flash power or a higher shutter speed), and in many cases it may be desirable to use less than full exposure from one type of light. In the tropics, for example, slightly underexposing background water can lead to a richer intensity of colour than that produced by the indicated exposure.

If the flat surface of a shipwreck in a wide-angle scene is poorly lit, it can be illuminated by flash. Positioning the flash perpendicular to the flat surface will illuminate the wreck evenly and allow the flash exposure to be set manually. A meter reading taken of the available light in the background will allow an appropriate shutter speed to be selected for the flash-determined aperture. As the wreck is poorly illuminated by available light in comparison with the open water, the available-light component of the subject is probably negligible and no further adjustment of the settings will be required. The resulting picture would show the wreck illuminated correctly and evenly, with blue water behind it. Although the two light sources have been considered independently, their interaction requires no further adjustment in this example.

By allowing available light to partially expose this close-up photograph of a snake pipefish (*Entelurus aequoreus*) from North Wales, context has been added to the picture.
Subal-housed Nikon F100 and 60mm micro-Nikkor lens. 1/15s at f/16 on Fuji Velvia 50 ISO

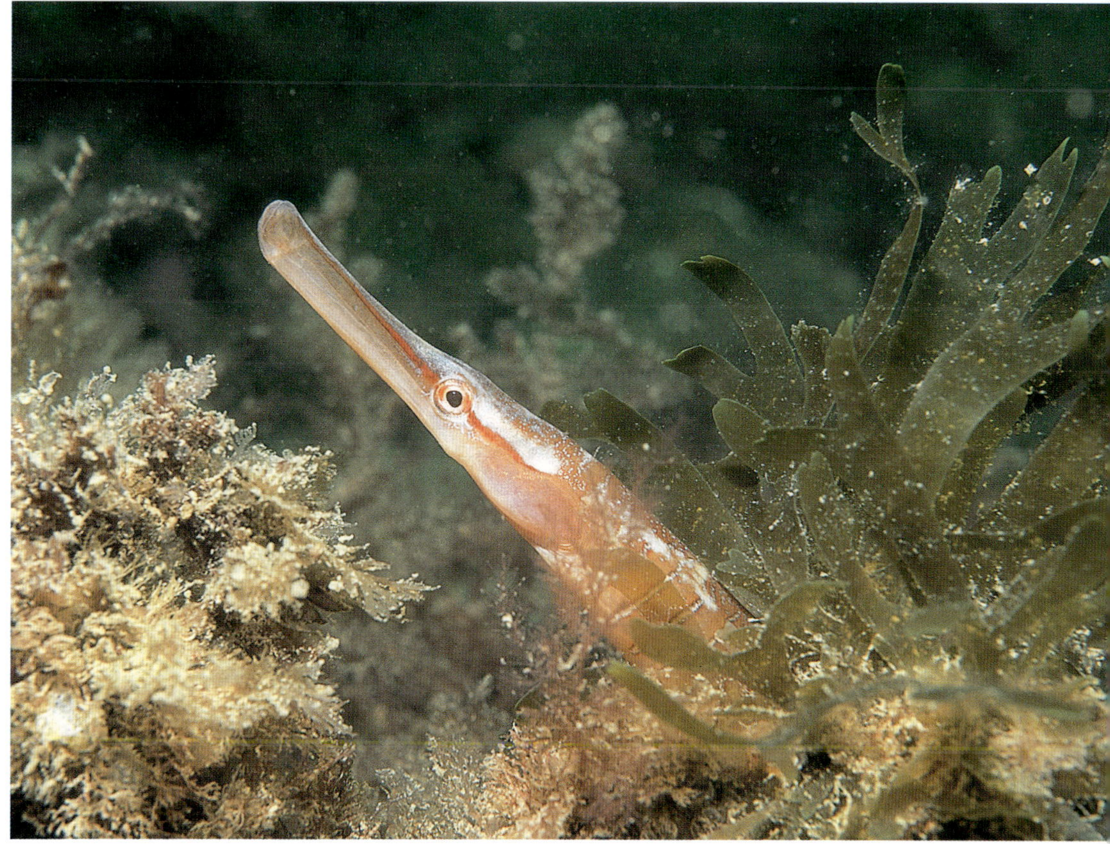

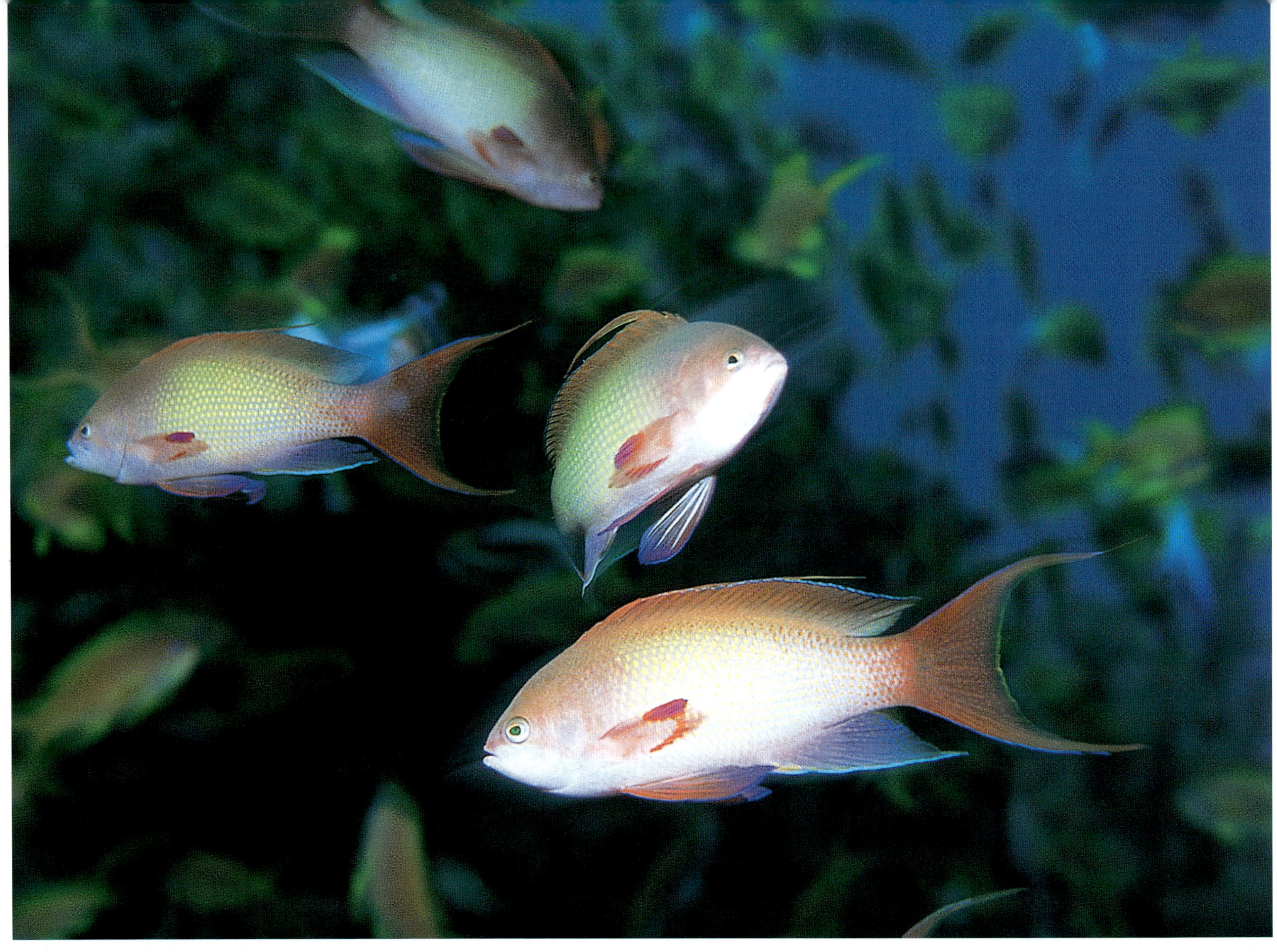

This shot of lyretail anthiass (*Pseudoanthias squamipianis*) from Aqaba, shows clearly the interaction between flash and available light. The fish would be slightly underexposed by flash alone, with available light adding a slightly dark (underexposed) background. ***Subal-housed Nikon F100 and 60mm micro-Nikkor, with a Nikon SB105 flash unit. 1/30s at f/16 on Fuji Provia 100 ISO***

Ultimately, however, subject matter is so variable that each photograph has to be assessed individually, and each photographer has to determine how best to adjust settings to produce the desired image.

Again, this is not as complex as it might sound. The important thing is to realize that when faced with scenes of the type used in the examples above, an automated fill-flash system cannot approach them in the same way as a photographer using manual settings. An automatic system will interpret the information supplied to the camera's microprocessor in the way that its designers considered best. This does not guarantee that the end result is what photographer intends at the time of exposure. In fact, automated flash is notoriously unreliable when used with wide-angle lenses, especially underwater, where contrast and light levels are low. This is because the camera's sensors are often provided with insufficient data about a scene to allow effective operation.

Understanding the concepts behind balanced-light underwater photography, and controlling a camera manually (at least to a degree), can help to overcome these deficiencies, even if the application of these techniques requires experience.

Rear-curtain sync flash

Normally, flash exposure takes place prior to ambient-light exposure. If rear synchronization is used this is reversed, and flash exposure takes place after ambient-light exposure. The effect that this creates can be useful when photographing moving subjects, as any areas not exposed to the flash, and blocked from ambient exposure by the moving subject, will remain unexposed.

An effect often produced by normal flash synchronization is an unwanted dark line in front of the subject, which looks unnatural. If rear-sync flash is used, any dark line produced will be behind the subject. While not ideal, the results are far more acceptable in most cases. If rear-sync flash is used on static subjects, the results are rarely significantly different to those produced by slow synchronization or using a manual ambient-exposure setting.

This rather striking portrait of an edible sea urchin (*Echinus esculentus*) has been achieved by using flash with somewhat underexposed available light. As a result, the tube feet (which are actually white) have been illuminated by greenish ambient light. Taken off Papa Westray in the Orkneys.
Subal-housed Nikon F801 and 60mm micro-Nikkor lens, with a Nikon SB105 flash unit. 1/15s at f/16 on Fuji Velvia 50 ISO

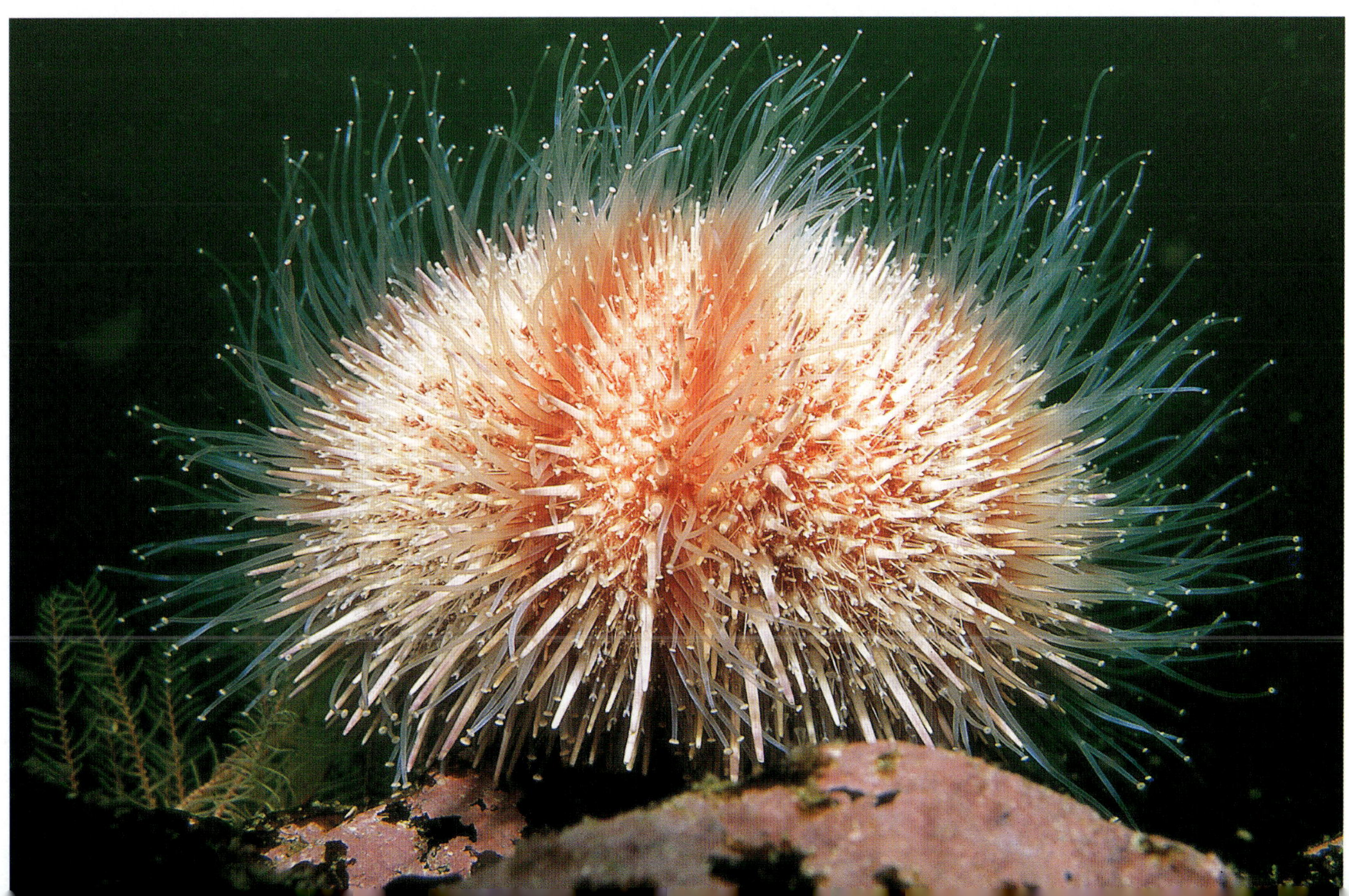

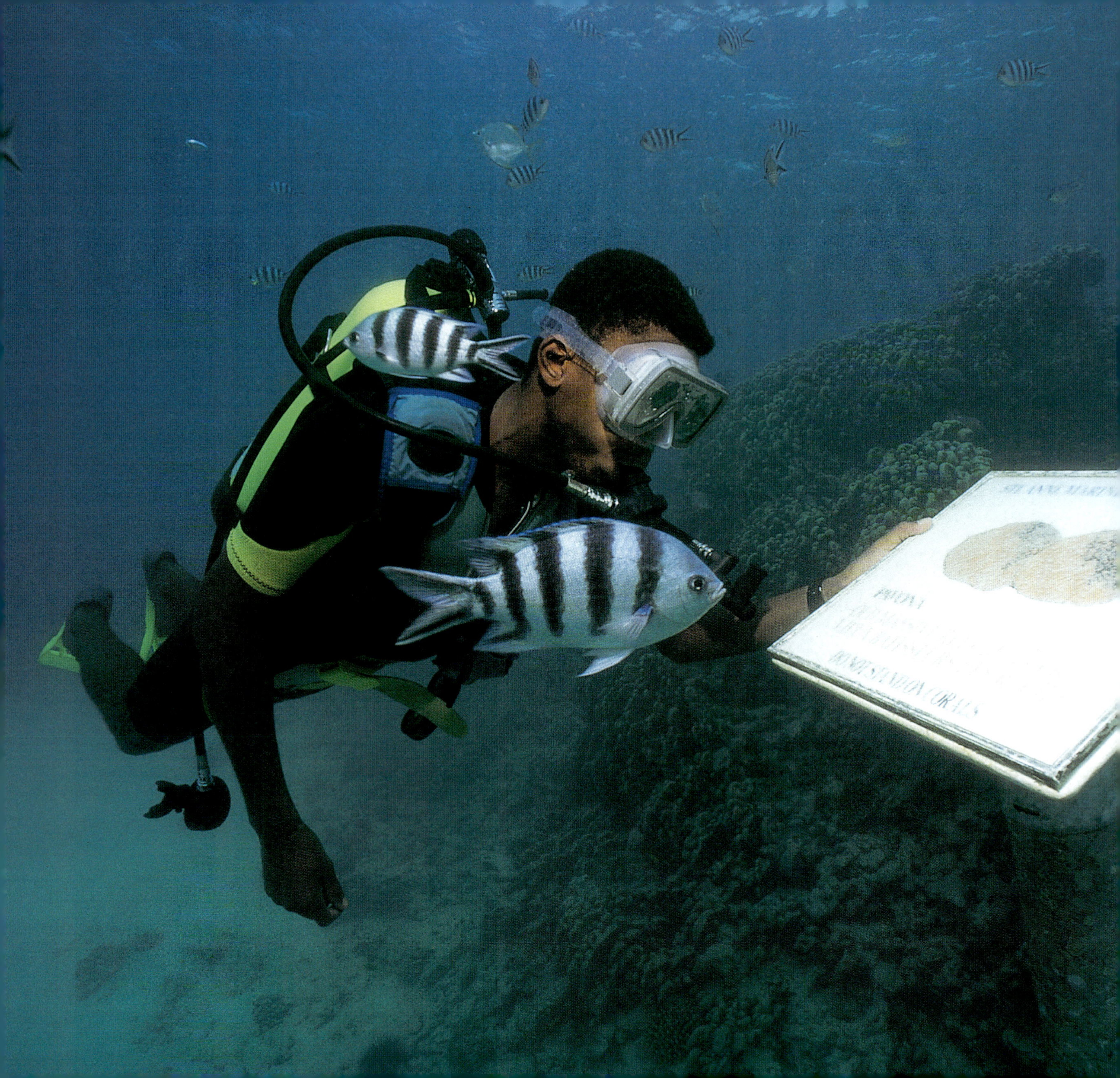

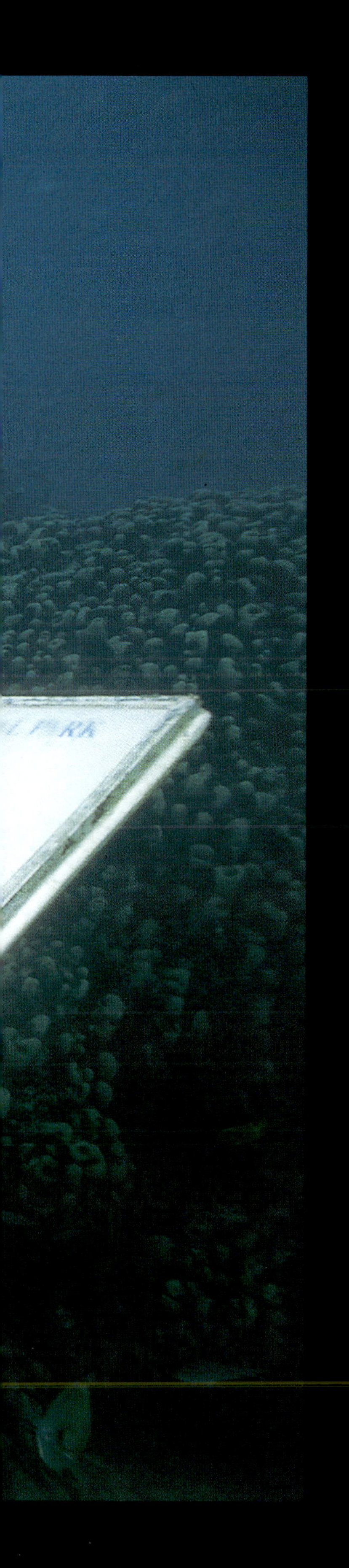

notes

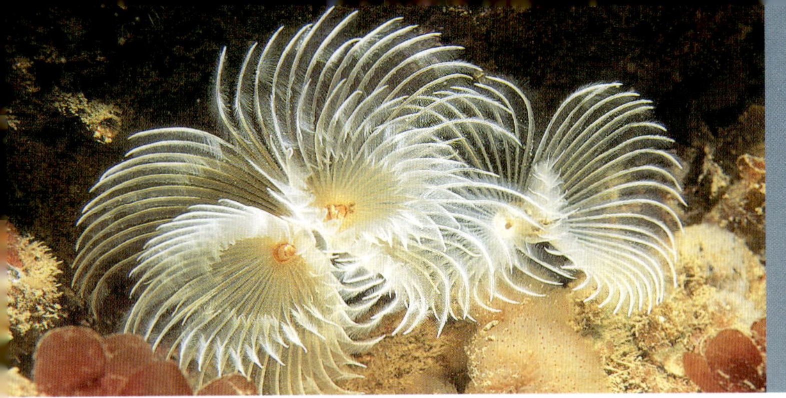

selling your photographs

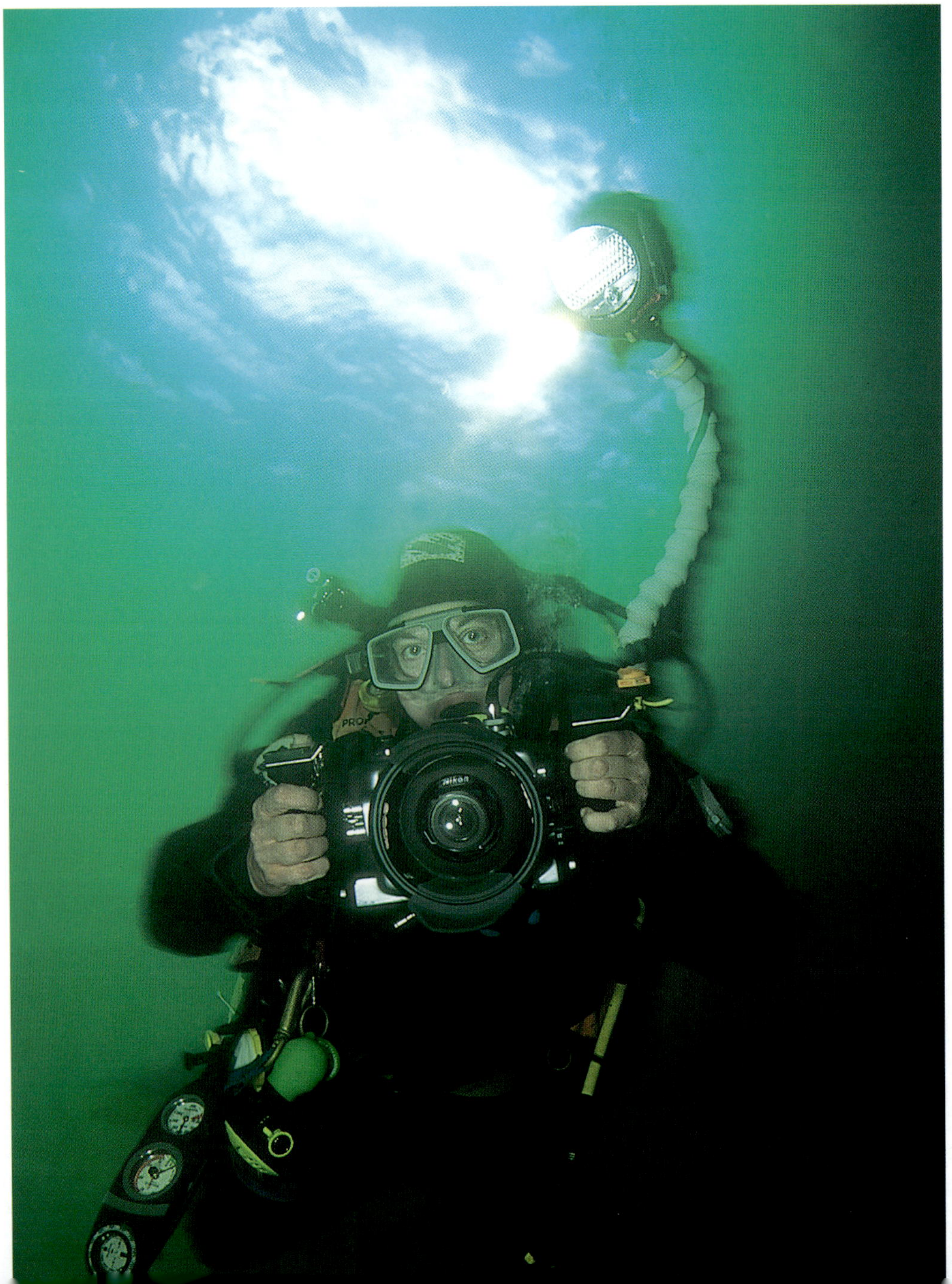

Many underwater photographers consider selling their photographs, which is quite understandable given the high cost of camera and diving equipment, and the expense of travelling to many locations.

However, as with many other moneymaking activities, it is not as easy to make a living by selling underwater photographs as it may at first appear. Legal requirements must be satisfied in order to comply with legislation in different countries. Such regulations cover diving, as well as aspects like insurance, taxation and record keeping. (See page 151 for more information on legislation.)

Only once these requirements have been satisfied can an underwater photographer go about selling his or her photographs. This is also time consuming, but the more effort put into selling pictures, the more likely sales become.

At this point, it is worth noting that there is a market for underwater photographs of the highest quality alone. Many underwater photographers try to make money out of their pictures, and standards are very high indeed. Only well-composed, technically adept photographs will make money. Even then, the subject must be a saleable one. For example, pictures of rare and beautiful sea slugs are – sadly – unlikely to sell very often.

This shot, taken inside the Sugar Loaf Cave in the Isle of Man, shows the freezing effect of flash, as it was a hand-held (although supported against rock) exposure of 4 seconds. It has been used as a magazine cover.
Subal-housed Nikon F100 and 17–35mm lens set at 17mm, with two diffused Nikon SB105 flash units. 4s at f/8 on Fuji Provia 100 ISO

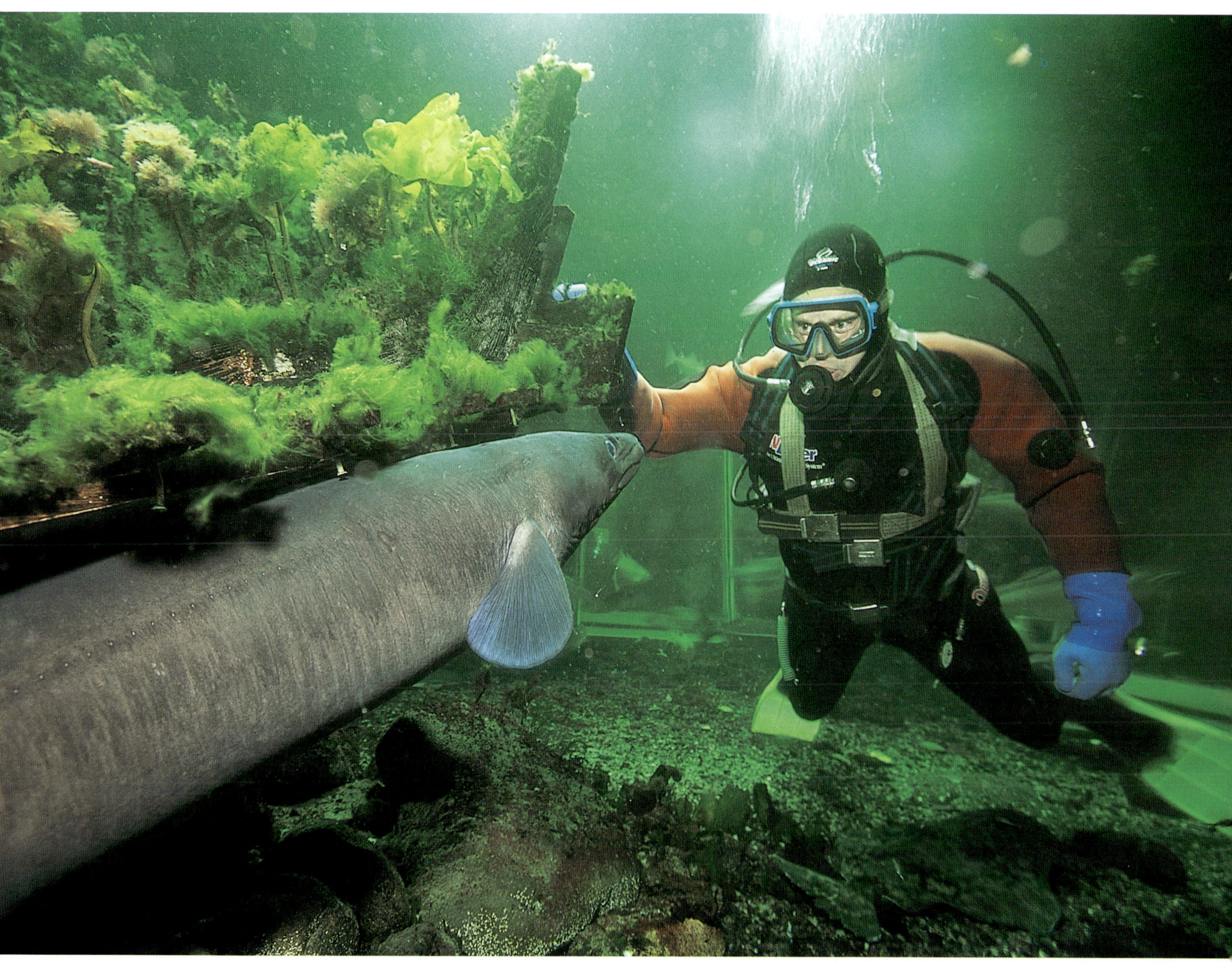

I took some publicity photographs for Exploris Aquarium in Northern Ireland, one of which was this picture of a conger eel and diver. Conditions were disconcertingly like those found in the sea – cold (less than 10°C) and dull – necessitating a slow shutter speed. The diver was a commercial diver acting as my 'stand-by', and did a good job of looking worried!
Subal-housed Nikon F100 and 17–35mm lens set at 17mm, with two diffused Nikon SB105 flash units. 1/4s at f/11 on Fuji Provia 100 ISO

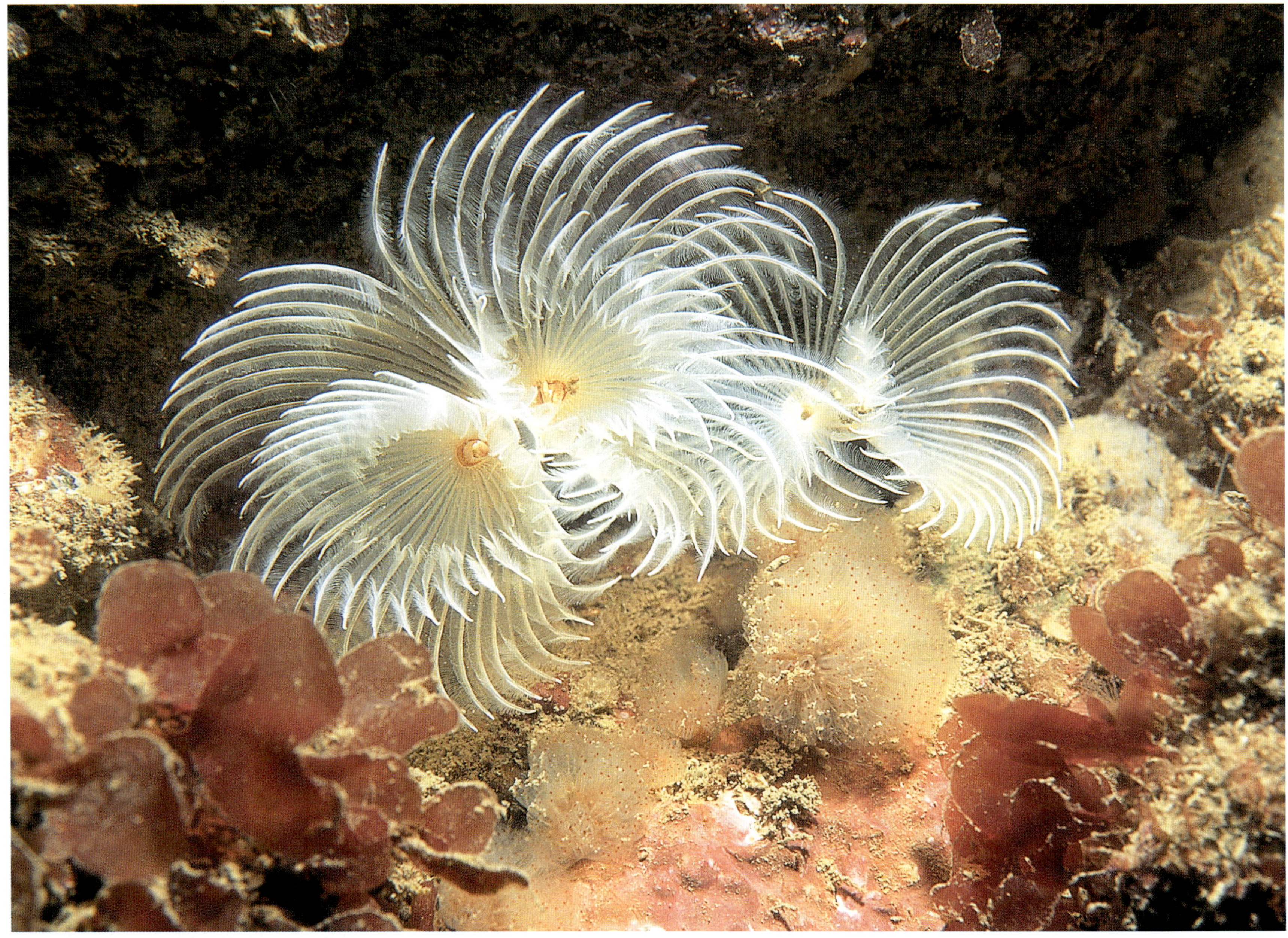

This shot has proved to be very successful, having been published many times. Double-fanned worms (*Bispira volutacornis*) are exquisitely detailed creatures, and not uncommon in the rocky areas of temperate waters, such as Bardsey Island, North Wales.
Subal-housed Nikon F801 and 60mm micro-Nikkor lens, with a Nikon SB105 flash unit. 1/60s at f/16 on Fuji Velvia 50 ISO

As many shots are of natural-history subjects, these have to be identified and captioned correctly, including the formal scientific name. This requires either detailed knowledge of the field, or a lot of research.

Perhaps one of the easiest ways of selling underwater photographs is to submit articles to diving magazines, thus supplying both text and pictures (although this is unlikely to provide a huge amount of income). To do so requires an understanding of the types of article that such magazines publish, and the style and content that they use. As this means using photographs to illustrate an article in a specific way, it is useful to have a subject in mind before taking them.

When taking photographs to illustrate an article, it is also important to consider accompanying above-water shots – it is not enough merely to take underwater pictures. Fortunately, diving trips often take place in locations offering marvellous opportunities for above-water photography.

Photographic agencies and libraries provide another outlet for underwater photographs. Most require a good throughput of very high-quality material, but while some will yield a steady flow of income, most are unlikely to provide more than a trickle.

Given the time and effort required to take and catalogue underwater photographs, it is difficult to make a significant income from them. (In terms of hourly pay, most

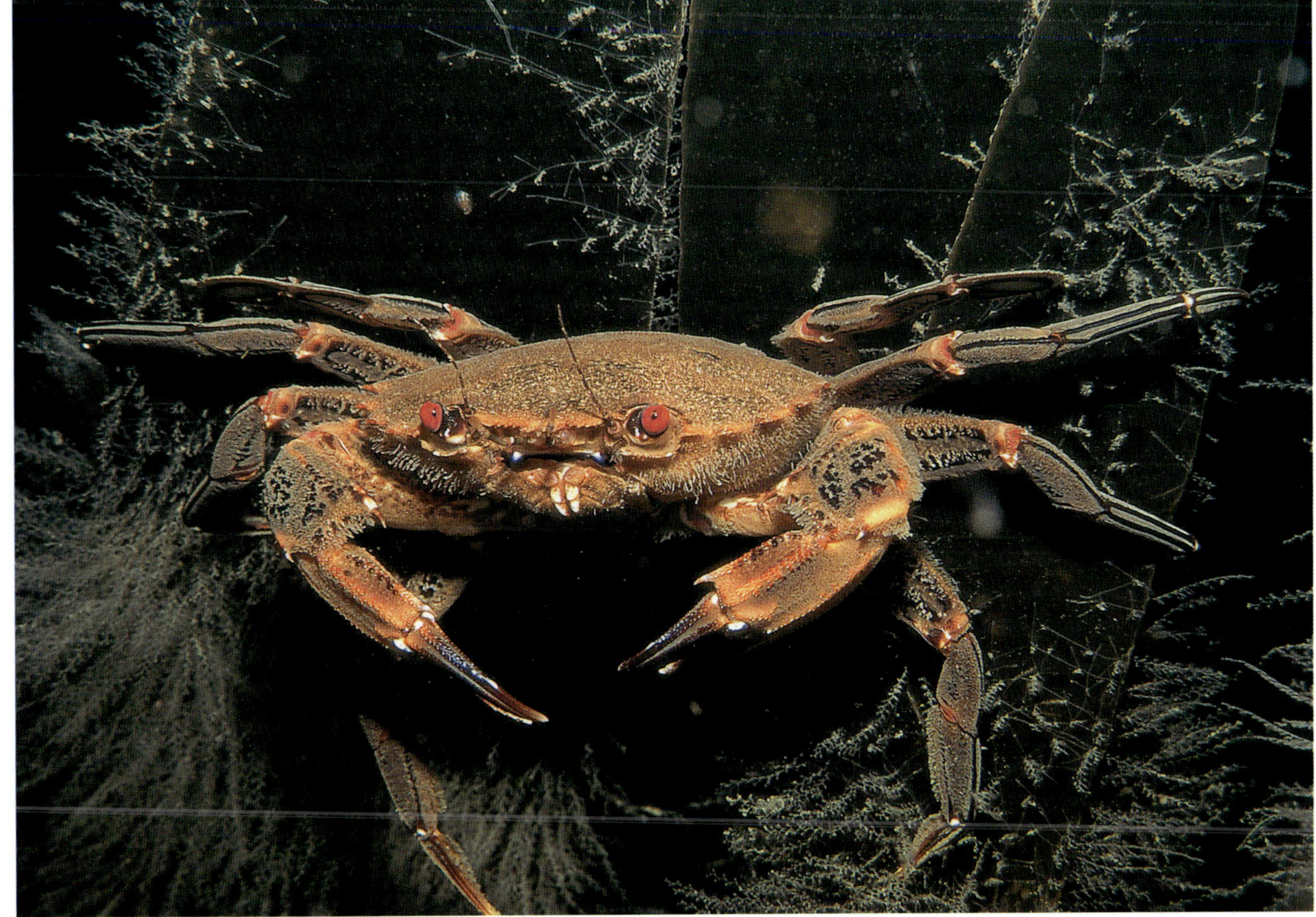

Velvet swimming crabs (*Liocarcinus puber*) are extremely photogenic. This composition, taken at St Kilda off north-west Scotland, is improved by an interesting but unobtrusive background of kelp. ***Subal-housed Nikon F100 and 60mm micro-Nikkor lens, with a Nikon SB105 flash unit. 1/60s at f/16 on Fuji Velvia 50 ISO***

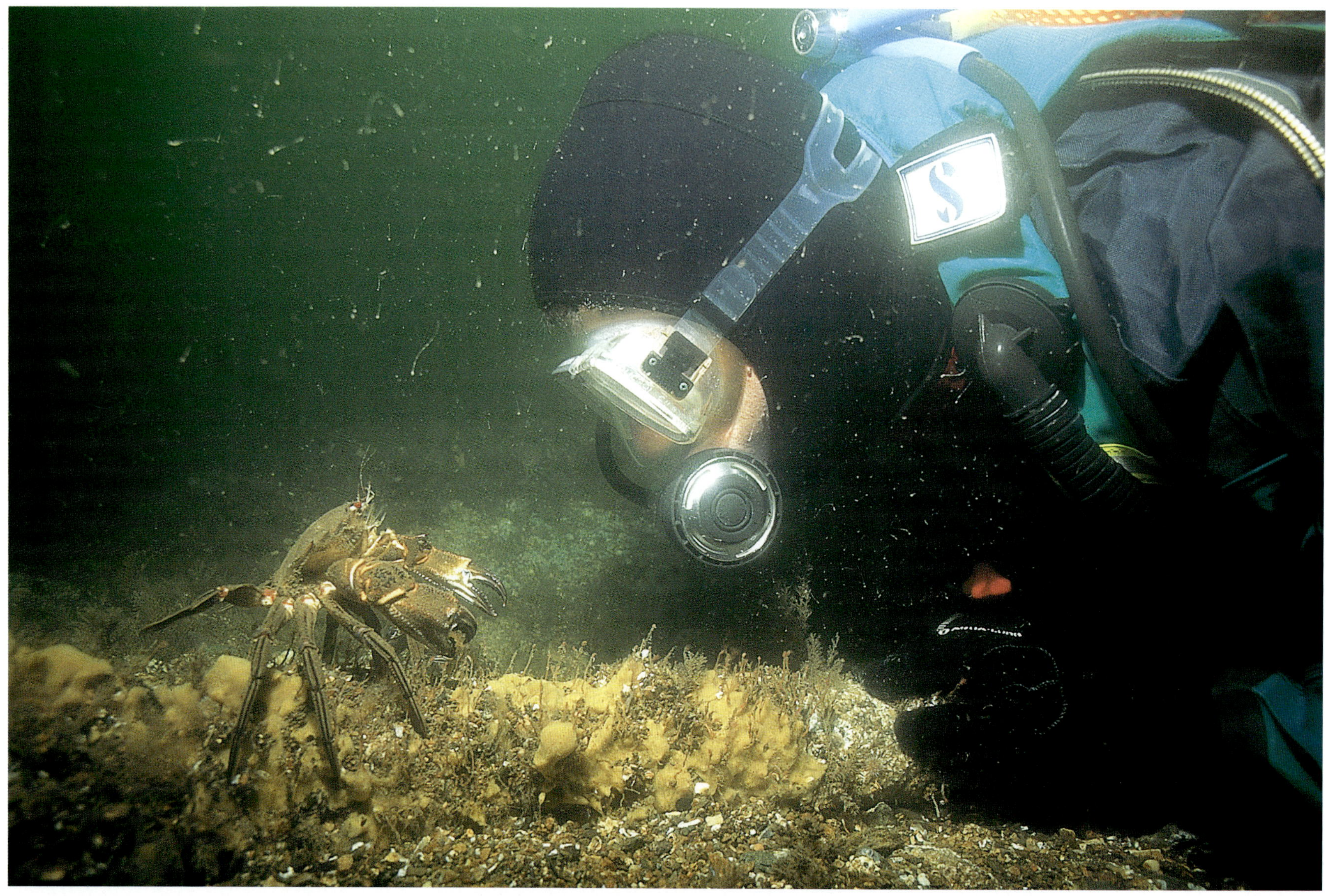

underwater photographers might well be able to earn more doing something else.) In fact, unless you are prepared to commit significant amounts of time and energy to marketing your photographs, it is unlikely that you will even recoup the cost of taking them. On a worldwide basis, very few underwater photographers make their living from underwater photography alone, and many have additional sources of income.

As a professional photographer, I prefer to enjoy my underwater photography, rather than having to consider it in a commercial light all the time. I do make money from it, but I am in the fortunate position of having a great deal of interest and experience in marine natural history and marine conservation. It is probably my knowledge of these areas, rather than my knowledge of underwater photography itself, that helps me to market my pictures successfully.

Human and animal interaction always helps to provide interest within a picture. The diver and crab are resting on an undersea cable that crosses the Menai Strait in Wales. Visibility was less than 3 metres.
Subal-housed Nikon F801 and 20mm Nikkor lens, with a diffused flash unit. 1/4s at f/11 with Fuji Provia 100 ISO

Legislation

Many countries place legal obligations on divers, and especially on anyone diving for profit. Operating as an underwater photographer and selling pictures may be viewed as diving for profit, and hence may fall within such regulations. It is essential to be aware of these and operate within them. Severe penalties can be imposed on those who do not comply with regulations.

In the UK, certain exemptions are required for specific types of diving. It is worth noting that all of these require divers to adhere to the safe-diving practices recommended by training agencies and governing bodies. This means that (at the time of publication) it is not possible to take pictures to sell while solo diving, or diving beyond 50 metres, in the UK.

Rock Cook wrasse (*Centolabrus exoletus*) are inquisitive but shy fish. They form small shoals around kelp areas, and are hard to photograph. This shot, from Ireland's Aran Islands, shows a shoal about to disappear under a large boulder. It is one of a very few pictures that I have managed to take of these fish.
Subal-housed Nikon F801 and 20mm Nikkor, with a diffused Nikon SB105 flash unit. 1/30s at f/11 on Fuji Provia 100 ISO

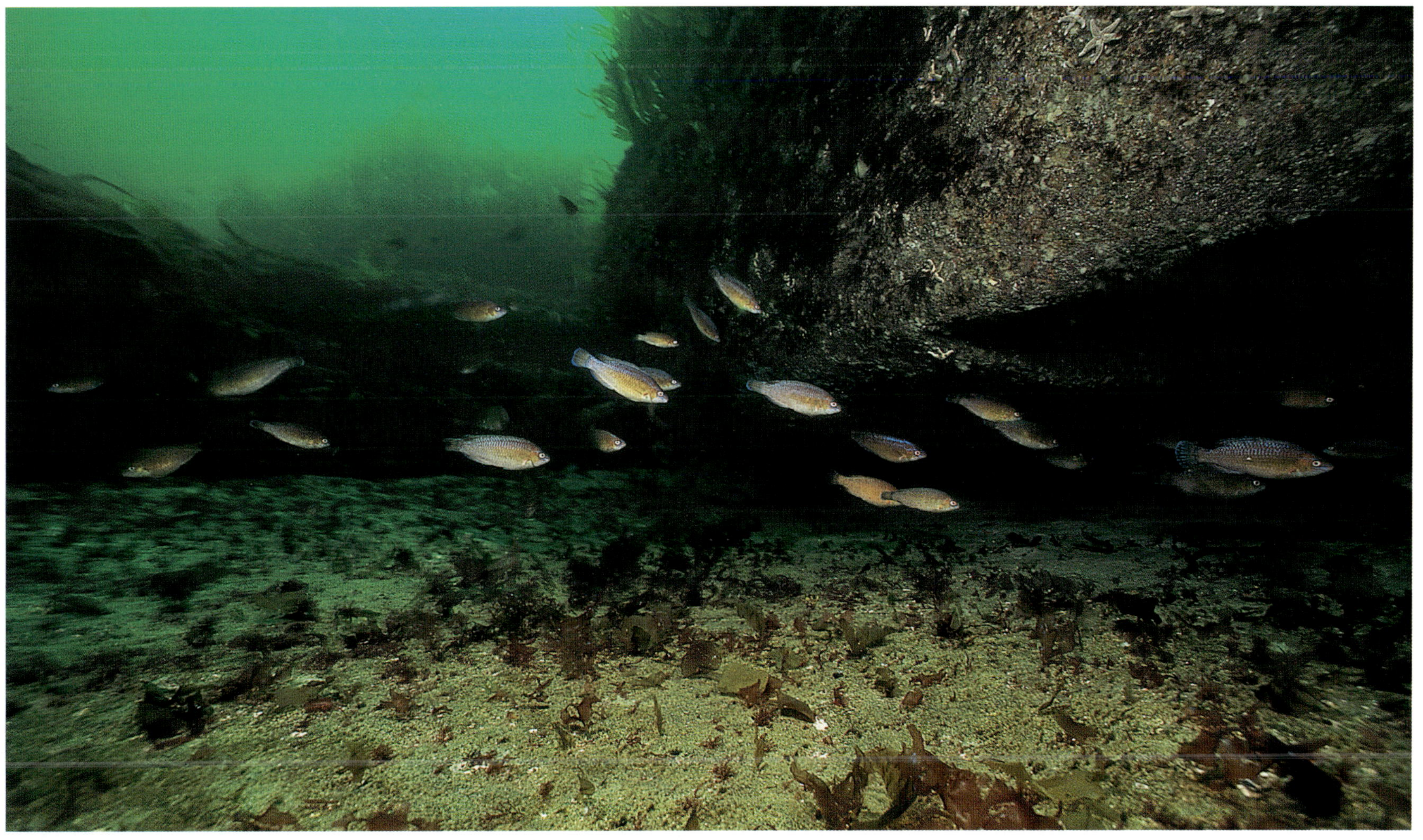

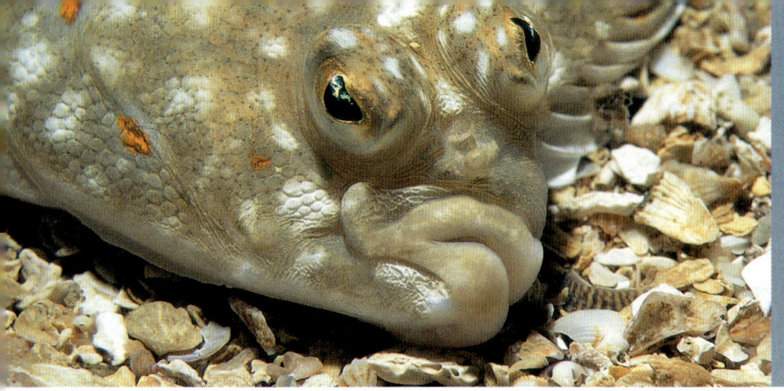

codes of conduct

Most underwater photographers make an effort to protect the environment in which they take their pictures, and to avoid disturbing marine creatures when they take their images. This is good for the marine environment and leads to better photographs.

This *Code of Good Practice* sets out good practices for anyone who aspires to take pictures underwater. Many aspects are also applicable to the general sports diver.

Unfortunately our dive-boat's anchor fouled the Red Sea coral reef on one dive site. This crown of thorns starfish appeared, probably attracted by the damaged coral. It provided an opportunity for a photograph to illustrate that bad practices have knock-on effects. ***Subal-housed Nikon F100 and 60mm micro-Nikkor, with a Nikon SB105 flash unit. 1/30s at f/16 on Fuji Velvia 50 ISO***

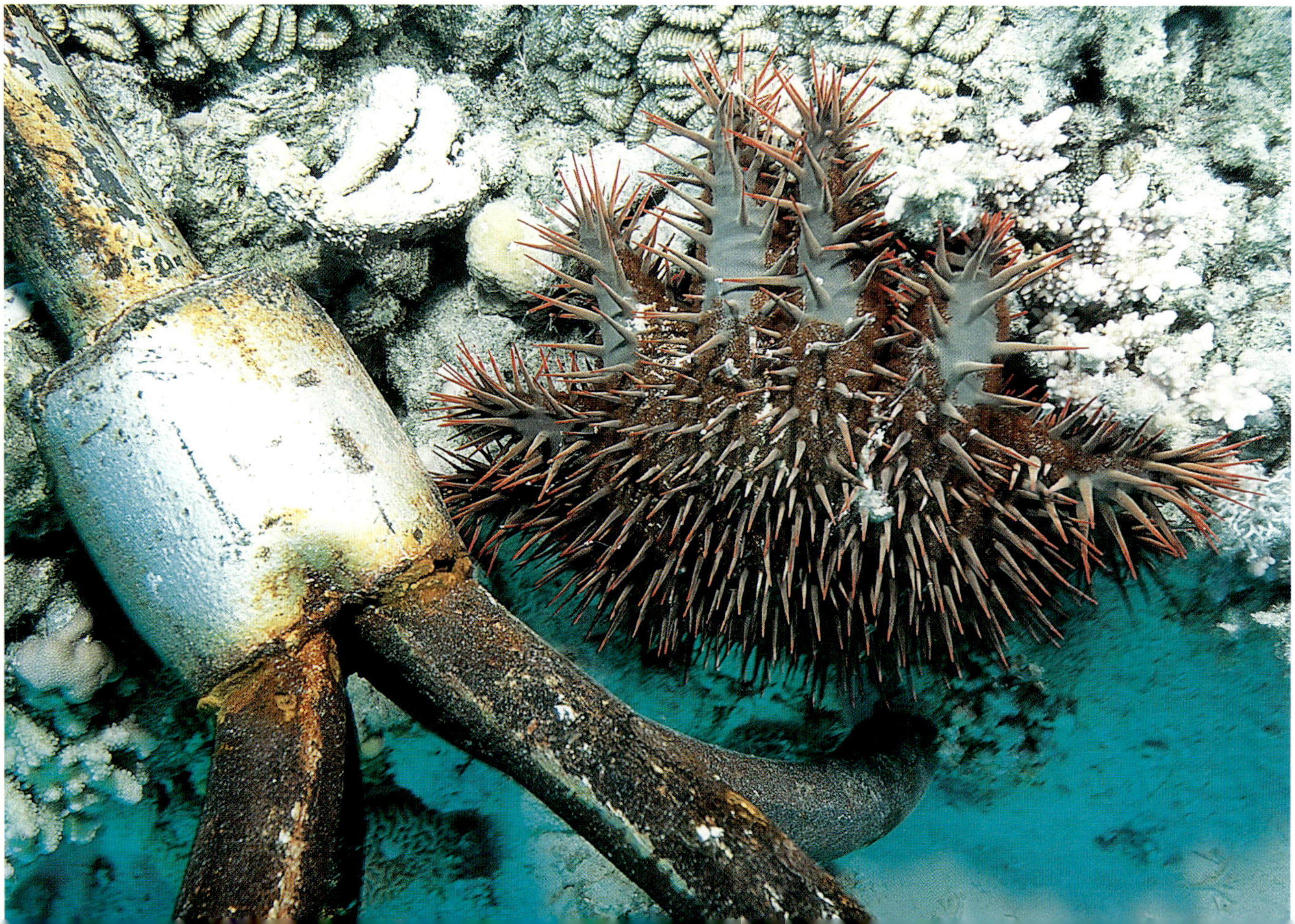

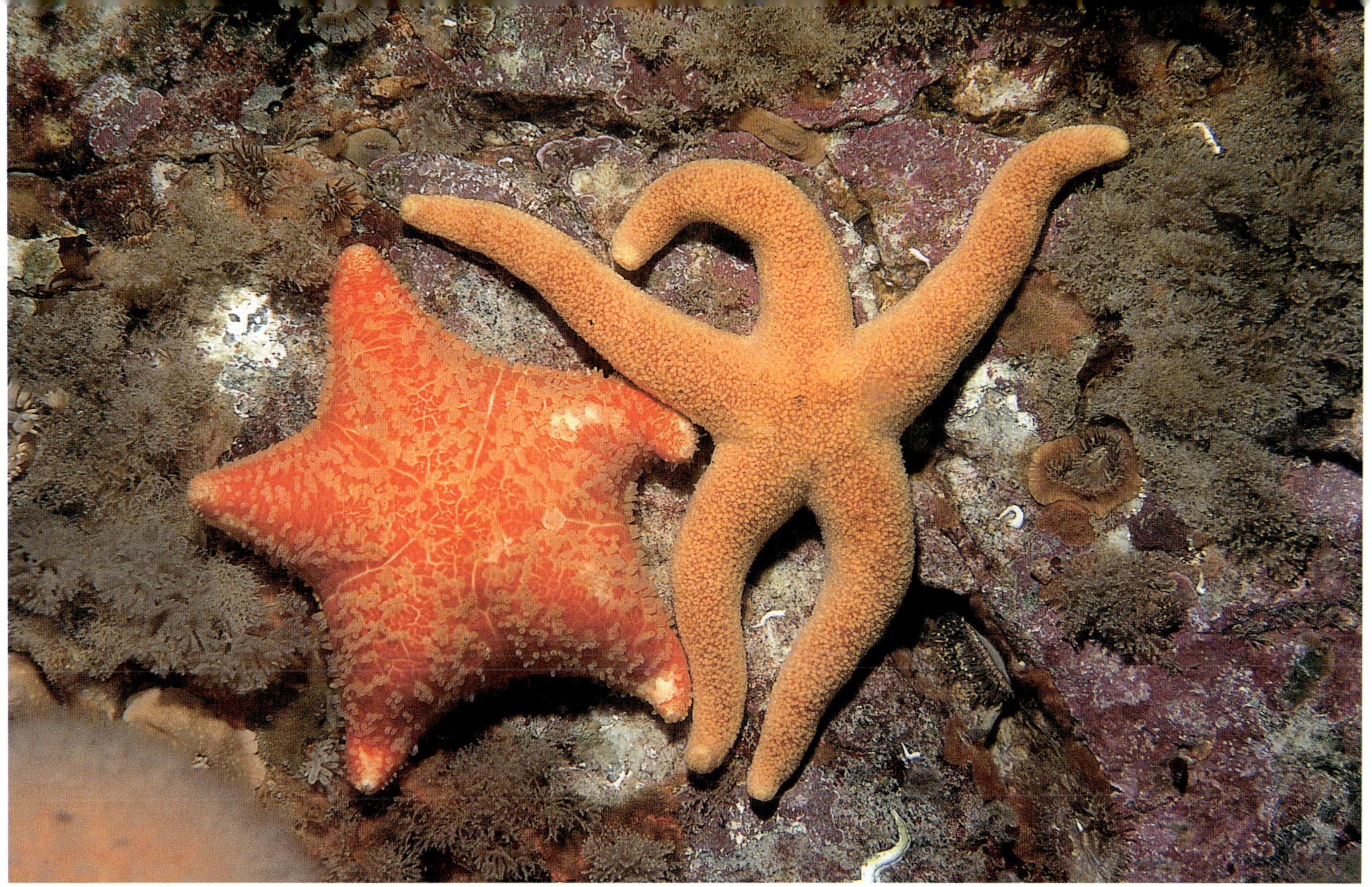

These two starfish look almost as though they are dancing partners. The shot was taken as seen and would be difficult to set up, as starfish tend to raise their arm tips when placed on a new surface. It is better to observe and photograph things as they are, rather than try to make adjustments (especially as this would contravene the *Code of Good Practice*).

Subal-housed Nikon F801 and 60mm micro-Nikkor lens, with a Nikon SB105 flash unit. 1/60s at f/16 on Fuji Velvia 50 ISO

1. No one should attempt to take pictures underwater until they are a competent diver. Novices who are conscious only of the image in their viewfinder, and subsequently unaware of the movement of their hands and fins, can do untold damage to the underwater environment.
2. Every diver, including photographers, should ensure that gauges, octopus regulators, torches and other equipment are secured so they do not trail over reefs or cause other damage.
3. Underwater photographers should possess superior precision buoyancy-control skills, to avoid damaging the fragile marine environment and its creatures. Even experienced divers and those modelling for photographers should ensure that careless or excessively vigorous fin strokes and arm movements do not damage coral or smother it in clouds of sand. A finger placed carefully on a bare patch of rock can do much to replace other, more damaging movement.

Sometimes it is possible to get close to a subject that is usually too timid. This plaice (*Pleuronectes platessa*) allowed several photographs to be taken without any sign of agitation whatsoever. It is important not to abuse such a privilege and to desist before upsetting such willing models. Taken in Connemara by flash illumination.
Subal-housed Nikon F100 and 60mm micro-Nikkor lens, with a Nikon SB105 flash unit. 1/60s at f/16 on Fuji Provia 100 ISO

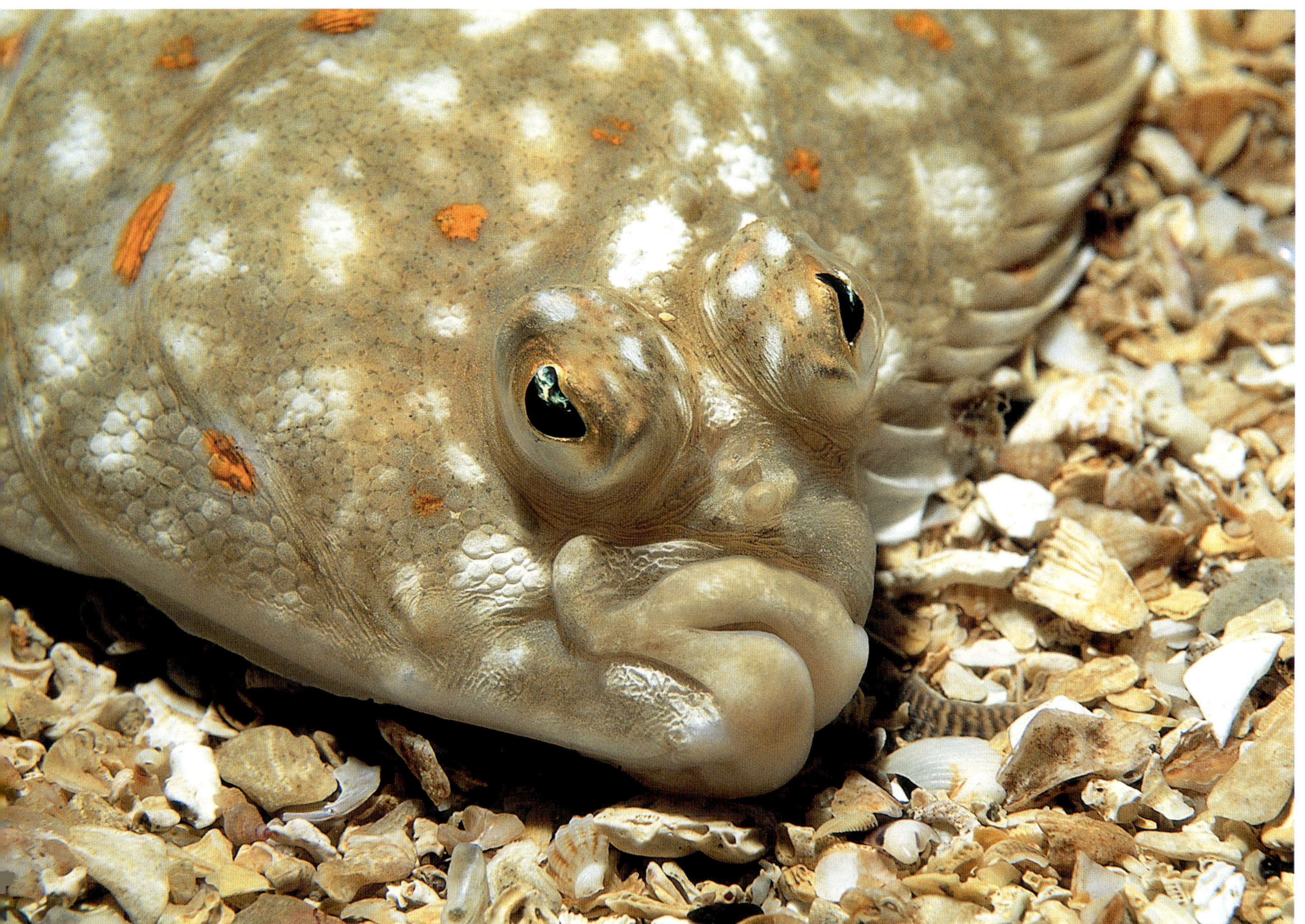

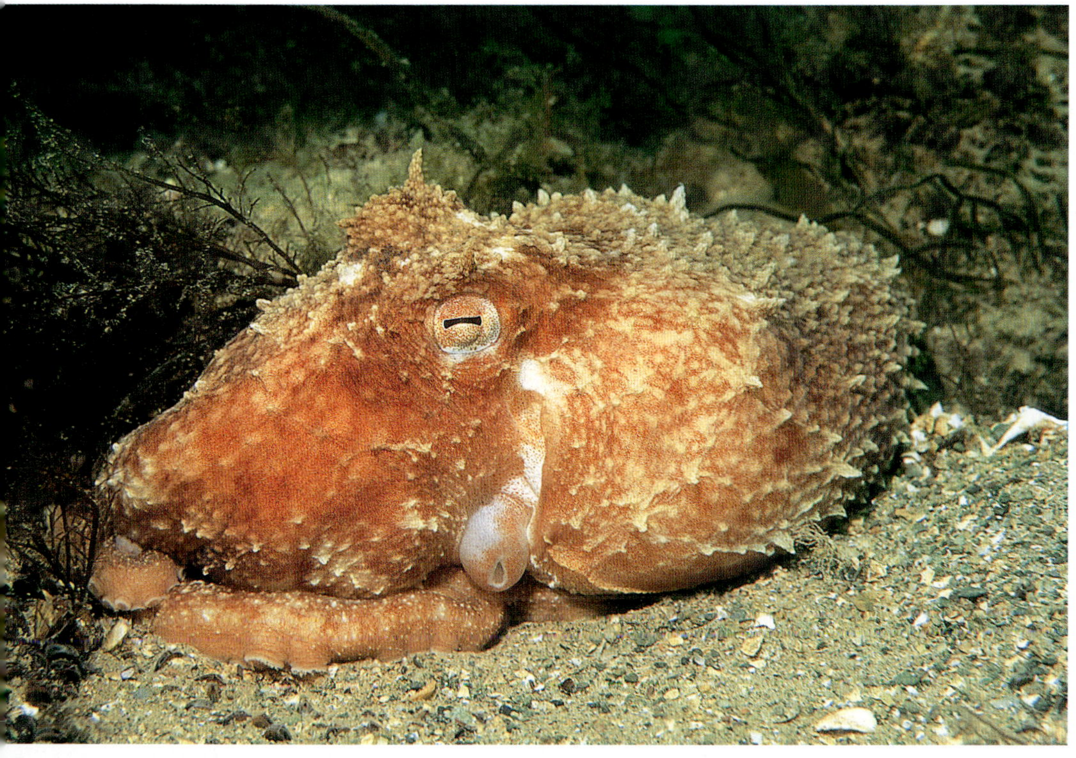

The spiky texture of this octopus's (*Eledone cirrhosa*) skin indicates stress – it doesn't like being photographed, and I try to minimize shots of such creatures. A little available light has been used, together with flash. Taken off of Trefor Pier, North Wales.
Subal-housed Nikon F100 and 60mm micro-Nikkor lens. 1/30s at f/16 on Fuji Velvia 50 ISO

❹ Photographers should explore the area in which they are diving carefully and find subjects that are accessible without causing damage to them or other organisms.

❺ Care should be taken to avoid stressing a subject. Some fish are clearly unhappy when a camera invades their 'personal space' or when pictures are taken using flash or other lights; others are unconcerned and so make better subjects.

❻ Divers and photographers should never kill marine life to attract other types to them or to create a photographic opportunity, such as feeding sea urchins to wrasse. Creatures should never be handled or irritated to create a reaction, and sedentary ones should never be placed on an alien background, which may result in them being killed or damaged.

❼ Queuing to photograph a rare subject, such as a seahorse, should be avoided because of the harm that repeated bursts of bright light may do to their eyesight. For the same reason, the number of shots of any individual subject should be kept to the minimum.

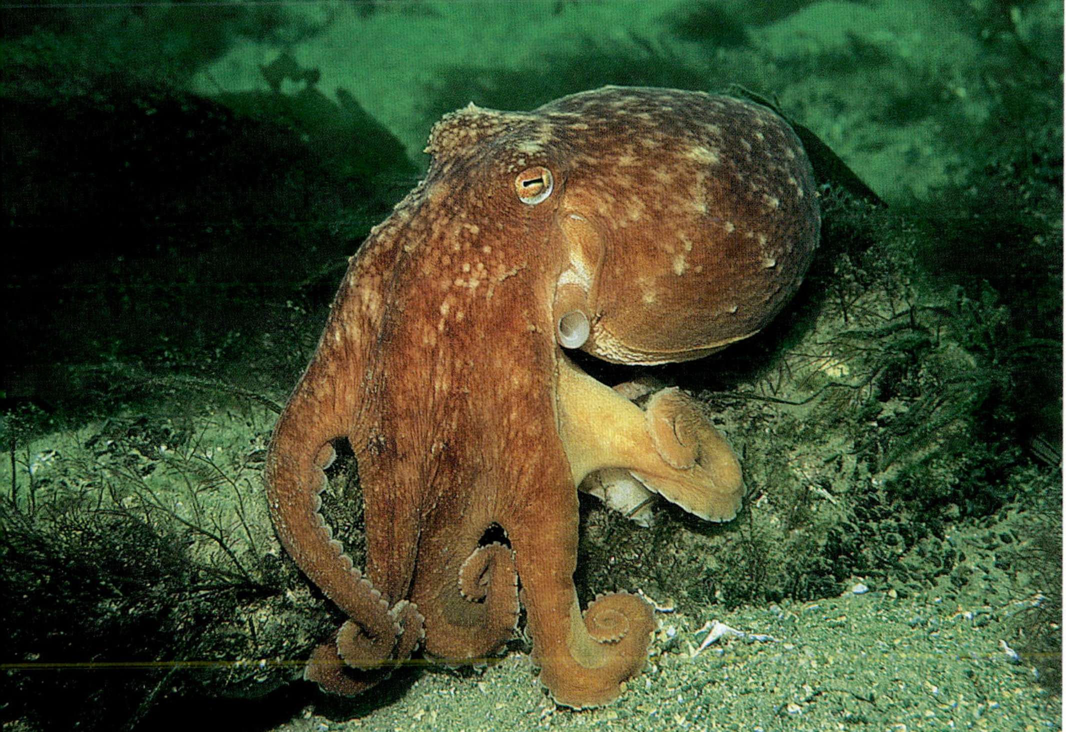

When an octopus changes colour, it is an indiction that it is worried and taking action to discourage attack. As it was becoming stressed, this was the last of three photos that I took of this specimen, despite the fact that the shallow, sunlit seabed off Trefor Pier provided good conditions for photography.
Subal-housed Nikon F100 and 60mm micro-Nikkor lens, with a Nikon SB105 flash unit. 1/60s at f/16 on Fuji Velvia 50 ISO

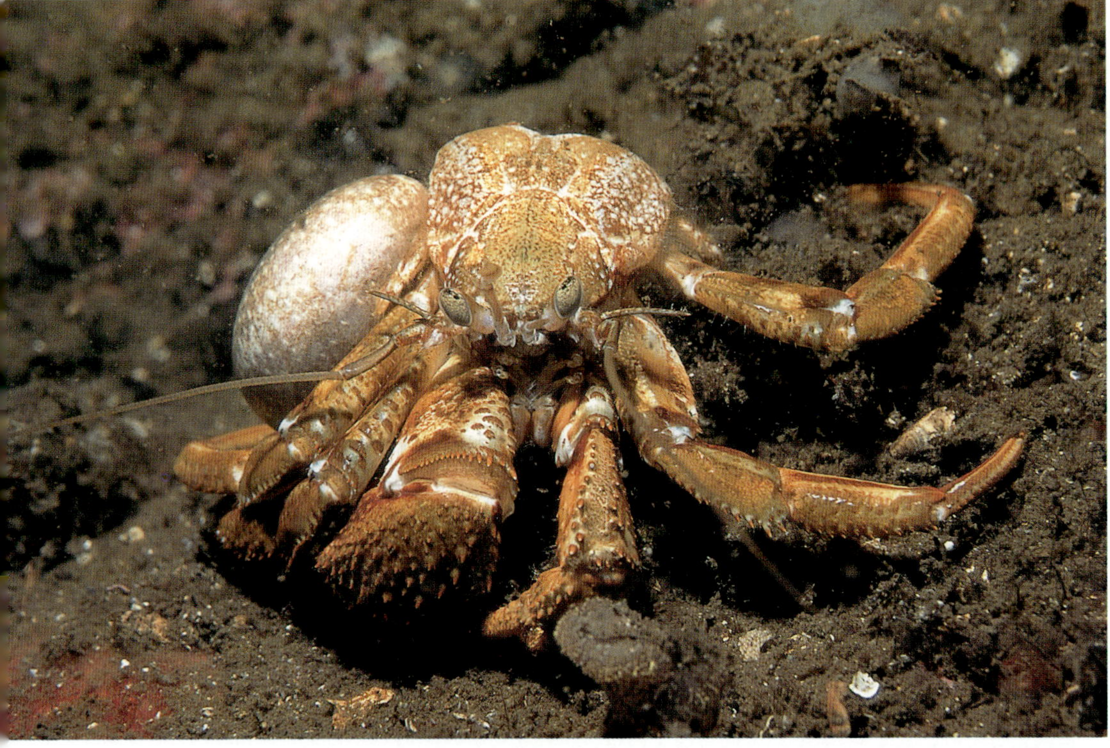

This hermit crab (probably *Eupagurus* sp.) has, unusually, lost its home (a whelk shell) and has been photographed while vulnerable. Sound of Mull, west Scotland.
Subal-housed Nikon F100 and 60mm micro-Nikkor lens. 1/60s at f/16 on Fuji Velvia 50 ISO

❽ Clown fish and other territorial animals are popular subjects but some become highly stressed when a photographer moves in to take a picture. If a subject exhibits abnormal behaviour, move on and find another.

❾ Night diving requires exceptional care because it is much more difficult to be aware of your surroundings. Strong torch beams or lights can dazzle fish and cause them to harm themselves by blundering into surrounding coral or rocks. Others are confused and disturbed if torch beams or lights are pointed directly at them. Be prepared to keep bright lights off subjects that exhibit stressed behaviour, using only the edge of the beam to minimize disturbance.

❿ Care should be taken when photographing in caves, caverns, or even inside wrecks, because exhaust bubbles can become trapped under overhangs, killing marine life. Even small pockets of trapped air that allow divers to talk to each other can be lethal for marine life.

⓫ The image in the viewfinder can be very compelling. Photographers should remain conscious of their position

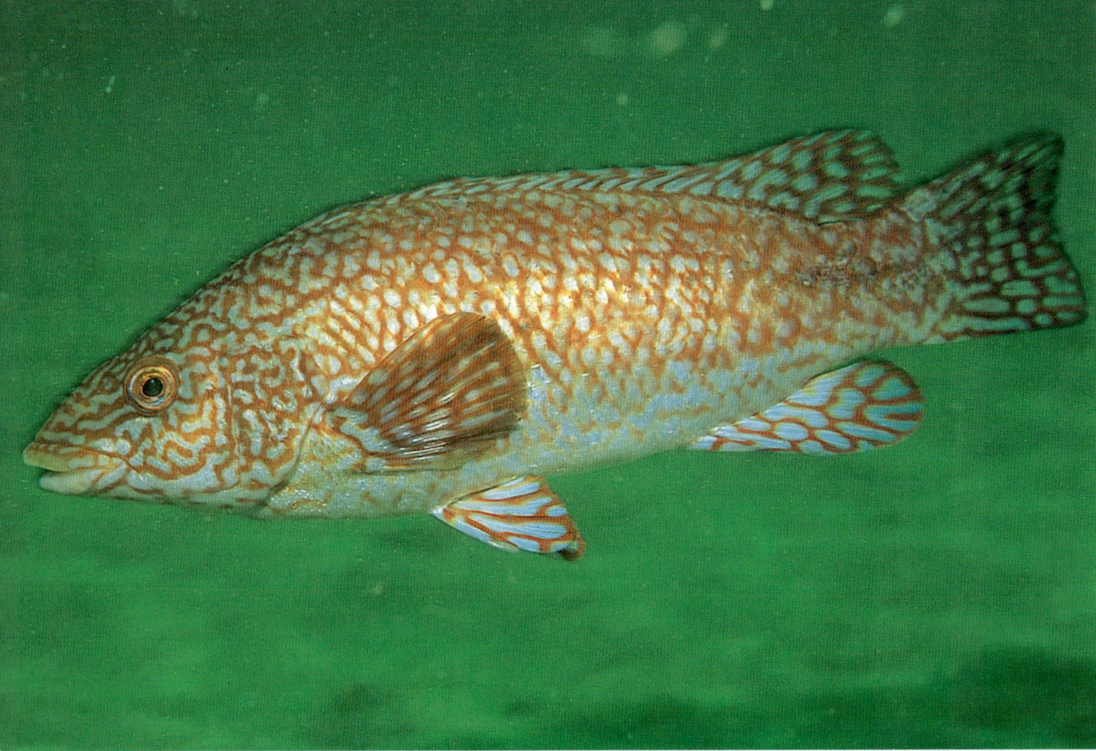

Port Erin breakwater on the Isle of Man has some of the friendliest fish in the world (possibly attracted by the bad habit that some divers have of breaking up urchins). This is an excellent place for trying balanced-background shots of moving subjects, like this big ballan wrasse (*Labrus bergylta*).
Subal-housed Nikon F100 and 60mm micro-Nikkor, with a Nikon SB105 flash unit. 1/4s at f/16 on Fuji Velvia 50 ISO

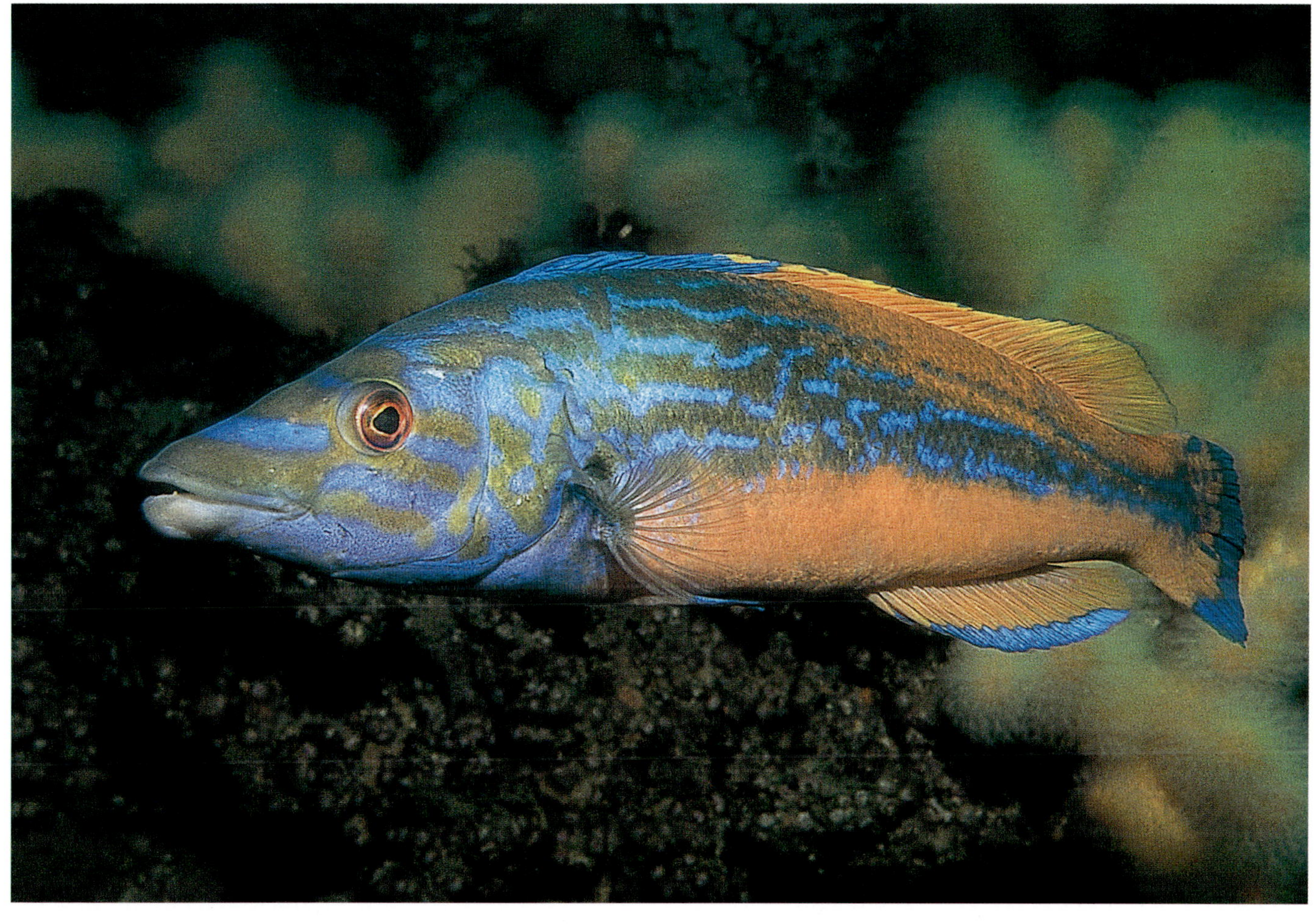

Male cuckoo wrasses (*Labrus mixtus*) are one of the most colourful of temperate fish. Despite being curious, they are fast moving and dart around close to divers, making them a very challenging subject. This one was wary of other territory-infringing males and had stopped to watch transgressors, enabling a good portrait. ***Subal-housed Nikon F801 and 60mm micro-Nikkor, with a Nikon SB105 flash unit. 1/30s at f/16 on Fuji Velvia 50 ISO***

and of the marine life around them at all times. In sensitive areas, they should avoid moving around on the bottom while their mask is pressed up against the camera viewfinder.

⓬ Areas of extensive damage or pollution should be reported to the appropriate authorities.

Today, when so many more divers are taking up underwater photography, both still and video, it is essential that the preservation of the fragile marine environment and its creatures is paramount, and that this *Code of Good Practice* is carefully observed.

This *Code of Good Practice* has been introduced by the Marine Conservation Society with funding from PADI's AWARE project. It is endorsed by the British Society of Underwater Photographers, the Northern Underwater Photographic Group and the Bristol Underwater Photography Group, as well as being supported by the Sub-Aqua Association, the British Sub-Aqua Club and the Scottish Sub-Aqua Club.

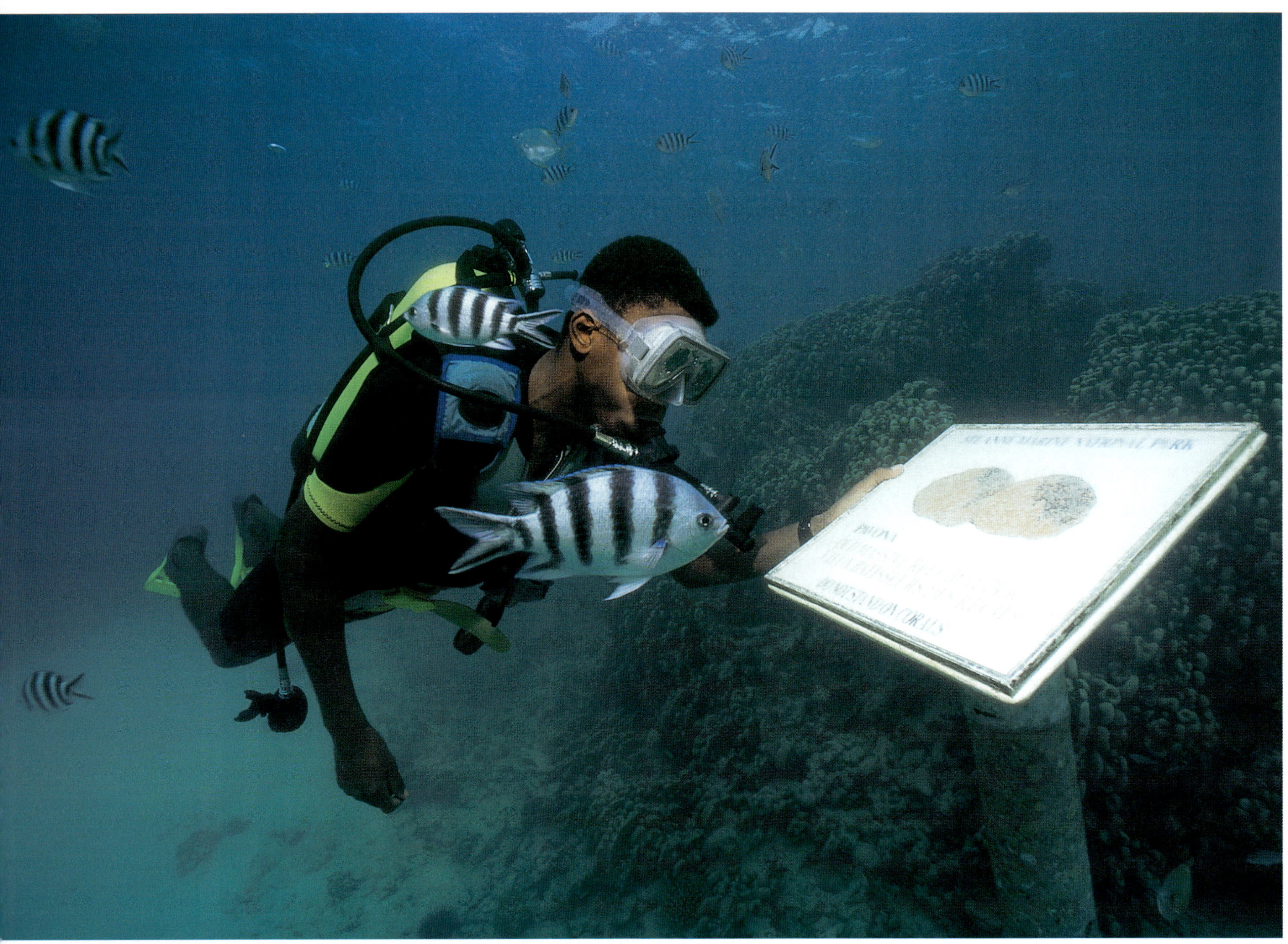

St Anne's marine park in the Seychelles has a snorkel trail complete with underwater interpretation boards. It appears from this picture that the park's inhabitants are keen to show visiting divers what is to be seen here. This shot is all about timing.

Subal-housed Nikon F801 and 20mm Nikkor lens, with a diffused Nikon SB105 flash unit. 1/30s at f/11 on Fuji Velvia 50 ISO

gallery

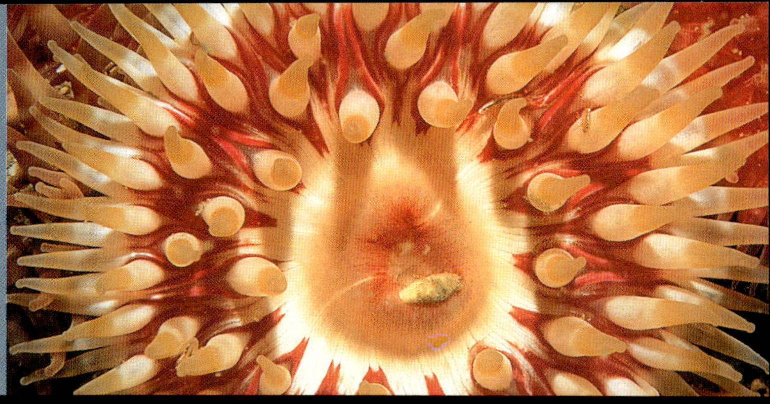

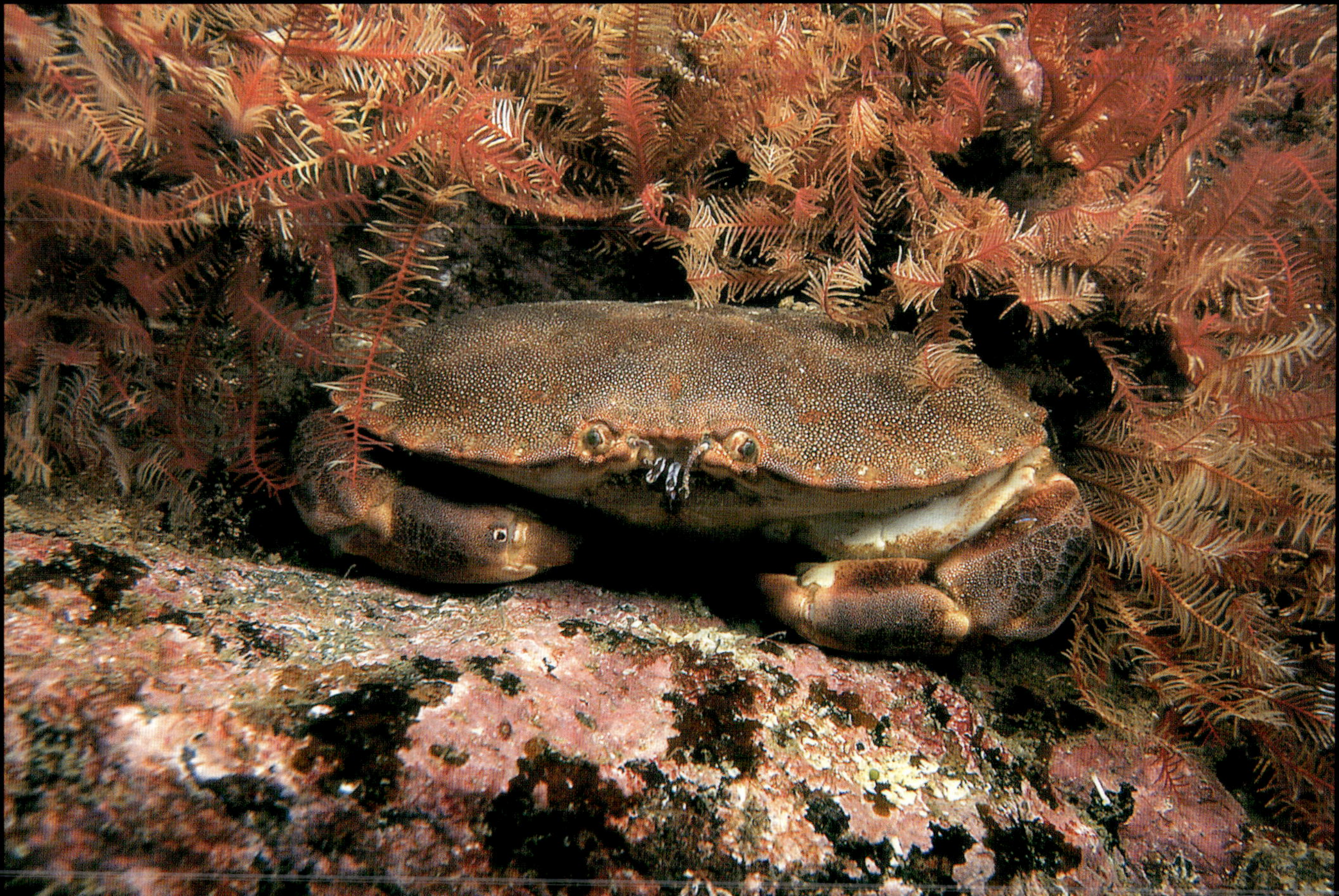

There is more to this picture of an edible crab in a crevice than meets the eye. Above are featherstars and below is pink algae-encrusted rock. This is a very typical photo of the west coast of Scotland.
Subal-housed Nikon F100 and 60mm micro lens, with a Nikon SB105 flash unit. 1/30s at f/16 on Fuji Provia III 100 ISO

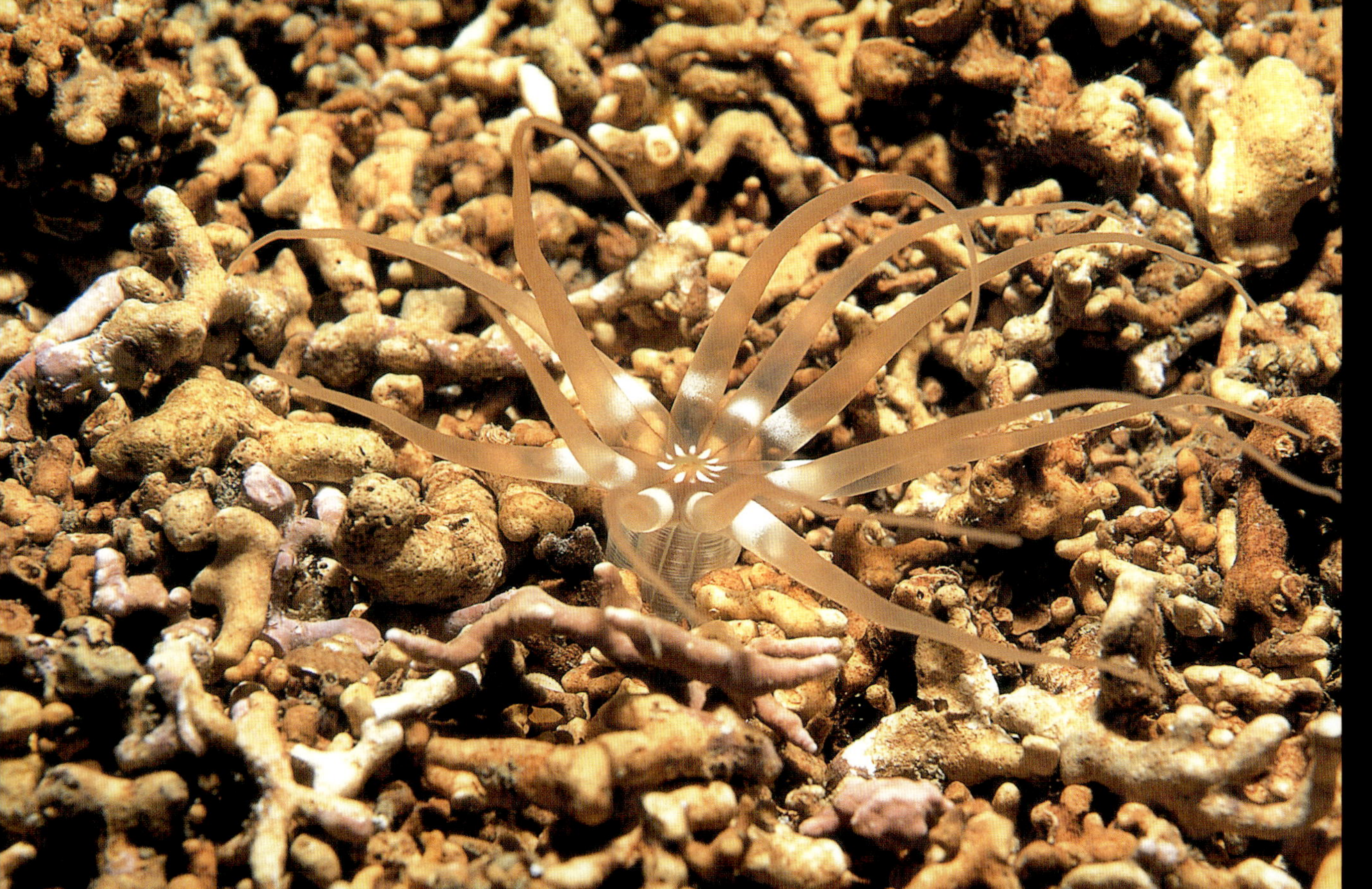

Some undersea creatures are nocturnal, like this burrowing anemone (*Halcampoides purpurea*), which also lives in current-swept maerl beds. This makes it a tricky subject simply because it is hard to find! ***Subal-housed Nikon F801 and 60mm micro lens, with a Nikon SB105 flash unit. 1/60s at f/16 on Fuji Velvia 50 ISO***

Mud may not appeal to many underwater photographers as a hunting ground, but does compensate by providing some whacky creatures, like this mud-runner crab (*Goneplax rhomboids*).
Subal-housed Nikon F100 and 60mm micro lens, with a Nikon SB105 flash unit. 1/60s at f/16 on Fuji Velvia 50 ISO

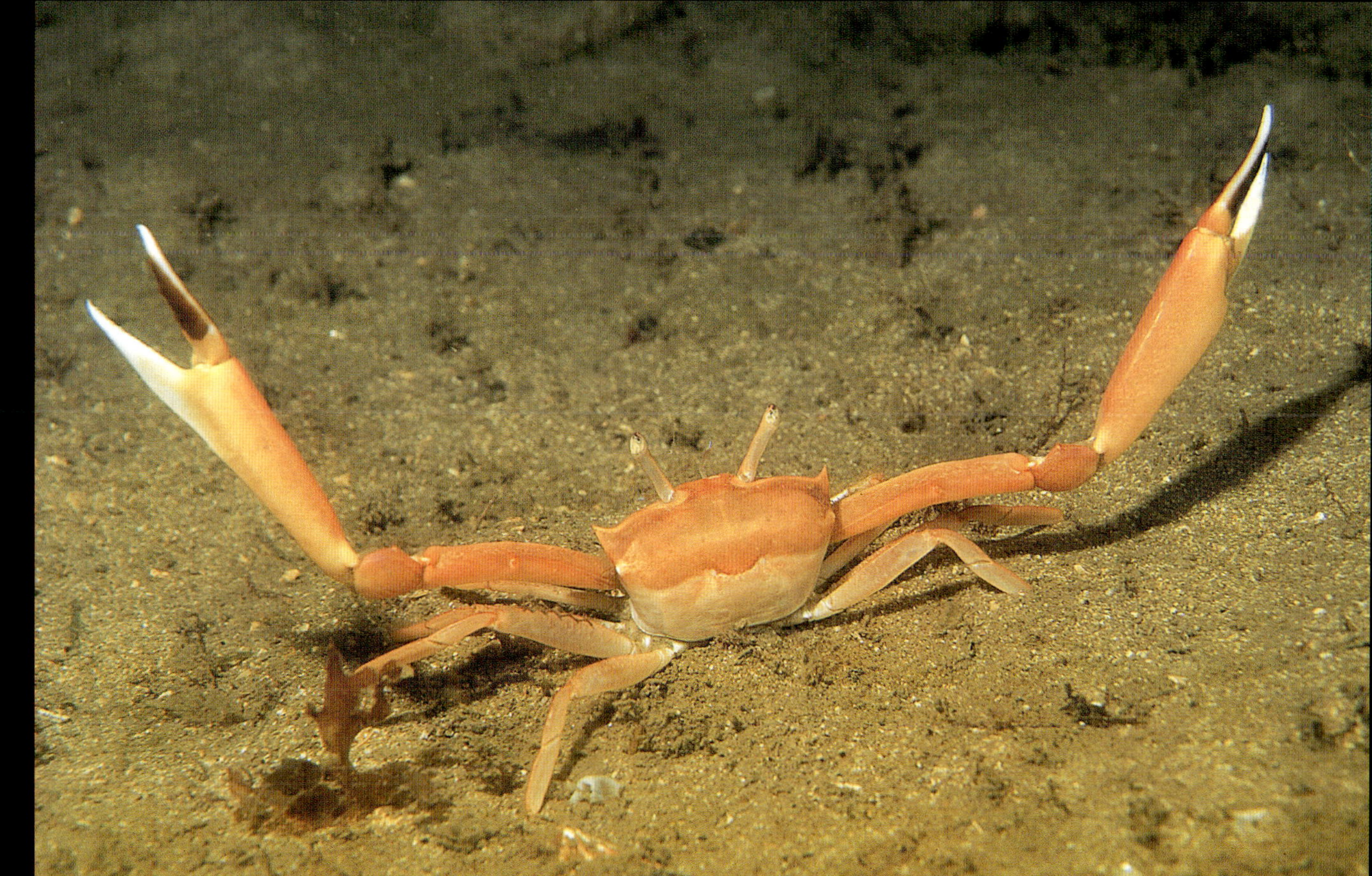

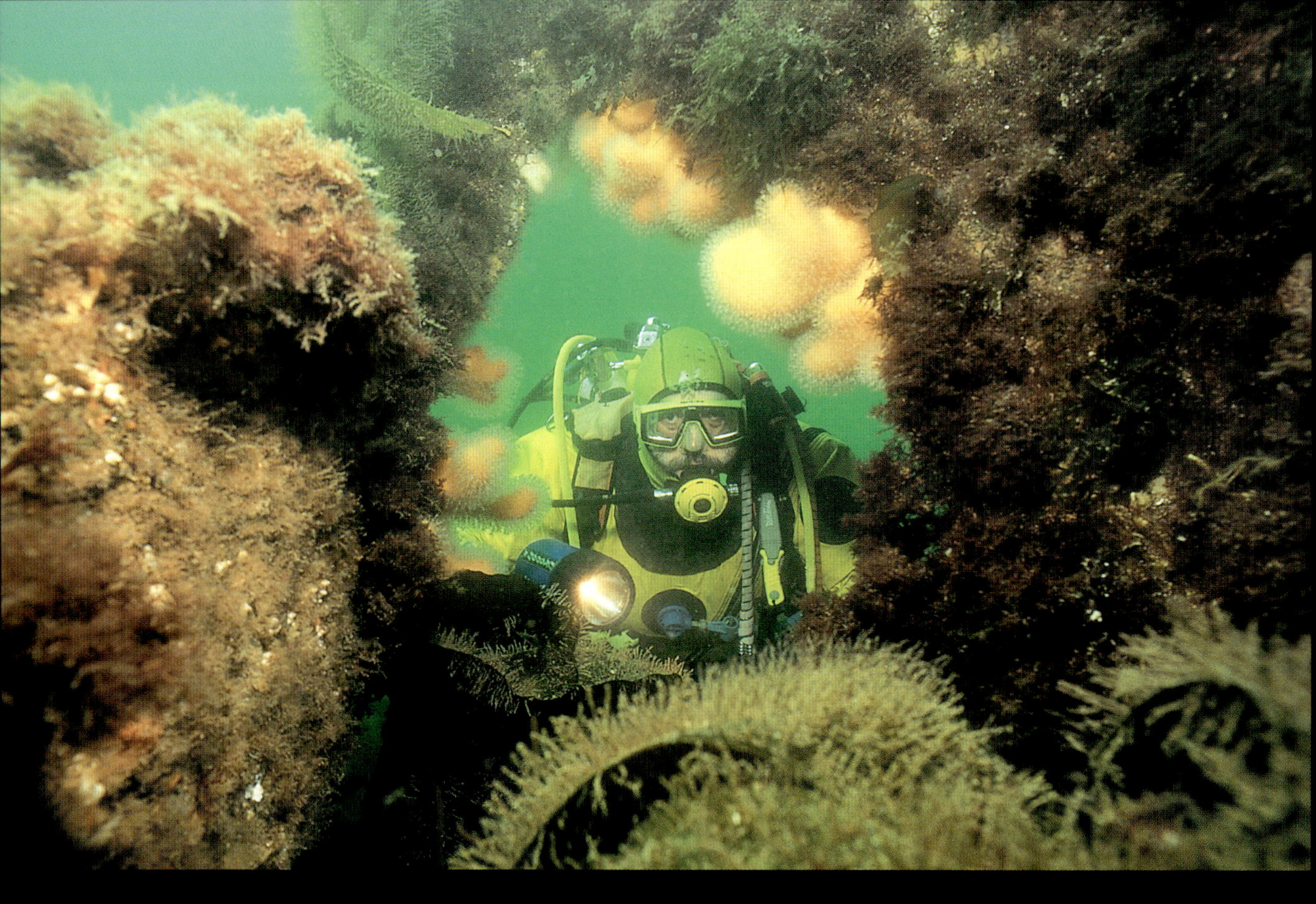

Wrecks can be photogenic when covered in marine life, as is the case with this Clyde puffer, lost off Islay in south-west Scotland. ***Subal-housed Nikon F801 and 20mm lens, with a diffused Nikon SB105 flash unit. 1/15s at f/11 on Fuji Provia II 100 ISO***

Fortunately for this ragged creature (a seven-armed starfish, *Luidia ciliaris*) starfish can regenerate their arms, and this one is in the process of doing so.
Subal-housed Nikon F801 and 60mm micro lens, with a Nikon SB105 flash unit. 1/60s at f/16 on Fuji Provia III 100 ISO

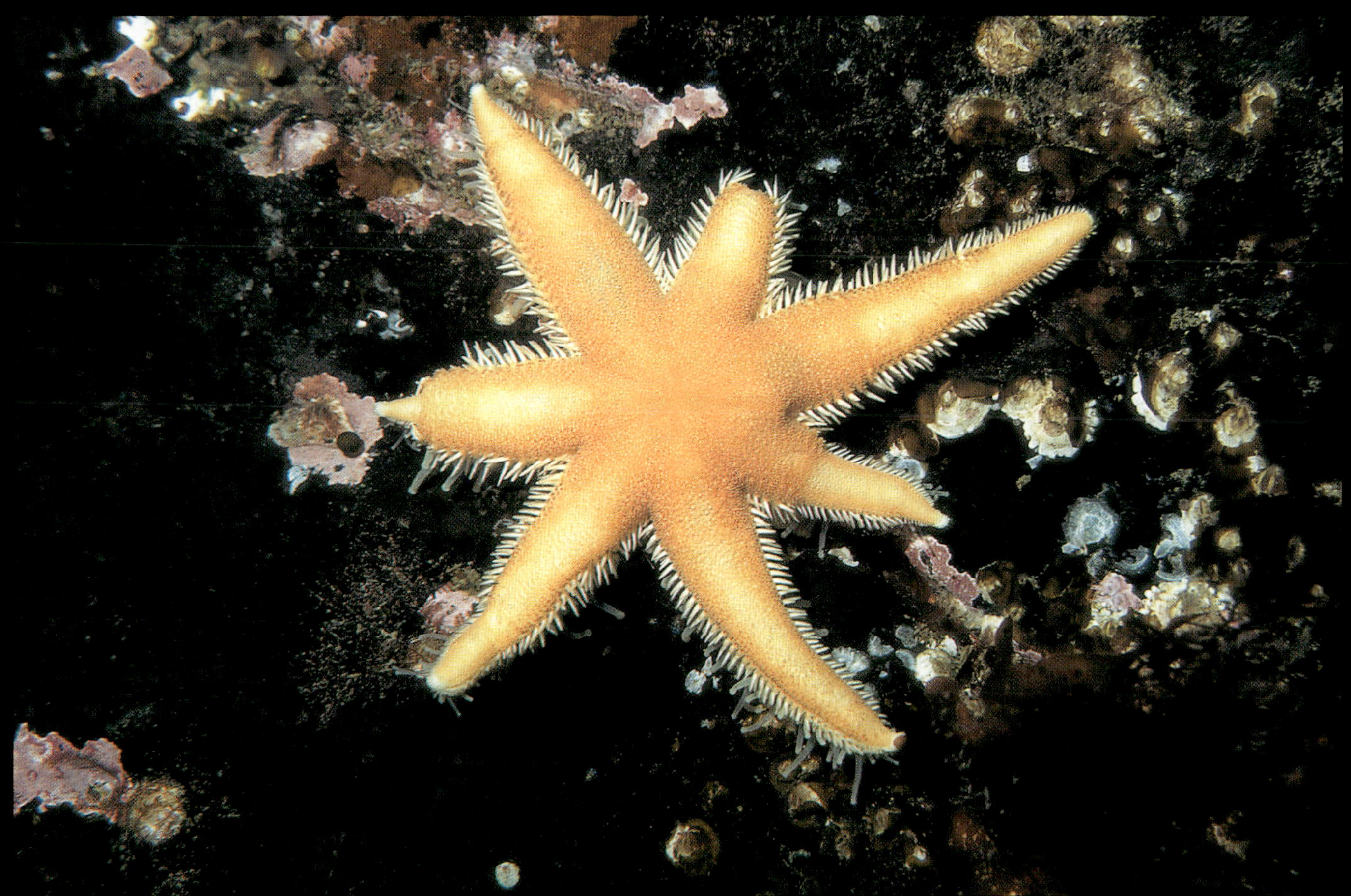

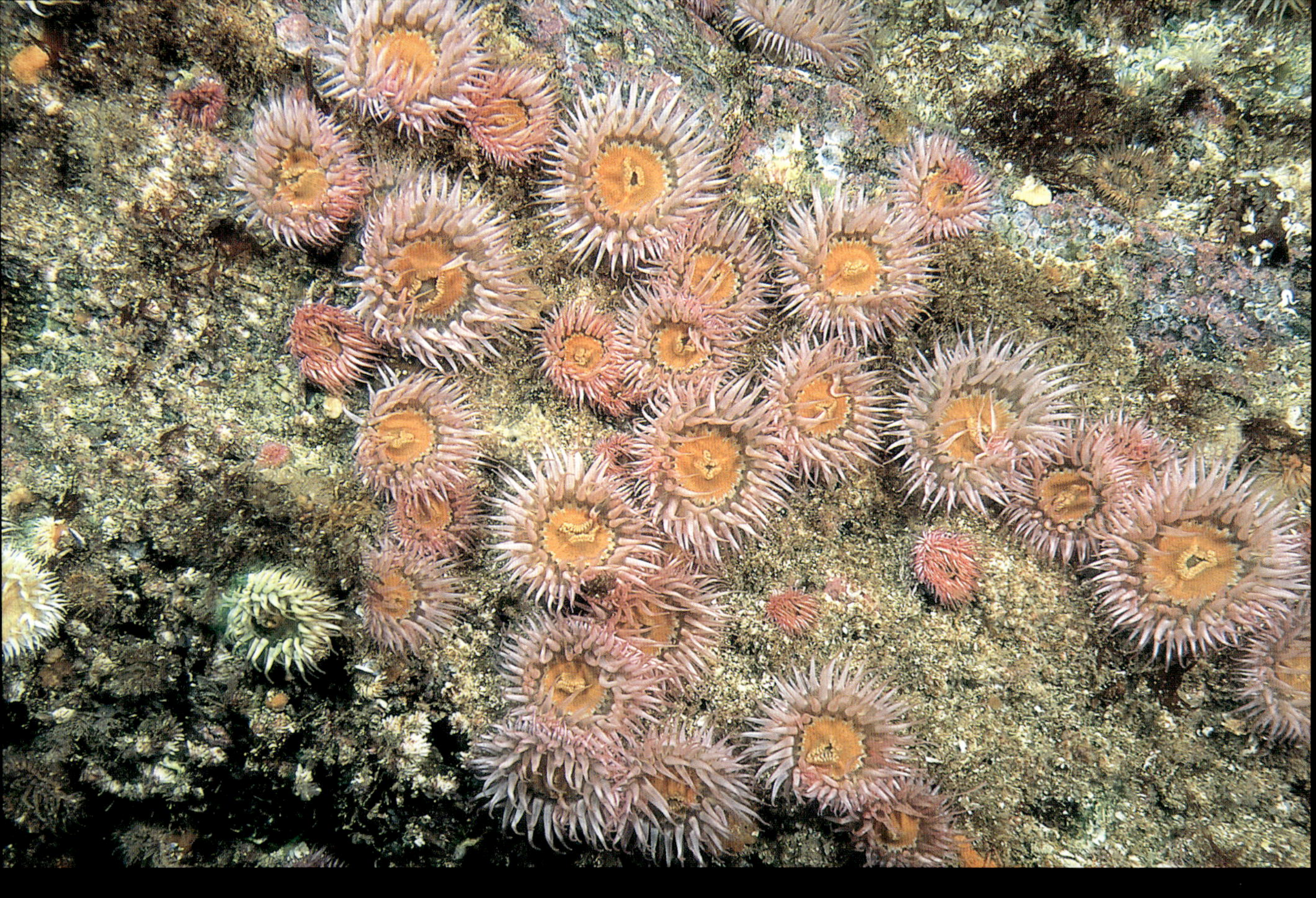

Sagartia elegans **anemones are very variable in colour. These are of the variety known as Rosea and were on a vertical rock wall west of the Outer Hebrides, Scotland.**
Subal-housed Nikon F100 and 17–35mm AFS lens set at 35mm, with two diffused Nikon SB105 flash units. 1/30s at f/16 on Fuji Provia III 100 ISO

Inland dive sites are difficult to portray on film. Here, a diver is captured in Vivien Quarry in Snowdonia, UK, by available light on a poor port/lens combination. Despite this, the shot still produced an interesting result.
Subal-housed Nikon F100 and 18–35mm lens in a 24–50mm port. 1/15s at f/8–11 on Fuji Provia III 100 ISO

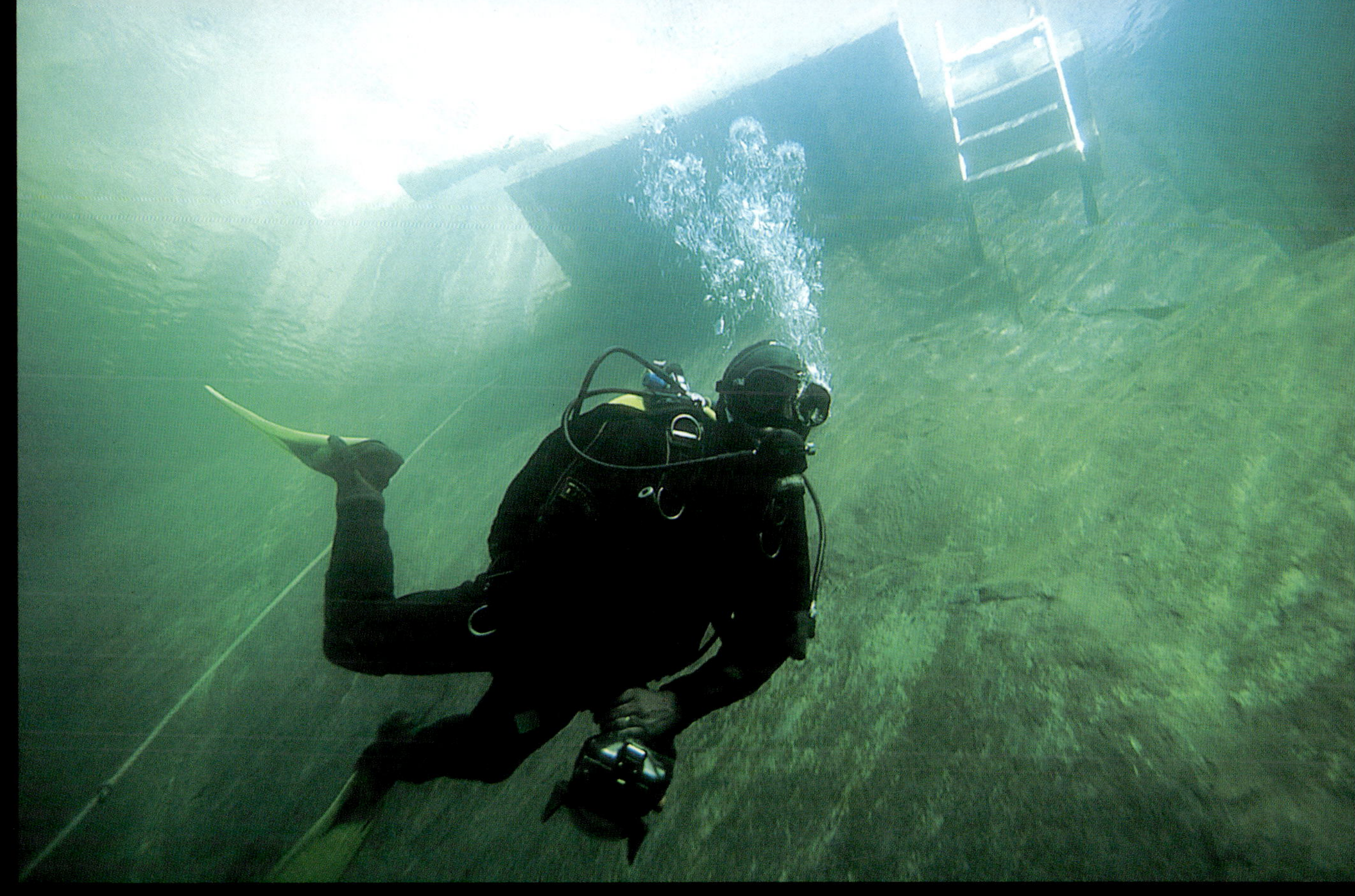

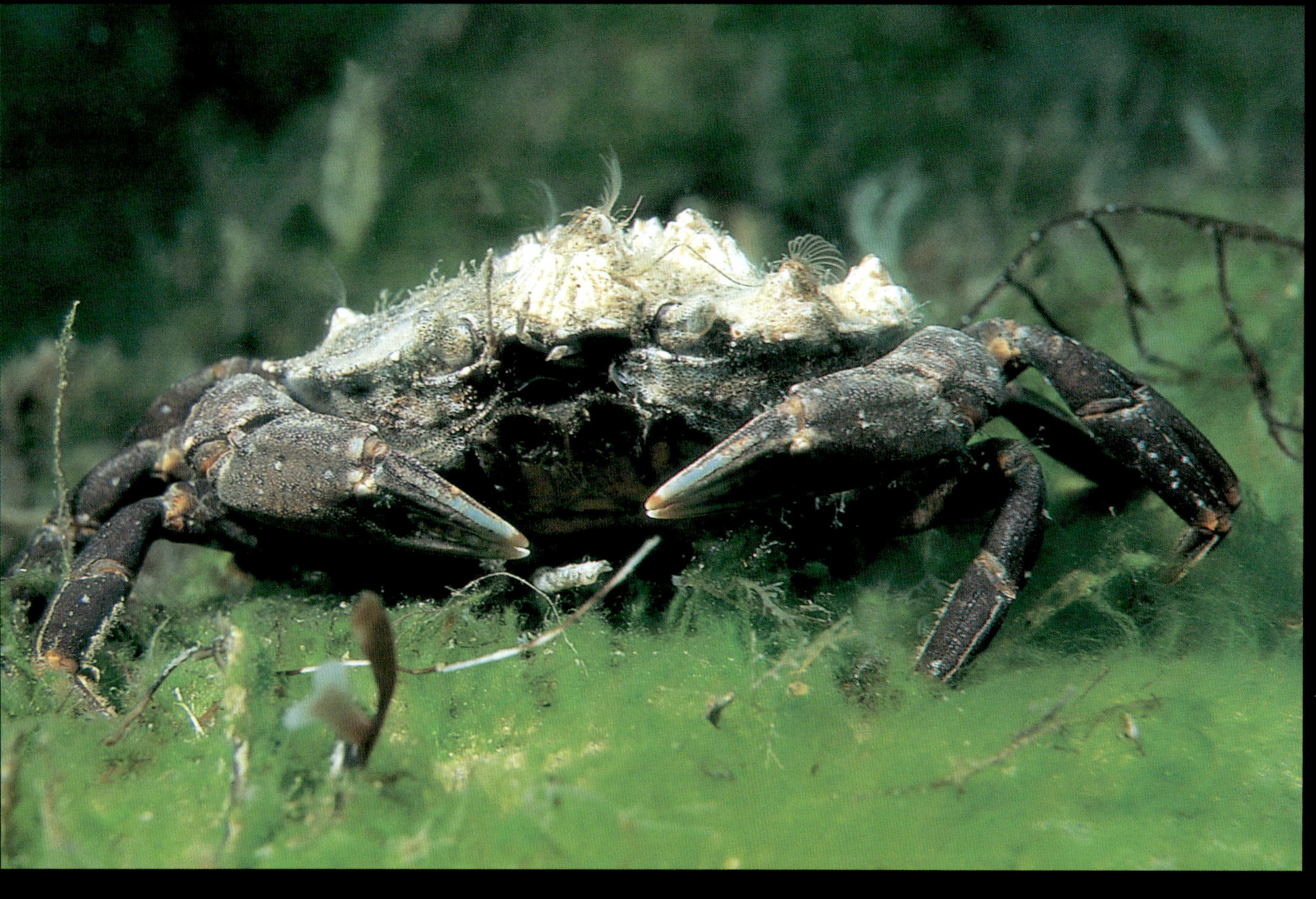

This photograph of a shore crab (*Carcinus maenas*) is helped by the vivid green of the seaweed on which it is standing.
Subal-housed Nikon F80 and 60mm micro lens, with two Nikon SB105 flash units. 1/8s at f/22 on Fuji Provia III 100 ISO

Even on a cold March day, underwater photography is still possible. Capernwray Quarry near Lancaster in north-west England has plenty of friendly trout.
Subal-housed Nikon F801 and 60mm lens, with a Nikon SB105 flash unit. 1/8s at f/11 on Fuji Provia III 100 ISO

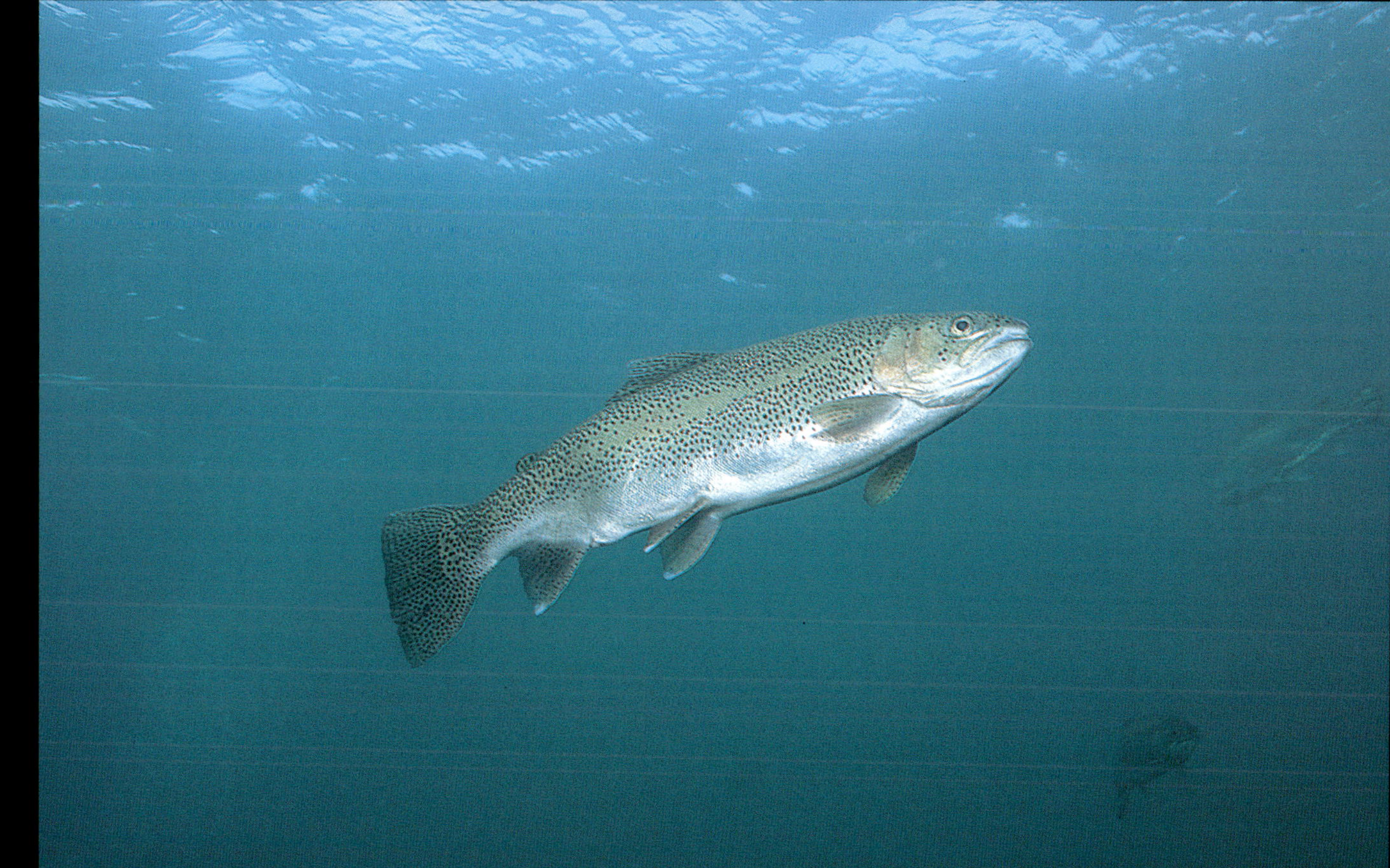

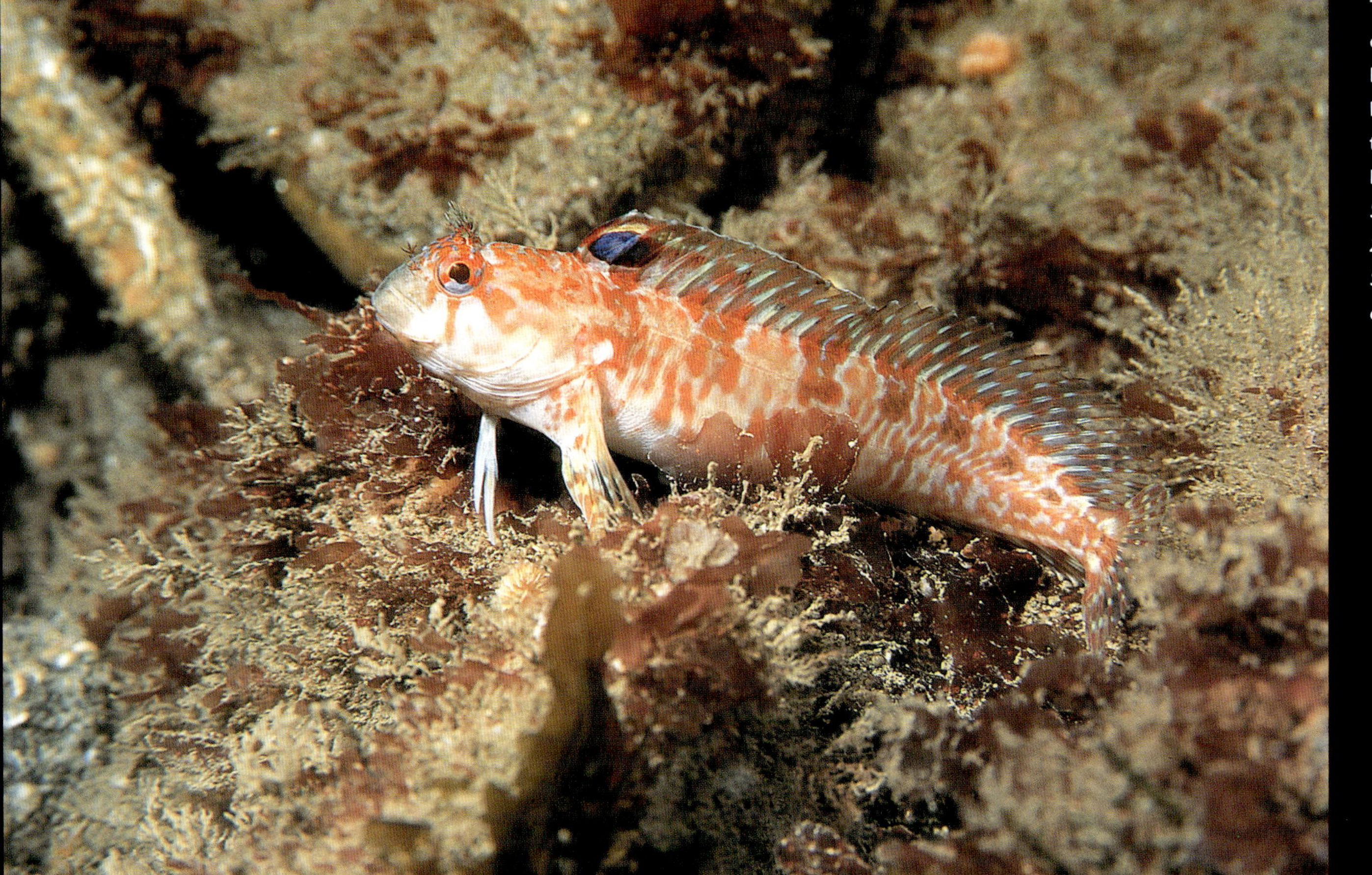

This is the first-known photo of a male Red or Portuguese Blenny (*Blennius ruber*) in breeding colours. Taken in temperate waters off the Aran Islands in Ireland.
Subal-housed Nikon F100 and 28–105mm lens, with two Nikon SB105 flash units. 1/60s at f/16 on Fuji Provia III 100 ISO

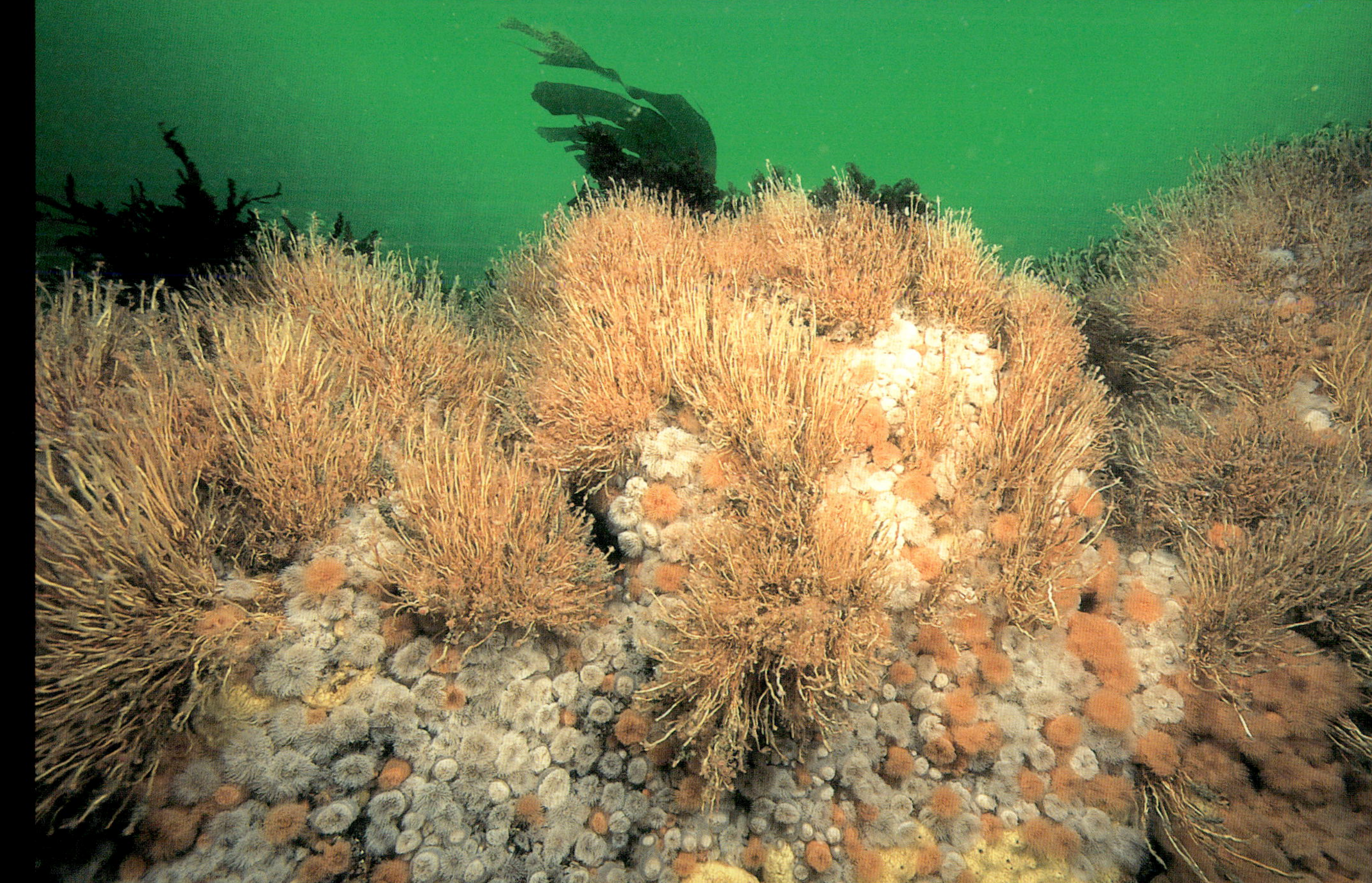

A heavily coated rocky reef off the Calf of Man in the Isle of Man, UK.

A balanced-light shot from a Subal-housed Nikon F100 and 17–35mm AFS lens set at 17mm, with two diffused Nikon SB105 flash units. 1/8s at f/11 on Fuji Provia III 100 ISO

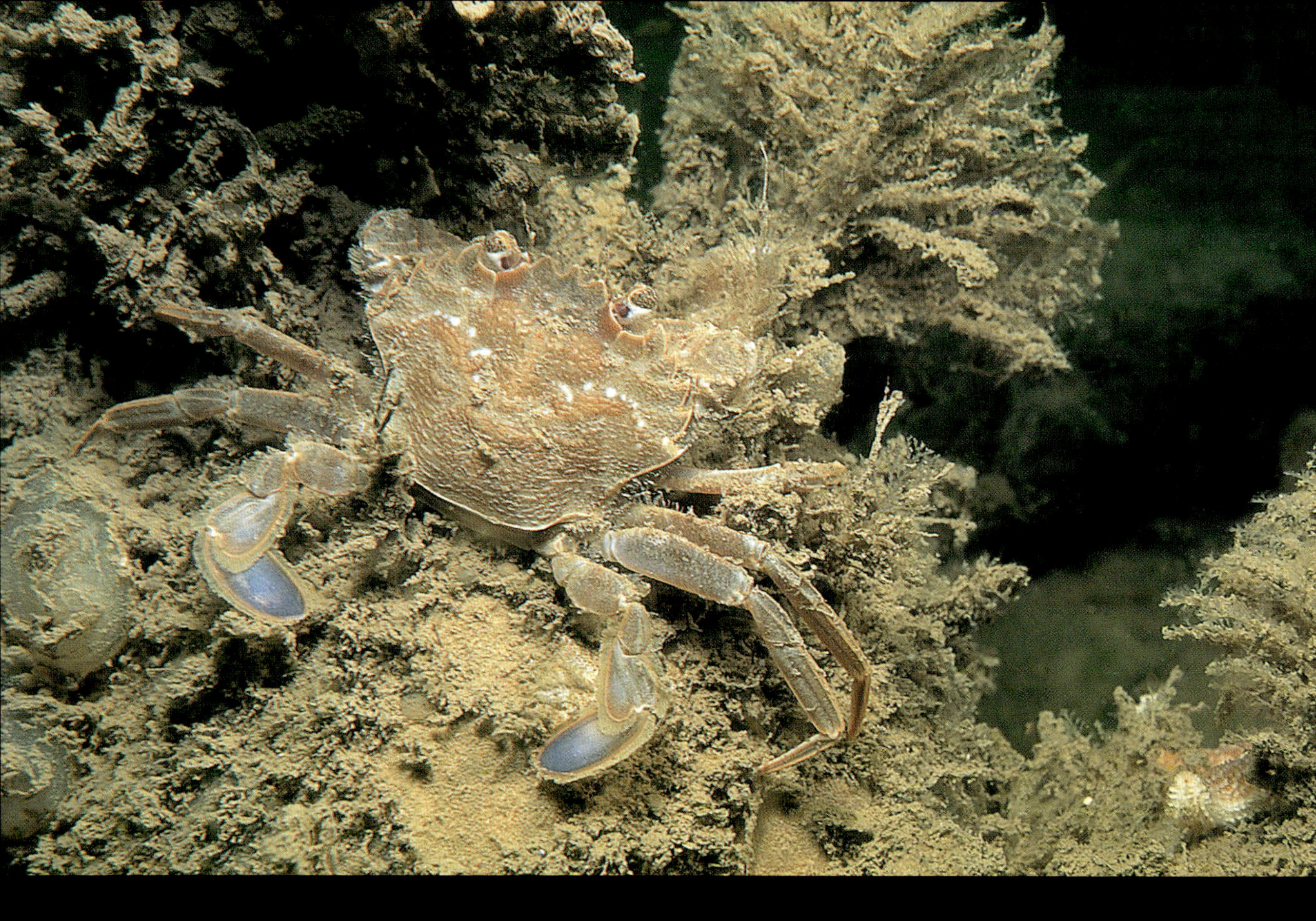

An unusual shot of a swimming crab (*Liocarcinus depurator*) taken during a scientific survey off the Fylde coast in north-west England, which is notorious for its poor visibility.
Subal-housed Nikon F100 and 60mm micro lens, with a Nikon SB105 flash unit. 1/60s at f/16 on Fuji Provia III 100 ISO

Dahlia anemones (*Urticina felina*) can be extremely photogenic.
Subal-housed Nikon F100 and 60mm lens, with a Nikon SB105 flash unit. 1/60s at f/16 on Fuji Velvia 50 ISO

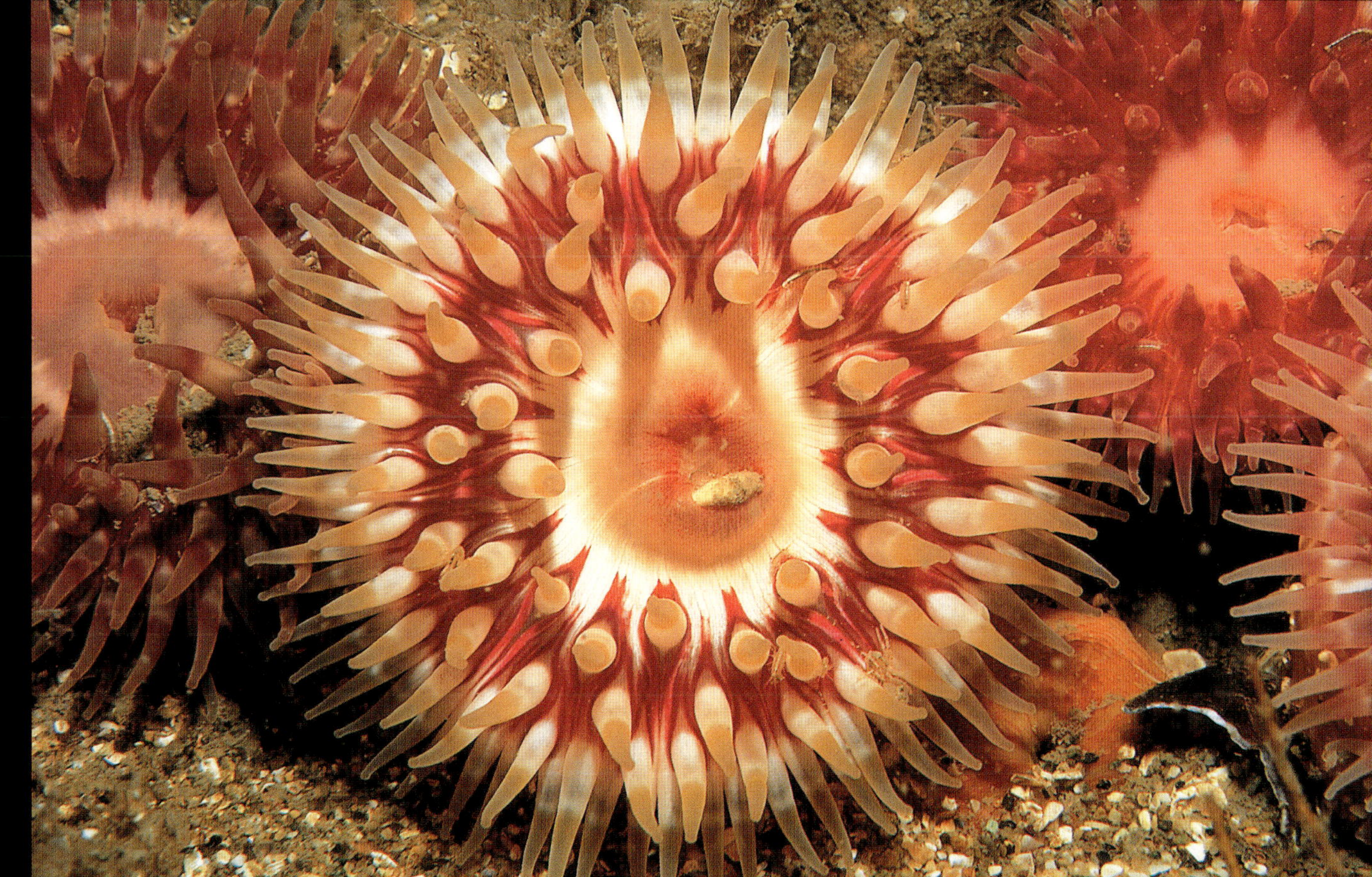

appendix

This diagram shows the interaction between the flash unit's 'cone' of illumination and the lens's pyramid-shaped field of view when using a simple macro set-up (for details see pages 123-5).

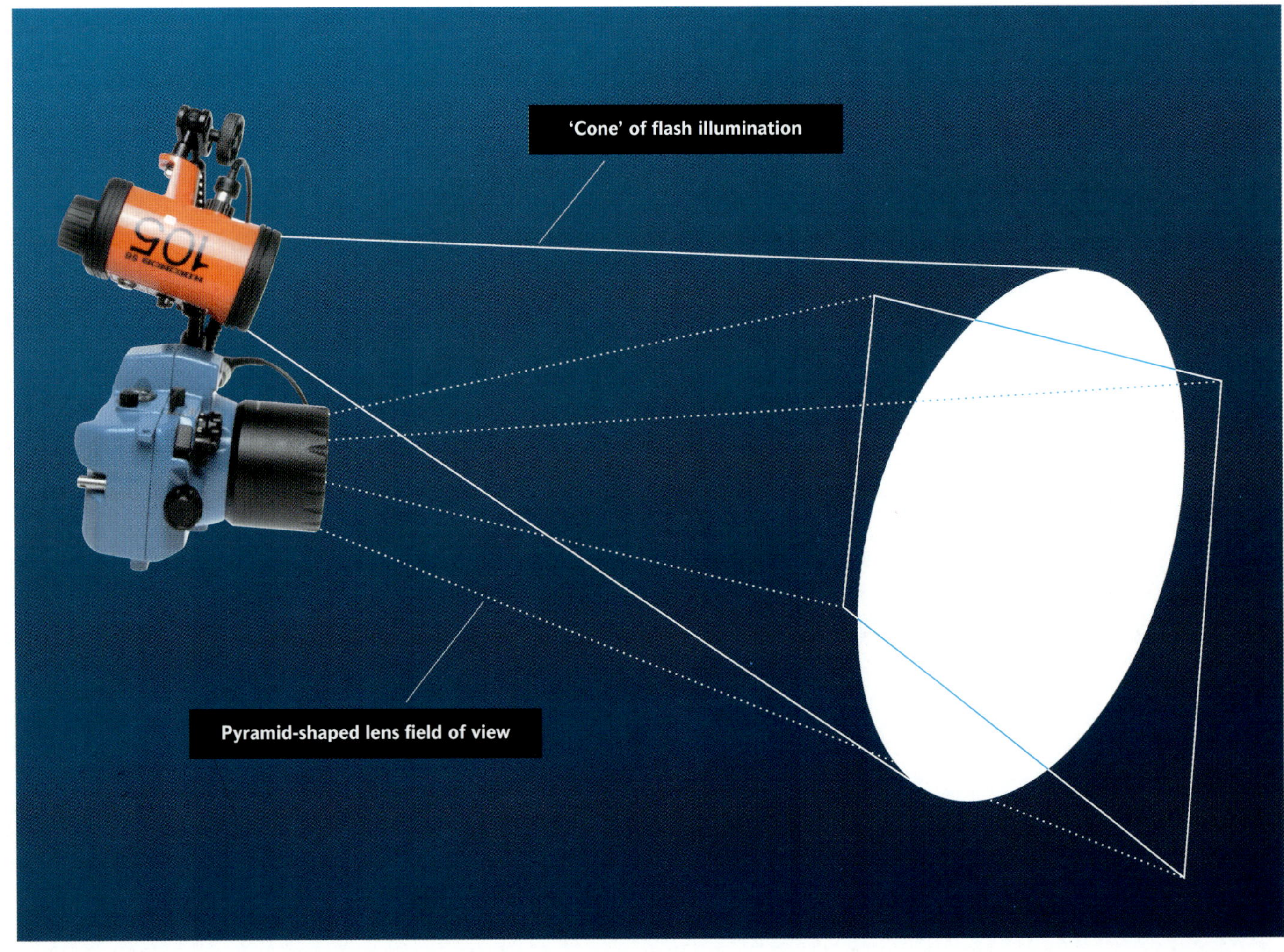

further reading

Some of these are out of print, but can probably be found through a book search service.

Underwater Photography by John Turner (Focal Press, 1982)
ISBN 0 240 51122 0

This is an old book, but it covers a wide range of basic information. It is well worth reading as it covers many aspects of underwater photography and is a good insight into the associated problems.

The Manual of Underwater Photography by Heinz Gert De Couet & Andrew Green (Verlag Christa Hemmen, 1989)
ISBN 3 925919 02 3

This book is almost a must-have for anyone interested in underwater photography. It is an extensive volume covering an enormous amount of information on underwater photography. It predates marginally the introduction of autofocus and as such is over-reliant on the Nikonos system, but it is very good on basic theory and lighting.

The Underwater Photographer (2nd Edition) by Martin Edge (Focal Press, 1999)
ISBN 0 240 51581 1

This is a popular book which explains many aspects of underwater photography, and which covers the author's distinctive 'think and consider' system.

A Manual of Underwater Photography by T Glover, GE Harwood & JN Lythgoe (Academic Press, 1977)
ISBN 0 12 286750 5

Although now very dated in some ways, this is one of the few books available that contains information and theory on the optics of underwater lens systems. It also gives details on sealing systems.

The Underwater Photographer's Handbook by Peter Rowlands (Van Nostrand Reinhold, 1983)
ISBN 0 442 27716 4

This is a very informative book, again somewhat dated, but with lots of useful and interesting information in it.

The Art & Technique of Underwater Photography by Mark Webster (Fountain Press, 1998)
ISBN 0 86343 352 9

A modern book showing the quality of images possible with modern autofocus cameras.

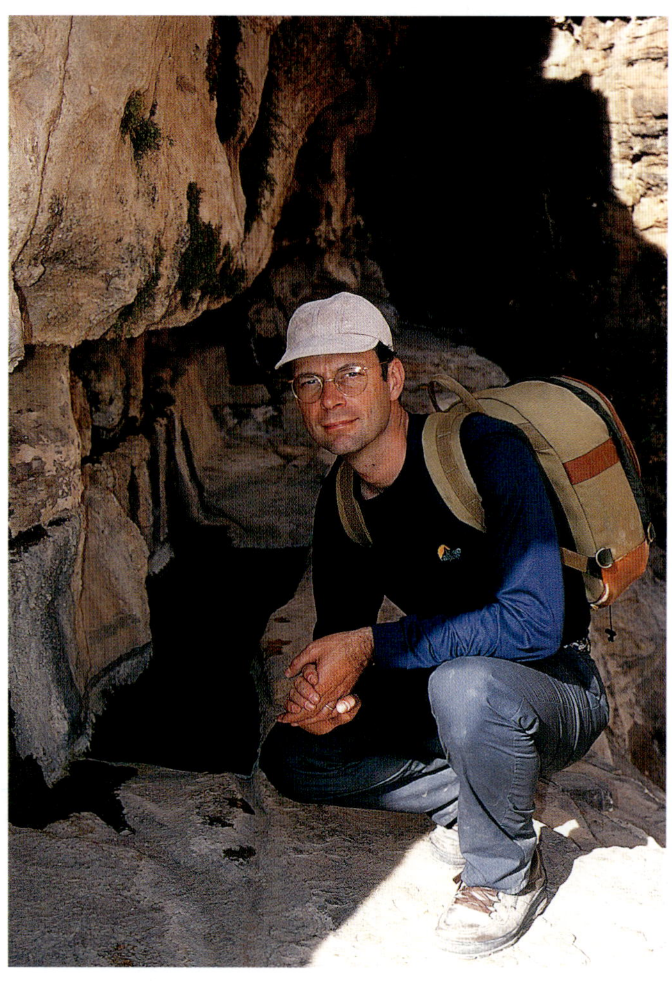

about the author

Paul Kay's credentials as an underwater photographer are second to none. After graduating from university in 1981 with a degree in photographic science, Paul achieved the distinction of becoming the first person to be awarded a fellowship by the Royal Photographic Society for temperate underwater photography. His pictures have been published worldwide and have won numerous awards in British and international competitions.

He has been a freelance photographer and writer since 1990, and is the author of many illustrated articles and several previous books including, most recently, *The Diver's Guide to the Lundy Marine Nature Reserve*, which he produced for English Nature. In addition, he runs photography courses, leads expeditions to both tropical and temperate regions, and plays an active role in several diving and photography groups.

Paul Kay lives in North Wales, where he runs his own image library, The Marine Wildlife Photo Agency. This is his first title for GMC Publications.

index

A

B

C

D

E

F

G

H

I

L

S

T

V

W

Z

TITLES AVAILABLE FROM

GMC Publications

BOOKS

A Beginners' Guide to the Dolls' House Hobby *Jean Nisbett*
Celtic, Medieval and Tudor Wall Hangings in 1/12 Scale Needlepoint *Sandra Whitehead*
Creating Decorative Fabrics: Projects in 1/12 Scale *Janet Storey*
Dolls' House Accessories, Fixtures and Fittings *Andrea Barham*
Dolls' House Furniture: Easy-to-Make Projects in 1/12 Scale *Freida Gray*
Dolls' House Makeovers *Jean Nisbett*
Dolls' House Window Treatments *Eve Harwood*
Edwardian-Style Hand-Knitted Fashion for 1/12 Scale Dolls *Yvonne Wakefield*
How to Make Your Dolls' House Special: Fresh Ideas for Decorating *Beryl Armstrong*
Making 1/12 Scale Wicker Furniture for the Dolls' House *Sheila Smith*
Making Miniature Chinese Rugs and Carpets *Carol Phillipson*
Making Miniature Food and Market Stalls *Angie Scarr*
Making Miniature Gardens *Freida Gray*
Making Miniature Oriental Rugs & Carpets *Meik & Ian McNaughton*
Making Miniatures: Projects for the 1/12 Scale Dolls' House *Christiane Berridge*
Making Period Dolls' House Accessories *Andrea Barham*
Making Tudor Dolls' Houses *Derek Rowbottom*
Making Upholstered Furniture in 1/12 Scale *Janet Storey*
Making Victorian Dolls' House Furniture *Patricia King*
Medieval and Tudor Needlecraft: Knights and Ladies in 1/12 Scale *Sandra Whitehead*
Miniature Bobbin Lace *Roz Snowden*
Miniature Crochet: Projects in 1/12 Scale *Roz Walters*
Miniature Embroidery for the Georgian Dolls' House *Pamela Warner*
Miniature Embroidery for the Tudor and Stuart Dolls' House *Pamela Warner*
Miniature Embroidery for the 20th-Century Dolls' House *Pamela Warner*
Miniature Embroidery for the Victorian Dolls' House *Pamela Warner*
Miniature Needlepoint Carpets *Janet Granger*
More Miniature Oriental Rugs & Carpets *Meik & Ian McNaughton*
Needlepoint 1/12 Scale: Design Collections for the Dolls' House *Felicity Price*
New Ideas for Miniature Bobbin Lace *Roz Snowden*
Patchwork Quilts for the Dolls' House: 20 Projects in 1/12 Scale *Sarah Williams*
Simple Country Furniture Projects in 1/12 Scale *Alison J. White*

CRAFTS

Bargello: A Fresh Approach to Florentine Embroidery *Brenda Day*
Beginning Picture Marquetry *Lawrence Threadgold*
Blackwork: A New Approach *Brenda Day*
Celtic Cross Stitch Designs *Carol Phillipson*
Celtic Knotwork Designs *Sheila Sturrock*
Celtic Knotwork Handbook *Sheila Sturrock*
Celtic Spirals and Other Designs *Sheila Sturrock*
Celtic Spirals Handbook *Sheila Sturrock*
Complete Pyrography *Stephen Poole*
Creating Made-to-Measure Knitwear: A Revolutionary Approach to Knitwear Design *Sylvia Wynn*
Creative Backstitch *Helen Hall*
Creative Log-Cabin Patchwork *Pauline Brown*
Creative Machine Knitting *GMC Publications*
The Creative Quilter: Techniques and Projects *Pauline Brown*
Cross-Stitch Designs from China *Carol Phillipson*
Cross-Stitch Floral Designs *Joanne Sanderson*
Decoration on Fabric: A Sourcebook of Ideas *Pauline Brown*
Decorative Beaded Purses *Enid Taylor*
Designing and Making Cards *Glennis Gilruth*
Designs for Pyrography and Other Crafts *Norma Gregory*
Dried Flowers: A Complete Guide *Lindy Bird*
Exotic Textiles in Needlepoint *Stella Knight*
Glass Engraving Pattern Book *John Everett*
Glass Painting *Emma Sedman*
Handcrafted Rugs *Sandra Hardy*
Hobby Ceramics: Techniques and Projects for Beginners *Patricia A. Waller*
How to Arrange Flowers: A Japanese Approach to English Design *Taeko Marvelly*
How to Make First-Class Cards *Debbie Brown*
An Introduction to Crewel Embroidery *Mave Glenny*
Machine-Knitted Babywear *Christine Eames*
Making Decorative Screens *Amanda Howes*
Making Fabergé-Style Eggs *Denise Hopper*
Making Fairies and Fantastical Creatures *Julie Sharp*
Making Hand-Sewn Boxes: Techniques and Projects *Jackie Woolsey*
Making Mini Cards, Gift Tags & Invitations *Glennis Gilruth*
Native American Bead Weaving *Lynne Garner*
New Ideas for Crochet: Stylish Projects for the Home *Darsha Capaldi*
Papercraft Projects for Special Occasions *Sine Chesterman*
Papermaking and Bookbinding: Coastal Inspirations *Joanne Kaar*
Patchwork for Beginners *Pauline Brown*
Pyrography Designs *Norma Gregory*
Rose Windows for Quilters *Angela Besley*
Silk Painting for Beginners *Jill Clay*
Sponge Painting *Ann Rooney*
Stained Glass: Techniques and Projects *Mary Shanahan*
Step-by-Step Pyrography Projects for the Solid Point Machine *Norma Gregory*
Stitched Cards and Gift Tags for Special Occasions *Carol Phillipson*
Tassel Making for Beginners *Enid Taylor*
Tatting Collage *Lindsay Rogers*
Tatting Patterns *Lyn Morton*
Temari: A Traditional Japanese Embroidery Technique *Margaret Ludlow*
Three-Dimensional Découpage: Innovative Projects for Beginners *Hilda Stokes*
Trompe l'Oeil: Techniques and Projects *Jan Lee Johnson*
Tudor Treasures to Embroider *Pamela Warner*
Wax Art *Hazel Marsh*

GARDENING

Alpine Gardening *Chris & Valerie Wheeler*
Auriculas for Everyone: How to Grow and Show Perfect Plants *Mary Robinson*
Beginners' Guide to Herb Gardening *Yvonne Cuthbertson*
Beginners' Guide to Water Gardening *Graham Clarke*
Big Leaves for Exotic Effect *Stephen Griffith*
The Birdwatcher's Garden *Hazel & Pamela Johnson*
Companions to Clematis: Growing Clematis with Other Plants *Marigold Badcock*
Creating Contrast with Dark Plants *Freya Martin*
Creating Small Habitats for Wildlife in your Garden *Josie Briggs*
Exotics are Easy *GMC Publications*
Gardening with Hebes *Chris & Valerie Wheeler*
Gardening with Shrubs *Eric Sawford*
Gardening with Wild Plants *Julian Slatcher*
Growing Cacti and Other Succulents in the Conservatory and Indoors *Shirley-Anne Bell*
Growing Cacti and Other Succulents in the Garden *Shirley-Anne Bell*
Growing Successful Orchids in the Greenhouse and Conservatory *Mark Isaac-Williams*
Hardy Palms and Palm-Like Plants *Martyn Graham*
Hardy Perennials: A Beginner's Guide *Eric Sawford*
Hedges: Creating Screens and Edges *Averil Bedrich*
How to Attract Butterflies to your Garden *John & Maureen Tampion*

Marginal Plants *Bernard Sleeman*
Orchids are Easy: A Beginner's Guide to their Care and Cultivation *Tom Gilland*
Plant Alert: A Garden Guide for Parents *Catherine Collins*
Planting Plans for Your Garden *Jenny Shukman*
Sink and Container Gardening Using Dwarf Hardy Plants *Chris & Valerie Wheeler*
The Successful Conservatory and Growing Exotic Plants *Joan Phelan*
Success with Cuttings *Chris & Valerie Wheeler*
Success with Seeds *Chris & Valerie Wheeler*
Tropical Garden Style with Hardy Plants *Alan Hemsley*
Water Garden Projects: From Groundwork to Planting *Roger Sweetinburgh*

Photography

Close-Up on Insects *Robert Thompson*
Digital Enhancement for Landscape Photographers *Arjan Hoogendam & Herb Parkin*
Double Vision *Chris Weston & Nigel Hicks*
An Essential Guide to Bird Photography *Steve Young*
Field Guide to Bird Photography *Steve Young*
Field Guide to Landscape Photography *Peter Watson*
How to Photograph Pets *Nick Ridley*
In my Mind's Eye: Seeing in Black and White *Charlie Waite*
Life in the Wild: A Photographer's Year *Andy Rouse*
Light in the Landscape: A Photographer's Year *Peter Watson*
Outdoor Photography Portfolio *GMC Publications*
Photographers on Location with Charlie Waite *Charlie Waite*
Photographing Fungi in the Field *George McCarthy*
Photography for the Naturalist *Mark Lucock*
Photojournalism: An Essential Guide *David Herrod*
Professional Landscape and Environmental Photography: From 35mm to Large Format *Mark Lucock*
Rangefinder *Roger Hicks & Frances Schultz*
Underwater Photography *Paul Kay*
Viewpoints from *Outdoor Photography* *GMC Publications*
Where and How to Photograph Wildlife *Peter Evans*
Wildlife Photography Workshops *Steve & Ann Toon*

Art Techniques

Oil Paintings from your Garden: A Guide for Beginners *Rachel Shirley*

VIDEOS

Drop-in and Pinstuffed Seats *David James*
Stuffover Upholstery *David James*
Elliptical Turning *David Springett*
Woodturning Wizardry *David Springett*
Turning Between Centres: The Basics *Dennis White*
Turning Bowls *Dennis White*
Boxes, Goblets and Screw Threads *Dennis White*
Novelties and Projects *Dennis White*
Classic Profiles *Dennis White*
Twists and Advanced Turning *Dennis White*
Sharpening the Professional Way *Jim Kingshott*
Sharpening Turning & Carving Tools *Jim Kingshott*
Bowl Turning *John Jordan*
Hollow Turning *John Jordan*
Woodturning: A Foundation Course *Keith Rowley*
Carving a Figure: The Female Form *Ray Gonzalez*
The Router: A Beginner's Guide *Alan Goodsell*
The Scroll Saw: A Beginner's Guide *John Burke*

MAGAZINES

Woodturning ◆ Woodcarving ◆ Furniture & Cabinetmaking
The Router ◆ New Woodworking ◆ The Dolls' House Magazine
Outdoor Photography ◆ Black & White Photography
Travel Photography ◆ Machine Knitting News
Guild of Master Craftsmen News

The above represents a full list of all titles currently published or scheduled to be published.
All are available direct from the Publishers or through bookshops, newsagents and specialist retailers.
To place an order, or to obtain a complete catalogue, contact:

GMC Publications,
Castle Place, 166 High Street, Lewes, East Sussex BN7 1XU United Kingdom
Tel: 01273 488005 Fax: 01273 402866
E-mail: pubs@thegmcgroup.com

Orders by credit card are accepted